KNOWING
and
REASONING
in COLLEGE

Marcia B. Baxter Magolda

KNOWING
and
REASONING
in COLLEGE

Gender-Related
Patterns
in Students'
Intellectual
Development

Jossey-Bass Publishers · San Francisco

For sales outside the United States, contact Maxwell Macmillan International Publishing Group, 866 Third Avenue, New York, New York 10022.

Manufactured in the United States of America

 The paper used in this book is acid-free and meets the State of California requirements for recycled paper (50 percent recycled waste, including 10 percent postconsumer waste), which are the strictest guidelines for recycled paper currently in use in the United States.

Library of Congress Cataloging-in-Publication Data

Baxter Magolda, Marcia B., date.
    Knowing and reasoning in college : gender-related patterns in students' intellectual development / Marcia B. Baxter Magolda.— 1st ed.
        p.   cm.—(The Jossey-Bass higher and adult education series) (The Jossey-Bass social and behavioral science series)
    Includes bibliographical references and index.
    ISBN 1-55542-467-8 (alk. paper)
    1. Learning—Longitudinal studies.   2. Knowledge, Theory of— Longitudinal studies.   3. College students—United States— Longitudinal studies.   4. Sex differences—Longitudinal studies.
I. Title.   II. Series.   III. Series: The Jossey-Bass social and behavioral science series.
LB1060.B4 1992
370.15'23—dc20   92-9889
                                                      CIP

FIRST EDITION
HB Printing   10 9 8 7 6 5 4 3 2 1   *Code 9264*

A joint publication in
The Jossey-Bass
Higher and Adult Education Series
and
The Jossey-Bass
Social and Behavioral Science Series

Consulting Editor
Student Services

Ursula Delworth
University of Iowa

To my husband,
Peter Magolda

Contents

Preface

The information is cut and dried. It is either right or wrong. If you know the information, you can do well. It is easy because you just read or listen to a lecture about the ideas, then present it back to the teacher.

—Jim

Genetics isn't an opinionated kind of subject. Genetics is, "These are the experiments; that's what happens. This is what we know now." You wouldn't sit around and have a discussion in calculus . . . or chemistry. In the AIDS class, it's just open discussion, and it makes you really say what you want and think through what you want to think about.

—Fran

I don't know [how I decide on my opinion]. Something works inside my head, and it's just there.

—Laura

I don't care if people feel this way or that way about it. But if they can support their stance and have some background and backing for that, to my thinking that is valid.

—Gwen

This book is about different ways of knowing. Jim, Fran, Laura, and Gwen express various ways of making meaning of their experience. Jim looks for right answers based on the assumption that knowledge is certain, whereas Fran sees some areas as uncertain and behaves differently when approaching them. Laura believes that knowledge is uncertain and creates her own perspective without attention to context. Gwen also develops her own point of view but takes into account evidence she judges as reasonable. These different perspectives prompt Jim, Fran, Laura, and Gwen to approach both curricular and cocurricular learning differently. My interpretation of their stories and those of their peers has resulted in the model presented in this book; called the epistemological reflection model because it is based on students' perceptions of the nature of knowledge, it describes the four ways of knowing and their development throughout the college experience.

Stories in this book also shed light on a second component of the epistemological reflection model: the role of gender. In addition, they reveal differences within ways of knowing, called reasoning patterns, that also affect how students think about knowing. Listen, for example, to these comments:

> I get into discussions; they are better for me to learn. You have an opening lecture where you have the professor discuss. Then students can contribute — listening to other students contribute their ideas and putting in my own — that makes learning better for me because it makes me think more.
> — *Kris*

> The debate and discussion process for me is really interesting. I learn a lot more because I remember questions. And I guess I learn the most when I sit and I'm actually forced to raise my hand and then have to talk. I have to sit there and think on the spot.
> — *Scott*

On the one hand, Kris approaches learning by immersing herself in the information and in peer interaction aimed at gaining access to it. Scott, on the other hand, distances himself from knowledge and interacts with other students to achieve mastery.

Scott's approach is closest to how educators have historically viewed learning.

Most educators would hope that the college experience could assist students to learn as Gwen does. Nevertheless, critics of higher education still charge that the undergraduate experience falls short in promoting critical thinking, empowering students to analyze and synthesize, preparing them for complex roles in society, and fostering appreciation of diversity and that responsibility to others so necessary in our interdependent world. Few educators disagree with these charges, but identifying shortcomings is far easier than finding solutions to them. Yet Jim, Fran, Laura, Gwen, and their contemporaries possess a wealth of insights about the problems. The curricular and cocurricular learning experiences that allowed these four to adapt the ways they learned and to discover a variety of approaches can also help educators develop possibilities for promoting complex ways of knowing.

Knowing and Reasoning in College tells the stories of 101 women and men whom I began interviewing in 1986, when they started their first year in college. Our conversations during each of their years in college and the first year after graduation have provided valuable insights about how ways of knowing develop, together with concrete examples of helpful or negative experiences. Because the study was longitudinal, we were able to discuss experiences, and students' reactions to them, as they occurred. The participation of seventy students for the full five years created an array of perspectives on the college experience, and the inclusion of both women and men yielded information not available from single-gender studies. For example, the approaches of Kris and Scott are equally complex. Their patterns of reasoning were used by both genders, but more often by one than the other. Thus, the students' stories reveal that different reasoning patterns are related to, though not defined by, gender and that they are equal in complexity. Taking these patterns into account has enhanced my understanding of how particular experiences affect individual students. Furthermore, their candid perceptions of what changed their thinking give rise to compelling ideas about how to transform educational practice.

Plan of the Book

Originally, I had planned to offer a specific plan for the redesign of educational practice, but these stories have changed all that. Now I invite readers to join the students in their experiences, and me in interpreting them. This change of purpose came about for two reasons.

First, despite many common themes, the interviews convinced me that these students' experiences cannot easily be described collectively. Development, as they portray it, fits better with Marilyn Frye's (1990) notion of charting the prevailing winds over a continent, realizing that they do not affect every part of the continent in the same way. There are some prevailing winds, captured here as the epistemological reflection model, but the differences in various students' experiences prohibit placing them in static categories. Instead, the experiences generate possibilities for effective practice, one of which is to listen to students in particular practice settings for guidance.

Second, one of the most powerful messages in the students' stories was that the ability to develop a distinctive voice stems from defining learning as constructing meaning jointly with others. Learning experiences of any nature were described as more powerful when students were free to relate them to aspects of their own lives, when learners were valued as capable of exploring knowledge and interpreting it, and when learners worked through their various ideas collaboratively to arrive at understandings or beliefs. These circumstances led to the empowerment of learners and, it is important to note, were valuable to students regardless of their way of knowing or their reasoning pattern.

After hearing students' stories, I no longer view the central task to be simply redesigning educational practice. Rather, *transforming* educational practice seems to be required. In my mind, transformation not only includes alterations in educational practice but also addresses the underlying assumptions on which practice is based. Historically, educational practice has been dominated by positivist assumptions; the result has been an objective pursuit of knowledge that is then generalized to other times and contexts. (The objectivist approach has been given several other names. Elsewhere in the book, I use both the terms *objectivist* and *paradigmatic;* see Bruner, 1986). In recent years, many educators have argued for social constructivism, which posits that multiple realities arise from negotiations among learners about the meaning of experience. (This approach is also referred to variously; I use Bruner's term *narrative* elsewhere in the book.)

The dominance of objectivism has fostered separation in educational practice: between teacher and student and between knowledge and experience (Palmer, 1987). This separation hinders students' ability to construct their own perspectives. The objectivist view of knowledge also separates curricular from cocurricular knowledge, thereby distancing the process of knowing from the arena in which students feel most comfortable. Transforming educational practice requires eliminating separation in favor of connection. Constructing one's own perspective requires encouragement, which often comes from interactions between teacher and student, between knowledge and experience, and between curricular and cocurricular life. Relational knowing necessitates a shift in assumptions to the social constructivist approach, which accommodates both Kris's and Scott's reasoning patterns, whereas objectivism validates only one of the two patterns. This shift would assist those who learn in ways not validated by objectivism. It is also important to help students develop both patterns because the patterns converge in the most complex way of knowing.

For these reasons, the format of the book relies heavily on students' stories to help readers relate the stories to aspects of their experience, to inspire possible meanings, and to allow readers to analyze and synthesize their interpretations and mine to arrive at insights that they can use in their practice. I wrote the book primarily using the narrative approach, because it accepts the students' stories as genuine, describes my own transformation, and reinforces the primary message of the book regarding relational knowing. I recognize, and so should readers, that different reasoning patterns and ways of knowing affect writers and readers as much as they did the students in my study.

Those who use the narrative approach will find validation in the story format and the invitation to come up with possible interpretations. Those who favor the objective approach may tire of the story format and ask why the findings are not presented more efficiently and objectively. Having been a proponent of both approaches (as the evolution described in Chapter One illustrates), I have tried to be sensitive to the preferences of both kinds of readers. However, my own transformation to social constructivism clearly biases my writing toward that approach.

Audience

This book is intended for an audience interested in promoting complex knowing during college. The stories offer rich data for student development educators about student organizations, living environments, informal student relationships, campus employment, internships, and the peer culture. Teaching faculty will find excellent examples of how instructional approaches, class expectations, peer interaction, and evaluation methods affect learning. The variety of the students' disciplines helps us envision how their ideas could be applied in diverse educational settings. The stories can affect educators' perceptions and attitudes toward students and how those attitudes contribute to or inhibit intellectual development. The interconnection of curricular and cocurricular learning necessitates exploration of the possibilities for collaboration between student affairs personnel and faculty members. Reading about students' perceptions of both curricular and cocurricular life will be valuable to student affairs and classroom educators. When I use the term *educators* throughout the book, I am referring to both student development educators and college faculty.

Overview of the Contents

Part One introduces the different ways of knowing. Chapter One reviews the literature on college students' ways of knowing and researchers' ways of looking at that topic. I discuss the transformations I have experienced to show how I arrived at the guiding assumptions for the book, which are also outlined in the first chapter. Also described there are the participants in and context for the study; further details on the methods of the study can be found in the resources. Chapter Two provides an in-depth introduction to two of the study participants as a means of presenting the epistemological reflection model developed from my interpretations of the collective data. Extensive quotes from the five years of interviews with Gwen and Mark (all student names are fictitious) illustrate the four ways of knowing that emerged from the data; the two patterns within the first three ways that appear to be gender-related; and the progression of ways of knowing throughout the college experience.

Chapters Three, Four, Five, and Six each describe one kind of knowing and the patterns evident within it. General characteristics are illustrated by students' comments about their role as learners; about the roles of instructors, peers, and evaluation of their work; and about the way they decide what to believe. I then explore each pattern, also drawing on student comments.

Because I argue in Chapter One that these stories chart prevailing winds rather than describe the experience of all students, I use Chapter Seven to discuss whether their experiences and the epistemological reflection model could be transferred to other contexts. I examine themes of dominance/subordination and socialization to entertain possibilities that these ways of knowing and the patterns within them might relate to other students. In particular, I rely on other research to discuss students in nondominant groups, because only three of my participants came from such groups.

Part Two of the book turns to transforming educational practice through acknowledgment of the relational nature of knowing. Chapter Eight summarizes students' advice to classroom educators. Chapter Nine discusses how to promote development of a distinctive, individual student perspective in curricular settings. Chapter Ten contains students' advice to cocurricular educators, and Chapter Eleven addresses developing student voice in cocurricular settings. Three overriding principles organize Chapters Nine and Eleven: validating the student as a knower, situating learning within the students' own experience, and defining learning as constructing meaning collaboratively with others. Student comments are used to generate possibilities for effective practice using these three principles. The concluding chapter (Chapter Twelve) summarizes the major findings of the study and discusses them in the context of the broader literature on and realities of student development and educational practice.

In the resources, readers will find background on Miami University, where the study was conducted (Resource A), an explanation of the methods used (Resource B), and the actual interview and questionnaire (Resource C).

I have made every effort to maintain the integrity of students' stories as I heard them and to convey them in as much detail as is reasonable. I have also tried to put into practice what I learned from the students: that is, I have attempted to avoid finding simplistic solutions to complex problems. My professional practice has been significantly shaped by the interviews. I am now able to listen more carefully in order to gain access to students' experiences as a continuing source of understanding. I hope that hearing the stories secondhand will produce a similar outcome for readers.

Acknowledgments

This book, and the research on which it is based, recount a journey — a journey for seventy students through college and one for me in understanding their intellectual development. Many people helped make the project successful. Patricia Baugher's computer expertise located the students who would participate. Former graduate students Ken Hudiak, David Johnson, Kim Ogle, and Carol Quilty made countless telephone calls to schedule interviews and remind students about questionnaires. John Vaughn, in audiovisual services, was indispensable in acquiring the necessary equipment for recording. In the beginning stage, five people helped with the large number of interviews: Randall Beachy, Lori Bennett, Robert Borden, Peter Magolda, and Kathy Lee Sandberg.

My research was funded through four sources. A grant from the American College Personnel Association Theory and Research Board launched my work in 1986, and a second grant from the same source helped me continue. The Miami University Faculty Research Committee provided both a grant to promote research and scholarship and a summer research appointment; these allowed me time to begin analysis of the results. A research challenge grant from the Ohio Board of Regents and Miami University provided substantial funding to continue the project. Additional funds were furnished by the American Association of Counseling and Development Foundation through their Professional Enhancement Grant Scholar/Research Award Program. Special thanks go to William Rauckhorst and Carol Willeke of Miami's Research and Sponsored Programs Office for assistance in acquiring these funds.

Many others offered invaluable assistance along the way. Jacky Lewis and William Porterfield rated questionnaires for the project. Janet Crump spent many hours recording ideas on index cards and meeting with me to talk about theme development. Insights from all three of these people were essential to understanding the students' comments. Betty Marak, who transcribed all 432 audiotaped interviews, was a mainstay of the project; her expertise in recording students' words verbatim contributed immeasurably to the integrity of the study. I was able to summarize my outcomes as a result of a faculty improvement leave, which I received thanks to the support of my department chair, Nelda Cambron-McCabe, and Dean Janet Kettlewell. The secretarial staff of the Educational Leadership Department, including Peggy Bauer, Jan Clegg, Lorene Moore, and Carolyn Walsh, contributed their support throughout.

Conversations with friends and colleagues, too numerous to mention here, helped me make sense of what I was attempting to accomplish. My graduate students' ideas and comments on my research helped spark new ways of looking at it. Many colleagues helped broaden my thinking — Cathann Arceneaux, Blythe Clinchy, Gary Knock, Nona Lyons, Laurie McDade, Judy Rogers, and Dawn Schrader, to name just a few. I am particularly indebted to Judy Rogers for challenging my quantitative perspective, providing the library books and intellectual stimulation to learn about qualitative research, and participating in the evolution of my thinking. Readers of the manuscript were also of invaluable assistance. George Kuh's guidance helped produce a successful book prospectus. Richard Quantz, Sally Sharp, and reviewers for Jossey-Bass (including senior acquiring editor Gale Erlandson) graciously read the entire manuscript and offered constructive suggestions. The support and helpful feedback I received from Ursula Delworth, consulting editor for the Jossey-Bass Higher and Adult Education Series, contributed significantly to its final form.

The strength to embark on a journey, particularly a long one, comes from loved ones as much as from professional colleagues. Much of my strength I acquired from my mother, Marjorie Baxter, whose outlook on and approach to life convinced me that anything is possible. My husband, Peter Magolda, has provided the unconditional support, professional expertise in interpretive inquiry, and willingness to participate in extensive dialogue that have made this effort possible and meaningful. These two people's support of my professional work has enabled me to devote the considerable time and energy that such an extensive project requires. Finally, persevering on a long journey is made easier by those encountered along the way—in this case, the students who participated in the study, who were in the midst of their own journeys yet willingly assisted me. Although I cannot name the participants, I wish to express my deepest appreciation to each of them for the insights into their own lives and into student development, and for the many enjoyable conversations.

Oxford, Ohio   Marcia B. Baxter Magolda
July 1992

The Author

Marcia B. Baxter Magolda is associate professor of educational leadership at Miami University. She received her B.A. degree (1974) in psychology from Capital University and her M.A. (1976) and Ph.D. (1983) degrees from The Ohio State University in college student personnel services.

Baxter Magolda's main research activities have centered on the issues of intellectual development and gender in young adults. Her experience with assessment includes creating and validating a measure of college students' intellectual development. The longitudinal study on which this book is based resulted from the author's involvement with gender issues.

In 1984, she received the Dissertation of the Year Award from the National Association of Student Personnel Administrators. She also received the Theory and Research Board Award from the American College Personnel Association in 1986 and 1989. She is the author of *Assessing Intellectual Development: The Link Between Theory and Practice* (1988, with W. Porterfield) and numerous research articles published in the *Review of Higher Education,* the *Journal of College Student Development,* and the *College Student Journal.*

Before joining the faculty, Baxter Magolda was a student affairs practitioner from 1976 to 1983 at The Ohio State University. She served on the American College Personnel Association Assessment Commission for five years and is currently a member of the editorial board of the *Journal of College Student Development.*

KNOWING
and
REASONING
in COLLEGE

PART ONE

Understanding Gender-Related Patterns in Knowing

Understanding how people make meaning of their experience stems from listening to what they have to say about it (Perry, 1970). Listening is difficult work, particularly given that all of us bring our own biases to the process and interpret what we hear through them. Listening requires suspending judgment to hear as accurately as possible what others are saying about their experience. I invite readers to listen to the stories in the next seven chapters to hear what students say about coming to know in college.

For five years, I listened to the stories of college students recounted here. Chapter One explains my own initial biases and how listening changed my perspective. Readers may thus get some idea of how my thinking influenced the way I retell students' stories in Chapters Two through Six. Two students whose experience is detailed in Chapter Two offer insight into absolute, transitional, independent, and contextual forms of knowing. Their comments also illustrate two distinct gender-related patterns within absolute, transitional, and independent knowing. Those perspectives and the gender-related patterns within them are the subject of Chapters Three through Six. Chapter Seven summarizes the themes of the students' stories and borrows stories from other research to extend insights to students other than those with whom I talked.

Listening carefully is particularly important in exploring how these students made meaning of their experience because the traditional value placed on objective or rational forms of

1

knowing makes it easier to hear stories consistent with those forms. The students whom readers will meet in Part One of this book tell stories that contain both objective and narrative forms of knowing and reasoning. Withrell and Noddings write: "The stories we hear and the stories we tell shape the meaning and texture of our lives at every stage and juncture" (1991, p. 1). The stories I heard broadened my perspective; the story I tell aims to shape readers' understanding of gender-related patterns in knowing.

Chapter One

Studying Ways
of Knowing

I think people [students] need to kind of get a chance to
talk about the things that they know, too.
                                                    — *Deirdre*

Understanding college students' intellectual development is at
the heart of effective educational practice. Students interpret,
or make meaning of, their educational experience as a result
of their assumptions about the nature, limits, and certainty of
knowledge. Such assumptions, referred to by researchers as
epistemic assumptions (Kitchener, 1983), collectively form "ways
of knowing." The four students quoted at the beginning of the
preface illustrate that students use different sets of assumptions
to interpret their experiences. Educators also interpret, or make
meaning of, their experience based on their ways of knowing.
Unfortunately, educators often use their own frames of reference to interpret behavior without understanding how a student's perspective may shape such behavior. For example, students who do not support their stance with evidence because
they believe that all opinions are equal are often viewed as lacking knowledge or arrogant. This interpretation stems from the
educator's idea that beliefs must be supported by evidence rather
than some students' notion that all views are equally valid. Effective educational practice requires gaining access to students' ways
of knowing to avoid misinterpreting their approach to learning.

   William Perry, a pioneer on this topic, advocated understanding students' perspectives by listening to them. Specifically,
he said, "People tend to 'make sense,' that is, to interpret experience meaningfully. The 'meaning' of experience consists of
some sort of orderliness found in it, and the nature of this orderliness in a given person's experience can often be deduced
by others from the forms of his behavior, including, especially,
what he himself has to say on the matter" (1970, pp. 41–42).
   What college students have to say on the matter is the
focus of this book. However, like educators, researchers interpret these learning perspectives within the framework of their
own assumptions. Different ways of knowing result in different
interpretations. Some commonly used approaches also place
more emphasis on what researchers conclude than on what students believe. Because much of this book is my interpretation
of what students have revealed, it is important for me to explain my perspective on college students and on research. I therefore begin the chapter by summarizing my understanding of
the current literature about college students' ways of knowing.
Because I experienced a transformation in my thinking on this
subject, I describe that transition to illuminate the biases inherent in my analysis. Although I suspect that readers who enjoy narratives might appreciate that discussion, those who favor
the objective approach might find it more useful to go directly
to the guiding assumptions at the end of the chapter. Finally,
the context of this study is described in detail because who the
students are, of course, affects what they have to say.

College Students' Ways of Knowing

I encountered the concept of ways of knowing for the first time
in graduate school. The setting was less than ideal for learning.
Our student development theory class met in a dilapidated building earmarked for demolition in the not-too-distant future. The
location's only advantage was proximity to the parking garage.
Despite the small, hot, basement room, the professor was usually
jovial and visited with us as we entered the room. Soon after
class began, my attention was captured by his theatrical imper-

sonations at various positions of the Perry (1970) scheme. In his southern drawl, he ventured this soliloquy: "Democracy is the right form of government, and it is my duty to defend it. There is a right answer to what caused the Civil War, and I just have to find it. There is one right career for me, and I just have to find it. There is one right person out there for me, and I just have to find her/him."

Repeating the same speech with substitutions such as communism for democracy, he showed that how the student thought was more important than what the student thought. His illustration of Perry's position two dualist complete, he launched into another impersonation, this one of a student posing questions like "How will we ever know what caused the Civil War?" "How can it be that people in other countries believe their form of government is best?" and "How will I figure out what career is right for me if the career counselors aren't sure?" The questions and his matching quizzical expression clearly demonstrated the position three student's perspective that discerning what was right was complicated when some things were uncertain. The professor's tone changed substantially as he turned to a new student character: "All forms of government are equally valid. People of a given country can believe what they wish. There are lots of interpretations of what caused events such as the Civil War, and all opinions are equally plausible. There are millions of careers I could pursue. I can always change my mind later if I find that I don't like what I'm doing. I'm enjoying doing my own thing!"

There was little question among those of us who had completed the reading assignment that this was Perry's position four student. The professor's performance captured both the freewheeling and slightly feisty nature of the position four thinker. His portrayal of the position five relativist was a little more serious in nature in an attempt to describe how that sort of person used evidence within a context to make judgments about what to believe. The professor did not offer soliloquies for the commitment stages of Perry's scheme, perhaps because they did not represent new ways of knowing beyond relativism.

I found myself enthralled with this explanation of how

college students learn, partially due to my professor's ability to bring the process to life and partially because it seemed compatible with my own experience. This understanding had been useful (and improved my patience) in my work in residence life, in which I often found myself mediating conflicts among students. I cannot recall how many times I heard "We just have a basic personality conflict" as the reason I should move someone's roommate elsewhere. Translated, this statement meant that the student viewed her or his roommate as being the "wrong" one; with the "right" one, all conflicts would disappear. In disciplinary meetings, I was sometimes asked, "What business is it of yours to decide what we should do in our own room?" or "What gives the institution the right to decide what we do in our hall?" At these times, I wondered if the position four perspective was really more complex than the position two point of view, at least in discipline situations.

After a few years of encountering these ways of knowing every day, I came to believe that someone ought to develop more practical, yet accurate, ways to assess students' thinking so that educators could identify and help provide the experiences that Perry and others said would aid movement to more complex ways of thinking. I arrived at this point at the same time that I began my search for a dissertation topic, so I soon found myself trying to figure out how to measure something that I had seen and heard on a daily basis. The idea of quantifying students' ways of thinking was so captivating that I did not notice a major conceptual issue until many years later.

It was an issue that I did not recognize even when the dissertation was complete. For the next few years, attempting to find the central themes and organize ideas into neat categories, I pored over students' short essays about the nature of knowledge and how they learned. After reading over one thousand student essays, I felt comfortable enough with the categories to publish them in the form of a rating manual to be used to identify students' ways of knowing. Anxious to hear the response of those in the field, I sent the manual to someone whose judgment I valued. The expert's response, in a nutshell, was, "The manual looks great, but there are some areas in which I ques-

tion the accuracy of your interpretations: they do not match
Perry and you might want to reevaluate them." Devastated does
not quite capture my reaction. Many thoughts raced through
my mind, among them, "How could I have misinterpreted the
responses? I was so careful. . . . " "How will I fix these problems now that the manual is published?" and "Why did I ever
start this project in the first place?" That the students themselves
had formed the manual, a fact that I stressed at presentations
and in class, did not come to mind at the time. Discussions with
other colleagues and substantial reflection on this issue eventually caused this important idea to resurface. Was it possible that
the manual was not inaccurate but different from the Perry
scheme because I had heard other voices?

My student development class helped me sort out this
question. One of the assignments for the course was to write
a paper on the evolution of their own ways of thinking from
the beginning of college to graduate school. After describing this
evolution, they were to address the degree to which their experience matched Perry's explanation. Many students, more often
than not women, expressed difficulty with the assignment. They
often reported that their thinking processes coincided with Perry's
description to a degree but had trouble matching all their experiences with his scheme. I concurred with their judgments,
as the students articulated situations that I could not place in
the scheme either.

Researchers studying women (Clinchy and Zimmerman,
1982) were reporting similar difficulties in interpreting women's
experiences using the Perry scheme. Some of the students' stories resembled those found in other research (Benack, 1982) —
namely, that women's thoughts appeared to be more tolerant
and flexible than Perry's positions would seem to indicate. When
Women's Ways of Knowing was published (Belenky, Clinchy, Goldberger, and Tarule, 1986), I was reminded by the authors that
Perry's work had been based predominantly on men. Although
the authors found many similarities between Perry's positions
and the women they studied, they described perspectives that
sounded somewhat different. To my delight, some of these differences matched the "inaccuracies" in my rating manual.

According to Belenky, Clinchy, Goldberger and Tarule, women's knowing could be organized into five categories. They described the silent women, who did not view words as tools for understanding. Other women they identified as listeners, who focused on receiving knowledge from others. Some women listened to their own internal voices — their own subjective understanding. Still others used different procedures: some were objective and separate from others, and some involved gaining access to others' experiences in a connected fashion. Finally, some women constructed knowledge by judging evidence within a context, an integration of both the separate and connected approaches.

I found it fascinating that Perry's research on men in the 1950s and 1960s had so much in common with Belenky, Clinchy, Goldberger, and Tarule's research on women in the 1980s. I was even more intrigued, however, about the degree to which gender similarities and differences existed. Another line of research (Kitchener and King, 1981 and 1990) that involved longitudinal study of both women and men described the nature of knowledge slightly differently than either Perry or Belenky, Clinchy, Goldberger, and Tarule. Because gender was not a central theme of this research, it occurred to me that I had discovered an important gap in the existing research in this field. One of my graduate school professors had emphasized finding the "cutting edge" for research. I remembered her insistence in the research proposal seminar that we not pursue questions already addressed in the literature. Invariably, as we reported updates on our projects, she would peer over her half–circle glasses and cite literature we had somehow missed in our visits to the library. She believed, as did I when I finished her course, that good research extended our knowledge and understanding. Having found the cutting edge in the area of how college students know, I therefore undertook a longitudinal project to follow their ways of knowing throughout college. I specifically planned to reveal gender similarities and differences in order to create a more comprehensive picture of students' ways of knowing. With my knowledge of the literature and research skills to confirm my confidence, I embarked on five years of interviewing students. That is where the transformation in *my* way of knowing began.

Researchers' Ways of Knowing

Most of my knowing as a researcher came from graduate study. In addition to the cutting-edge lesson, I absorbed a great deal about ways of collecting and analyzing students' ideas about themselves. I learned that most researchers who studied how people make meaning of their lives thought that the best results were obtained when people were given the freedom to talk about what they perceived as important in an interview. Although the interviewer could guide the discussion to cover relevant topics, the situation could be open-ended enough for the students to express themselves freely.

I had learned how to analyze interview data from Jane Loevinger and Ruth Wessler's (1970) work. They advocated organizing students' ideas into categories and themes that could then be used to understand future responses. Their approach entailed always being open to new ideas, which were added to the categories and themes as they arose; the integrity of the students' voices was thus maintained. This rather fuzzy process was made more quantitative by assigning numbers to the categories and using these numbers to summarize students' responses. The feature of adding new ideas as they arose accounted for the "inaccuracies" that I had included in my earlier description of students' ways of knowing. I had incorporated all of these ideas in the interpretation system for my longitudinal interviews. Thus, I organized students' ideas by matching them to the categories that I had developed, adding new categories as need be. The categories were then assigned numbers that allowed me to enter data into the computer, develop profiles of students' responses, and explore differences by year or gender.

After I had entered data and examined printouts for three years, a significant event took place. The volume of data was nearly overwhelming and took countless hours to sort through. Of the hundreds of printout pages strewn around my study, one page caught my attention: it showed a statistical difference between women's and men's ways of knowing. I tried to contain my excitement: this was the type of finding publishable articles are made of. I read the table carefully to make sure that my computer program statements were accurate and gleefully showed my printout to a few colleagues. One particularly honest colleague pointed out that despite the statistical difference, women and men fell into the same categories; even in the few cases that were different, the numbers were very close. I returned to my office somewhat deflated, remembering a statistics professor's admonition about distinguishing between a statistical and a meaningful difference. I also had a nagging sense that my experience with the students in the study suggested more similarity than difference in ways of knowing.

Often, as I sat with students during the interviews, I heard ideas that did not automatically fit into the categories that I carried around in my head. For example, some students (usually men) described debate and argument as a way of learning, even though they believed that knowledge could only be obtained from instructors. I rarely worried about these instances. Instead, I concentrated on clarifying what student meant, so that when it was time to examine the typed transcript of the interview, I would be able to understand it.

Later, during the many hours I spent reading interview transcripts, I often struggled with how to sort ideas. New categories were easily added, but often ideas overlapped — the boundaries between them were too indistinct to enable me easily to make assignments to one category or another. Sometimes, when students described a particular area of knowledge as uncertain, it was difficult to tell whether that perception applied only to that area or to all knowledge. I made my best calls in these cases, but questions that arose in my mind at these times stayed with me. I decided to reread the data in light of the statistical difference to see whether it was meaningful and evident in the sound of student voices. This proved to be a turning point in my thinking about the study.

Rereading the data, I became immersed in the students' stories. I lost track of the categorization system that had become so ingrained in my thinking as I listened to their experiences and what they thought about them. The experience transformed my thinking. It was a transformation similar to that described by Robert Coles (1989) in *The Call of Stories*. Recounting the tale of his residency in psychiatry, he talked about two supervisors whose approaches differed considerably. One supervisor, Dr. Binger, encouraged Coles to diagnose his patients' psychological health using the tools at his disposal. In their sessions together, they generated various hypotheses about particular patients. The second supervisor, Dr. Ludwig, discouraged this kind of diagnosis. He gently tried to get Coles to set aside his knowledge about psychological health and listen to what his patients had to say. He told stories about patients during their sessions and encouraged Coles to do the same. In Dr. Ludwig's attempt to convince Coles of the value of this approach, he offered what Coles referred to as a brief lecture during one of their sessions: "The people who come to see us bring us their stories. They hope to tell them well enough that we understand the truth of their lives. They hope we know how to interpret their stories correctly. We have to remember that what we hear is their story" (p. 7).

Although Coles's situation differed considerably from mine, Dr. Ludwig's message seemed to convey what I had come to understand in trying to reconcile students' stories with my computer printout. The stories were richer than my statistical operations were able to communicate for two reasons. First, all students assigned to one way of knowing appeared the same within their numbered category; in reality, however, some were just arriving at that way of knowing, and others were nearly ready to leave it.

Second, statistical operations could only be used for categories, not for the themes within them (an explanation of this limitation can be found in the resources). Thus, the varied themes of student stories that existed within the categories were hidden when this type of interpretation was employed alone. For example, the student who emphasized listening and recording information and the one who stressed participating in order to express interest to the teacher both belonged to the same category of knowing, as they believed that knowledge came from the authority figure.

The students had told their stories well enough for me to understand them. Now my task was trying to interpret the stories *correctly* (to use Coles's term), keeping in mind his advice that "what you are hearing is to some considerable extent a function of 'you' hearing" (1989, p. 15). Recognizing that the story I was constructing could not be totally correct because it was a combination of the students' stories and my interpretation of them, I tried to focus on arriving at a *reasonable* interpretation. Reflecting on the data-analysis process that I had learned from Loevinger and Wessler, I realized that it was centered around interpreting student stories reasonably. The provision for revising interpretive categories according to student stories kept the focus on constructing the story based on the students' ideas. Yet by the same token, rereading the stories helped me see that my interpretation of the statistical procedures resulted in a story constructed with less attention to their ideas — one that reduced these to levels in which their differences were exaggerated. My statistical procedures allowed generalizations that were incompatible with reasonable interpretations of the stories. I decided that using the evolving-category system was appropriate, as was summarizing the percentage of students whose stories could be fitted within various categories and themes. However, statistical analyses of gender similarities and differences were less helpful than the actual words and stories of the students.

This transformation in my thinking had significant implications for my interpretation of the interviews. Fortunately, they had been open-ended from the beginning and had become more so over the years as I became increasingly intrigued with the students' stories. Fortunately, I had thousands of pages of interview transcripts that reproduced the students' own words and ideas. I was therefore able to reinterpret the stories reasonably. The process of reinterpretation of existing stories and the subsequent interpretation of new ones in the last two years yielded three important changes.

The first change was to view ways of knowing from the students' frames of reference rather than those of the literature. Although there were not major differences between the two, the flavor of my students' stories was not entirely captured by previous labels. In order to concentrate on the students' ideas, I renamed each perspective to reflect the content and flavor of what I had heard. This process resulted in the identification of four ways of knowing used by both women and men in the study. Variations in the themes of the stories also appeared. These themes took the form of reasoning patterns, or ways that students justified their thoughts. I had recorded reasoning patterns within ways of knowing throughout the study and now organized them into patterns that captured the variations.

The second change had to do with interpretation of the reasoning patterns within ways of knowing, particularly as they relate to gender. The student stories had shown from the beginning that the women tended to use one pattern more than did the men and vice versa. I had described the patterns as gender-related rather than dictated by gender to reflect this situation. Rereading the stories increased my awareness of the fluidity of the boundaries between patterns. Following the development of individual students over the five years, I discovered that some consistently used similar patterns over time, whereas others moved back and forth between patterns. Some who used one pattern fairly consistently would still occasionally exhibit reasoning from the other pattern. I began to understand the patterns as a continuum bounded by a pattern on each end, with numerous variations and combinations in between. That enabled me to portray the nature of gender similarity and difference reasonably in light of the students' stories. My purpose was transformed; it was now to interpret the students' stories as accurately as possible.

The third change I did not accept easily. In reviewing my statistical data (which I continued to generate) and the transcripts, I had to accept that there was more similarity than difference in these women's and men's ways of knowing. This recognition, initially a disappointment, opened the door for viewing similarities and differences between genders in a new light. Once free of my original set of biases, I was able to see the value of being able to say that women and men in this group were "equal" in their ways of knowing. Moreover, it was valuable to be able to say that in this group, different reasoning patterns led to equally complex ways of viewing the world. This change helped me see new possibilities and avoid coming to premature conclusions. It was comforting to come across other work in my reading that also suggested that gender-related differences were more likely to exist within than between particular perspectives (Colby and Kohlberg, 1987; Gibbs, Arnold, and Burkhart, 1984; Walker, 1984).

Researchers' Ways of Knowing: Alternative Perspectives

I cannot, in all honesty, claim to have arrived at these important insights totally independently. My reconciliation of the students' stories with my computer printout occurred at a time when I was also exploring two other bodies of knowledge: naturalistic or constructivist inquiry and postmodern feminist literature. The exploration of naturalistic inquiry was sparked by my colleagues' and my decision that it was an essential component of our master's-level research course. One of my colleagues, an avid reader, had checked most of the qualitative research books out of the library, and we immediately began the task of enlightening ourselves. I was particularly motivated because the class was my responsibility.

As I read the basic assumptions of naturalistic inquiry (Bogdan and Biklen, 1982; Eisner and Peshkin, 1990; Lincoln and Guba, 1985), I began to view these ideas as closer to my thinking than the quantitative research assumptions with which I was so familiar. I suppose my flexibility in this regard was influenced by the increasing criticism of logical, abstract forms of knowing and the growing acceptance of alternative forms based on lived experience (Eisner, 1985; Withrell and Noddings, 1991).

The naturalistic notion of multiple realities instead of one objective one matched the data on student reasoning patterns. Even students who shared basic assumptions about knowing went about it in very different ways. What was perceived by some as an ideal environment was perceived by others as the worst possible one. The naturalistic idea that knowledge was determined by context seemed reasonable because the students' stories were clearly tied to their own unique experiences and thus differed accordingly. The naturalistic concept that entities shape each other was borne out in students' stories as well. Because they used various ways of knowing or reasoning patterns, students experienced learning situations differently. Subsequently, their instructors sometimes altered the nature of learning situations in response to students' reactions. Finally, the naturalistic idea that research observers could not be separated from what they observed was certainly supported by my study. Some students told me that reflecting on their experience in the interview changed their thinking about it and made them more aware of it during the intervening year.

Recognizing the similarity between naturalistic inquiry and certain aspects of my study still left many issues unresolved. Qualitative research in student affairs being difficult to come by, I offered one of my conference papers as an example for discussion in one of the naturalistic-inquiry sessions of my graduate research class. The students asked numerous polite questions, routinely commenting on the value of the research. Toward the end of the conversation, one woman queried, "I am not certain I understand how to combine your quantitative data analysis and your qualitative data analysis. Could you explain this?" I began to explain the purpose of each, but as I talked, doubts began to emerge. Apparently, my attempt to concentrate on the explanation was unsuccessful, as a sea of puzzled faces soon filled the room. Or perhaps my own lack of conviction had somehow slipped into my response.

As I taught these concepts over the next few semesters, the limitations of quantifying students' ways of knowing became clear to me. Organizing students' stories into categories and themes was a useful process through which to obtain a better understanding of how they view the world. Yet at the same time, any findings based on these categories had the potential to imply that they were discrete, generalizable, and objectively true. This potential was heightened when quantitative analysis techniques (like my statistical procedures in the printout) were applied to qualitative data (like my interviews). The questions my graduate students asked about these ideas and their ramifications for my research forced me to think through this dilemma.

My shift from assumptions of objectivity, generalization, and cause-effect relationships to assumptions of subjectivity and context-bound, and jointly shaped relationships led to my pursuit of feminist writers' discussions about gender. One of the major themes evident in these writers' work was the view of gender as a socially constructed concept. They denounced the idea that gender-related behaviors were a result of maleness or femaleness; rather, they believed that these behaviors were developed (constructed) through interactions with others in particular contexts. This conceptualization of gender is more complex than the usual male-female dichotomy in two important ways. First, it recognizes that variability exists among members of a particular gender—not all women are perceived to be alike and not all men are considered to be alike. Second, it recognizes that gender-related behavior is fluid; it changes depending on context and other factors that interact with gender-related behaviors, such as race, class, or ethnicity. This conceptualization leads to a view of gender differences as context-bound rather than as enduring, universal entities (Deaux and Major, 1990; Thorne, 1990). Reading Marilyn Frye's (1990) remarks on this issue made it clear for me: "Schematically and experientially the problem of difference in feminist theory is simple: a good deal of feminist thinking has issued statements and descriptions that pertain to 'women' unmodified for distinctions among them. These are the sorts of statements their authors want to be making. But when such statements and descriptions are delivered in public they meet with critics, who are women, who report that the statements are appallingly partial, untrue, or even unintelligible when judged by their own experience and by what is common knowledge among women of their kind, class, or group" (p. 177).

As I read her comments, I imagined encountering this criticism had I made general statements on the basis of my statistical procedures. Fortunately, I had already discovered that the generalizations did not accurately capture the stories students told me. The reason for the discrepancy is also Frye's main point: that the particulars of each person's experience make generalization problematic.

Frye suggests that the idea of patterns is a more useful way to make sense of experience. These patterns are constructed from communication in which people uncover the events of their lives by naming them. As each person provides a context for other stories, they together discover, recognize, or create patterns to make sense of their collective experiences. Frye describes this process as one of opening up possibilities rather than drawing conclusions because the interaction creates new situations that alter the pattern being constructed. The pattern is an overarching concept that does not attempt to describe each person's experience in the same way (Frye's "charting the prevailing winds"). Thus, patterns can be used to make sense of experience but stop short of characterizing it in static and generalizable ways. As I studied Frye's ideas, I recognized that they were the same as the original intent of my interpreting student's ways of knowing. My interpretation process did involve creating categories and themes based on putting ideas that were similar together, but it simultaneously entailed keeping the categories and themes fluid to accommodate new ideas as they arose. My interpretations therefore made sense of the stories that the students had told me but did not apply identically to each story or student.

The difficulty of balancing the attempt to chart the prevailing winds against necessary attention to the particulars of people's experiences was another theme that I found in this group of writings. As this issue relates to women, some writers believed that minimizing gender differences by emphasizing the variability among women would hinder attempts to achieve their equality (Hare-Mustin and Maracek, 1990; Freedman, 1990). Yet emphasizing differences could also encourage inequality. This latter concern took the form of describing women's ways of knowing as intuitive and experientially based; this description implies that other ways of knowing (such as rationality and logical abstraction) are male. Identifying certain characteristics as male or female could lead to women's being viewed as incapable of other kinds of knowing and subsequently devalued (Hare-Mustin and Maracek, 1990). In this light, a balanced use of patterns and the particulars of experience became even more important. The challenge was to construct patterns that avoided oversimplification and prescription — to construct those, as Frye suggests, that generated new possibilities for interpretation.

Recognizing a challenge and being able to meet it are two different things. I was aware that other researchers, whose ideas were similar to mine, had been criticized for overgeneralizing (however unintentionally). For example, authors of journal articles had found fault with Carol Gilligan's (1982) work for overgeneralizing gender differences (Broughton, 1983; Hare-Mustin and Maracek, 1990). At a national conference that took place just as I was trying to decide how to meet this challenge, I attended a presentation on gender issues at which both presenters cited Gilligan's work as evidence that gender differences had been overgeneralized. One of my colleagues, an expert on Gilligan's work, also attended. She indicated surprise and frustration that the presenters had, in her view, misinterpreted Gilligan's research.

The presentation and conversation with my colleague left me wondering how I would avoid oversimplifying the students' stories in my attempt to find organizing themes. One of the first things I did after returning home from the conference was pick up my well-worn copy of *In a Different Voice* (1982) to see how Gilligan had approached the issue. Perhaps she had underemphasized the flexibility of relational and autonomous thinking in a way that had led others to misinterpret her intentions. I only had to read to page two to find the following paragraph:

> The different voice I describe is characterized not by gender but theme. Its association with women is an empirical observation, and it is primarily through women's voices that I trace its development. But this association is not absolute, and the contrasts between male and female voices are presented here to highlight a distinction between two modes of thought and to focus a problem of interpretation rather than to represent a generalization about either sex. In tracing development, I point to the interplay of these voices within each sex and suggest that their convergence marks times of crisis and change. No claims are made about the origins of the differences described or their distri-

bution in a wider population, across cultures, or through time. Clearly, these differences arise in a social context where factors of social status and power combine with reproductive biology to shape the experience of males and females and the relations between the sexes. My interest lies in the interaction of experience and thought, in different voices and the dialogues to which they give rise, in the way we listen to ourselves and to others, in the stories we tell about our lives [p. 2].

So much for my underemphasis theory. I turned to my equally well-worn copy of *Women's Ways of Knowing,* another work that had been cited as representing gender differences as "essential, universal (at least within contemporary Western culture), highly dichotomized, and enduring" (Hare-Mustin and Maracek, 1990, p. 23). Perhaps the authors of *Women's Ways of Knowing* did not directly state their assumptions. In the introductory chapter, I found this statement: "We recognize (1) that these five ways of knowing are not necessarily fixed, exhaustive, or universal categories, (2) that they are abstract or 'pure' categories that cannot adequately capture the complexities and uniqueness of an individual woman's thought and life, (3) that similar categories can be found in men's thinking, and (4) that other people might organize their observations differently" (Belenky, Clinchy, Goldberger, and Tarule, 1986, p. 15).

So much for my theory of indirectly stated assumptions. How was it possible that these works were construed as representing universal, enduring, dichotomous conceptualizations of gender difference? (It was important for me to understand how readers had arrived at this conclusion, because it was one I wished to avoid about my own writing.) I thought of two possible explanations. The first was that readers skip the introduction to get to the heart of the story. The second was that careful explanation of methodology and language leaves readers with an impression different than the perspectives outlined in the introductions. Both books contain discussions of the (naturalistic) methods used that aim to assure the reader of the rigor of the research. Both also use the term *women* in statements that describe the patterns they observed, probably because all of the participants in these studies were women. Taken together, efforts to convince the reader of the quality of the study, constant use of statements that characterize women in a particular way, and many people's natural inclination to generalize produce an impression other than that intended. Most of us probably share a tendency to draw conclusions rather than to envision the new interpretive possibilities Marilyn Frye wrote about. As a result, I have emphasized my attempts to avoid overgeneralization throughout the book rather than relying on the preface alone to make the point.

Returning to Frye's discussion of patterns, I paid closer attention to her cautionary advice that using patterns created the danger of misjudging the scope of the pattern (or overgeneralizing). Her recommendation for avoiding this danger was communication. Although by *communication* she meant discussion among persons who, through sharing their experiences, were generating patterns, my use of the term refers to communication with my readers. This takes two forms: first, stating unequivocally the assumptions that form the basis of my interpretations; second, avoiding generic language that could be misread to imply enduring, universal gender differences.

Guiding Assumptions

The following discussion outlines the principles that have guided my work.

1. *Ways of knowing and patterns within them are socially constructed.* Students' own ways of seeing the world come into contact with professors' and peers' frames of references in various contexts. The meaning that students make of these experiences depends partially on their original view of the world, partially on the other views they encounter, and partially on the context in which the experience takes place. For example, during a discipline interview, a student who believes that knowledge is certain might encounter an authority figure who thinks that knowledge is relative. Because the student probably perceives the

authority figure as an adversary, the likelihood of the student's changing her or his view within this context is slim. If, however, the difference of views occurs in an interaction with a trusted adviser, the student may be more likely to consider reevaluating the original opinion. How forcefully held the view was to begin with, how strong the authority's opinion was, and how salient the difference in views is to their interaction are also factors. Patterns within ways of knowing are further dependent on other issues like race and class, social relations, and the nature of individual experiences. Though gender may play a role in these experiences and interactions, it does not in and of itself account for the variation in patterns within ways of knowing.

This concept of ways of knowing as socially constructed is consistent with Piaget's (1932) explanation. He suggested that individuals hold perspectives that make sense of their experiences. They respond to experiences in light of these perspectives until the two become irreconcilable. At that point, the person revises the perspective so that it takes into account the experiences that did not fit into the previous one. Thus, points of view depend on the nature of people's experiences and reaction to them. Although I agree with the process that Piaget described, I am not arguing that it results in a set of ways of knowing that applies to people in general.

2. *Ways of knowing can best be understood through the principles of naturalistic inquiry.* Viewing ways of knowing as complex, socially constructed entities leads to the assumption that these processes can best be understood through the principles of naturalistic inquiry. Because students' ways of knowing and their experiences jointly shape each other, ways of knowing are context-bound. The fluidity of reasoning patterns indicates multiple realities rather than one single truth about students' perspectives. Naturalistic methods maintain the richness of the students' stories that is lost to a degree when the stories are quantified. The methods used in this study are thus consistent with naturalistic assumptions and rigorously apply them. Adopting the naturalistic framework leads to my next three assumptions.

3. *Students' use of reasoning patterns is fluid.* Because ways of knowing are socially constructed, reasoning patterns within them

may change as students encounter different experiences. Some students may use "pure" versions, whereas others use a mixture of patterns. Pattern use may change over time as ways of knowing evolve. Data to support this assumption is described in Chapter Two.

4. *Patterns are related to, but not dictated by, gender.* Although women in the study use some more than men (and vice versa), none of these patterns was employed exclusively by one gender or the other. Data to support this assumption is also described in Chapter Two.

5. *Student stories are context-bound.* The stories told here are bound to a particular context beyond which the interpretations cannot be generalized. The group is largely homogeneous along race and class lines, and the college environment has a distinct character. The reader must judge to what degree these stories and my interpretations of them can be transferred to other contexts.

6. *Ways of knowing and reasoning patterns within them are presented here as patterns in Frye's terms.* The five previous assumptions culminate in this definition of ways of knowing and patterns within them. While recognizing the fluidity and variation among and within members of the group, I have attempted to chart the predominant ways of knowing in this group's experience. Although within those, women and men in the study did show differences in their use of reasoning patterns, these are not essential, universal, or enduring—a fact I stress throughout the book to avoid the appearance of overgeneralization. The patterns are not dichotomies but continuums containing various possibilities. Their value is to open up new ideas for dialogue in education that values these and future possibilities. I will argue in Part Two of the book that the process of charting these patterns is potentially more important than the patterns themselves.

The second part of my plan to avoid overgeneralization hinges on language and types of information. I have named the patterns in ways that I think capture their essence. My discussion uses those names rather than gender-related language to remind the reader throughout the book that the patterns are not gender-exclusive. The variability in students' use of patterns is described in Chapter Two to emphasize their fluid nature. Examples used in Chapters Three through Six include quotes from both women and men, though each pattern contains more examples from the gender using it most. This approach should help avoid overgeneralizations, both by readers and by me. A more detailed explanation of the method of the study is located in the resources.

The Context: Miami University

The six assumptions just outlined emphasize the importance of context in interpreting students' stories. Just as the stories told in this book were influenced by my ways of understanding as a researcher, they were also influenced by the context in which these students attended college. The remainder of the chapter offers what Lincoln and Guba (1985) call the "thick" description of that context. Although the characteristics of the students are of primary importance, the broader student body, the student culture, and the institutional culture all play a part.

Study Participants

One hundred and one students, selected randomly from the entering class of 1986, participated in the study. Details of their selection and interviews are discussed in the resources. All were traditional-aged students, and fifty were male. Three of the 101 students in this study were from nondominant populations. Although I never asked them directly about this subject, many volunteered in the course of our interviews that they received above-average grades. Students often expressed concern over what normally would be considered above-average grades. For example, Scott recounted the following:

> I did really well last semester. The only thing that bummed me out was that I was borderline A-B on the final in political science. Really, all that I needed to get an A was a 90 percent on the final, or an

89 really. And I got a B. So that upset me a lot
because that would have raised my GPA.

Only one or two students reported a serious struggle for
academic survival, and those instances were usually at a particular period of time rather than during most of the college experience. Students in the study declared majors in all six university divisions, and many changed their major at least once.

Involvement in college was a high priority for the students in the study. The stories told in this book are peppered
with references to leadership positions in student organizations,
active involvement in organizational and service activities, and
membership in Greek organizations. Many students reported
participating in the honors program, and three were from the
Western interdisciplinary program. Fifteen of the students took
part in Laws Hall and Associates (a student advertising organization), and nine took advantage of international study opportunities. Many students held part-time jobs in local businesses
or in campus offices such as the computer labs, the Outdoor
Pursuit Center, residence life, and campus dining halls.

Despite their involvement in academic and cocurricular
pursuits, these students maintained a giving attitude. They invested time and effort in this particular study to help Miami
faculty learn more about how students come to know. They were
candid in their sharing of experiences in hopes that future students unknown to them would benefit. Their commitment was
evident in their persistence in the study. Of 101 students interviewed in their first year, 95 returned for the sophomore-year
interview, 86 for the junior-year interview, 80 for the senior-
year interview, and 70 for the fifth-year interview. Two students
who transferred to other institutions their junior year stayed in
the study. The group was balanced by gender during the first
year (fifty-one women and fifty men) and remained reasonably
so throughout the study. Students rarely complained about their
frustrating experiences, usually couching their criticisms in constructive suggestions. Although many had periods that shook
their self-confidence, they generally had the same high expectations and confidence as their larger peer group.

The Student Body

As the prevailing winds metaphor would suggest, the study participants were not exactly representative of the larger student body but shared most of its characteristics. Miami's participation in the Cooperative Institutional Research Program (American Council on Education and the University of California, Los Angeles, 1986) yields information on demographic characteristics, student experiences, and student expectations. The profile of the 1986 entering class summarized this information for the class of which my study participants were a part. The information was based on a 44 percent male and 56 percent female student response.

The majority (80 percent) of the students were eighteen years old. Ninety-seven percent were white, and 3 percent were from nondominant populations. Thirty percent lived within one hundred miles of Miami, 61 percent from one hundred to five hundred miles away, and 10 percent more than five hundred miles away. Seventy-five percent were residents of Ohio. The majority of students reported parental income as either between $40,000 and $74,999 (47 percent) or between $75,000 and $149,999 (23 percent). Thirty-four percent of these parents had four dependents. Eighty-five percent of the students stated that their parents lived together. Although the data did not clearly indicate how many students came from the first generation in their family to attend college, only 13 percent of their fathers and 22 percent of their mothers had not attended college.

The group was highly involved in academic and campus activities. Most studied with other students (93 percent) and had been bored in class (97 percent). The majority had attended religious services (86 percent), had attended a recital or concert (95 percent), and drank beer (80 percent). Many engaged in volunteer work (74 percent) and reported having stayed up all night at least once (78 percent). Sixty percent earned a varsity letter in sports, and 50 percent played a musical instrument. Thirty-five percent were president of one or more student organizations. (It is no wonder that 78 percent had stayed up all night.)

Miami was the first choice for 78 percent of these students, 85 percent of whom had one to four other acceptance offers. They reported going to college to get better jobs (86 percent), make more money (71 percent), gain a general education (62 percent), and prepare for graduate school (51 percent). They selected Miami for two primary reasons: academic reputation (89 percent) and graduate job placement (62 percent). They were well prepared, with 98 to 100 percent meeting or exceeding requirements of four years of English, three years of math, two years of a foreign language, and one year of history. Seventy to 78 percent met or exceeded requirements of two years of physical science, one-half year of computer science, and one year of art or music. Forty-eight percent met or exceeded the requirement of two years of biological science. Many earned advanced placement in English (39 percent), math (44 percent), social studies (37 percent), and natural sciences (26 percent).

The profile for this class published by the Admissions Office in 1986 described the typical student as having a high school grade point average of 3.4, as being in the top 14 percent of her or his class, and as having a 25.8 on the ACT or a SAT score of 533 verbal and 600 math. These students had high aspirations and expectations. Highest degrees planned included bachelor's (25 percent), master's (46 percent), doctorate (12 percent), medicine or veterinary medicine (7 percent), and law (7 percent). The majority expected to get their degree (84 percent), and find a job in their field (73 percent). Most also anticipated being satisfied with college (64 percent) and making at least a B average (52 percent). Their perceptions of themselves were equally strong. The majority saw themselves as above average or in the top 10 percent in academic ability (90 percent) and in drive to achieve (74 percent). Many also held this perception as it related to leadership ability (61 percent), physical health (65 percent), intellectual self-confidence (67 percent), and social self-confidence (49 percent). It seems that their expectations were well founded.

Finally, a few of the Cooperative Institutional Research Programs questions about values add to the profile of these students. Seventy-four percent expected to become an authority in their field, raise a family, and be well-off financially. Ninety-three percent (97 percent of women and 87 percent of men) supported job equality for women. Approximately 65 percent believed that the government was not promoting disarmament or controlling pollution and that abortion should be legalized.

The stories in this book were constructed in this context. (In the interest of describing the context thoroughly, I have provided additional information regarding the student culture and the institution in Resource A.) Although this context differs from that of many higher education institutions, the stories can inspire understanding of students in other environments. The study participants' contribution to our comprehension of ways of knowing and how various college experiences affect knowing is substantial. I invite you to listen carefully to their stories in hopes that they will spark new possibilities for all educators.

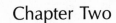

Chapter Two

Gender-Related
Patterns in Knowing

Before, it was getting a lot of the facts down. And now, it's truly trying to analyze, trying to really think. Looking back, I can see that steady progression from freshman year, where you took a basic chemistry class and a math class and an English class and that sort of thing and a history class, and they said, "All right, well, here's the history of the world." And although it can be approached in different ways, there're certain things that are pretty cut and dried. You can look at an issue from both sides, and it's still history, and you're still getting those facts and different people's different opinions about things. And then that's kind of the basis. And now, taking that and working with it to come up with some sort of conclusion, or maybe not a conclusion, and that's the conclusion in itself.

— Lowell

Lowell's reflections on college are only a small part of his story, but they clearly express the transitions he encountered in his assumptions about knowing. Like Lowell, students in this study told their stories in a way that demonstrated their awareness of, reflection upon, and interpretation of their particular experiences. As I listened to and studied seventy longitudinal sets of stories, I identified assumptions about knowing in each story. To interpret the meaning of the collective stories, I grouped

28

similar assumptions into categories called ways of knowing and charted their progression. The result is the epistemological reflection model.

The overarching story that emerged from this process includes four qualitatively different ways of knowing, each characterized by a core set of epistemic assumptions. Each leads to particular expectations of the learner, peers, and instructor in learning settings, as well as to an understanding of how learning should be evaluated and how educational decisions are made. An overview of the epistemological reflection model appears in Table 2.1 to serve as a guide to our exploration of the four ways of knowing. These, however, are best explained within the context of the students' own experiences rather than by the abstract form they take in Table 2.1. The same is true of the gender-related patterns that emerged within three of these ways of knowing.

To illustrate the general development of ways of knowing, two students' stories are recounted in detail in this chapter. Gwen and Mark represent individual examples of the greater story discussed in this chapter because each espoused all four ways of knowing over the five-year period. The pace of their development differs from that of some of their counterparts, particularly in Mark's case. Although Gwen and Mark are not prototypes of the entire group, their experiences serve to help us grasp the developmental process from their view of the world. Interludes are inserted to draw connections between their particular experiences and the overarching story.

Absolute Knowing

We first encounter Gwen and Mark during their freshman year, when they were both absolute knowers.

Gwen

Gwen entered college in the fall of 1986. It was October 9 when she arrived at my office to participate in my research interviews. I could immediately tell from her demeanor that she was an ener-

Table 2.1. Epistemological Reflection Model.

Domains	Absolute Knowing	Transitional Knowing	Independent Knowing	Contextual Knowing
Role of learner	• Obtains knowledge from instructor	• Understands knowledge	• Thinks for self • Shares views with others • Creates own perspective	• Exchanges and compares perspectives • Thinks through problems • Integrates and applies knowledge
Role of peers	• Share materials • Explain what they have learned to each other	• Provide active exchanges	• Share views • Serve as a source of knowledge	• Enhance learning via quality contributions
Role of instructor	• Communicates knowledge appropriately • Ensures that students understand knowledge	• Uses methods aimed at understanding • Employs methods that help apply knowledge	• Promotes independent thinking • Promotes exchange of opinions	• Promotes application of knowledge in context • Promotes evaluative discussion of perspectives • Student and teacher critique each other
Evaluation	• Provides vehicle to show instructor what was learned	• Measures students' understanding of the material	• Rewards independent thinking	• Accurately measures competence • Student and teacher work toward goal and measure progress
Nature of knowledge	• Is certain or absolute	• Is partially certain and partially uncertain	• Is uncertain—everyone has own beliefs	• Is contextual; judge on basis of evidence in context

getic, friendly person. She volunteered that her initial educational experiences were in Canada, where she lived until junior high school. She described herself as involved in many high school activities and always busy. Asked to describe how she learned, Gwen responded:

> I try to keep ideas real separate. And when I'm taking my notes, definitely, so I can visually see a breakage between ideas and subtopics of a main idea. I think that when you read over your notes so many times, you remember what they look like — so sometimes you almost find yourself looking in your mind as to what the page looked like and how your notes were arranged. I try to summarize what the teachers say. I don't like to write out everything that they say by any means at all. A lot of times, I'll just put little notes in the margin about how this relates to something that they spoke of before, to try and get a bigger perception of whatever it was.

Ways that teachers could help Gwen learn emerged next in the conversation:

> I like teachers that hit highlights in a section after you have supposedly read it. Sometimes teachers themselves will come up with little learning devices, like little word relations or things like that. I can do that on my own, but it's helpful if the teacher has one that works well, and they use it for years. And I like teachers who will give you as much as you need and not just leave you with a little small idea and try and have you talk it out. I like it when they give you a lot of information. Then you can discuss. Doing quizzes that don't count or a game of some sort helps.

From here, the conversation moved to the interactions Gwen had with other students. She reported that she found students who lived in her residence hall or were in her sorority to study with outside of class. She described these interactions as working on calculus problems with someone, quizzing each other in botany, and asking others to read her English paper to see how it sounded. Describing how peers helped her learn in class, she said:

> They can sit next to me. I think it's helpful just to have people around you, so if the teacher's whizzing through stuff, you can quickly ask somebody next to you and hope they're paying real close attention. It's nice to compare notes and see how they take notes after class is over. As far as during class, I don't really know what can be done without distracting the professor totally.

At this point in the conversation, we began to discuss how students' work was evaluated. Gwen remarked:

> I really prefer the professors that have weekly quizzes, then a big test, then more weekly quizzes, then a big test. Because then you've got those quizzes; you see generally what he's looking for; and you can go back and study those, work some problems through. If you have any questions about what you missed on the quiz, you can correct it for the test.

Gwen also had adamant feelings about tests:

> I hate true-false tests. Multiple choice is okay depending on the subject because I've had some teachers that are just impossible on multiple choice. When I thought of those classes it was very easy to say that I would much rather have an essay test. You're learning it, you're reading a lot, and you just have a general or a good idea of a certain subject — you could write and write, and sometimes that would be easier as opposed to just pulling out little tiny tidbits of it for an objective test.

Toward the end of the interview, we came to the subject of how Gwen was approaching educational decisions. She described her thoughts about career choices in this way:

> In the beginning, I was thinking in terms of what kind of environment could I see myself spending the majority of my life in. I tend to look at my parents. My dad is in banking. My mom was a teacher for many years and is now in real estate. So in those three areas there's a lot of diversity. I don't want a career that's going to be the same every day or that is limiting in any way. I want something that will be challenging, yet fulfilling. I'm always listing positive and negative aspects and what will happen to me if I do this. I heard a speaker just yesterday who said, "Today is all we know we have for sure. Tomorrow may never be here." And I tend to believe that a lot. But then I know I can't totally stick to that and expect my career is just going to fall into place. So I have to really just sit down and think, "What do I want to do, where am I going?"

As it turned out, this question would remain with Gwen for the next few years.

Mark

Mark also entered college in 1986. As the clock approached 2:00 P.M. on October 14, I heard a knock at my office door. I turned to see a thin, serious-looking student, who had also come to participate in my research interviews. When he immediately began asking questions about what my perspective on the study was, I knew it would be an interesting five years. As we settled into the interview, Mark described himself as growing up in an innovative grade school in the 1970s and as the beneficiary of parents who believed in taking him to cultural events as a young child. He described both as "broadening the mind for a youth." Asked how he learned at the present time, Mark responded:

In my opinion, the best way to learn is to listen in
class, not be distracted. If I want to learn, then I'll
sit in the front row or front third and try to concentrate and look at the teacher. There is a tendency
to daydream when you're in the back. So just concentrating on the class, in my opinion, is the way
to get ahead.

On the subject of teachers, Mark had this to say:

I like teachers with a sense of humor. As far as
presenting ideas, I like concrete examples. For a
class atmosphere, I like participation. Challenge the
student. Don't give him an answer. Let's say I
respond to a teacher. She plays devil's advocate and
tries to dig more out of me than just my first response — dig deep into the theory, you know, "Why
did I say that?" Then I think, "Why *did* I say that?"
If I get tongue-tied — it's fairly rare, but if I do —
then I know I'm really thinking. And when I'm
stumped, I'll admit it and say, "I don't know." When
I say I don't know, I don't quit thinking about it.
It's just that I don't have the answer yet.

Asked what students could do to help him learn, Mark
said:

Basically, if some of them would just shut up. You
hear chattering in the background, and that's kind
of distracting. As an adult, you're at this age now
where there's a big difference, I guess, between
those who have a mature outlook and those who
don't. If they could just keep their mind on class
while they're in class, that's all I ask. In grade
school, I was the one getting in the way — a little
in high school too. But now, if you're in college,
you're here to learn. And supposedly, we're real
smart, everybody here says. Let's just try to keep
it under control for an hour and fifteen minutes.

After a short conversation about social interactions involving study versus parties, the topic of evaluating students' work arose:

> Some classes just don't lend themselves to teachers' comments on papers, like physics and math. They're very straightforward. But in papers where you're writing, if a teacher can pick out a triple mixed metaphor, or whatever, then go ahead and do it. Overall evaluations, not just on what you're handing in for homework, would really help. If the teacher wrote a comment on how I was doing in class, not just on that paper, then that could be what I need to work better in the class. You think of a physics and a math course — you're filling out little squares for the test. It's such a factual thing, you know where you messed up. Whereas in English, there's a lot more theory and structure behind papers, so you can mess up and not see it.

Later, the conversation turned to how Mark approached educational decisions. Describing his decision-making process, he offered:

> This university is big enough that there's a lot of bureaucracy, so I try to beat the system however I can. I sign up for more credits than you're allowed to see if you can do it. As far as discerning what courses I want, I made a personal rule that I'm only going to take two courses a semester that I don't like. I have a luxury because my major is very flexible. I'm going to law school, so I could study music and get into law school.

On the subject of why he chose this particular institution, Mark explained that his mother had pressed him to consider it. He had really wanted to go to a smaller school, but a few considerations changed that:

I had this romantic idea about being on academic scholarship. And when it was offered, I figured I might as well take it. Plus, like it or not, this is the future, the real world, white, upper-middle class. You're looking at the future leaders of America, like it or not. And I know the director of my major. He kind of swayed me—he's a really cool guy.

As the interview came to a close, I asked Mark if there was anything that he thought was important that we had not yet covered. He responded:

Sure. Well, there's an issue of gender in here. From what I've heard, girls learn better because they are more linguistically oriented, and that's how the teacher teaches, basically. Knowledge is maturity, so if girls are learning more, then they would be more mature in their midteens than guys. But I also think that some of that discrepancy is made up for in the way teachers treat guys. They expect us to be more aggressive and to raise our hands all the time. [For] girls, I think they don't encourage aggressive learning. Guys pick up things in their mind, mechanical reasoning—I don't know.

On that note, we adjourned, agreeing to meet again the following year. I wondered how his thinking about gender would evolve and what I would learn about the subject from Mark and his peers.

The Nature of Absolute Knowing

Both Gwen and Mark were categorized as absolute knowers their first year. Absolute knowers view knowledge as certain. They believe that absolute answers exist in all areas of knowledge. Uncertainty is a factor only because students do not have access at the time to absolute knowledge. Neither Gwen or Mark introduced the idea of uncertainty in their first-year interviews.

Some absolute knowers acknowledge that differences of opinion sometimes exist among authorities, but they do not view these instances as changing the facts. Instead, they interpret such situations as differing degrees of detail, different opinions about the facts, or misinformed authorities.

Students with this perspective believe that authorities, particularly instructors, have all the answers. Thus, absolute knowers view their role as learners as obtaining knowledge from the instructors. This point of view translates into learning methods that focus on acquiring and remembering information. For example, Mark's comments about sitting in the front row and Gwen's note-taking plan both represent techniques to accomplish this goal. Gwen's endorsement of games to help her remember and Mark's preference for being challenged also place the responsibility for learning on the instructor. Because the teacher holds the knowledge, it is the teacher's task to transfer it to the student.

Evaluation is perceived as an opportunity to reproduce for the instructor what the student has acquired in order to see if it is correct. Mark described getting feedback to "see where you messed up," and Gwen wanted a series of quizzes so that she could correct questions before the major exam. Peers' role in learning is limited by the fact that they do not possess knowledge other than that obtained from authorities. Recall Mark's comment "Basically, if some of them would just shut up" and Gwen's comment "They can sit next to me." Peers can share materials and explain what they have learned in order to help each other in the acquisition process.

Patterns characterized by different justifications of epistemic assumptions emerged within absolute knowing. These patterns are related to gender (they were used more often, but not exclusively, by one gender). They are best viewed as a continuum, because some students' reasoning clearly represented one or the other, whereas others' fell in between. Reasoning patterns represent qualitative differences in how students justify epistemic assumptions within the same way of knowing and, thus, different but equally valid approaches to knowing.

Receiving and mastering knowledge emerged as the two

patterns within absolute knowing. The receiving pattern was used more often by women than by men in the study; the mastery pattern was used more often by men than by women. Receiving-pattern students took a private approach to acquiring knowledge, whereas mastery-pattern students took a public approach. Receiving-pattern students describe listening and recording as their primary role in class, do not expect interaction with the instructor, view peers as a support network to help listen and occasionally ask questions, value evaluation that offers the best opportunity to demonstrate their knowledge, and rely on their own interpretations of discrepancies in knowledge claims rather than consulting authority. Gwen illustrated this pattern through her comments on taking notes, sharing notes with peers, preferring weekly quizzes, and having limited expectations of teachers.

Mastery-pattern students embrace a public role in class to demonstrate their interest to the instructor, expect interchanges with teachers, view peers as partners in arguing and quizzing each other to master the material, value evaluation that helps them improve their mastery, and appeal to authority to resolve differences in knowledge claims. Mark illustrated this pattern clearly in his first-year interview, particularly in his comments on the subject of teachers. His expectation to be challenged is clearly aimed at mastery. This theme carries through his desire for "a comment on how I was doing in class" to help him "work better." More details about absolute knowers in both of these patterns are provided in Chapter Three.

Transitional Knowing

Gwen's sophomore and junior interviews and Mark's sophomore interview showed that both students had exchanged absolute for transitional knowing. Their comments reveal what transitional knowing entails.

Gwen's Sophomore Interview

When Gwen came to her second-year interview in October of 1987, her thinking was no longer absolute. True to her previous year's description of herself as busy, Gwen reported at the outset that she had taken a resident-assistant position in addition to her other activities. After a brief conversation about balancing studying with that type of responsibility, we turned to her current approach to learning, which she then described:

> I have started using different color pens, and I find that helps me. It helps me particularly in classes with a lot of overheads — like economics graphs. For me, to use the different colors — it's just much clearer; I can see things better. I can highlight points with different colors. It sounds really silly. I started doing it last year when I had an aeronautics class. He would be doing all this draftsman stuff in all one color. Nothing made sense in all one color.

The notion that material should make sense carried over into her description of the most effective teachers:

> When they can break down things into simplistic terms and give you — like my economics professor talks about pies a lot. He talks about apples and oranges and things that make it more tangible and easier to grasp. I have a professor this semester who puts a daily outline on the board of things he's going to cover. That way, even if I don't have the clearest notes — at least I know what he intended to cover. My French teacher is getting away from the book exercises because everyone falls asleep. So she's started getting us into group discussions using our reading, but she corrects our tenses and sentence structure. It's much more real, much more practical, and I think that's what we need. People are saying, "Let us learn something we can actually use."

Hoping to hear about her interaction with her peers, I asked Gwen to elaborate on the group discussions in French class. She said:

It's interesting because she's forcing us to think in
French. It's interesting, too, because she's very
French, and a lot of things we'll be talking about
she doesn't understand—our terms and things we
are trying to get across. She'll say, "Someone tell
me in French; I don't know what you're talking
about." We've been getting off on different topics.
Something about the women's movement in France—
everything from them getting their voting rights
through things that are going on now. And a lot
of controversy—like we went through a big thing
about what is the image of today's woman in France
here? How is it portrayed in the media and TV and
stuff like that? That's an interesting topic. The open
discussion is very helpful.

On the subject of evaluation, Gwen had mixed feelings.
Reflecting on her feelings from the year before, she said:

I like scan-tron [computer-scanned] tests; I've gotten to like them. I used to hate them. I've gotten
to a point now that I'm used to it. I like to see the
possibilities and work from there; seeing the words
keys things in your mind that help you, actually.
I used to have a problem with being able to make
sense of too many of the answers. In economics,
we have a workbook that has a lot of multiple-choice
pretests. You get used to that line of thinking. I
have essay in another class. I have a professor who,
if you were just slapping stuff down, would tell you
that you were doing that. It takes the pressure off
when you have multiple choice.

A short while later, Gwen commented that if she had a choice,
she would choose writing papers. She explained:

I'd rather write a paper than do anything else. Not
anything else, but than a test or anything like that.

> I like to write creatively. I don't particularly like
> to do analysis. I do [it], and that's all right, but I'd
> rather do something that's different. I've had some
> creative-writing classes that have just let me let my
> imagination go, and I really like that a lot. I think
> that sometimes it's more frustrating because you
> have nothing really to compare it to. On an exam,
> it's all cut and dried right in front of you.

Gwen's desire to let her imagination go reappeared in our discussion of how to choose between conflicting ideas. Although
she had not encountered any such instances in class, she described what she would do if they occurred:

> If it was the same class, I would talk to the profes-
> sor and try to make a link for myself. If it was two
> different classes, I'd just separate them. My expe-
> rience has been that when they [the teachers] have
> an idea and they keep talking about that idea—
> work with it, because that's what they want.

Asked how she would decide personally what to believe, Gwen
said:

> Basically, whatever made more sense to me, which-
> ever seemed more reasonable. They [the ideas]
> could be totally wrong. I probably wouldn't go into
> much more of it. I wouldn't go so far as to research
> it or anything. I really don't have interest in com-
> ing up with things like that.

Near the close of the interview, Gwen reported that she
had changed her major from business to English. Asked how
that came about, she explained:

> I got to thinking about what I wanted to do in my
> life and the kinds of things I wanted to see hap-
> pening. Business was not a part of that. I worked

in a bank this summer and liked it, but when I think of other possibilities and things I could be doing, English feels much better to me. I'm thinking about a lot of things — teaching high school, counseling, writing. But my dad is in banking, and he said his bank is interested in hiring people with liberal arts backgrounds. So I don't feel limited. I'm taking economics and accounting. I'm trying to keep as many doors open as I can because I really don't know what I want to do.

I wondered, as Gwen left, how her plan to keep doors open would work out over the next year.

Gwen's Junior Interview

By her junior year, Gwen had exchanged her resident-assistant position for a major leadership role in her sorority. As of October, she had not yet exchanged her transitional way of knowing for a new one. Early in the interview, she volunteered that she was taking all classes for her English major and found herself in "all different class settings and test taking." Intrigued, I asked her to continue. She started off with her views on tests:

> I hate multiple-choice tests. I go into an exam thinking that I know everything, and I'll get back a C. For the most part, my exams in the English department are essay. I can write, and I get A's. That's one of the biggest things — you can know that you know the material, go into the exam, and do well. You get a question, and you know how to answer it, and you can instantly relate [to] it in a way that best suits you.

Gwen's preference for tailoring evaluation techniques to her needs was also evident in her perspective on grading systems. She explained:

> One professor realized that three grades were not enough. He switched to three exams and two pap-

ers. It was better because the more that they have
to pull from gives the student a better chance to
do well in the course. I've had professors who give
you the option of tests or papers. For those students
who don't feel that they can do well on multiple
choice, the harder the exams are going to be. I have
the option in two of my courses. I think that's a
much more fair, objective way to evaluate the students' knowledge of the course matter.

Her relationships with instructors were more personal-
ized as well. Commenting on what she viewed as helpful from
instructors, Gwen said:

Every single one of my professors this semester
knows my name, inside of class, outside of class.
That makes it more comfortable to go in and talk
with professors, and you get the feeling they are
going to say hi because they know your name, and,
"Come on in and sit down." That's something I
never experienced before. My professors, for the
most part, want me to do well. They are willing
to help you; they are willing to do whatever it takes.

When the conversation turned to what classes were like,
Gwen described her role in her current classes:

My classes have both lecture and discussion. You
can't [just] sit there; there are always issues being
raised. You're always free to ask questions, in class,
out of class—to respond to other students' responses
to the professor. A lot of interaction, which not only
helps you understand but keeps you awake, keeps
you interested.

Part of what Gwen found interesting about this learning environment was students' views on various topics. She continued:

It's always interesting—if you know the material
well enough. See, I like to disagree and debate, and

a lot of it is just interpretation, the way you would
see character development, character analysis. Different people have different views on the character.
When people share these views, that to me says they
did their homework; they know what they are talking about.

Asked how she formed her views in these discussions, Gwen said:

It depends. Sometimes I will have my mind made
up before I go into class; sometimes I listen to this,
listen to that, evaluate it with what I think, and say,
"Well, I'll adapt or switch." And a lot of professors
don't say, "You have to say that it's this way." If
you can support it [another] way, they're open
enough to be able to accept that interpretation —
both interpretations.

Finally, Gwen talked about her enjoyment of her English
classes and her overall satisfaction with her major. That prompted
me to inquire about the impact of this satisfaction on her career
decision making. She responded:

I have always liked to write. I've written several
short stories. And that is my goal: that I will do
that someday. But I have worked for a bank the
last two summers. And talking to several other people, the liberal arts majors are of interest to them.
So it gave me a much broader selection of future
paths to take, law school, grad school, working for
a bank, stock company, corporation, or whatever.
It was always what I wanted to do all along.

Thus, although Gwen professed to want to be a writer, she was
continuing her open-door policy to avoid limiting her options.

Mark's Sophomore Interview

Mark had moved to transitional knowing by the time he came
to see me in September 1987. Inquisitive about the study as

ever, Mark was a little more relaxed for his sophomore interview and started off on a personal note by stating that he was happy because he was getting along well with his girl friend. After hearing about how his program was going and how he felt about school, we began to discuss learning. He maintained some of his approach to learning from the previous year:

> Always attend class, I think I said that, but it helps. Look at the instructor, keep eye contact — I always sit in the second row. The first row is too far — the instructor's looking past you. Don't sit in the back. You just can't function then.

But he also added a new dimension:

> Keep up when you can. Some classes you know you don't need to work in. Take that extra time and put it into classes that are really challenging. The challenging classes I'd say would be honors classes, small seminars where there is more give-and-take. The students make the class.

Asked to clarify the teacher's role in this setting, Mark responded:

> Take what we've read and don't just apply it within the context of the book. Apply it at least in the context of other books you've read in that class so there's a theme going through, a theme that we can always look at and grasp.

Returning to his thoughts on peers, Mark continued:

> The best classroom experiences are when the exchanges are wholly between the students and the instructor is more of a bystander. One instructor taught us some ways of looking at material, and then about midway through the semester he said, "Why don't you go ahead and discuss it?" He sat on the side and said, "I'm not going to say anything

unless you guys get way out of line." The students
can learn a lot from each other because students
have learned from different teachers all this material. We've gone to different schools, and we all
learn a different perspective.

Reporting an interesting evaluation technique he encountered, Mark shared his thoughts on evaluation of his work:

In my honors class, the instructor didn't give out
any grades for the whole semester until a year-end
conference, where he went over every paper and
told you what you got. He'd just write comments.
It made it more experimental for me because I
didn't have this shadow over my shoulder of grades
on each paper. So I was a little more experimental
in the structure of what I wrote, which helped me
a lot. I wouldn't want that in every class, though.
I wouldn't want things that uncertain. One a semester, yeah.

Eventually, the conversation turned to whether the information he had encountered was consistent. Mark speculated,
not remembering an exact incident:

If I encounter discrepancies, I think my mind is — I
want to be a lawyer — so I've concentrated on making it logical. What I do is make it fit logically. It
would really bother me if material didn't fit together. I don't think it's happened because I'd definitely remember it because it would frustrate me.
I'd go to the teacher and say, "This does not fit to
me. Explain it." I'd say they're totally responsible.
Unless they give you two things and you should be
able to figure it out on your own. That's fine with me.

Finally, in response to other ideas he might have, Mark
summarized his view on learning as a sophomore:

College shouldn't be a thing for buttressing things you've already learned. What it should do, in my opinion, is tear down and challenge some of those things. You can't do it all the time; you can't tear down everything when a person's grasping for straws. Challenge them, I mean, and tear things down and really question what they think. That's the job of the teacher. Build them back up a little.

The Nature of Transitional Knowing

Gwen's sophomore- and junior-year interviews and Mark's sophomore interview describe the assumptions inherent in transitional knowing. These differ from the absolute perspective in accepting that some knowledge is uncertain. Although transitional knowers still believe that absolute knowledge exists in some areas, they have concluded that uncertainty exists in others. Discrepancies among authorities in these uncertain areas are viewed as a result of the answers being unknown. Categorized as moving between transitional and independent knowing as a sophomore, Mark expressed a transitional explanation of knowledge differences in his comments about making material fit logically. Learning is more complex in the uncertain areas, a situation that prompts students to believe that understanding takes precedence over acquiring and remembering information. Gwen, categorized as a transitional knower in both her sophomore and junior years, showed a shift in her approach when she revised her note-taking plan (involving use of colored pens) to "make sense" of the material. Simply recording it was no longer sufficient.

Transitional knowers expect instructors to go further than simply providing information; they should employ methods that focus on understanding and application of knowledge. Students' investment in learning is dependent on their perception of how useful it will be in the future. For example, Mark suggested as a sophomore that the teacher use material in the context of other books to identify a theme for students. Gwen viewed her sophomore French class as effective because the students learned something practical. Evaluation is expected to measure students' understanding, rather than their acquisition of information. Issues of subjectivity in evaluation arise from the acknowledgment that even the instructors do not know the answers in some cases. This view of evaluation was expressed by Gwen's sophomore preference for writing creatively and her recognition that "slapping stuff down" on an essay was insufficient. As a junior, she wholeheartedly endorsed essays to "relate in a way that best suits you." The role of peers is expanded because involvement is seen as a way to learn in this uncertain arena. Classmates still do not know the answers, but discussion and hands-on activities can help promote understanding. Gwen endorsed this type of learning in her descriptions of her sophomore French class and her junior courses that combined lecture and discussion.

Interpersonal and impersonal describe the two patterns within transitional knowing. On this continuum, the interpersonal pattern was used more often by women than by men in this study; the impersonal pattern was employed more often by men than by women. Interpersonal-pattern students prefer to be involved in learning through collecting others' ideas, expect interaction with peers to hear their views and provide exposure to new ones, seek rapport with the instructor to enhance self-expression, value evaluation that takes individual differences into account, and resolve uncertainty by personal judgment. For example, Gwen appreciated discussion in her sophomore French class, liked evaluation in which she could "write creatively" and react in a way that worked for her, appreciated knowing her junior-year instructors, and made decisions based on "whatever made more sense to me."

Impersonal-pattern students want to be forced to think, prefer to exchange their views with instructors and peers via debate, expect to be challenged by instructors, value evaluation that is fair and practical, and resolve uncertainty by logic and research. Challenge was a major theme of Mark's sophomore interview. He also clearly demonstrated a use of logic in how he dealt with discrepancies. Although he did not mention debate in his comments on student-oriented discussion, we will hear in later interviews that debate was his approach as a sophomore. Gwen also began to show an interest in debate in her junior interview, saying, "I like to disagree and debate." Her purpose is more aligned to the collection of ideas (consistent with the interpersonal pattern) but contains elements of the impersonal one as well. Chapter Four contains more detailed stories of transitional knowers within both of these patterns.

Independent Knowing

Gwen's senior year and Mark's junior year marked their transition to independent knowing. The interviews that follow also illustrate two patterns within independent knowing.

Gwen's Senior Interview

Catching up with a college senior is not an easy task. When I finally did see Gwen at the start of the second semester of her senior year (January 1990), she was already preoccupied with graduation and postgraduation plans. The postgraduation plans remained flexible, as was evident in these comments:

> I'm looking for a job and applying to grad schools. I'm planning to go back to graduate school at some point. I'm looking at things like industrial psychology, English. I've even thought about law school and an MBA program. Lots of different things. But right now, I'm just trying to find some direction— get some grounding and go from there. Sometimes it's exciting. And then you think, "Ah, this is my future," and you panic. I think I'm going to enter a training program with a company that I've interned with the last two summers. I think I'm going to get into the training and development aspect of the human resources department, which is what I want to do. So I'm excited about that. They also encourage you to go back to school while you're working for them. So I've even thought that I could do some preliminary stuff—you know, even just sampling different things. And if I find something finally, then go back and do it.

Turning to her experience as a senior, Gwen described a new relationship between student and teacher:

> As you get towards upper-level classes, there is a lot more one-on-one contact with the instructor and the students. The pedagogical relationship is not the same as it was when you were a freshman and the professor stands at the front of the room and lectures to the class. It's more of an interchange and interplay. They try to know you personally; you call them by their first name. It's much more casual, informal, and, I think, more effective: seminars, a lot of active participation in discussions. I'm not opposed to lecture because I think sometimes it's the most effective way to get stuff across. But I think as far as actively taking it in, you have to give something back as you're learning it. I appreciate instructors who try to get to know you on your level rather than trying to set up the hierarchical structure. The student is less intimidated. And although you know that your experience and your background and your knowledge of the subject are not what your instructor's are, you still feel that your opinions and your ideas are valid.

Gwen added that several instructors had invited students to their homes for wine and cheese and informal discussion. They also encouraged students to talk to each other, rather than to the instructor, in class. Gwen found this valuable. She described peers' views:

> Very diverse views, diverse opinions. It's funny. You read the same thing, and yet people see three different stories or three different meanings or interpretations. And although you might have grounded yours, it's very easy to see how they might have come up with that reading. It helps you either reaffirm your own opinion, modify it, or whatever is neces-

sary. I'm rarely tight on my opinions. Once I form one — a lot of times I'm kind of fuzzy about it — but when I do have one, someone has to give me a really good argument to make me sway a little bit from mine. In that case, all these other opinions of people help me form my own.

After this line of conversation, I asked Gwen to talk about how the existence of different meanings was a factor in the evaluation of students' work. She replied:

I don't think that they judge whether your perspective is good or bad. I think they want you to make a stand, and they want you to support it. They want to see that you've thought about it. And if you cover those bases and express it clearly, then I think you'll do well. That's the opinion I get, at least. But they're not saying that your opinion will be right or wrong, that your ideas are right or wrong. It's just if you have ideas and can get them across, then you're successful. I think this is so much better because, particularly when you're talking about literature, there's no right and wrong. I mean, certain professors have certain ideas. And, yeah, you have to reflect those back because there are big things in certain pieces. But to say that there's a right way and a wrong way to read something — it's just, I think, insane.

The impact of this new relationship between teachers and students and of the learning environment just described was our next topic of conversation. Gwen described it in this way:

It's amazing how much different it is when you really are interested and involved. Before, I would read the material and say okay. Now I read the material, and I think about it. There's the difference, because before you would read the material and be familiar with it and they'd tell you what to think,

as opposed to now, when they say, "What do you
think?" and you [say to yourself], "Oh, I'd better
think of something."

Asked whether she could still learn from lecture classes, given
her perspective, Gwen replied:

> It depends on the class. For an anthropology class,
> it would be no problem. I think it's just that I've
> been trying to read things, as far as literature. Opin-
> ions versus facts, you know. There are certain
> things in anthropology that are true. And in liter-
> ature, that's not necessarily so. It's a much freer
> structure, and I think the classes in each are reflec-
> tive of that. So what works for something that is
> point, point, point is not going to work the same
> for the other. But when I was a freshman, I didn't
> know that. You didn't know that it was any differ-
> ent than being a student and listening to the profes-
> sor and raising your hand from time to time when
> it was appropriate. Maybe you had a little bit of
> involvement, but it wasn't the same. You know,
> when the teacher says, "I reject this role as pro-
> fessor."

Gwen called her experiences from this year the "capstone of four
years." There was certainly no mistaking the difference between
the woman who separated ideas via colored pens and the one
approaching graduation, who wanted to discuss different meanings of literature.

Mark's Junior Interview

Mark started off the junior-year interview (September 1988) with
the conclusion that students were more likely to adapt to teachers
than the reverse. Intrigued with this view I urged him to continue:

> I definitely have been more attuned to seminar-type learning because I have had teachers in that setting whom I admired. Now it's become entrenched where if I get in a lecture class, I will definitely be one of the more vocal ones because I'll want the exchange with the teacher and other students. I need that. I can't sit quiet too long, whereas I could originally.

Explaining further the importance of seminar-type learning, he said:

> I can go beyond the material with it. The teacher does not know what I am thinking, so he or she will present the material that is important to them. They don't know my interests. The teacher can address them if I bring it up. And then I learn, and also the professor might learn a few things because I have a diverse background, whereas he or she may be more specialized.

Following up on the earlier comment about exchanges with other students, Mark remarked:

> I want to be challenged. I'm in a gender theory course that has a lot of women's studies students in it. There I feel challenged. My own politics are closely like theirs, but I don't have the background in women's studies that they do. When I speak up, I really have to concentrate on what I think, communicate it effectively, and then if there is a discrepancy between what I think and what someone else thinks, then I feel I can grow. But in another class, sometimes I can say anything, and everybody just turns into, "Yeah, that sounds good."

Asked to talk more clearly about the role he played in this learning process, Mark responded:

You have to target a class and get a subject that
you're interested in. Then narrow it down to who's
good at that subject. Listen to the professor and
challenge his stuff. What is he or she saying that's
different from what I think? Look at journals. See
if there's other ways to look at the material that the
professor is ignoring, maybe. You have to try to
fix their politics early on. You have to set priorities. Do you want to expand your mind? I do, so
I really put a lot of emphasis on academic performance myself.

On the subject of evaluation, Mark described the reality
of grading, as well as ways to make the most of it.

I like something more than just a number on a
paper. I like an invitation from a professor to make
an appointment to come in and talk. Just so you
can get beyond, "I've got an A. That means I did
good. Why?" You can't be too idealistic as far as
saying, "Grading's horrible. It's just part of our
meritocracy." Maybe it is, but we can't change that
overnight. So, you know, you're going to law school.
If they don't want C's, you get A's. Just find out
what's behind it. And see what you can do to improve it.

Toward the end of the interview, Mark reflected on the
similarities and differences between his current views and those
he held the previous year. He said:

I'm a little more understanding and more personable.
It goes back to an experience I don't want to get
into — it was an experience outside the classroom that
was very enlightening. It gave me a little more compassion and a little more idea of the pressures people are under sometimes. And not quite be, as I was
freshman year to a certain extent, holier than thou.

The Nature of Independent Knowing

Gwen was moving from transitional to independent knowing her senior year; Mark was thinking independently in his junior year. Independent knowing represents a shift to assuming that knowledge is mostly uncertain. Viewing knowledge as uncertain changes substantially the learning process and the sense of where knowledge resides. Differences in the opinions of various authorities represent the range of views possible in an uncertain world. Moreover, these authorities are no longer the only source of knowledge; instead, students begin to see themselves as equals and hold their own opinions as valid. Gwen described this shift in her senior literature class when she said that believing there was a right or wrong way to read literature was insane. The emerging ability to create one's own perspectives focuses attention on thinking through and expressing one's own views, as well as hearing those of others. Gwen again demonstrated her intellectual autonomy in her comments on how she thought about material in her senior literature class.

Independent knowers appreciate instructors who promote this independent thinking and the exchange of opinions in class. The instructor's responsibility changes from providing the knowledge to providing the context in which to explore knowledge. Mark had such an experience as a sophomore, when his teacher stayed out of the conversation; as a junior, Mark advocated exploring knowledge by bringing up his interests in the class. Students who think independently also believe that evaluation should reward this kind of thinking and should not penalize anyone for holding views different from those of the instructor or authors of texts. Gwen directly addressed this issue as a senior when she said, "I don't think they judge whether your perspective is good or bad. They want you to make a stand and support it." For the first time, peers are a legitimate source of knowledge rather than part of the process of knowing. For Gwen, "other opinions of people help me form my own." In the excitement over independent thinking, of course, the idea of judging some perspectives as better or worse is overlooked. Students during this phase stress being open-minded and allowing everyone to believe what they will.

The two forms of independent knowing are interindividual and individual. The interindividual pattern was used by women more than by men in this study; the individual pattern was used more by men than by women. The interindividual pattern is characterized by students' dual focus on thinking for themselves and engaging the views of others. They emphasize thinking for themselves and having their own interpretations; simultaneously, however, they espouse sharing views with peers, expect instructors to promote exchange of opinions, and view evaluation as a joint process occurring between student and instructor. Gwen's senior interview reveals this pattern. She described class as "more of an interchange and interplay," involving active discussion that made her "feel that your opinions and your ideas are valid." In discussing her classmates, she suggested that their diverse views led her to reaffirm her own opinion or to modify it.

Individual-pattern students also value interchange with peers and instructors, but their primry focus is on their own independent thinking. They emphasize thinking for themselves (and ways to think), expect peers to think independently, prefer instructors who allow students to define their own learning goals, and view evaluation as based on independent thinking. In Mark's junior interview, this individual pattern is manifest in his focus on "expanding your mind," going beyond the material, and being challenged. He valued being challenged by classmates in his women's studies class and felt he could learn more from debate than when students automatically agreed with him. His closing comment hinted at a change in his interactions with others (and possibly his reasoning pattern) that he talked more about the following year. Chapter Five contains detailed stories of independent thinkers within both the interindividual and individual patterns.

Contextual Knowing

The fifth-year interviews with Gwen and Mark, as well as Mark's senior interview, revealed another way of knowing. Gwen's and

Mark's comments typify contextual knowing and show how patterns of knowing that appeared to be gender-related in previous ways of knowing seem to converge in the contextual perspective.

Gwen's Fifth-Year Interview

I looked forward to my January 8, 1991, telephone interview with Gwen due, in part, to my overwhelming curiosity about her career decision. As luck would have it, her most significant recollection of her senior year was the job search. Describing its ups and downs, she finally came around to how she decided what to do.

> There's certainly nothing scientific about it; gut feelings were a lot of it for me. I tried to talk to as many people as I possibly could in different areas — everything from people who were involved in HR [human resources] to people who were accountants, [in] advertising, banking — all different realms of responsibilities — and try to come up with an assessment based on what I heard from them. "What do I think of all these different opportunities?" I continued to interview. A lot of that was also just trying to say, "Could I really see myself here, doing what they're telling me this job would do?" I really believe that you can make of a situation more than it seems to be. You make of it whatever. In my case, I thought that there were a lot of things that I could have been happy doing, and it was just trying to pick the best opportunity at that time. I learned senior year that it is essential that I always maintain the ability to think critically. To become too accepting in my mind is very dangerous because it allows room for things to go overlooked or unseen. I was looking for an opportunity that was going to give me room to grow, that was going to provide the immediate type of program that I was

looking for, in addition to being a good place to
be from also in the event that I wanted to move
on. I wanted to be from a good, solid background
that I knew would be worth something someplace
else. So I guess that's how I wound up at this job.

The job was underwriting insurance at a major insurance company. We went back to her senior year before talking about her
experience in this new job.

Asked what was important for us to talk about regarding
her senior year, Gwen started with this statement:

I think that *interactive* would be probably the best
way to describe it. I had a couple of seminar classes,
my history class, and a human sexuality class which
was big lecture. All, with the exception of the lecture class, were very interactive—where it's very
evident if you are not partaking in the discussion;
if you don't have things to offer, to bring to class.
I think it was that from the beginning, you are
evaluated on your participation in the class, and
please do not come if you are bringing nothing with
you. Those types of expectations, when everyone
else is contributing. Also it's the instructor. He or
she in all these instances really made me want to
be a part of that.

Gwen appreciated it when her peers took assignments seriously
and brought their valuable ideas to class. On the subject of how
to make sense of these contributions, she commented:

In some classes, particularly when you're talking
politics, you have people that are super fired up on
the left and people who are super fired up on the
right. And you know every day that comment X
will trigger the person on the left and comment Y
the person on the right. Those people who are so
totally impassioned by their thoughts and feelings

help to offset each other, so you can kind of arrive at something in the middle. You have to take it in and let it process before you form a reaction.

After a moment of reflection, she added:

> A response as opposed to a reaction — a reaction being something that is sudden and spontaneous and a response being something that has taken more facts into account and allowed them to kind of gel. As you hear more people's opinions, you piece together what you really think. Who has the valid point? Whose point is not valid in your opinion? And come to some other new understanding from a more dimensional perspective. It's super subjective. A lot of it is weighing people's opinions and their facts against what you yourself have previously processed. I don't care if people feel this way or that way about it. But if they can support their stance and have some background and some backing for that, to my thinking that is valid. If they're just shooting off at the mouth because they like to hear themselves talk and want to get in the stir, that is not valid. That's annoying.

Gwen took this perspective, which she labeled the ability to think critically, into her work in the insurance business. Becoming quickly bored with the technical learning involved in underwriting, she was unwilling to accept that she would be doing it for six months. She described what she did next:

> I started looking at the management training program as a whole and identifying strengths and weaknesses. I tried to talk to as many people in different areas of my company — networking if you will — and made a lot of noise to the people who it mattered hear me: my managers; my supervisors; my HR manager, who was responsible for the pro-

gram. One day, I got called into my manager's office, and she closed the door and said, "I want to talk to you about your progress and your path here." And I thought uh-oh. She said, "You've done well. We are going to move up your move."

Gwen subsequently moved into her human resources responsibilities four months ahead of schedule. She learned from the experience, saying:

I learned that it is important to try and improve the process. To accept it as is, is not good enough for me. I wanted to know the whys and why nots and to challenge those things and come up with some constructive feedback. I really think to be passive and sedate — for some people that's fine. But that's not the way I learn, and that's not the way I feel challenged — to just work by someone else's set of objectives on their agenda. I like to have a little bit more to do with that.

Reflecting on her work experience thus far, Gwen said:

When I first started, I really pushed and tried to stretch and tried to grow in this position. I was really bursting and made that very open with my manager: "Please give me something else to do. I'm anxious to take on a new project." It's persistence, it's the ability to be patient and squeaky at the same time. And there's a fine line between being persistent and challenging and being abrasive. That's something I'm conscious of, and I think I do pretty well.

Gwen credited much of her success to date to what she learned during her senior year in college, which included coming to terms with her career expectations. She remarked:

I realized that it is ongoing learning and that every time you think you are comfortable and think you understand—for me, those are always the times when I try to shake things up again so I'm forced to push a little further. I thought originally that I should know what I wanted to do at the end of four years. And now I see that I don't really need to know exactly what I want to do. But I should be getting some good experience that I can—that sounds kind of funny. It sounds very directionless. But I really think that you work with the opportunities that you have and try to make the most of them at that time. When those opportunities seem to be dwindling, you look for new opportunities. And if you've made good use of your time to that point, you've certainly not wasted any time. So that's my outlook, I suppose.

Mark's Senior Interview

I was fortunate enough to see Mark as a senior in September 1989. Mark immediately took charge of the interview and said that he would definitely like to discuss having had the best professor of his career. He struggled to describe what it was about her that was so powerful:

> I've never seen such control in the classroom; effortless, though, and not authoritarian control. Absolutely perfect timing on comments. I was absolutely amazed with her.

He quickly realized that I wanted more details:

> Well, okay. There'd be a movie. She'd sit on the side of the classroom—out of the position of asymmetrical relations—the power source being in front of the room. She'd throw out a question and have

us discuss it. If she thought the reactions were getting a little major or whatever, she'd throw in a
voice of support. But she'd suggest something to
keep it going. Just perfect comments to make sure
that the class used the correct critiques or the critique she was teaching them to view the film with.
It's hard to describe, but she had a real sense of
when to step in and when not to. Very intelligent.
It's hard to describe.

Mark turned the conversation to another rewarding classroom
experience, which led us to the issue of other students:

There was a lot of unity in one class; we discussed
personal issues. I think that's important regardless
of what classroom you're in. It's important to know
something about other students in the classroom
and get a sense for them. Even if you don't agree
with that student, if you know where the person's
coming from, you can divorce the critiques of their
views from critiquing the person. It's a fine line between getting too far away from the material and
getting it just personal and then engaging the material so much that your personal views don't come
into it. It's a tough negotiation. It's rare, but it
happens.

I asked Mark to elaborate on the idea of engaging the material.
His response:

If it resonates with your personal history — that's
what I mean by engagement. And also on an intellectual level. If the material speaks across disciplines to what you've learned in the past and also
speaks between each book you read. Believe it or
not, with supposedly good professors, sometimes
the material just does not interlock, as far as I can
see. Fine, you have a historical progression between

this writer and this writer, and they're addressing to a certain extent the same subject, but there's not much there to interlock them. The material needs to speak to larger issues, much bigger than any classroom can address in and of itself.

Returning to the idea of interactions with other students, the conversation took an interesting turn. Mark commented:

> The interchanges — this sounds horrible, but I'll say it, I'll be as honest as I can — the interchanges that really stimulate my brain come from the teacher; they don't come from other classmates. When I say something in class, to a certain extent it's me showing how smart I can be. I'm proud of this. I suppose there's a lot of ego involved in it. That's one reason that when I would get attacked by somebody I didn't know, I'd wait for them [and attack their views at the next opportunity]. I don't do it quite as much now. I've changed during college; I'm not quite as insensitive or antagonistic. I understand people more. But I don't want to get in one of those situations in the classroom where everyone's voice is validated; you know, everybody gives everybody a hug, either. Everybody needs to be interrogated; I do, too. But when I learn something from what's said in class, it's the teacher interrogating my voice, not so much other students, although occasionally that will happen.

Mark did, however, qualify his view that instructors were "supposedly" the experts:

> They don't know everything, just because they have a Ph.D. I can bring things to the class and other students can bring critiques to the class that are important and significant that the instructor won't acknowledge, even though they're just as valid as what the instructor would say to be the correct critique.

Mark's ideas on evaluation continued to emphasize feedback from the instructor. He described his best experience in this way:

> In one class, we constantly during a semester put in these little opinion papers. So you're constantly getting feedback throughout the semester, as opposed to one huge project at the end, where there's no chance for you to go back and redo. He takes a cassette, and he'll put it in there, and he'll read your paper. And then he'll talk to you for five minutes, and then he'll give the cassette back to you. That's a great way to do it. He goes into much more depth than written comments can. You get the immediacy of his feelings, too. He'll put [emphasis] on certain words. If you saw it on a page, you wouldn't get the same sense of what was going on.

Mark continued, however, to say that the instructor's feedback was sometimes less valuable:

> If you get a paper late in the semester and you've written a really good paper that works with the new critiques the professor's shown you — and you know it's an A paper, but the professor says, "There're still some problems with it" — I still won't agree with the professor, because I know it's a good paper. I don't care what the professor says. So sometimes there will be a disjunction between what you feel and what the professor feels. But it's still valuable to get feedback because the professor will have some kind of valid critique on it.

The conversation again turned to how Mark had engaged others in class in previous years, a topic that had emerged every year. This year, it led to his thoughts on how he dealt with various views in trying to determine his own.

I'd take extreme positions early on. I'd look at their position and extrapolate on that, take it to its farthest reaches, and make their argument ridiculous because of these implications. Then I'd show my position, trying to undercut all their positions. Now I'd maybe suggest there are some ramifications that we don't see for understandable reasons, and then try to find some common ground. Instead of shifting our arguments away, bring them together. I definitely think that people are more willing to build toward some common ground than stake out their own place against it. Guys are more prone to stake out their ground and dominate.

Naturally, my interest in gender issues prompted me to encourage Mark to continue with his theory on the subject. He ventured to say that he was glad to have attended a coeducational institution:

You need that other, gender's input. I feel more comfortable talking with women sometimes because of that building-towards-community attitude they have because of the way they've been socialized. They're very good to sit and talk to. You can tell they're listening and care.

Toward the end of the interview, we arrived at the subject of what Mark planned to do upon graduation:

I'm committed to law school. I had some questions over the summer about whether to pursue my Ph.D. I don't know. I think tht law is such a big field that there'll be plenty of opportunities for me to find my niche and do things as valuable as I could do in anything else. I've definitely made that decision, but it's not a lifelong decision. I can change it. You can make significant contributions in almost any setting.

As Mark left my office, I was struck by how different the decision to attend law school sounded than it had four years earlier.

Mark's Fifth-Year Interview

Just as he had said at the senior-year interview, Mark had gone to law school. After two weeks of playing telephone tag in November 1990, we finally found a convenient time for a telephone interview. After a brief exchange about how things were going, we discussed observations about his senior year that I had missed by interviewing him in the fall. About effective learning expriences, he said:

> Independent studies projects that let you go at your own pace. You study what you want to study. Independent studies working directly with a mentor, a professor—those are good. Independent study groups, even of students who will get together and talk about issues they're interested in without a professor even being there.

Mark described having had these experiences and suggested that informal meetings with the professor were sufficient for guidance and evaluation, particularly if that person had intimate knowledge of the project and the student. He suggested that students should get all their requirements out of the way early in order to be able to do independent work because "coming out of high school, you're attuned to lecture-type learning. The talking head is all right. But, as you go on, you really don't respond to it at all."

As we made a transition to talking about Mark's current experiences in law school, he said that he had made ten minutes' worth of notes in preparation for our conversation. His notes covered instructors, the Socratic method, grading, and his hopes for law school. Regarding instructors, who for him had provided the most important learning experience thus far, he remarked:

> These folks are brilliant. But I think if you have intelligence without some sense of humanity in a

professor, or [showing some] kindness and respect
to students, I think that can defeat a lot of the intelligence. Luckily, there are only a couple of professors that are of maybe average humanity. Everyone is of superior intelligence.

Clarifying this notion of humanity in the context of the Socratic
method, Mark continued:

For instance — and none of my professors did this
the first day, but I thought they should have — if
they had said something like, "*We're engaged.*" And
I think people could do this at the undergraduate
level, too, to make it clear to the student that the
teacher's also a student and that we're all in the classroom engaged in kind of a joint venture. "I can learn
from you, you can learn from me" approach. Say
something to the extent, "If you answer a question
and it later proves to be wrong or questionable,
don't be embarrassed." It's a little different because
it's a totally new discipline, and the professor does
have all the answers. But I think it's more admira-
ble for a student to stick to her guns than just say
"oh, okay." Unfortunately, the professor's approach
sometimes will deter the student from saying anything else.

Mark's tendency to hold his own view emerged in his discussion about his classes. He explained:

These are introductory courses, like required courses
in undergraduate, so I'm not really interested in
them. The classes assume that law is this extremely
powerful force in society. And, the way I see it, law
permeates a lot of relationships. You know, when
you order a hamburger, you make a contract — all
that. I think the actual power in society is part of
culture. Creation of gender identity would be one

example of power that would be more influential
than law. In that way, the subject matter is just not
as stimulating. But I hope that it will get more
stimulating.

Mark also had a note about the grading system on his
list of important characteristics about law school. After saying
there were "no grades, basically," he explained the system and
its impact on competitiveness.

First semester is mandatory credit — no credit. The
rest of the semesters are graded on pass and fail.
There's no class rank ever computed, no GPA ever
computed. I think that helps students work together. You're already dealing with hypercompeti-
tive people. The grading system encourages people
to work together and not be selfish about note sharing or helping with projects or whatever. Another
advantage is that without the pressure of grades,
I underline things that I think are important even
if they aren't mentioned in class. If I was being very
efficient about this, I would just study what I need
for the exam in order to get through. It allows you
to put your studying where you want it to be.

In response to my question about whether he worked
together with other students, Mark responded:

Everyone here is very intelligent and articulate. And
I feel honored to be here because you can knock
on your neighbor's door and discuss anything. In
that way, it builds community, and at the same time
you're constantly learning outside a classroom.

At the close of the interview, Mark said that this atmosphere
was prompting him to reevaluate where to spend his energy and
opening new avenues of intellectual stimulation for him.
Contextual knowing, rarely evident during college, was

the approach Mark used as a senior and law student and the one Gwen used after graduation. The nature of knowledge remains uncertain in contextual knowing, but the "everything goes" perspective is replaced with the belief that some knowledge claims are better than others in a particular context. Judgments of what to believe are possible, although not absolute, based on reviewing the evidence. Gwen illustrated this kind of judgment in her distinction between a response and a reaction in her fifth-year interview. Mark similarly described judging the expertise of instructors and students in his fifth-year interview.

When all perspectives are no longer equal, learning changes from thinking independently to thinking through problems and integrating and applying knowledge in context. Although the student still creates a point of view, it must be supported by evidence. The instructor is expected to foster learning environments that promote application of knowledge in a context, evaluative discussion of perspectives, and opportunities for the student and teacher to critique each other. Reflecting on her senior year, Gwen appreciated instructors who set up interactive environments in which students were expected to make worthwhile contributions. Mark was impressed by the senior-year teacher who guided the class in effectively critiquing material.

The two-way nature of instructor-student interaction is evident in the idea of evaluation as a process in which the student and instructor work together toward a goal and measure their progress. Evaluation takes on a more flexible nature; any type is appropriate as long as it accurately measures competence in a particular context. Mark expressed this view in his description of working with a mentor in independent studies, and he also made it clear that his opinion of the quality of his work might differ from his instructor's. These notions about the exchange and comparison of views include peers as well. Classmates are judged to be assets in learning if they make worthwhile contributions — in other words, if they can support their views with evidence. Gwen emphasized the need for valuable contributions, and Mark lamented that his peers' comments were often unstimulating.

In the year following graduation, contextual knowing was

evident in only 12 percent of the interviews, resulting in too little data to explore gender patterns. In Gwen's and Mark's cases, aspects of patterns they had used infrequently earlier became increasingly apparent in more complex ways of knowing. Mark described trying to find common ground with others as a result of becoming more compassionate over the years, a matter of some import to him as he advocated a "degree of humanity" in his law school classes. Gwen described becoming more active over the years, enjoying debate as a senior, and taking the initiative to meet her own needs in her professional position. Thus, though their preferences within ways of knowing illustrate gender-related patterns, they simultaneously reveal that students' thinking is not restricted to one pattern.

Evolution of the Four Ways of Knowing

Both women and men experienced the four ways of knowing that I have described. Although movement from one way of knowing to another differed at some points over the five years, the pace of women and men was more similar than different.

Following students from college enrollment to the year following graduation made it possible to determine whether the four ways of knowing occurred in any particular order. Figure 2.1 shows the percentage of students exhibiting each intellectual perspective during each year. Absolute knowing was most prevalent in the first year of college (68 percent). Fewer students were absolute knowers as sophomores (46 percent) and very few as juniors (11 percent) and seniors (2 percent). This approach to knowing had disappeared by the year following graduation. Whereas absolute knowing decreased with each year, the transitional perspective increased during the first three years of college. Thirty-two percent of the first-year students were transitional knowers. This number rose to 53 percent for sophomores and 83 percent for juniors. Transitional knowing declined slightly for seniors (80 percent) and substantially the year following graduation (31 percent). Thus, transitional knowing was most prevalent in the junior and senior years.

Independent knowing was not evident in the first year of

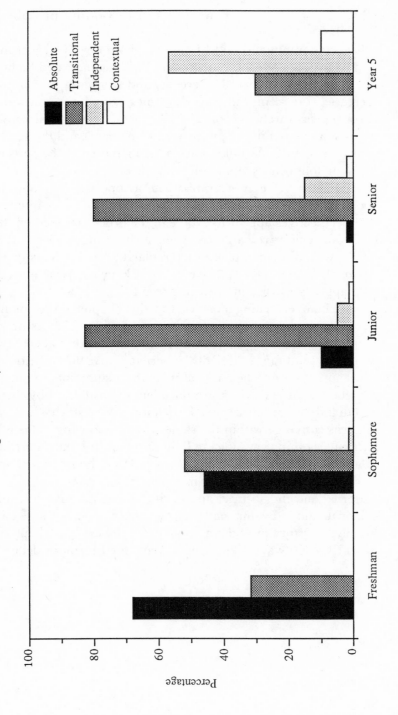

Figure 2.1. Ways of Knowing by Year.

college and minimally evident in the sophomore (1 percent) and junior (5 percent) years. Independent knowing increased slightly during the senior year (16 percent) and showed a substantial increase (57 percent) the year following graduation. Contextual knowing was rarely evident during college. Contextual knowing first appeared in the junior year (1 percent) and the senior year (2 percent). As noted earlier, it increased to 12 percent the year following graduation.

Figure 2.1 demonstrates that, as one way of knowing declines, the next becomes more prevalent. The four intellectual perspectives appear to evolve in the order expected on the basis of previous research (Kitchener and King, 1990; Perry, 1970), with more complex forms replacing less complex ones. Although there is little data on contextual knowing, what is available appears consistent with this trend.

The overarching story told in this chapter serves many purposes. It charts the "prevailing winds" of students' assumptions about knowledge and names the patterns that affect how we understand many students' experiences. At the same time, the chapter captures the fluid nature of the assumptions by showing that Gwen and Mark are not identically affected by them and that they shift over time. The chapter suggests that diverse patterns converge within the same ways of knowing. This is a particularly important idea in light of the traditional deference to abstract, logical modes of knowing. Here the relational approach (seen in the receiving, interpersonal, and interindividual patterns) and the abstract approach (seen in the mastery, impersonal, and individual patterns) have been described as equal. Finally, the story provides a preview to the next four chapters, in which each way of knowing is recounted in more detail.

Chapter Three

Absolute Knowing: Receiving and Mastering Knowledge

I like to listen — just sit and take notes from an overhead. The material is right there. And if you have a problem, you can ask him, and he can explain it to you. You hear it, you see it, and then you write it down.

— Toni, a sophomore

I like getting involved with the class. Just by answering questions, asking questions. Even if you think you know everything, there're still questions you can ask. When he asks questions, you can try to answer them to your best ability. Don't just let the teacher talk but have him present questions to you.

— Tim, a freshman

Toni and Tim have different perceptions of their role as learners. Toni sees hers as receiving information from the instructor and asking for clarification only if it is necessary. Tim takes a more active approach, emphasizing the importance of asking questions even if he knows everything. Inherent in both responses, however, is the notion that knowledge is to be gained from the instructor. Both Toni and Tim believe that knowledge is certain and that it is known to authorities. Thus, their role as learners is to obtain that knowledge. The students that we meet in this chapter express these common assumptions and at the

73

same time illustrate the gender-related patterns within this way of knowing.

Absolute Knowing

The core assumption held by these students is that knowledge exists in an absolute form. Uncertainty occurs only when the student does not know the answer. The functions of instructors, peers, and the learners themselves all hinge on the view that knowledge is the domain of the instructor. As learners, absolute knowers focus on obtaining information. They expect instructors to communicate knowledge clearly to them to aid in their acquiring it. They do not expect peers to have legitimate knowledge, although they can share what they have learned from authority figures. On the subject of evaluation, instructors are expected to determine whether students have acquired the necessary information. Instructors' ability to do so stems from their mastery of knowledge. Students interpret any discrepancies that they encounter in the learning process as variations in explanations rather than as true differences. Finally, they approach educational decisions by looking for the right answers about educational programs, majors, and career directions. These core assumptions are summarized in Table 3.1.

Gwen, whom we met in Chapter Two, illustrated the belief about the certainty of knowledge in her response to the question, "When two instructors explain the same thing differently, can one be more correct than the other?" She replied:

> No. Yet one can be clearer than the other. I take the simplest way possible to understand. For example, in calculus, one professor puts it in simpler terms, whereas the other tries to make it tough. Usually, they are both accurate, just on different levels of thought.

In response to the same question, Lowell said:

> One could be. But unless you had some background on the subject, the student would not be able to tell.

Table 3.1. Epistemological Reflection Model.

Domains	Absolute Knowing	Transitional Knowing	Independent Knowing	Contextual Knowing
Role of learner	• Obtains knowledge from instructor	• Understands knowledge	• Thinks for self • Shares views with others • Creates own perspective	• Exhanges and compares perspectives • Thinks through problems • Integrates and applies knowledge
Role of peers	• Share materials • Explain what they have learned to each other	• Provide active exchanges	• Share views • Serve as a source of knowledge	• Enhance learning via quality contributions
Role of instructor	• Communicates knowledge appropriately • Ensures that students understand knowledge	• Uses methods aimed at understanding • Employs methods that help apply knowledge	• Promotes independent thinking • Promotes exchange of opinions	• Promotes application of knowledge in context • Promotes evaluative discussion of perspectives • Student and teacher critique each other
Evaluation	• Provides vehicle to show instructor what was learned	• Measures students' understanding of the material	• Rewards independent thinking	• Accurately measures competence • Student and teacher work toward goal and measure progress
Nature of knowledge	• Is certain or absolute	• Is partially certain and partially uncertain	• Is uncertain—everyone has own beliefs	• Is contextual; judge on basis of evidence in context

I would try to do some research on my own, as well
as talk to each of the teachers about the other teacher's ideas. By doing this and drawing a conclusion
based on what evidence has been discovered, one
could probably be able to draw a fairly accurate
conclusion—one that satisfied all three different
sources.

Gwen demonstrated her view that knowledge is certain by her
hesitation to recognize any real discrepancy between her two
calculus professors. Although Lowell initially acknowledged the
possibility that one instructor could be wrong, he believed that
research and discussion would resolve the differences. The certainty of knowledge was central to both students' views.

Given that certainty, the role of instructors is to provide
knowledge and that of students is to accept it. This idea is clear
from Hugh's comments:

Things that seem really difficult, that teachers have
known that students have had problems with in the
past—just maybe make sure that the student really
knows that. Lots of things in class, you can go over
quickly, and it's obvious the students can grasp that
quickly. Other things, it's obvious that it takes more
time for the student to understand it. If they go over
that again, I think that would help.

Hugh's remarks implied that the teacher should not only provide the knowledge, but should also make sure that students
understand it. The instructor's responsibility to get the information across was also evident in Sandra's response:

Instructors should be there if you want to ask a
question. I expect that they won't make fun of you
if you ask a question in class. Some of the professors are so into their subjects that they get a little
fast. They should talk more on our level.

Although Hugh and Sandra both indirectly alluded to the student's role, others expressed it more directly. In talking about her preference for classes based on factual information, Eileen said:

> I have to see what I'm learning, and I have to know why. I have a good memory, and it's very easy for me to memorize facts. The advantage is that it is kind of cut and dried. The information is there — all you have to do is soak it into your brain.

Jim also preferred factually oriented classes and described his function as learner similarly:

> The factual information is cut and dried. It is either right or wrong. If you know the information, you can do well. It is easy because you just read or listen to a lecture about the ideas. Then you present it back to the teacher.

Although Eileen and Jim focused on factual information, other students described acquiring information in classes emphasizing ideas and concepts. Marla said that she learned best in classes concentrating on ideas because "I can remember better if it is logical, and I have thought it out (as opposed to pure memorization)." She saw the advantage as "it makes you think . . . . you remember it for a long time," whereas the disadvantage was "it takes longer and a little more effort." Carmen also liked a focus on ideas and concepts because she could "see where all the information can relate to each other — I can associate the ideas and concepts with other areas I am dealing with." Carmen cautioned, though, that a disadvantage was that "you have to be in the right state of mind — fully alert and wanting to learn." The common thread in these students' comments was that the learner acquired and remembered the information provided by teachers, whether it was facts or ideas.

Students' responses regarding the function of the learner

contained very few remarks about what students should do in class (with the exception of a few suggestions discussed under the mastery-pattern section of this chapter). Most centered on attending class and paying attention. Beyond that, most students saw learning as occurring outside of class. The most prevalent ideas were that students should study regularly, keep up with class work, and get help from the instructor or a tutor if needed. All of these suggestions illustrate learning as a process of acquisition.

The belief that authorities are in charge of learning was perhaps most evident in Kyle's response about the advice he would give others regarding successful learning. He said, "I, as a freshman, am still learning how to learn in college course work and therefore do not feel that I could be handing out advice to anyone on this subject matter."

As one might expect, students who believe that knowledge is obtained from authorities did not expect their peers to play a significant part in learning. When asked what role classmates played in learning, Rich replied:

> I don't know. I never have thought of that. I guess if I had a problem or something—instead of wasting the teacher's time, I could just go to them and ask them to explain it to me. Or if I miss notes that day, I would hope that person would be willing to let me borrow them. The one thing that a lot of kids could do is if you have a question—you don't understand something, and the professor's answering it—the people right around you shouldn't talk to each other, or else you just won't learn it.

Lindsey expanded on the notion of students explaining to other students:

> I like working with other students and hearing what they have to say, because sometimes if you don't understand something, it's easier to have a student explain it to you than a teacher. Not that the teacher

can't explain it, but a teacher doesn't always understand what you don't understand. And it's hard
to explain what you don't understand. A student
might be on the same level as you, may have just
understood that same problem himself. So I like
that.

Thus, although these students saw their peers as helping by sharing notes and explaining ideas, neither suggested that classmates
were a source of knowledge in and of themselves. The source
of knowledge remained the instructor.

Students' views of effective evaluation also took into account this view of the instructor. When asked about how college course work should be assessed, most students embarked
on a discussion of tests as though tests and evaluation were synonymous. Despite most students' dislike for tests, they rarely
questioned their use as an evaluation tool. Lynn's comment
demonstrates her assumption that examinations are a necessary
part of the assessment process:

I always feel like I'm too pressured in a test, but
I guess that's the best way for a teacher to evaluate
you is by seeing what you've learned on the test.
I don't know what other ways there are, though,
of a teacher seeing what you've learned other than
giving an exam. There's really no other way.

Lynn's conclusion that tests were the only option was most likely
a result of her inherent trust in teachers, who knew how to help
students learn and how to assess learning. Faith in the teacher's
ability to judge learning accurately was evident in Art's thoughts
on effective evaluation:

You can ask questions about math problems. But
in chemistry, you get your score, and that's it. What
I did was I went through, and they [tell you what
you missed], and I was circling the right answers
on my tests because we got to keep that (the exam)

after we were done. But in English, the professor
writes comments and stuff. I think that really helps.
Instead of just giving you a grade and saying, "You
did this and this wrong," they give you some good
points.

As Art stressed the benefits of knowing what he did right, he
also implied that, in math, chemistry, and English, the teacher
knows what is right and what is wrong.

Reliance on authorities for knowledge extended beyond
classroom learning and was most evident in students' discussions of educational decision making. New students often chose
to use college choice as an example in response to questions about
how they made decisions. Art described his college choice as
his decision, but the role of authorities was an important component of the process:

I had a lot of athletic offers from smaller schools.
A lot of my high school teachers went here, so I
heard about that. I also knew a student here, so
I was getting pumped full of information. But I had
the decision of a small school with sports or this
school. My chemistry teacher gave me some information on paper science. I wasn't really sure what
I wanted to do, but I didn't want to go to college
undecided. So I looked into this, and it looked like
a good thing. So I thought sports in high school,
but that's over now. It isn't going to make me any
money, so why stick with it? I decided to come here.
It's got a good reputation, obviously. There're people from New Jersey and all over the place here
now, so I think it was the right choice.

Art's closing comment, "so I think it was the right choice," illustrates a crucial part of most students' views of decisions in
the first two years of college. Thinking that knowledge is certain leads to believing that there are correct choices. Students
who discussed decisions that they had made expressed the be-

lief or hope that they were right; those who described being in the midst of a decision often had not yet come to a conclusion because they were not yet sure what was right.

These absolute knowers shared core assumptions about the nature of knowledge, the role of various players in the learning process, and authorities' influence in their learning and decision making. Despite these basic similarities, distinct gender-related patterns emerged in students' reasoning about these assumptions. These patterns are represented in Table 3.2.

Table 3.2. Absolute Knowing: Receiving and Mastering Knowledge.

Domains	Pattern	
	Receiving	*Mastering*
Role of learner	• Listens and records information	• Participates in interesting activities • Shows instructor that student is interested
Role of peers	• Talk to create relaxed atmosphere • Ask questions to relieve pressure	• Act as partners in debating and quizzing each other to further learning
Role of instructor		• Uses interesting methods
Evaluation	• Is based on knowledge of material • Affords multiple opportunities to show knowledge	• Provides feedback from instructor to help student improve • Can be inaccurate
Nature of knowledge	• Involves different opinions regarding the facts • Is resolved by personal interpretation	• Involves different degrees of detail • Is resolved via research and asking authorities

The Receiving Pattern

As noted in Chapter Two, patterns within ways of knowing were used more often by one gender than the other but not exclusively by either. In this study, the receiving pattern was employed more frequently by women. Perhaps the most striking characteristic of the receiving pattern is its internal approach, as shown by Toni at the beginning of this chapter. This approach involves minimal interaction with instructors, an emphasis on comfort in the learning environment, relationships with peers, and ample opportunities to demonstrate knowledge. Exploring how this perspective weaves through their perceptions, it is possible to see that the way these students see themselves and the world interacts with their learning preferences and their intellectual development.

The receiving pattern was most clear in students' descriptions of their role as learners. Nancy, like Toni (whose quote appears at the beginning of the chapter), saw her role as acquiring information:

> When I first came, I started recording all my classes because I found that most of my exams were based on the lecture. And if I knew my lecture material, I would do well on the exams. Then I found myself spending at least an hour every night recopying my notes and relistening to the tapes. It just didn't work out because I would get behind. It wasn't worth it, so I stopped doing that. But generally, if I just try to write down things that I think are important, I miss out on a lot of information. So I just write down every point that he or she gives me. Not word for word, but every point.

Nancy's original approach was to note everything that was said in the lecture. When she found that impossible, she turned to writing down every point. She did not change her perception about what her role was but adjusted it to be more realistic. Bev expressed a similar concern in her attempt to record everything in her classes:

> When the teacher lectures, I take notes and try to understand what he says. I have a teacher right now

who won't quit zipping out facts, and it's really hard for me to get them all down. Sometimes, I focus in on more of what he's saying, and I can go back and find the facts myself. I try to understand just the important points. I am trying to take down both facts and concepts. But if I have trouble because the teacher is going too fast, I try to concentrate more on what they are trying to get at. That's the important part of the lecture.

Similarly, Dean stated, "You have to make sure you pay attention to everything the lecturer says because you can miss what he's going to put on the test." Dean also said that because the instructor was "not going to write [the answers] down for you, always try to listen to the professor for the answer you're looking for." Dean also recommended taking notes on chapters and remarked, "The only way to learn every single thing possible is to read the book and stay caught up."

These students described a process for learning that involved recording in some fashion the information presented by the instructor. When the ideal recording system was not feasible, they adjusted to try to obtain as much as possible, particularly those pieces of information they thought were important. They did not suggest any change on the part of the instructor or indicate any interaction with the teacher. Thus, their emphasis was on receiving knowledge by listening more than by speaking. Amy described the balance of listening and speaking out in class:

I like to listen to what the teacher has to say, and it depends on the class I'm in whether I speak out or not. In high school, I felt comfortable with everyone in the room, and we were encouraged to speak out. Some of these classes are larger, so you don't have a chance to speak out. I usually listen. But if I have an idea or I know what the teacher's asking, then I'll speak. I usually don't speak out just for the sake of speaking out.

Amy saw no point in talking other than to offer an idea
or an answer. Considering these four students' comments together, it appears that verbal participation was of minimal importance to them. The value of a limited role was most apparent in their views on the behavior of peers.

In reply to a question about what classmates could do to
help her learn, Megan's initial reaction was "Be quiet." She continued in order to describe how peers could be useful:

> Asking questions — when other people ask questions
> it helps because I'm very shy. Sometimes I'm hesi-
> tant to ask questions first. I mean, I realize if I want
> people to ask questions, they probably want me to
> ask questions, too. But it's [better if] the outgoing
> people kind of start with questions. And if some-
> body asks a question, then I can ask a question.
> And I'll be like, "Well, I'm not the only one who
> doesn't understand."

Jim also found peers helpful. He said:

> People asking questions is very important because
> you might have the same question. If they ask the
> question, you don't have to worry about asking. It's
> kind of another thing about being comfortable. And
> that helps. And paying attention. When somebody
> gets distracted, then everybody becomes distracted.

As we saw in Chapter Two, Gwen offered a similar response:

> I think it's helpful just to have people around you
> so, if the teacher's whizzing through stuff, you can
> quickly ask somebody next to you and hope they're
> paying real close attention. But as far as [commu-
> nication] during class, I don't really know what can
> be done without distracting the professor totally.

Megan, Jim, and Gwen thus viewed peers as being supportive. They stressed that they should play a limited role to

avoid interfering with the instructor's lecture. Verbal participation of self and others in learning — restricted to speaking out
on occasion, asking questions, and sharing notes — was clearly
secondary to listening. However, the importance of knowing
other people in the class was a clear theme in receiving-pattern
students' comments. Gale captured this idea in her statement:

> It's good to have a small class because it's more in-
> timate. You feel closer to the class and to the peo-
> ple in it. So you get to know the personalities — it's
> easier to ask questions.

The perspectives of these students revealed that the authority of instructors was taken for granted. Instructors were
not criticized for presenting information too fast and were very
· rarely given any responsibility beyond conveying facts or ideas.
Although no recurring ideas about student expectations of instructors were evident, Gwen in Chapter Two described an approach that she valued in a teacher:

> Sometimes teachers themselves will come up with
> little learning devices, like word relations or things
> like that. I can do that on my own, but it's helpful
> if the teacher has one that works well and they use
> it for years. And I like teachers who will give you
> as much as you need and not just leave you with
> a little small idea and try to have you talk it out.

Even here, Gwen saw the teacher as facilitating the students'
reception of information. Gwen acknowledged that she could
generate learning devices on her own but preferred the proven
techniques of her instructor.

Just as receiving-pattern learners emphasized taking in
knowledge, they also stressed reporting it in the evaluation
process. Their only expectation was that appropriate conditions
exist to enable them to make clear what they knew. Bev explained this approach:

> Testing is kind of standard. You get lectured on
> the material; you memorize it; you learn so much

of it. Then you get tested on it and get a grade.
I think that it's necessary, but I would like to—I
guess—be evaluated on, not really attitude things,
but how much you're understanding about the concepts that are not coming out on the test material.
I just came back from a class in which we took a
test last week. I understood all the material. And
I've paid attention to the lecture in class, and I knew
everything they were talking about. But when it
came down to the test questions, they were kind
of ambiguous. We haven't gotten the scores back
yet, but I know I didn't do as well as I wanted to.
And I know that if I sat down with the instructor
and the person asked me questions (instead of just
multiple choice), I could explain the answers. It
probably would have been better. So I think a lot
of times testing can be misleading. I may not understand the way questions are phrased, even though
I would understand the concepts.

When asked to elaborate on her statement that testing is
necessary, Bev said:

I don't know. I guess it's the easiest way for teachers
to get people to learn. If you take a class and you
know you're not going to be tested on things, maybe
you won't pay attention.

Bev's trusting attitude toward authority overrode her concern
that the structure of testing did not always afford her the opportunity to express what she knew.

Other receiving-pattern knowers suggested that students
be given multiple opportunities to show what they had learned.
For example, Terry expressed his interest in labs:

Tests, for some people, work—for some others,
don't. Some students freeze on a test. They might
know all the information beforehand. But when a
test comes, there is too much pressure, and they're

just blank. Labs will show what you've learned. You
have to basically know everything that's been going on in the semester or the year to complete it.

Lorene thought that tests could allow students to express what
they knew under certain circumstances:

Multiple-choice exams are fine if they aren't ambiguous. Sometimes, you have four choices, and
two could be right — or none could be right — or all
of the above or none of the above. I hate those. I'd
rather have fill in [the blanks] or something where
you can put in your own words what you know,
rather than interpret what they're saying.

Holly also suggested alternatives:

I think [work] should be evaluated through the
whole course; the grade shouldn't be weighted so
much on one test score. Maybe a variety of ways,
because some people aren't good at one way — so
there could be a mixture of regular tests and essays.

Though these students suggested various methods that would
help different students demonstrate their knowledge, the idea that
evaluation showed what students learned remained unchallenged.

The perspectives of receiving-pattern students on the nature of knowledge initially appeared to contradict these students'
sense of the infallibility of authority. They routinely suggested
that students have their own feelings or values on subjects and
should use these to settle competing knowledge claims. Bev explained discrepancies in knowledge in one of her classes as follows:

A lot of what our honors prof presented was not
so much raw facts as it was how you felt about a
certain issue at a certain time. Maybe that was a
contradiction to what a lot of people in the class
believed morally, but it was just hearing something
you were taught.

This quote makes two major points. First, there is a difference between "raw facts" and "how you feel about an issue." Bev seemed to suggest that the differences that arose in her honors class involved opinion rather than information. Second, the professor's attitude toward knowledge (as evidenced in what she or he presented) could differ from the students'. "It was just hearing something you were taught" implies that there is no need to compare the two perspectives to make any decision about which one to adopt. Similarly, Ross said:

It was only on statements of opinion. I don't think there was any discrepancy as far as factual information. Basically, I took what the professor said because that's what he believes, but I guess in the end I had my own view. I did respect his decision or his belief but based mine on my own values — just what my parents instilled in me.

Another woman, Jill, said:

I use my best judgment to decide what to believe. Everyone has different ideas and values, and no two people can have the exact same explanation for something if it is a personal view. A student must use his own ideas and values to choose.

Despite the seeming independence of these students' perspectives on knowledge, on closer examination they can be interpreted as versions of absolute knowing. Of course, absolute knowers would need to reconcile different explanations (or what a professor said with what they believed morally) if these differences called knowledge into question. Bev, Ross, and Jill use their own values in making decisions in ways that do not affect knowledge itself, implying that students' reactions to knowledge do not challenge its validity. The authority's status remains unchanged; students simply process how they feel about the knowledge they are taught. Said another way, people can have different opinions about the facts, but the facts remain unchanged.

The receiving pattern's deference to authority was also

evident in students' descriptions of educational decisions. Most decisions were based on what the person believed to be a *right* choice. One approach to determining the correct choice was to rely on authority, which took on a variety of forms. Barb described her decision about which college to attend:

Question: What alternatives were available to you?

Barb: High school counselors, books, and pamphlets.

Question: How did you feel about these alternatives?

Barb: All literature written about other colleges was helpful, but there were so many to choose from.

Question: How did you go about choosing from the alternatives?

Barb: I thought about which would suit me best — which ones were right, financially, academically, et cetera.

Barb described her alternatives not in terms of the colleges themselves, but in the form of information about them. In any case, her response demonstrated the strong role that authority (in this case, counselors and brochures) played in her decision. She was, in the end, searching for the right college. Carmen stated the role of authority more directly in discussing her choice of college major:

> I did not really decide. My mother suggested majoring in zoology, so I did. An alternative was majoring in psychology. Psychology was interesting, but I really didn't know what I wanted to do. Premed in zoology is more productive and more challenging. If I become a doctor, I could become very proud of what I am. I would get personal satisfaction out of knowing that I worked hard and deserved to be where I am.

Although Carmen provided a rationale for a decision, she clearly stated that *she* did not make it. Her response implies that she had found reasons for her choice after acting on her mother's suggestion.

Pamela's parents also played an important role in her college choice. She said:

> My parents set up the following criteria for me in choosing a school: six hours driving time from home, cost (negotiable but under $7,000), and the school had to have a good science department. I agreed with all of the alternatives and helped my parents make them. I then went to the library where I had access to a computer that listed the colleges that would be good for me based upon the criteria that I gave it.

Pamela's parents' criteria probably resulted in a variety of options. However, her perception of the decision was that, after she helped establish various alternatives, it was up to the computer to provide the right colleges. She did not explain how she chose from her list.

Finally, some receiving-pattern knowers mentioned authorities as figuring in their decisions but focused even more on the rightness of the choice. Tracy indicated that she consulted authorities (in the business world) in trying to ascertain what major was right for her. In considering a number of areas within business, she described the uncertainty as intimidating and worried that she might not make the correct decision. Describing her final decision, she said:

> I like working with numbers and statistics, but I don't want to work with just columns of numbers (such as accountancy). I want to work with money, stocks and bonds. Therefore, finance was my choice.

Thus, after consulting with others, Tracy finally determined what is right for her based on a pre-existing interest. Carl similarly chose paper science and engineering as a major because "I like chemistry. And when I was talking to the director of paper science, he told me it was related to chemistry."

The receiving-pattern students are recognizable by their internal approach, a participation in learning not discernible by observing their class behavior. They participate through the act of listening and adjust their ways of listening to increase the likelihood of acquiring information. Their expectations of instructors are few, although these learners appreciate an instructor who eases the task of information acquisition. They rely instead on peers for support. Peers can make class more comfortable; they make it easier to ask questions, share notes, and help others acquire information. Classmates' support in class, however, is limited to what does not interfere with the instructor's lecture. Once information is acquired, the receiving-pattern students focus on reporting it in the evaluation process. Although they clearly prefer the types of tests that offer them opportunities to express what they know, they defer to the authority's judgment about how evaluation takes place. This deference to authority is clear in their decision-making processes as well.

Thus, these students seem to be receivers — of information from instructors, of support from peers, and of judgments about their work from tests. One could argue that their "voice" is silent in light of the descriptions offered here. The only area in which these learners seem to have more independent perspectives involves their view of knowledge. These perspectives become clear in their focus on personal interpretation for resolving conflicting knowledge claims. Phrases like "how you feel about an issue" and "if it's a personal view" denote the existence of feelings or opinions about knowledge. It is striking, however, that these ideas are detached from knowledge itself. These students seem to describe personal interpretation as their reactions to information but assigned no role for them in the construction of knowledge.

The evidence of a personal view raises the question of why it is not expressed in the learning process. Perhaps, as Belenky, Clinchy, Goldberger and Tarule (1986) suggested, "Believing that truth comes from others, they still their own voices to hear the voices of others" (p. 37). The receiving pattern's emphasis on not interfering with the instructor's lecture further reduces the chances of expressing personal views. As Amy explained earlier, speaking out is only useful when you know what the teacher is asking.

Another possibility is that socialization restrains receiving-pattern students, particularly those who are female, from expressing their views. Brown and Gilligan (1990) have described adolescence as a crisis of connection for girls. They report that, upon confronting Western culture's expectations of women, adolescent girls experience a loss of voice. Whereas younger girls speak from their experience, girls at the edge of adolescence "engage in difficult and sometimes painful personal battles around issues of voice and authorization, unsure of the accuracy of their perceptions, afraid that speaking up will damage relationships or compromise their image in the eyes of others" (p. 7). Brown and Gilligan provide narratives of girls who choose not to express themselves in order to maintain harmony with others and the image that they perceive is expected for them. This internalization of voice, in conjunction with the assumptions of absolute knowers, may in part account for the receiving pattern described here.

The Mastery Pattern

The mastery pattern was used more often by men than by women in this study. Characteristics of this pattern reveal that these students prefer a verbal approach to learning, can be critical of instructors, and expect interactions with peers and instructors that aid mastery of knowledge. A more interactive perspective permeates most aspects of the learning process. It appeared initially in students' discussion of their role as learners. For example, Clark emphasized making the teacher aware of his presence:

> I like to ask questions in order for the professor to become associated with me, be aware of who I am, how much I'm trying, how interested I am in what they're teaching. Usually, someone teaching a subject in college is pretty interested in that area.

Cherylyn showed that she was engaged because it "works better." She added:

> I sit in the front of the class. I try to get to know
> my prof. I try to ask questions and answer ques-
> tions. I try to show that I'm interested. If I'm sit-
> ting in the front, maybe he'll see me in class, too.

Rich preferred a similar approach but for slightly different reasons:

> I like to participate because it shows the teacher that
> I'm awake and I'm eager to learn what they hand
> out. I sit in front of the class. I think if the teacher
> says this and this and "give me some input on it,"
> then I try to give him my opinion. I like to ask a
> lot of questions so they know I'm awake. If they
> say, "Come on up to the board and do this prob-
> lem," I volunteer, or I volunteer to read something.
> This way, I usually feel more a part of the class.
> When I feel more a part of the class, I pay more
> attention, and then I remember more.

Rich, Cherylyn, and Clark wanted the teacher to know that they
were interested in learning and implied that this kind of involvement had some impact on the process. They expressed interest
by asking questions, and Rich attempted to show his progress
through volunteering an opinion or doing a problem. All three
students seemed to believe that learning requires more than
merely taking in the information. An exploration of their expectations of instructors and other students adds another dimension to this learning pattern.

In addition to assuming that teachers possess knowledge
and will share it with students, mastery-pattern students expected
instructors to teach in an entertaining fashion. Bryan began his
discussion of teachers by noting that they have different abilities in lecturing. In describing an effective instructor, he said:

> Obviously, teachers who keep people interested are
> doing their job. No matter how much teachers know
> and how many degrees they have after their name,

it doesn't really matter if everyone's asleep in the
class. So even if it's just a graduate student—if they
can keep the class interested, they're probably going to have a lot better time getting the point across.
They should mix it up from day to day. Involve
the class in discussions or movies, so people don't
get in a rut of doing the same thing.

Marge preferred teachers with a "dynamic personality." She said
that she had "a hard time getting the inspiration unless they're
really interesting." Frank went a step further in suggesting that
the instructor should push students:

The teachers I've done best with are a happy med-
ium between the teachers that are hands-off kind
of learning (we present the material, and if you
learn it, you learn it; if you don't, you don't) and
a little bit of thought-provoking kind of thing, where
you know that you have to learn the material. I
don't want to be babied through a subject but want
a little bit of pushing. And the teacher needs to provoke interest, so that I want to go to class.

These comments reveal that the students hold the teacher responsible for giving them incentive to attend class, keeping them
interested while they are there, and letting them know that they
have to learn the material. The teacher was supposed to challenge
students, and students were responsible for demonstrating their
interest. Although the teacher had the greater share of the
responsibility, the relationship had a mutual flavor, requiring
action on the part of both instructor and student. This mutual
dimension was also evident in students' conversations about
evaluation of their work.

For Rich, as a college freshman, this relationship took
the form of the teacher's critiquing his work and his trying to
improve it as a result. Rich said:

In my opinion, when teachers grade a paper, they
shouldn't go through it with a fine-toothed comb

and take every nook and cranny that's wrong with it
and downgrade you for it. Kids are here to learn. And
if they really knew everything, then they wouldn't
be here. To a point, it's good — teachers should put
a lot of comments on your paper. Comments that
say what you could have done better and little questions there that get you thinking and saying maybe
I could do it this way in the future and improve
on the mistakes.

It is clear from Rich's comments that he felt a responsibility to
respond to the teacher's critique in his future work. He did not
always take responsibility for not understanding the material,
though, as was obvious later in the interview:

If the teacher gives the class a test and they do really
badly on it — the class average is really low, and it's
not scaled or something — that makes the students
feel that he doesn't care. I don't think that is right.
I think if the whole class does badly, that's obviously saying something — whether the teacher's not
getting the point across or kids aren't understanding it. I wouldn't say it's the students' fault for not
studying because it's the whole class.

This excerpt suggests that poor performance on the students'
part can stem from ineffective teaching, as well as from lack
of studying. Collectively, Rich's ideas indicate that the teacher
should make effective presentations, students should study the
material and submit assignments, teachers should then assess
these efforts, and students should use the teacher's guidance to
improve their work in the future.

Whereas Rich's plan relied heavily on written communication between the teacher and student, some of his peers emphasized a need for more interactive communication. For example, Andrew proposed:

An evaluation conference allows the students to
see what they've really learned beyond what letter

grades say. It helps identify your strong and weak
points so you can improve even more.

Genesse also liked conferences based on this experience:

My physics teacher last year would call us up there
after every couple of tests, and we'd get our grades.
And then we'd talk about where we were at that
point in the quarter and what we needed to do. So
if you knew what you were shooting for and what
you needed to get for the next grade, that helps.

Kyle also preferred direct communication but for a different reason. He said:

Evaluation should be done by the instructor but
with feedback from the students because the instructor can make mistakes in grading. Communication
between instructor and student would save a lot of
trouble when mistakes in grading appear.

Two common themes emerged from the discussions of
evaluation. One was the idea of mutual responsibility: teacher
and student each have a distinct part to play in the learning
process, and their interchange is essential if it is to be successful. The second theme demonstrated the students' reliance on
authority as the guide in this interchange. Although instances
of their shortcomings in teaching and grading were taken into
account, teachers were generally trusted to provide accurate information about student progress. This dependence on authority is consistent with the view of the teacher as responsible for
getting students to come to class and keeping them awake and
the idea of the importance of their showing interest.

Reliance on authority took on a more subtle form in perceptions about the nature of knowledge in general. Mastery-
pattern students attributed discrepancies in knowledge claims
to different degrees of detail and relied on doing research or asking authorities for resolution. In response to whether one in-

structor could be more correct than another if they explained the same information differently, Phillip explained:

> I believe so. All material is derived from some source, and no two instructors derive their knowledge from the same source. I would locate other sources, get different opinions. If I were unsure, I'd go to the library, find materials on the subject, and evaluate it myself. You can be certain about what to believe if the instructors state their sources.

Phillip assumed that authority resides in the sources of information. If he cannot resolve a discrepancy by talking to others, he can always look at the sources. His response implies that absolute knowledge exists within these sources, despite the fact that they appear different; Phillip also seems to indicate that he, as a student, is able to evaluate the sources he reviews. Mark agreed that students can judge knowledge claims. Recall, in Chapter Two, he used the term *logic* to describe how he would resolve competing ideas:

> If I encounter discrepancies, I think my mind is — I want to be a lawyer — so I've concentrated on making it logical. What I do is make it fit logically. It would really bother me if the material didn't fit together. I don't think it's happened because I'd definitely remember it because it would frustrate me.

When asked to elaborate further on how he "makes it logical," Mark explained:

> I'd go to the teacher and say, "This does not fit to me. Explain it." I'd say they're totally responsible. Unless they give you two things and you should be able to figure it out on your own. That's fine with me.

Carmen also used logic to sort out knowledge claims:

> If I think I know a lot [about the subject], I hunt,
> try to [reason] it out. And then if I don't, I try to
> look at the sources themselves. And then if neither
> of those work, I just kind of say, "Well, he says this,
> and he says that, and I don't know which one to
> believe." Either I'll look it up or talk to other peo-
> ple about it.

Mark's and Carmen's emphasis on logic can be viewed as reliance on the way both have been taught to think. Knowledge
has traditionally been defined as objective, rational, and logical. Students are taught by authority figures that looking at
knowledge claims objectively or logically will result in seeing
the truth. Thus, their responses to differing information can be
interpreted as internalized forms of trust in authority. Mark
holds the teacher responsible for the discrepancy but allows for
his own responsibility if it is a "test" that he should be able to
master.

This approach to thinking and learning was prevalent in
mastery-pattern students' interactions. The combination of the
certainty of knowledge, the use of logic to arrive at answers,
and the view of self as autonomous led to a style of interaction
that appeared on the surface to be competitive. Ned viewed interaction with other students as helping him learn. He remarked:

> I prefer students talking in class. I can get a better
> view of the situation when the students are debat-
> ing it. Since they are debating, they must know
> what they are talking about. Students must be
> communicative — nothing can get done in a tight-
> lipped group that doesn't interact.

Marge also learned from this type of interaction:

> I like classes where people get involved, where peo-
> ple are talking back and throwing things at you that
> make you think a little bit harder. It does help to
> have people around you. Basically, just ask ques-
> tions and raise them in my mind.

Another student extended this idea to studying with classmates. Rob found studying with others beneficial because "they help you in areas you are weak in and vice versa. Having a person drill me over things I am to know lets me know how well I have really learned it." Ned, Marge, and Rob's preferences initially sounded like competitive interchanges but, upon further analysis, seemed to be a system for learning. If students know what they are talking about, they can work through the material to absorb it and check each other's level of mastery. Michael's comment revealed the symbiotic nature of this relationship.

> In math and physics courses, we get together to do homework problems. We put our minds together and get the problem. I also have somebody in the class ask me questions. They may ask questions I didn't think to review myself. Then I do the same for them.

Collectively, these preferences illustrate that these students challenged each other to master the knowledge at hand and took turns providing this opportunity for each other. The challenge inherent in words like *debate, drill,* and *quizzing* was not threatening to their view of themselves or their relationships with each other. Challenging each other was preferred over a "tight-lipped" group experience.

Finally, the unique blend of reliance on authority and value assigned to their own preferences appeared in their descriptions of educational decision making. Hugh described his decision to change his major:

> I changed my major from economics to finance because I wanted to be a stockbroker. I've seen that there are more opportunities than just stockbroker, and I'm just interested in finance. I went to a finance club meeting the other night [and I agreed with what the adviser said]. I must be a finance major.

Hugh's own interest propelled him into the new major, but he confirmed the choice based on his agreement with the finance club adviser. Similarly, Paul used his identification with coaches and his own personal preferences in his choice:

> I still want to coach wrestling because I like it a lot. I'd really enjoy being a coach and teacher. Helping kids wrestle makes me feel good, and I like being around coaches.

These students' own inclinations played a major role in their respective decisions, but the influence of authority figures was central to the process.

The hallmarks of the mastery pattern within absolute knowing are the verbal stance of these learners, their expectation of exchange with the teacher, their preference for opportunities to master knowledge and to show their command of it, and an interaction with peers characterized by mutual challenge. Students expected the instructor to know the necessary information, to have skill in presenting it, and to be able to judge the students' achievement. Simultaneously, however, the students saw themselves as responsible for expressing their interest, making the teacher aware that they were engaged in learning, trying out various tasks in class to aid their mastery, and working to improve their performance on the basis of instructor feedback. The students extended their testing of various learning activities into interaction with peers. Both in and out of class, peers were viewed as partners in mastering the material and testing progress.

These perceptions clearly illustrate the value that mastery-pattern learners place on achievement. Their responses concentrated on how to master their course work and learn from their instructors. They were willing to take risks in class to express an opinion or do a problem in order to achieve their goal. Even though it could be discouraging, they wanted feedback on what they could do better. They were willing to expose their degree of mastery to classmates in an effort to enhance it. This interactive approach may be what they think that teachers expect of them. One male student said, "Teachers expect us to be more aggressive and raise our hands all the time. They don't encourage aggressive learning with girls."

This perspective may also result from their socialization in previous learning experiences, where they have been rewarded for showing an interest, trying out their skills, and succeeding. The identification of mastery-pattern students with authority, a thread intertwined throughout their comments, encourages use of the learning process that authorities prescribe. Risk taking, volunteering in the classroom, and practicing logic all seemed to be part of the mastery pattern. These students were self-confident enough to engage in these activities and perceived no conflict between them and their values.

Receiving and Mastery Patterns of Knowing Compared

Absolute knowers shared the belief that knowledge is certain and held by authorities. Beyond this common set of assumptions, receiving- and mastery-pattern students differed in three areas: voice, identification with authority, and relationships with peers. Though there was no real student voice in absolute knowing, mastery-pattern students attempted to express themselves, whereas their receiving-pattern counterparts remained essentially silent. Mastery-pattern students seemed to imitate the voice of authority figures and worked hard at reproducing it in an effort to join them as knowers. Receiving-pattern students listened carefully to the voice of authority and repeated it in an effort to show that they had acquired the information.

Moreover, receiving-pattern students exhibited much less identification with authority figures than mastery-pattern students. Students in the receiving pattern showed a detachment from authority. They described learning as a transaction largely devoid of interaction with authority unless clarification was needed. Despite their motivation for receiving knowledge, they did not view interaction with authority as a central part of that process. Yet students in the mastery pattern showed a desire to take their place "next to" authorities in the arena of knowledge. Their learning behaviors resembled those of the active apprentice trying to master the trade.

Relationships with peers was a third point of difference

for receiving- and mastery-pattern students. On the one hand, receiving-pattern students valued classmates as adding comfort to the learning atmosphere. Collaboration took the form of support and the sharing of notes and information. Mastery-pattern students, on the other hand, valued peers as partners in striving for and testing achievement. They assisted each other in mastering knowledge and took turns testing each other's progress. Collaboration in this form was characterized by individual autonomy.

The path from absolute to transitional knowing involves the realization that not all knowledge is certain and that authorities are not all-knowing. As the students' stories in the next chapter reveal, mastery- and receiving-pattern students encounter this experience differently. Mastery-pattern students' identification with authority prompts them to persist in using certainty and logic as much as possible to confront uncertainty. Receiving-pattern students' detachment from authority makes it easier for them to relinquish the idea of certainty and accept uncertainty. Accepting uncertainty leads to an increase in these learners' participation beyond listening. Peers are important to students of both patterns, but those embracing uncertainty more readily assign legitimacy to classmates' ideas.

Chapter Four

Transitional Knowing: Interpersonal and Impersonal Patterns

I just always assumed they were honest. I thought that they would never do anything wrong. I believe in what they say. Isn't it kind of hard to believe that he just wasn't going to say anything? It's unbelievable. I was just amazed that someone would actually do that. I was shocked.

— *Marla, a junior*

Marla's surprise was occasioned by an instructor she had the second semester of her sophomore year. She and a friend received lower course grades than they expected. When the friend approached the instructor about her grade, he acknowledged that he had lost the midterm marks and just assumed that they were B's. Asked about the effect that this discovery had on her, Marla said, "Well, I wouldn't judge everybody on the basis of him, but I will be a little bit more questioning of the grades or testing." It is this fundamental discovery—that authorities are not all-knowing—that seems to mark the change from absolute to transitional knowing.

Often, authorities themselves set the stage for this revelation. Marla's articulation of her and her friend's experience describes this transition particularly well. Bob named the instructor as a key element in his discovery:

I took a different teacher in the sophomore level of the subject, and I learned to interpret things

103

differently. When you have someone else give you
a different interpretation of the same subject, you're
forced to go back and do comparisons. And I thought,
well, why would this person teach this subject this
way and be successful and at the same time there's
a person teaching it a different way but still being
successful? It begins to change you a little bit. You
go, "Obviously, there're two different interpretations
here. Maybe there are different ways of looking at
things than the way I'm looking at them." That was
more significant to me than anything else.

Sean described an experience in which the role of peers
overshadowed that of the instructor in initiating the discovery.

As far as any one influence within my classes — if
I had to put it in a word, I'd say *perspective*. Just
finding out through a whole bunch of experiences
the idea that [for] any one thing, whether it be a
book or topic, there are going to be fifty to a hundred thousand viewpoints going at that. And to the
people who have derived them, they're all right or
at least justified. If you want to be a thinking person, you have to take them into account, instead
of just saying "that's right" because my teacher said
it. I learned this mostly through two honors courses.
We studied human development from age fifteen
to twenty-five. We read about two hundred pages
a night. And what we'd do is — he never taught anything really. We'd start class all having read it, and
he'd walk in and say something obnoxious and completely wrong. One shout would break out from one
end of the room and one from the other, and we'd
just start knocking at each other, going back and
forth at the same topic for the entire class period.
And after doing that for a semester, it just ingrains
in your mind that no matter how right you think
you are, you've got to hear somebody else out be-

cause they're to some extent right, too. When you've
got fifty other people in the room challenging your
views every ten seconds, it just goes back and forth,
and you learn to assimilate everything. You try to
piece out what you think is the best out of a con-
glomerate whole. That's the best. It's not normally
like chemistry class. That's sit down, take notes,
ask questions.

Bob and Sean clearly articulate the discovery of multiple points
of view — Bob, through comparing two successful teachers who
approached a subject differently, and Sean, through hearing his
peers challenge his views. Marla's experience is similar in that
she now sees that things are not always one way. Despite these
revelations, these students did not immediately abandon the idea
of absolute knowledge in all areas. Sean's closing comment reveals that his new-found uncertainty does not extend to all topics,
and Marla notes that she will not judge all teachers by the actions of one. A new balance of certainty and uncertainty un-
derlies transitional knowing.

Transitional Knowing

The shift in their view of knowledge sparked changes in the roles
that students perceived for themselves and others. Students altered their focus from acquiring knowledge to understanding
it. This focus required that instructors use methods aimed at
understanding, many of which included applying knowledge
within class and to life in general. Peers took on more active
roles, perhaps because understanding was described as neces-
sitating more exploration than that required for the acquisition
of knowledge. Evaluation was seen as appropriate to the extent
that it measured students' comprehension of the material. Uncertainty permeated decision making as well, as students struggled to figure out options for the future. Processes believed to
lead to future success replaced direct reliance on authorities for
educational decision making. These core assumptions were held
by both women and men. The core assumptions are next de-

scribed in greater detail prior to exploring the gender patterns within transitional knowing. The assumptions are summarized in Table 4.1.

The existence of two categories of knowledge—certain and uncertain—is evident in transitional knowers' accounts of their learning experiences. Megan explained that she handled knowledge discrepancies in two ways:

> I don't like to just let things sit and not understand why one person says one thing and why another says another. And if *he's* wrong and *he's* right, then I want to know what way it really is. But then I'd get to looking at it—since it hasn't happened, I don't know—but it just seems like if it's a theory or a philosophy [where] there are different ways of looking at situations, if it were something like that, I could probably accept both opinions. But if it's like factual information or something, then I'd probably want to know what's right.

Megan had not yet come across contradictory or uncertain information, but she projected that it would be either a case of right and wrong or one of varying perspectives. Carl had actually experienced this situation, so he described the two categories more definitively. He said:

> I don't particularly care for humanities, English or stuff. There's a lot of—the answers are—they can vary. There's no right or wrong answer. I like things where there's a right answer. Like in chemistry, there's a right answer, but in other classes there's not. I guess it could be easier if there's not a right answer, but I feel uneasy in classes like that.

Al described what he thought should take place in areas of uncertain knowledge:

> You do something like accounting; it's not subjective. But marketing is more subjective. When we

Table 4.1. Epistemological Reflection Model.

Domains	Absolute Knowing	Transitional Knowing	Independent Knowing	Contextual Knowing
Role of learner	• Obtains knowledge from instructor	• Understands knowledge	• Thinks for self • Shares views with others • Creates own perspective	• Exchanges and compares perspectives • Thinks through problems • Integrates and applies knowledge
Role of peers	• Share materials • Explain what they have learned to each other	• Provide active exchanges	• Share views • Serve as a source of knowledge	• Enhance learning via quality contributions
Role of instructor	• Communicates knowledge appropriately • Ensures that students understand knowledge	• Uses methods aimed at understanding • Employs methods that help apply knowledge	• Promotes independent thinking • Promotes exchange of opinions	• Promotes application of knowledge in context • Promotes evaluative discussion of perspectives • Student and teacher critique each other
Evaluation	• Provides vehicle to show instructor what was learned	• Measures students' understanding of the material	• Rewards independent thinking	• Accurately measures competence • Student and teacher work toward goal and measure progress
Nature of knowledge	• Is certain or absolute	• Is partially certain and partially uncertain	• Is uncertain—everyone has own beliefs	• Is contextual; judge on basis of evidence in context

> analyze a case, there're different ways to go about
> it. At least from the classes I've had, there's a process
> you go through to analyze the case. In one class,
> he gave us a process, but we don't know what to
> do with it because he never gives us a concrete [idea
> of] what you should do. There have to be more
> guidelines or structure, I think. You have to have
> something more firm there; there's never a straight
> answer.

All three students separated knowledge into certain and uncertain categories. The uncertain one complicated the learning process because straightforward acquisition was not feasible. Perhaps this complexity explains transitional knowers' emphasis on the process of learning (defined as understanding) in their role as learners.

Both the learner's and teacher's functions are focused on understanding in transitional knowing. Students usually described understanding as requiring some type of meaningful encounter with the subject. For example, Ned had this view of what was involved:

> I think I [did] a lot more abstract thinking last year.
> I think I need more concrete thinking. This is basically because of the research I did this summer.
> It was slower than the book work. But as you do
> it, you actually — it's imprinted on your mind. It's
> not [that] you skim over a few sentences. You can
> talk about the reactions in two sentences, but it takes
> actually a week and a half to do it in the lab. The
> concrete experience helps to visualize and finalize
> it in your head instead of just some kind of abstract
> concept that you really don't understand.

"More concrete" does not necessarily mean lab experience, as evident in Marge's comment:

> I can see it, practically, at home. A lot of it is hands-
> on. It's not like studying all these classes at the theory

level. When it's not applicable to me, I am not interested because I don't see where it is going. I'm
interested in my current classes because as I learn
about interpersonal relationships—it's like my roommate and I or my boy friend and I are like that in
our relationship. My mother and I were like that.
I have these examples in my head when I'm studying it. It's so much easier to learn, so much easier
to understand.

Marge's lab was her relationships with friends and family. The
concrete application of what both students were learning made
it more understandable.

As would be expected from the previous perspectives on
learning, transitional knowers expected instructors to use methods concentrating on understanding and applicability. In describing a class she loved, Alexis gave the credit to her instructor:

The instructor would start by giving us straighfor-
ward definitions of the terms we were going to talk
about during class. He gives us lots of examples.
Then, when we were talking about radio commer-
cials, he was going through and showing us the
different techniques. Then he'd play them for us.
He'd play two or three examples that were used in
different ways. It was really easy to understand just
because he explained it in so many different ways.
He showed us in action. He also gave us extra information (like how many radio channels people
listen to on the average) that will help us in our
work.

Spencer also gave his lab instructor credit for making a computer lab an effective learning experience. In describing the lab,
he said:

It was really hands-on. We had a fairly detailed lab
book, and we were given all the equipment we
needed, and we just had to kind of piece it together.

You could open up a computer and actually see how
everything tied together. It made everything meaningful; you'd hear about all these transducers, but
we would actually get to build them and use them
to make a thermometer or something. That's why
I thought it was effective — because we were actually producing something that was worth using in
the business world.

These students appreciated the ability to engage actively with
the material that they were studying and to apply learning to
real life. Transitional knowers' comments about their role and
that of teachers reveal recognition of a purpose for learning that
was not present in absolute knowing (which concentrated on
reproducing information).

Consistent with the active description of learning in transitional knowing, active exchanges with peers in class were
preferred. Alice explained the value of two students with different perspectives in one of her classes:

One student is from Japan. And when we talk about
small towns and culture here, she talks about Japan.
It makes you think about stuff a whole new different way. And what's funny is that I figured if you
took a class on rural America, there would be more
people in there from a small town. But it turns out
that I'm the only one. There're a lot of stereotypes
that everyone thinks about small towns, and I've
been refuting them right and left. But then I have
a lot of stereotypes about big cities. It's just interesting to see everyone's point of view.

Bryan expressed the same interest in hearing other perspectives
and applied the idea to classes in general.

I like discussion classes much better than lecture
classes. Even though there is only one person in
the classroom with a Ph.D. — if you can get twenty

> to thirty people to give their input, you can learn
> more. Everyone here is in college; everyone has a
> brain; everyone has some opinion to give. And it's
> nice to hear. I have learned a lot from students who
> can offer insight—even the professor can't cover
> everyone's opinion. Some people will just approach
> something completely differently and shed a little
> light on it.

These comments show that classmates insights had taken on increased importance in learning. This is the beginning, particularly for interpersonal-pattern students, of the recognition of the student voice as something more than an echo of authorities. Listening to peers was, however, still limited to uncertain areas of knowledge.

Understanding is also a vital part of transitional knowers' perceptions about effective evaluation. Measuring students' understanding of a subject was central to effective and fair evaluation. For example, Megan explained:

> You have to know the rules to apply them. If you've
> applied them correctly and you know them, you're
> going to get a good grade. I mean, it's not just like
> memorize this and write it down. You have to know
> how to be able to use it, which I think just may
> be more effective than sitting down at a lecture, get
> notes, memorize them, and spit them back with-
> out really knowing. I couldn't tell you half of what
> I learned now because I memorized it for the exam.
> If you have to apply it, I feel I'm learning it more.

Dawn concurred by saying, "When you really have to take a chance, stop and think, and put down what you know and how it all works together, you learn more." Some students noted that the process of applying knowledge had superseded getting the right answer. Sidney offered an illustration with this statement:

> Essays are probably the fairest way of evaluating.
> It sees what you actually know, and it gives you

a chance to express what you know. My last cost-accounting exam, I didn't get one right out of five questions. I still got an A, because grading is based on how you present the answer and how you explain yourself. I think that was the highest form of learning in that class. It wasn't getting one specific answer; it was understanding everything that went into it and being able to use different pieces to get to a result, which is what he graded on.

Focus on the process of understanding in evaluation seemed to provide an alternative to not having a certain answer in all cases. The process took precedent over the answer in educational decision making as well. Although considerable concern was invested in the outcome of a decision, the discovery of uncertainty made finding the right answer difficult. Students talked about what was best for the future as the central element of their decision making. In debating whether to attend school near home or in a new environment, Rich said, "I decided that the new environment would allow me to grow the most in the future; it would yield the optimum result." In describing her choice of a major, Adrian said:

I had many alternatives. But realistically, I had to choose from business department offerings. The alternatives were diverse, and I had a hard time knowing exactly which one was right for me. I talked to each of my professors for my business classes to try and get a feel for what I could do as a career with each major. The most important considerations involved my interests and the type of fields I could go into upon graduation.

Despite the uncertainty of the future, transitional knowers attempted to ensure that they chose what would work out best.

"What would work out best" seemed to be an all-around substitution for the absolute knowledge that these students found did not exist. In approaching knowledge, transitional knowers suggested a process that would enable them to use information in the absence of a right answer. A hands-on role for the learner was viewed as promoting understanding of how to apply knowledge. Teaching methods that aided understanding and application were also preferred. Appropriate evaluation hinged on measuring students' ability to understand and use knowledge. The opinions of peers could shed additional light on topics. Thus, transitional knowers seemed to be doing the best they could to prepare for an uncertain world.

Beyond the core assumptions described above, transitional knowing took on different gender-related forms. The impersonal pattern, used more often by men in this study, is a logical extension of the mastery pattern in absolute knowing. The interpersonal pattern, used more often by women in this study, involves a greater attachment to learning than we saw in absolute knowing's receiving pattern. The characteristics of the interpersonal and impersonal patterns are summarized in Table 4.2.

The Interpersonal Pattern

Within the dichotomy of certainty and uncertainty, interpersonal-pattern students tended to focus on the uncertain areas, though their comments consistently revealed the existence of the certain category. Marla, whom we met at the outset of this chapter, described her interest in the uncertain arena in these comments about a psychology class:

> In psychology, there are conflicting views — there are so many different ways of looking at things and so many different theories. One professor told us that he was saying it was one way but others would tell us it was different. If you were taking math and this happened, you'd begin to wonder! But our psychology professor kept his own views secret throughout the class. I think that's good; it doesn't give you a biased view. You get the feel of all the different theories — he made all of them sound correct. There is another teacher that only teaches his area of ex-

Table 4.2. Transitional Knowing:
Interpersonal and Impersonal Approaches.

	Pattern	
Domains	*Interpersonal*	*Impersonal*
Role of learner	• Collects others' ideas • Is involved in learning • Stresses learning prac- tical material	• Understands versus memorizes • Is forced to think • Exchanges views via debate
Role of peers	• Provide exposure to new ideas • Become involved with others, hear their views	• Express their opinions • Debate views
Role of instructor	• Creates rapport with student • Allows student involve- ment and self-expression	• Focuses on understand- ing versus memorization • Challenges students to think
Evaluation	• Should make personal decisions based on individual differences	• Is fair, based on practi- cality
Nature of knowledge	• Focuses on uncertainty • Resolves by personal judgment	• Involves balanced focus on certainty/uncertainty • Is resolved by logic and research

pertise. That's not good because you're not giving students a chance to look at the theories and decide for themselves.

Asked how she decided for herself in this class, Marla responded:

It's hard. They all sound right. I can honestly say that parts of each make sense. There's no one right theory. There's no way one can possibly explain all behavior. But certain things, just the overall picture, you thought, "Yeah, I can see that that really makes sense to me." You put yourself in the situation, and you say it makes sense.

Marla's comments suggest that uncertainty should be acknowledged when it exists. Her brief quip about math reveals that she thinks there are still some sure areas. She believes that instructors should hide their biases to let students decide for themselves. Her decision process involved personal judgment. Art also used personal judgment to decide, saying:

> If I believe something—if we were talking about a class not so technical, if I were taking a religion class or something—and somebody believed one way and I believed another, I don't know how you solve that. You can't say, "This is the right way." For me, I just say, "Well, that's what you believe; you believe it. And I'll believe what I want to believe."

In the same way, Alice relied on her own judgment:

> I've noticed that a lot of things professors say are opinion, and it's their own experience. It has to be because it's not real factual material. If it is a definite fact or statistic or a definition, they'll say. But in general lecture, you can tell that it's from their personal experience. I think that's good in a lot of ways, though, because it makes me think, "What have I ever done that fits into this?" If one made more sense to me personally, that's probably the way I would go with it. Just take it on a personal basis, really.

Applying things to one's own experience was also evident in Cherylyn's remarks:

> You can disagree in psychology, like in evolution. You can't really disagree with Spanish or zoology. But in psychology, we studied evolution. I'm a

Christian, and I don't agree with evolution. I just
look at the two, try to see what makes sense, what's
reasonable, and why I feel a certain way or why
I don't. Think of exceptions, think about situations
in my own life and how things have happened
there — what I've found to be true in my own experiences. And then what support other people may
have.

All four students briefly acknowledged certainty but were more
concerned with uncertainty. Disagreement with authority was
possible in these cases. Finding a similar pattern in their study
of women, Belenky, Clinchy, Goldberger, and Tarule (1986)
speculated that women's freedom to explore their own voice and
"release" from authority's monopoly on knowledge accounted
for their enthusiastic embrace of uncertainty. This idea could
hold true for interpersonal-pattern students as well.

Judgments about educational decisions reflected the same
emphasis on personal experience. Here is Kelly's description
of her choice of major:

At first, I wanted to make money. But the courses
didn't thrill me that much. I started thinking about
education because, the summer before I came here,
I taught swimming lessons. And I had such a good
time doing that. I got such a high off the kids. I
can't describe it; it just makes me feel so good just
watching them and how far I could take them in
two-week sessions. Then I thought, teachers don't
make money; this is crazy. I went to the Majors
Fair and talked to the department chair there. I
finally decided that I'd rather do something to make
me happy.

Her choice was based on dislike of the courses in her original
major and the pleasure she found in teaching swimming. Her
interest took precedence over the goal of making money.

Uncertainty also opened the door for more interaction in

learning because the instructor was no longer seen as the source of absolute truth in all cases. These students' preference for more interaction was obvious in their remarks about both the role of the learner and that of peers. Interpersonal-pattern learners emphasized collecting others' ideas, being involved and learning practical material as their role. Kris's comments capture the idea of collecting others' thoughts:

> I get into discussions. Classroom discussions are better for me to learn. You have an opening lecture, where you have the professor discuss. Then students can contribute. Listening to other students contribute their ideas and putting in my own inputs — that makes learning better for me because it makes me think more and try to come up with more generative ideas as to what I would do in a situation. We react to the material, look at ideas and relate them to ourselves, look at what kinds of action we can take. It's a hands-on type class.

As Kris continued, she began to see a change from her previous experience. She said:

> We're working in groups, whereas other professors just lecture. This is weird — because I can hear myself saying this, and I used to live for lectures. All through high school and into my freshman year, lectures were it. I learned best from lectures. They told me what I needed to know, and I could just put it right down. And now it seems where I'm internalizing — this is good! — internalizing and making this stuff my own. I'm growing up, I guess. I don't know.

She seemed unaware of any change until she heard herself talking about it, and she interpreted the difference as a good one. Tracy expanded Kris's definition of involvement beyond taking in others' ideas:

I know classes where I've been involved and discussed—like either small discussion groups, or if
a group has been assigned a project and we've had
to go out to the library, research it, work together,
bring it back and present it to the group. I've learned
more, and I remember the material a lot more. I
guess it's more of an in-depth study of that material.

A practical emphasis was subtly present in Kris's comment. It was more clear in other comments such as Adrian's:

I have a professor who has worked in the business
world and knows which of the principles and things
that are presented in the book are actually used.
If there are things in the book that are either out-
dated or if there are computer programs that do
the same things, he eliminates them. I did much
better in the class than my friends who were in
another section—they had to learn everything in
the book. I think it is important that you learn what
is actually happening instead of just something
somebody happened to write in a textbook.

The focus on collecting ideas and being involved led to
the perception that classmates should participate actively in
learning. Interpersonal-pattern students interpreted their peers'
role as providing exposure to new ideas, being involved, and
expressing their views. Monica explained how ideas were shared
outside of class:

In English, we read all the same stories, and we'd
come back from class and have excellent discussions
because we all sort of had different opinions on it.
We'd take what we had in class and say, "What if
this had happened?" And four or five of us would
say yes and no. I wish these discussions were in
class, because when people talk about things and
work things out that way, you can see other peo-

ple's views—it's not "prof talk." Not like, "Oh, the esteemed professor knows what's right." Obviously, we wouldn't be discussing it if there wasn't more than one interpretation.

For some students, the sharing of ideas had taken place both in and out of class. As Marla explained:

> When others share their experience, you just see a different viewpoint or something maybe you never thought of. Someone else had an experience that maybe was totally contradicted in yours, and you never saw it that way. People sharing with me—it makes you think some original thoughts, not necessarily in class, but just later on. I think about it a lot; like after I walk out of the class. So I definitely learn from other people. I don't know if I really necessarily learn anything more about the material in the book or anything like that.

A more specific example of in-class sharing came from Adrian, who said:

> We saw a movie about Webster Grove. And there happened to be a student in the class who lives there. We talked about that forever, because it was so interesting that there's someone who lives there and could say how it has changed. If the class had been lecture, we wouldn't have gotten that perspective. There are so many people here from all over; they've done all sorts of things. I think that's one of the most important things about going to college—meeting people from other places and hearing other things.

The variety of perspectives was an advantage according to Steve, who remarked:

I'll have my thought, and then someone else will
say something. And I try to be pretty much open-
minded about it: "Well, you know, is that right?
That's a different point of view I hadn't thought of."
The more input you have, the more variety you'll
be able to see.

In these quotes, it is important to note that the ideas of others
were used to supplement these students' own thinking and in
some cases to "work things out"; the environment was not perceived as adversarial. The idea that certainty remained in some
areas subtly remained in Monica's "obviously, we wouldn't be
discussing it if there wasn't more than one interpretation" and
Marla's "I don't know if I really necessarily learn more about
the material in the book."

For these learners, it was necessary that instructors provide support for this new level of activity both in the form of
relationships with students and in class structures that allowed
for self-expression and involvement. In describing the type of
teacher that she preferred, Marla said:

A teacher who seems to want to relate to you. You
can tell who's sincere and who's not — like if they're
wanting to deal with students. Those who say "call
me anytime." They know your name and talk to
you about life. You know that they are a real person and they really care about you and if you're
learning.

Similarly, Reginald described rapport as stemming from being
on a first-name basis with instructors. He said, "I got to call
Henry, Henry — I got to call Steven, Steven; it made a closer
connection with the instructor." Reginald believed that calling
instructors by more formal academic titles distanced them from
him, and he found it harder to open up to them.

Cherylyn defined support as helping students express
themselves. She remarked:

Two of my professors have good teaching styles.
My Spanish professor tries to pull things out of you,

which I think is very effective. We only understand
so much, so he acts things out and helps people if
they're struggling to say something. He'll just start
them off—not just saying, "You don't know what
you're talking about" and go on. But he has the patience to stick with the student and bring the answer out of him with his coaxing.

The importance of students' voices was also inherent in one of
Kris's statements. She explained:

A small group of us sat together, and we would
whisper back and forth, discussing what the professor said. If we felt that what the professor said was
not very valid or wasn't right, we would let the
professor know. Or amongst ourselves we would
say, "Well, we think this." The professor was pretty
receptive. Never did our professors say, "Hush, I
don't want to hear that." They would always listen
to us and let us speak our piece. Sometimes they
would reconsider and say, "That might be an alternative." Sometimes they would just prove us
wrong.

The instructor's receptiveness to and concern for students seemed
to take on additional importance as they tried to use their own
voices to learn.

For interpersonal-pattern knowers, the focus on personal
judgment and experience evident in previous areas permeated
perceptions about effective evaluation. They stressed that individual differences should be considered in judging students'
knowledge and that the instructor should make personal judgments about their progress. For example, Kelly suggested:

I like more personal things, just so the prof can get
to know [me]—I don't know, maybe this encourages
profs to play favorites. But I think the person's attitude in the course should count. Because if someone's got a bad attitude but can ace all the tests—

versus someone who's got a really good attitude but doesn't test very well—I don't know, maybe that's really weird.

Gwen thought individual differences should be taken into account in the type of testing used. She talked about professors who offered students the option of taking a midterm or writing a paper. She thought this approach was more fair for the students who felt they could not do as well on the test. Al held a similar opinion:

> Essay tests tend to favor someone who's a better writer. I might understand what's going on better than someone, but maybe I can't express it very well in writing. Maybe if I could tell them, they would see that I have a good understanding.

The dominant theme of the interpersonal pattern in transitional knowing was access to one's own and others' personal experiences. The discovery of their voice—articulated here as using personal judgment, deciding for themselves, or thinking original thoughts—seems to preoccupy the students' learning efforts. The expression of voice is more likely in a supportive atmosphere, often created by familiarity with classmates. Anita clearly described her struggle to express herself in the following excerpt:

> I'm not real apt to speak out in class, especially because I'm always afraid that what I'm going to say is wrong and I'll feel dumb in front of everybody. But I know more people in my classes now, so I don't mind speaking in front of people I know. I'm trying to do more of that and finding it easier because I know some of the faces. I'm trying to speak up because I've always admired people who could do that in class. I'm working on self-confidence, which I think I had a lot of when I was younger, but I started to lose it somewhere along the way. And I think being able to speak helps me.

The connection to peers as a source of knowledge was another striking characteristic of the interpersonal pattern. Peers helped the students expand their thinking by offering their personal experiences. It is important to note that the descriptions of interpersonal-pattern students do not even hint at any friction resulting from collecting different views. Different views were embraced; often, students said that someone contradicted their point of view, and they subsequently saw it in a new way. The focus, however, was on collection and not on challenging other ideas.

The place of authority is difficult to assess in the interpersonal pattern. On the one hand, authorities still maintain a hold on the truth. On the other hand, their role has shifted in some uncertain areas to facilitating the expression and sharing of students' experiences. Other than to create rapport, authorities seemed to play a minimal part in learning. Thus, a distancing from authority seems to have taken place. The receiving-pattern student in absolute knowing had little identification with authority other than as the keeper of truth. Perhaps when this role was assigned less importance, the interpersonal-pattern students turned to the source that they readily identified with: friends and peers. The integration of their preferences with learning probably accounts for the increased interest of transitional knowers in the learning process.

The Impersonal Pattern

In the impersonal pattern of transitional knowing, learning is still individually focused. Although impersonal-pattern students intensify their interest and participation in debate with peers, the purpose of these exchanges is still to master learning. Yet an important difference exists between the concept of mastery here and in absolute knowing: here it is mastery of the process, not of the material. This change has occurred because of the discovery of uncertainty in some areas of knowledge. Impersonal-pattern students, however, put equal emphasis on the certain and uncertain categories. Sean's response to the question about how he reacted when two instructors gave different perspectives illustrates this point:

The key, for me, anyway, in deciding is that I start
with the premise that there is some body of truth.
And there's one of a couple of possibilities. Either
one's got it and the other one missed it, or they're
both hitting on different sides of the same ball, and
the complete picture is parts of both. So what I try
to do is see what correlates with what. If it's in a
science textbook, was it written for people who have
to know it for real, or is this an easy, oversimplified
way of explaining it to someone who's just beginning? I try to take into account every possible little view on what might be going on and why the
views might be different. If I still don't have an answer at that point, the only authority I have left
is other books or the professor. As a student, it
makes you think. It's good to have to sort out what's
good and what's not. If it's a fundamental issue, then
I go to the professor and talk to him about it.

Sean acknowledged uncertainty, beyond "some body of truth,"
but still worked toward an "answer." At the same time, he valued
sorting things out. The focus on mastering the learning process
is clear in Andrew's discussion of the same question:

I like to hear both sides and make my own decision. I like somebody to challenge me and make
me defend where I'm coming from. If you have
different ideas, you have to weigh them for yourself. One of my profs encourages you to debate it
and disagree with him, as long as you can defend
your position. That's what he wants you to be able
to do. A lot of times, if there're two things I don't
understand, I'll go in and talk to the teacher. You
know, something that's not going to be on the test,
but to discuss things. And sometimes, I actually just
go to the library and look something up just because I want to know the why and the way things
are.

Andrew emphasized defending his position and deciding for himself. However, he still relied heavily on sources of authority. He was learning from his instructor how to strengthen his point of view, as well as consulting the instructor or library for information. The continuation of the role of authority in this pattern was directly stated by Ned:

> The number-one reason to take an opinion would be consensus and authority. If enough people say it that are in a position of authority — well, maybe there's some merit to the idea. Is cold fusion really possible? Who knows? But if enough scientific authorities say they have the results and it is possible, then maybe I'll believe that. If an undergraduate says it, then you are going to doubt that opinion.

Ned reserved the prerogative to decide what he would believe, but it is clear that "enough authorities" will be able to convince him. In many cases, the idea of authority was inherent. For example, Justin said, "You can't question chemistry — it is just the laws of nature." In other cases, logic was substituted for authority in making decisions about what to believe. Tonya said, "I like logic. And if it makes sense to me, I'll believe it, and I'll understand it."

Reliance on authority and the importance of deciding for oneself reappeared in educational decision making. The impersonal-pattern students focused on a process that they believed would yield the best decision for the future. Ned's example of this process was typical of the impersonal-pattern students:

> The best way to decide is talk to a lot of people. It's like smart shoppers — get as much info as you can. Get involved in what you are thinking about doing. Take a class — there's no substitute for not knowing. After that, talk to a professional, an adviser, your father, your mother — somebody you trust. There're probably millions of places you could go to help make your career decisions, but mostly

I consider professional advisers that know you well
enough. I mean, they really have to know you.
That's why a parent would be good. Even a professional. If they know you well, they have enough
background that they can make a decision that you
don't know about yet. You get ten worthy opinions.
And after that, it's your own decision.

The process of gathering worthy opinions to augment what Ned
could not know increased the probability of a successful decision.

Mastering a process was also the theme in these students'
understanding of their role as learners. They stressed understanding instead of memorizing, being forced to think, and exchanging views through debate. Tony's experience in physics
underscored the value of understanding:

In physics, there were a lot of formulas we had to
know. I did go in and ask him how one worked.
And I tried to understand why it worked. And on
a test, there was a two-part problem where you had
to work around the formula to get another formula
for the second part of the problem. And I think it
helped there. Because if I just had memorized the
original formula and not really understood why it
worked, I could have never thought how to manipu-
late it to use it the way he wanted us to.

Understanding came through being required to think and
debating the material. Scott described the result of being forced
to think:

The debate and discussion process for me is really
interesting; I learn a lot more because I remember
questions. And I guess I learn the most when I sit
and I'm actually forced to raise my hand and then
I have to talk. I have to sit there and think on the
spot. I learn it better than in a note-taking class
that is regurgitation.

Similarly, Holly noted how discussion forced her to think:

> Just the fact that you are thinking about it, rather
> than taking notes and memorizing things. I guess
> hearing what other people have to say—and then,
> if you're called on to respond, you have to do some
> thinking. You definitely learn more if you're think-
> ing about what you're learning rather than just rote
> memory.

Terry gave a more detailed description that illustrated the debate idea further:

> In management, basically, he will ask a question,
> and then we just argue amongst ourselves. No an-
> swer's really directly stated, but we complain and
> bitch to each other, so we kind of get the idea. It's
> a decent class. He'll mention something, or he'll ask
> a hypothetical question that has no direct answer.
> And then we'll just argue amongst ourselves. He'll
> kind of bring out the major points that we say, but
> he won't actually state anything. So it's up to us.
> The class is more interesting, and we do learn quite
> a bit more, at least *I* do.

Tony focused on manipulating material the way the instructor
wanted him to, whereas the others relied on debate and discussion to help them grasp the material. All four students emphasized the process rather than a right answer.

Peers had a major part in making this type of discussion
possible. Their role was to express their opinions and engage
in the debate. Vincent described this environment in one of his
classes:

> We were talking about the way women are treated
> in society. We would split into groups and then
> come back to the large group and discuss what we
> had discovered in the small ones. I got to learn what

people actually think. You get everybody's opinion, the whole entire class's opinion on a certain
subject, which is good. We would sit around at a
table and just discuss our material and what people thought about it. Sometimes, we'd sit through
a whole class on one topic, just arguing back and
forth — which was neat because there were some
things people brought up that I wouldn't even have
thought of.

Although it sounds as though Vincent was interested in the opinions of his classmates, in response to a question about how he
decided what to think, he said, "I try not to let anybody else's
opinions influence mine. It could, I imagine, but I try not to."
Again, the process takes precedence over the outcome. The same
was true for Kurt:

As soon as one question is asked by the students,
that usually raises four or five more. I think that's
neat when that happens, because you get discussion between the students, and the teacher might
play devil's advocate. That's fun because you get
to see the whole different side, and you get to represent a side. And you get to learn more — the knowledge that you're talking about, certain theories or
whatever — you get to learn more about them because you're defending them.

For Kurt, it was defending ideas that promoted learning. Candace agreed, saying:

If you're in a group and you have to discuss and
defend and understand — I've changed my opinions,
and I've changed people's ideas like that because
when you're forced to sit down and discuss it and
defend your position, you have to listen more. You
think, "Well, that's true," or "No, come on, that's
not the way it is."

Impersonal-pattern students relied on their classmates to create the setting for debate but were really interested in their own opinions and learning (hence the term *impersonal*); interpersonal-pattern students, by contrast, were more interested in connecting with their classmates' ideas.

Impersonal-pattern students expected the instructor to take some responsibility in guiding this learning process by focusing on the students' understanding. This dimension was evident in Mark's expectations:

> In a seminar, I demand that the class be good — go past the material he or she has presented. Take what we've read and don't just apply it within the context of the book. Apply it at least in the context of other books you've read in that class so there's a theme going through, a theme we can always look at and grasp. Because sometimes we'll go into a class, and we're lost by the middle of the year. And at the end of the year, there's a summary, and your head is spinning sometimes.

A second major theme was the expectation that instructors challenge students to think. For example, Terry described the following criteria for effective teachers:

> Obviously, the fact that they got the class involved. And a lot of questions were asked. But they wouldn't directly state them — they made you think. Whereas in less effective classes, even if there is class participation, it's basically a straightforward question. It's just rattling off facts; it doesn't make you think at all. I prefer having to think somewhat because then I'll at least absorb some more knowledge.

Rosa also commented on the value of being challenged to think:

> I really don't think about it too much, unless it's asked in the class, and I'm like "oh." I hear other

people's views, and I can throw my views in. As
the classes get higher up, you get more into the subject; they get more controversial, and the discussion is needed. I have this really good teacher, and
he'll just say something just to tick everyone off in
the class, just to get people going — which I think
is great.

Chuck expressed a similar perspective but went a step further:

In political science, we question the guy — what he
says. You should question something that you don't
agree with to get a better understanding. And I find
myself doing that all the time. In political science,
we ask him if he really agrees with what he just said.
Sometimes they say no, they don't agree with it.
They want you to get a wide base of knowledge in
college; they want you to be able to think for yourself. I think it helps you think for yourself if you
know how others think and you know that everything the prof tells you is not necessarily what he
believes. It makes you think, "Maybe I shouldn't
have to believe it."

Terry and Rosa viewed thinking as helping them learn more,
whereas Chuck viewed it as increasing his understanding and
raising the issue of whether he should believe what he hears.
Although Chuck was beginning to consider thinking for himself, at this point he was still mastering the learning process.
     The focus on process was consistent; nevertheless, when
discussing evaluation, impersonal-pattern transitional knowers
sometimes emphasized outcomes because of the difficulty of judging the process. Fairness and practicality were the hallmarks
of appropriate evaluation, as evident in the following perceptions. Jim described the situation in this way:

I have a philosophy that I'd like to be able to have
everything — all the grades — put on [the basis of]

effort. Unfortunately, that's never going to work
because you can have probably the guy who tries
the hardest in the whole world, but he's never going to be able to run the company or something
like that. I'm sorry you can't give him all A's, but
nobody's going to hire him if he can't do [the work].

Jim then discussed a disappointing academic outcome:

I'm now into the learning process and not really
worrying about the grades that much. I think if
you're really into the learning process a lot of times
the grades will just kind of come. But I've found
it doesn't [always] happen that way, though. I
worked hard in one class and got a C. I really feel
like I learned a lot more than the average student.
But there's not too much you can do about it because objective things are the way they're going to
measure the grades. If you leave it up to the professor to say, "This person was here at night, and he's
a pretty neat kid so we'll give him an A"—that's just
not going to be real consistent. So you have to go
with the objective kinds of things. I don't like it,
but it's got to be done because how else are you going to give grades?

Hugh discussed the same issue in the course of a discussion about
essay exams. He said:

I hate subjective classes where it's totally up to the
teacher what your grade is—like an English class.
The fact that the teacher decides if something is
right or wrong just because of his past personal experiences. I just can't believe someone can say, "My
way is right and your way is wrong." It's kind of
aggravating. I'm contradicting myself. I like essay
exams, but I don't like subjective grading. You want
to be able to express yourself, but you don't want—I

don't know. It seems impossible. Maybe if you had
more than one professor evaluate your test. Like
on the Supreme Court, you have your conservative
judges and your more liberal judges, and there're
seven of those. How can you just have one teacher?

Those students who were able to think about evaluation apart
from grades put more emphasis on the learning process. This
was clear in Derek's comments:

I think that essay tests are the best kind—subjective
tests, because on objective tests you can guess. I
don't think that's going to improve your knowledge.
Essay tests make you sit down and analyze the question more. It makes you think through it. I think
the biggest thing is being able to write your thoughts
in words, just comprehension. I prepare more for
essays; it makes me not just memorize the material. It helps me develop the kind of thinking for
when you're into the real world. I mean, you aren't
going to have many tests after you get out of here.
You're going to have to know what you want to say
and how you want to say it.

Adrian described a good exam as focusing on practical information. Referring again to her professor who had worked in the
business world and eliminated principles not used there, she said:

I did much better on the exam than my friends did
[in other sections of the course], and I think it's for
that reason—that the essentials were on the exam.
They [her friends] had to learn everything that was
in the book for the exam.

The struggle between learning and judging the outcome
represents a broader problem in the impersonal pattern. Although learning was adjusted to account for the discovery of
uncertainty, many expectations were still aimed at closure. In

their attempts to understand, the impersonal-pattern students often returned to the voice of authority. Despite intense interest in debate, they often did not seriously reconsider their viewpoints. Thinking about the material was aimed at being able to learn it better. All of these observations suggest that impersonal-pattern students do not relinquish certainty easily and hold onto it whenever possible.

Authority figures by and large retained their status for impersonal-pattern knowers. Though they also stressed deciding about knowledge claims or educational choices for themselves, the students trusted authority figures completely in areas deemed certain and relied on them heavily in uncertain areas. Often, instructors or books were noted as the source of a solution if one was not found through other means. These students also followed the instructors' lead in the practice of disagreeing or questioning what to believe. Authority figures were also viewed as central to creating the preferred discussion-and-debate atmosphere. Thus, their role changed from providing knowledge (in absolute knowing) to creating a process for learning. Impersonal-pattern students had less interest in rapport with the instructor than did their interpersonal-pattern counterparts. The only friction with authority involved grading. Although they most commonly accepted the necessity, objectivity, and fairness of grading, the attitudes of some students (like Hugh, quoted earlier) bordered on questioning the instructor's authority. Hugh's question "How can you have just one teacher?" marks the beginning of true challenge to that authority.

Identification with authority did not inhibit student voice for the most part. Impersonal-pattern students shifted from giving answers (in absolute knowing) to giving opinions—a fact obvious from the involvement in thinking and talking so prevalent in transitional knowers' descriptions. However, their voices seemed to develop in conjunction with those of authorities. These students followed the lead of authorities even in the exercise of doubting and questioning. They did not value their peers' knowledge, only their contribution to an environment where debate could be used as a personal learning technique (recall Vincent's statement about not letting his peers' opinions influence his).

Relationships with peers represent an extension of their role in absolute knowing. Peers are a vehicle for engaging in the learning process. The nature of peer interaction may have changed because the nature of the learning changed. Yet even though the interaction is more intense, it has remained impersonal, largely because of these students' focus on themselves as individuals. Their interest is in discussing and debating to increase their understanding, not in sharing and adopting others' views. Each student gains the same benefit from the debate process.

Interpersonal and Impersonal Patterns Compared

Students in both patterns develop their voice more in transitional than in absolute knowing. The impersonal-pattern voice, though it now reflects the process of learning rather than the answers, remains close to authority. The interpersonal-pattern voice diverges more from authority; the discovery of uncertainty seems to be viewed by interpersonal-pattern students as an opportunity to increase both their involvement and their exercise of personal judgment in knowing. Inequality of knowledge between the interpersonal-pattern knower and authority may still exist, but the interpersonal-pattern voice has become more independent than that of the impersonal pattern. If we take the relationship with authority as a point of departure on the way to independent knowing, interpersonal-pattern students seem readier to adopt their own voice.

The fundamental differences between the two patterns are clear. Interpersonal-pattern students care about their classmates' perspectives, want to know their peers, and hope that instructors will care about them. Relationships are central to the learning process because knowing others promotes sharing perspectives and sharing perspectives increases knowledge. If instructors are uncaring, teaching (and thus learning) is ineffective. For impersonal-pattern students, challenge is more important than relationships. This emphasis appears to reflect the impersonal-pattern students' concern for individual learning, whereas the interpersonal-pattern students focus on the relationships made possible during learning. Considering peer relationships as a point of departure toward independent knowing, we could expect that interpersonal-pattern students will have little difficulty accepting peers' views as valid. For them, acceptance will be an extension of knowing in the uncertain arena. For impersonal-pattern students, the addition of peers (and themselves) to the ranks of authority will be required.

Chapter Five

Independent Knowing: Embracing and Subordinating Others' Ideas

> A friend who is a physics major said he was going to a physics seminar. When I heard the word *seminar,* I thought, "Physics has seminars? I mean, you can debate physics? And not be right and not be wrong?"
>
> — *Reginald*

Reginald's surprise about his friend's physics seminar was due to his sense that in the sciences things are sure. Reginald's reaction: "Why did I never have the chance to be in an open situation with physics? I hated it — couldn't stand it because I couldn't use my own ideas." The revelation that physics could be debated illustrates the shift from transitional knowing, where some things are still certain, to independent knowing, where most things are uncertain. Laura described her discovery of prevailing uncertainty in this way:

> Everything's relative; there's no truth in the world — that sort of thing. So I've decided that the only person that you can really depend on is yourself. Each individual has their own truth. No one has the right to decide, "This has to be your truth, too." If everybody is stuck on, "What do the other people think?," then you just waste your whole life. You just do

what you feel like you have to do. Sometimes I felt
that I had to get into business because everybody
was going into business. I don't think the world ro-
tates around the business world and money and
materialism. Now I'm relaxed, and I'm thinking of
what I want — what's best for me and not for anybody else.

Both Reginald and Laura have made a discovery that will
make independent thinking possible. Whereas knowledge previously was composed of things established as certain or what other
people thought was right, it will now consist of what Laura and
Reginald decide to believe. Other students' revelations took various forms. Recall Gwen's account of the professor who said "I
reject this role as professor." Gwen described that experience
as contributing to her understanding of literature as a subject
where no right and wrong existed. Reginald encountered it
through his friend. Sheila experienced it through an international exchange program. Describing the effects of her time in
Spain, she said:

I don't set anything that I feel in cement, which is
what I did before. I've found that my foundations
completely crumbled out from under me, and I had
to rebuild them for myself, which is the best thing
that ever happened to me.

Regardless of the nature of the experience that sparked the discovery, the result was the same in each case — thinking for oneself. This individual approach to knowledge stems from the core
assumption of uncertainty in independent knowing.

Independent Knowing

The basic assumption of uncertainty changes both the process
and source of knowing substantially. Differences among authorities represent the variety of views possible in an uncertain world.
Authorities are no longer seen as the only source of knowledge;

instead, students view themselves as equals and hold their own opinions as valid. The ability to create their own perspectives focuses students' attention on thinking for themselves. Instructors are expected to promote the expression of personal viewpoints; they are responsible for providing context for exploration, not knowledge. In the same way, evaluation should reward independent thinking and should not penalize a student for holding views different from the instructor or authors of texts. Peers become a legitimate source of knowledge, rather than part of the learning process. Independent knowers emphasize being open-minded and allowing everyone to believe what they will, as illustrated by Laura's comment at the beginning of this chapter. These core assumptions are summarized in Table 5.1 and illustrated with students' accounts of their experiences.

Uncertainty presided over most realms of knowledge for independent knowers. Laura, quoted in the introduction of this chapter, offered an example:

> I became very skeptical about what the "truth" was. It's amazing how you can influence statistics. Statistics are supposed to be really the truth. You can't manipulate statistics. But then I learned you really can manipulate statistics to have a point of view to be the truth.

Amy portrayed the same idea in the area of religion. Describing a class that she had taken on death and dying, she said:

> People had very strong beliefs one way or the other. We discussed AIDS and homosexuality and the nuclear problem — and people's beliefs in God and beliefs in the afterlife and things like that. You've got people who've been raised in Catholic schools all their life and do believe this one way. And then other people, who just do not believe in any god. And you have people arguing. I do not think that anybody felt that one way was better than the other. I think most people were very open-minded, though they had their own beliefs.

Table 5.1. Epistemological Reflection Model.

Domains	Absolute Knowing	Transitional Knowing	Independent Knowing	Contextual Knowing
Role of learner	• Obtains knowledge from instructor	• Understands knowledge	• Thinks for self • Shares views with others • Creates own perspective	• Exchanges and compares perspectives • Thinks through problems • Integrates and applies knowledge
Role of peers	• Share materials • Explain what they have learned to each other	• Provide active exchanges	• Share views • Serve as a source of knowledge	• Enhance learning via quality contributions
Role of instructor	• Communicates knowledge appropriately • Ensures that students understand knowledge	• Uses methods aimed at understanding • Employs methods that help apply knowledge	• Promotes independent thinking • Promotes exchange of opinions	• Promotes application of knowledge in context • Promotes evaluative discussion of perspectives • Student and teacher critique each other
Evaluation	• Provides vehicle to show instructor what was learned	• Measures students' understanding of the material	• Rewards independent thinking	• Accurately measures competence • Student and teacher work toward goal and measure progress
Nature of knowledge	• Is certain or absolute	• Is partially certain and partially uncertain	• Is uncertain—everyone has own beliefs	• Is contextual; judge on basis of evidence in context

Amy extended the notion of uncertainty to accepting all opinions. Steve offered a similar point of view in explaining that
he had become more liberal:

> I think a lot of it was my history classes, just be-
> cause you realize that — I don't know — just let peo-
> ple be their own person. That doesn't cause a lot
> of problems, you know. And not bothering with
> other people's world or what they're doing, as long
> as it's not affecting you.

Barry also had his own beliefs but noted that it was not always
to his advantage to express them. He described a class in which
he did not believe the instructor's perspectives because he had
worked for a company where these ideas did not work. In order
to get a good grade, however, he wrote down things he did not
believe on the test. He said:

> I'd be writing it down, really thinking, you know,
> questioning it. But I knew it was the right answer.
> In class, I'd bring it up and just ask the teacher
> about it. There're always some different ways to go
> about it. I basically tried to put my other thoughts
> away when I was taking the test. I didn't want to
> think during the test. Sort of spit it back out.

In most cases, however, independent knowers did feel free
to express their new-found voices. The belief in the validity
of their own voices, made possible because of the uncertainty of
knowledge, prompted them to focus on thinking for themselves.
Reginald described his favorite learning experiences as a senior
like this:

> Mostly, they were the kind of situations where the
> entire responsibility for learning was given to me
> and I had to take that responsibility. And that's
> where I started to learn that I had to start thinking
> for myself and saying what I felt and realizing that

you're going to be wrong—not necessarily wrong—
you're going to be critiqued, and there's going to
be discussion about what you think. But that doesn't
necessarily mean you're bad, evil, wrong, because
you said the wrong thing and so forth.

Sandra described her best senior classes similarly and then explained how she approached learning as a senior:

I guess I would kind of internalize things [from lec-
tures] and then talk about it with people. I was
really lucky to have a lot of friends in classes senior
year, so I had people to discuss things with.

She characterized learning in her hospital staff position after
graduation in much the same way:

I'm kind of a sponge. I guess I take everything in,
and then I go home at night and kind of sort out
what I want and what I don't want. Some things—I
guess maybe because of my morals and values—
will sit better with me and will seem like fact for
me. And other things, I'm just like, "I don't really
think so." And I throw them out.

Although Sandra did make decisions about what she thought,
she still tried to absorb everything and made her decisions on
the basis of her own values.

Both Reginald and Sandra found themselves in environments where they could think freely. Laura, by contrast, offered
an example of the fear encountered by independent knowers
when they feel their thinking is restricted. Describing her graduate classes in economics, Laura said:

I'm very high in imagination. I feel like they're trying to hit me on the head and make me think one
way. I see this image of them going chunk, chunk,
chunk—you know, hitting me, trying to form the

way I should think. In international studies, there
were so many fields that I could take that they weren't
able to hit me in a certain way to form this way
of thinking. But when you're taking all economics,
a lot of mathematics, they're shaping the way you
think about things. I really am fearful of that.

These students' focus on uncertainty and their investment
in thinking for themselves prompted them to prefer instructors
who promoted independent thinking. Phillip described how his
mass-media instructor promoted intellectual independence:

The way that my prof told me to analyze things —
critically analyze them and tear them apart — I think
probably helped a lot. He actually sat us down and
just broke stuff apart. He would take example upon
example and make us think about what the message in these ads on television or in print was saying.

Phillip characterized the class as an "eye-opener" and described
how it had helped him in buying a car after graduation.

Gale recounted similar preferences as she complained
about an instructor that she disliked her senior year. She said,
unequivocally:

He's one of those teachers where maybe you have
to believe his way in order to do well. I hate those
kinds of teachers. You can put that on the record.

Asked if she had many teachers like this one, she replied:

No, not at all. Everyone was pretty open, you
know — you have your own opinions. There was the
one who would insert his views. And I really don't
want to know. Not that it was really that important to me, but I really don't think they should tell
us. Because that might affect us, and it shouldn't.
But I didn't really come into contact with people

that persuaded my opinion one way or the other. They just are there to give you the general outlook on the whole thing.

In addition to promoting independent thinking, these learners wanted instructors to encourage the exchange of views among students. Kurt, a fifth-year senior, explained the value of peer interaction in these comments:

Interaction with your peers is very important, because obviously you get a whole different perspective from different people. I think it's also important to be able to disagree with your peers. And to not be defensive about that is very good, to be open-minded when somebody says, "Kurt, I disagree with what you just said." I would be like, "okay." I think I've developed — there was a time when I was defensive about somebody saying I was wrong. You know, it provides you with a different perspective you can take to something.

Sandra felt that other perspectives helped her to clarify her ideas. She explained the peer interaction in one of her senior classes:

We got to see how other students felt and kind of bounced our own ideas off of them. And then you didn't feel like you were the only one getting upset about these issues. You got to discuss others' ideas, not just what was in the reading material. You got to discuss — not argue — but discuss different points and figure out exactly where you stand on different issues. It was just a clarifying thing for me.

Asked to differentiate between arguing and discussing, Sandra said: "It's more like discuss different points, but we don't always agree. But that was all right too; we didn't all have to come to the same point." Thus, the common emphasis in Sandra and Kurt's comments was on exchanging viewpoints with others without trying to persuade them to adopt their point of view.

Maintaining a variety of perspectives was also important to independent knowers in the evaluation of their work. In retrospect, Valerie described her senior-year classes in this fashion:

> Senior year, they weren't really expecting an answer — they just wanted your input or output, whatever. Your output about what you thought, and there really wasn't a right answer. Things were evaluated by how you explained yourself. It's essay questions. If you'd come up with a completely wrong answer, a wrong answer compared to what the teacher thought, and you came up with a good idea about how to back it, then you would get credit for it. The answer wasn't the main thing; it was how you explained it.

Lowell was less fortunate than Valerie in one of his senior-year classes. In his fifth-year interview, he described the frustration that resulted from his instructor's approach:

> The first day, he said, "Everybody's views are good." And then it turned out not to be the case at all. It showed up in one of my exams where I had a question. I said, "I don't understand why this is wrong." And he said, "Well, it's not wrong; it's just not what I would have put." And I said, "Well, do I get credit for it, then?" He said, "No, it's *my* class." Turned me off for the whole class right away.

Both Valerie and Lowell wanted to express their own voices and expected instructors to reward their independent thinking.

The interest in maintaining an open mind is evident in the stories told here. This open-mindedness manifests itself in career decisions as well. Scott shared his perspective on career direction during his fifth-year interview. He had majored in political science and secured a job in his field. However, one graduate class that he took as a senior caused him to see political science differently. Although the class was "interesting and exciting," his assessment was, "It didn't catch me." This disappointment resulted in his career decision being what he called "one of the big 'I don't know' questions." Asked how he felt about his quandary, Scott replied:

> I've put it on the back burner more than I've actually resolved it. I've just toyed with ideas, "Oh, that might be kind of neat. Why don't I pursue that?" I feel like a freshman all over again. It's different. I thought maybe when I would graduate that I would actually have a direction and I'd be ready to go. But I'm finding more and more that the direction isn't there at all. So I'm just testing the waters and just trying to keep myself going right now until I see something that really sparks something in me. It's kind of odd, hearing it from a person who spent four years of education and then coming out finally deciding, "Well, I learned that I really don't know what I want to do."

Monica's story of her career decision was also centered around her open-minded approach. Being a public relations major, she had engaged in many extracurricular activities related to that field and fully planned to pursue a job in it. During her senior year, however, she received an invitation for an interview with an insurance company. Due to pressure from her housemates, she signed up for the interview. Although she described herself as having no idea what her interviewer was talking about in the first meeting, she was invited back for a second interview. She described what happened next:

> You know, my little voice was saying to me, "What the hell are you doing? You don't know." But it was going well; it was the only second offer that I had had. I thought, "Well, why not just go with it?" I got the job offer, don't ask me why, because I'm very, very public relations–oriented. But I think

eventually, I just sort of looked at it. I knew nothing about insurance. But I know a little bit about
PR. I'm young; when I'm twenty-five or twenty-
six, it won't be too late to change careers. I'll still
know some people in PR. Why not try it? If I absolutely hate it, I can do something else. But I will
have known that I tried something else. So that's
why I did it.

Monica and Scott's stories demonstrate that independent knowers not only embraced the idea of uncertainty but carried out
this perspective in their actions.

The word *openness* captures the essence of the core assumptions of independent knowers. They believed that knowledge
was open to many interpretations, that people should be receptive to others' ideas, that instructors should be open to students'
ideas, and that many possibilities existed in the choices confronting them. This openness facilitated the emergence of individually created perspectives because the risk of being wrong was
eliminated. Because knowledge could be seen in so many ways,
there was also no obligation to make judgments about various
views. Although independent knowers did make decisions about
what to believe, they rarely identified criteria upon which these
should be based. Thus, the independent knowers were free to
think for themselves, and they could use their voices with mini-
mum risk. Subsequently, they valued expressing their opinions
in all realms of learning and expected others to do the same.

Gender-related approaches were also detectable in the independent knowers' stories. The interindividual-pattern students
placed equal value on hearing others' perspectives and thinking for themselves, the two components being intertwined.
Individual-pattern knowers focused primarily on thinking independently; they appreciated exchange with others, but it was
secondary to thinking for themselves. These patterns are summarized in Table 5.2.

The Interindividual Pattern

This pattern was used more often by women than men in this
study. Interindividual-pattern knowers believed that different

Table 5.2. Independent Knowing:
Interindividual and Individual Approaches.

	Pattern	
Domains	Interindividual	Individual
Role of learner	• Thinks for self	• Thinks for self • Focuses on a way to think
Role of peers	• Share views	• Think independently
Role of instructor	• Promotes sharing of opinions	• Allows student to define learning goals
Evaluation	• Is mutual process between student and instructor	• Is based on independent thinking
Nature of knowledge	• Contains discrepancies due to interpretation or bias	• Contains discrepancies because everyone has own beliefs

perspectives resulted from each person's bringing her or his own interpretation, or in some cases bias, to a particular knowledge claim. They simultaneously advocated listening to other interpretations or biases and espousing their own; they described how the interaction of the two helped them form their own viewpoint. Alexis offered an example during her fifth-year interview. Reflecting on her senior-year classes, she commented that the senior year was a time "when you should be most open because you should be able to listen to what other people say and then come up with your own opinion on how you feel about a particular thing." Asked how she formed an opinion, she replied:

I listen to their arguments for it; then I listen to other people's arguments against it. And then it's just my own personal view, really, whether I can establish the credibility — so I guess it really stems from the credibility of the person who's saying it also, as well as just the opinion on it. I listen to both sides. I usually throw some of my own views

into it as well. So I'm influenced by other people —
like each member of the group should be influenced
by each other. But when the final vote comes in,
you should go with what you believe.

Alexis clearly valued hearing others' ideas and felt that people
should be influenced by each other. She simultaneously held
her own view and tried to integrate it with the opinions of others
that she perceived as credible.

A second example of the importance of simultaneously
hearing others and holding one's own view is inherent in Sheila's
account of her job as a flight attendant during her first year after graduation. Sheila had described herself as very strident about
her views until an experience with other cultures caused her to
focus less on converting people. She noted that as a flight attendant it was important to respect the beliefs of passengers and
co-workers. She described the impact of interaction with passengers and co-workers on her own perspectives:

Mine are perpetually changing, about who I am
and about what I want and about what I believe.
Everything is very gray before me. I am perpetually changing, and I like that. I think it's much more
natural than to kind of set yourself between guidelines and have to shove your life in between them —
try to make everything fit in. I'm with different people every day of the week. And I'm so affected by
everything everyone has to say to me; I'm so open
that it's good. I pick up so much about everything —
about countries, about the cultures, about just absolutely everything. That's what college was about,
knowledge for knowledge's sake. Everything is important as long as you can find a place for it and
understand what its impact is. That's the wonderful thing about this job that many people don't understand. I don't think I understood that when I
took this job; I don't think that I realized how much
I would be affected by meeting so many different

> people and coping with different cultures. I had a
> lot of the same prejudices that everyone has about
> flight attendants. You're just basically a bimbo, and
> you pass out Coke and peanuts. You don't realize
> what kind of diplomacy it takes and how much you
> do represent the country, the company.

These comments demonstrate Sheila's intense openness to other ideas. A few minutes later in the conversation, the subject of her impact on other people came up:

> I used to think that I could conquer the world and
> change the world and make it a better place. I think
> that I can do that now, but I realize I can only do
> that by changing myself. I don't want to change
> anybody else. Hopefully, if I do, it's only through
> my own actions and my own beliefs. I realized that
> the only change that ever is going to happen in the
> world is going to be through each individual striv-
> ing to be the best they can be, hopefully by doing
> so through understanding and compassion instead
> of zealousness and righteousness.

Though Sheila had renounced any desire to change people, she was willing for them to be affected by her beliefs, understanding, and compassion. She was unwilling to force her beliefs upon others, yet readily accepted theirs.

At the same time that interindividual-pattern knowers were open to other ideas, they were less concerned about what people thought about them. Thinking for self was described by many as "finding a voice" as a result of decreasing worry about the reactions of others. Lauren explained it as being "less afraid to learn" because "as a freshman you're very concerned about what other people are going to think; by the time you're a senior, it just really doesn't matter." Stephanie described a similar attitude:

> By the time you get to your senior year, you feel
> that if people are going to criticize you, it doesn't

matter because you're a lot more confident in yourself. And you also know that you're leaving within
nine months—whereas if you had to be critized by
someone for the next four years, that's a lot different. By the time you're a senior, if you feel you have
something worthwhile to contribute, I felt that I
could just go ahead and do that and not really care
if other people thought that was a little forward or
if they didn't agree with me. It didn't really matter.

Eileen extended this notion beyond learning in the classroom:

I'm a little more outgoing as far as if I have an opinion. Before, I would either go along with everyone
else, or I would just keep quiet. Not that I walk
around telling everyone what I think, but I'm just
more outgoing socially. And if I have an idea, I'm
not afraid to say what it is. A lot more confident
than I was before. That's me. I don't think there's
anything that I believe in that people just couldn't
accept, but I think it's just important to be honest
with people. If they don't like it, then they can do
what they want.

These comments imply that these students had thoughts of their
own all along but had refrained from expressing them due to
their fear of how they would be received. Prior to these fears
subsiding, they listened to others but did not give voice to their
own ideas.

A second condition that supported the emergence and expression of voice was the connection between academic life and
personal life. Deirdre experienced this connection as a result
of writing a journal in one of her classes. She said:

In school, you kind of leave your personal life and
your personal experiences out of what you do academically. And everything's supposed to be kind
of detached and formal. In the journal, you didn't
pay any attention to what you were writing. I think

any time you can learn about something and then somehow relate it to your personal life or some kind of experience you've had, it doubles — it makes the experience stronger. I think people need to get a chance to talk about the things they know, too.

She went on to say that some of the things she read in the class also had an impact on connecting her own life with what she was learning:

I began thinking about things that I had read in high school and how everything I had learned had been from a very specific viewpoint that wasn't mine, that made me kind of look at myself as some kind of other, foreign thing. I look at my mother and my stepfather and the way they interact. And my brother and sister. And being able to look at the world personally and then publicly. And things just starting to click.

The connection between academic and personal spheres and decreased concern over what people thought freed the voice of the interindividual-pattern student. Learning was thus transformed into a truly interindividual process because it made possible a dialogue between personal ideas and those held by others.

Interindividual-pattern students viewed peers as a source of the dialogue, as illustrated by Justin's comments:

When you're in a discussion with someone else — if you say your ideas and someone else says their idea and gives it in a different viewpoint — well, that's going to make me look at my perspective and say, "Well, maybe he's right." Or "Maybe I could change — maybe my idea is a little skewed," or, "I can see your point of view." And that might affect the way I feel about it. I think sometimes five or ten brains are better than one. It's really helpful to get insights from other people to help you shape your own.

Sandra assigned value to her peers' views in her job:

I've learned ten times more in one year of working
than I did in four years of college. It's hard to explain, but every day I learn something new about
alcoholism or about teenagers or about people in
general. I also learned a lot from the people that
I work with, especially recovering alcoholics that
I work with. They're able to give insight on the dis-
ease. I learn most from the patients, and they don't
even know that they're teaching you. I do learn a
lot from my staff. They're able to share what they've
learned and give advice.

Interindividual-pattern knowers appreciated instructors
who promoted the sharing of views in class. Tracy, a fifth-year
senior, discussed her social psychology professor:

We get into a lot of—I hate to use the word *meaningful* because that sounds kind of trivial—but we get
into deep discussions. Everyone has something to
say. We get feedback from everybody, not just the
professor. I like it because it's not just the professor saying, "Here's what's here—what major critics
have said about it. And, then, here's what I say
about it." He says, "I'm interested in this stuff;
otherwise, I wouldn't be teaching it. But I want to
know what you all think about it." And we get to
express it throughout, every day that we're in class—
rather than just an exam being the only way to express our thoughts, which I think is important.

Jim described instructors in his upper-level courses senior year:

The professor is up there saying, "I've got an opinion; the book's got an opinion; and you've got an
opinion. And yours is just as good as the two opinions that I've said before." And the ability of the
instructor to say, "Hey, that's a great idea. Let's
expand on that," and to allow students to talk and

express their opinions and their ideas. It's real
neat—you go in, and they actually ask you what
you think about it.

Alice illustrated the same point while discussing a multicultural
counseling class in the graduate program that she had recently
entered. Her experience, however, was the reverse of Tracy's
and Jim's because she felt that the instructor did not allow the
open exchange of ideas. Alice complained that he was impolite
to students and called their comments stupid. Asked to elaborate, she said:

> It's not effective for me at all. Now for some peo-
> ple it is. I've seen it be effective for people because
> he attacks them and then they come back and de-
> fend themselves and it's a real learning process for
> them. I mean, I've seen it occur. But for me it's
> not. I get angry, and I just tune him out. I don't
> participate from that point on. It just turns me off.
> We do keep journals. And a lot of it I express in
> the journals. It has been real thought provoking,
> especially a lot of the racial issues, because I've
> never really thought about my own biases before.
> I do express it in the journals, and I try to sort out
> my own things.

Although Tracy preferred to share her thoughts in class and hear
those of her peers, the nature of the environment obliged her
to turn to her journal to sort out her thoughts.

The desire to express personal views and hear those of
others was woven into comments about evaluation. Interindividual-pattern knowers endorsed the idea that both teacher and
student should contribute to evaluation. For example, Rosa
described why her student-teaching evaluation was effective:

> My cooperating teacher and I, we did it together.
> We sat down together and wrote it. A lot of posi-
> tive things were said. She said, "If you think of any-

thing else you'd like for me to put in there that you
feel was a good strength of yours," and things like
that. And that really helped because it was my
evaluation. And I know myself also—she tried to
leave me pretty independent in that room. That
helped because those kids had to get used to me and
they had to respect me as the authority. So it was
in those times that I would really evaluate myself.
So I felt, "Yeah, my opinion should count in that
evaluation because I know what it was like when
it's just me and I'm in charge of that whole room
and there's no one else there that I can turn to."

Stephanie described this kind of evaluation in a more informal
way in a senior class that simulated an actual management team.
She was part of a smaller group called General Management
because she had been on one of the teams previously. Describing what was effective about the evaluation, she said:

We did peer evaluations. But since there're only
five of us and we do meet every other day with the
professors, the professors are more able to see how
much work we're doing. And if it was a problem
with someone on General Management (the people there are supposed to be a little bit more sea-
soned) somebody—either a peer from General
Management or a professor—would say something
to the person and try to get things straightened out.

As was true of all independent knowers, interindividual-
pattern learners were more content to take in information than
to sift through it to make decisions. Career decisions for these
students hinged on eliminating choices that had negative characteristics. Anne conveyed this perspective as she described how
she decided on her job after graduation:

I had a couple of offers from fairly big firms, like
Fortune 500–type companies. I had three different

offers, and it was really a hard decision. It came
down to two companies. One was in my home
town, and I just kind of needed to get out of there
for a while, so I turned that one down. I had an
offer from a firm in Chicago, and I'm kind of a big-
city type. So that was really hard to turn down. But
I didn't like the job that much. This job, I finally
decided on it because I'm out at one of the paper
mills; it's a paper company. They own thirteen
mills; they only put a few accountants at each one,
so they really give you a lot to do. We wear jeans
to work, and everyone is really laid back and nice.
I got out in the mill a lot, and I interact with the
people out there. And I'll be talking to engineers
one day and people that work on the machines the
next. That's a big part of the reason I took it — just
the whole atmosphere about the place I really liked.
I guess I wasn't ready for a big, uptight corporate
job in a big city where you wear suits to work and
it's really high-key pressure.

Anne implied that all three offers were good but eliminated two
because of characteristics she did not like. She preferred her current position because it allowed her to maintain the interindividual approach to learning and knowing.

The interindividual pattern has as its defining theme a
connection between the knower and others that maintains the
integrity of both. For the first time, this student has become
an equal member of the intellectual community. Transitional
interpersonal knowers held their opinions in abeyance while they
collected the ideas of others, whose real or expected reactions
constrained their voices. Independent knowers, however, either
expected others to accept their views (as Eileen explained) or
no longer cared what others thought. As Lauren and Stephanie
put it, "It really doesn't matter."

Their decrease in concern about what others thought
about them resulted in an environment in which dialogue about
ideas was possible. The belief that everyone should be open to

a variety of viewpoints and the lack of focus on evaluating ideas formed a context for discussion that did not strain connections and relationships. Although increased self-confidence was noted by some as a factor contributing to their willingness to express themselves, the equality of ideas removed the component of judgment that could create friction. The introduction of an individually formed perspective changed the dialogue from interpersonal to interindividual.

The role of authority in the interindividual pattern was also one of interchange with the learner. Interindividual-pattern students viewed authority figures as partners in sharing ideas and evaluating learning. The detachment from authority evident in transitional knowing was less evident, perhaps because these students saw themselves as equal to authority figures. This view would allow for an identification with authority not evident in previous ways of knowing. Although authority figures were included in the interindividual exchange, they were no more important than peers.

The Individual Pattern

Individual-pattern knowers, like their interindividual-pattern counterparts, espoused independent thinking and the exchange of views with others. However, their primary focus was on their own thinking, and they sometimes had to struggle to listen carefully to other voices. Fully acknowledging that everyone had his or her own beliefs, students in the individual pattern described the dominant role of their ideas when differences of opinion took place. Lowell shared an experience in which he and other students had conflicting ideas:

> I'd consider myself conservative. And there was one guy in our group who was quite liberal and acknowledged it. I guess it gave me another viewpoint, another aspect to look at this. Like it or not, we're all kind of ingrained one way or another, whether it's the liberal end or the conservative end. He looked at it in this way, and I looked at it in another

way. And everybody in the group had their own
ways on it. [You had] to try to get your point across
without sounding too dominating—I'm searching
for words and not finding them. To try to listen
to theirs, to *really* listen, not to just hear it and let
it go through. And then to try to take that into account and reach a compromise. There was quite
a bit of discussion. But I don't think the attempt
was to try to change each other's mind. It was just,
"Your point is all right, but you've got to look at
this part, too, because this is as relevant."

Lowell's genuine attempt to hear his liberal classmate and his
insistence that his conservative perspective also be taken into
account did not result in a change in either perspective. Reginald
reported a similar struggle in his first year in the seminary. He
encountered some ideas in his liberation theology class that
caused him concern:

I don't expect everybody to believe the same things
I believe or to be where I'm at in terms of how I
think. But I usually had more people in the community that perhaps knew a little bit more about
the feminist issues. I was excited about these perspectives. But when I bring that out, I'm not considered someone interested in women's issues; I'm
just considered someone who might be gay. And
the male discussions are sometimes very inhumane.
I got this feeling of dislike—it's a feeling of the shut-
ting off of dialogue with another person. And I
know how detrimental that is, and I really struggled with it. The instructor helped me work out how
to confront them without jumping on them. I was
just turning it off; I didn't want to listen. They did
bring up good questions, though, and I hope that
I'm going to be able to develop the sense of being
able to put those antagonistic feelings aside and be
able to confront in a positive way and learn from

these people. Because I hope they're learning from
me, from the way I'm speaking, from the way I'm
not being derogatory about human beings.

Reginald hopes to be able to learn from his peers who think
differently, and he implies that he hopes to change their perspectives as well. Both Lowell and Reginald found it easier to
maintain their perspectives than to listen to those of others. Dawn
stressed the importance of listening to others but did not know
how to decide whether to accept their ideas. She said:

There are oftentimes disagreements. That's kind of
an education in and of itself, to know that not everybody's opinion counts. Or, yes, they all count, but
what you take in is what you choose to take in. I
suppose it depends on the validity of what they're
saying. And I suppose that you're going to ask me,
"How do you judge the validity of what they're saying?" And I don't know if I know the answer to that
question.

Thinking for themselves played the main role in learning for individual-pattern students. Chuck described it in the
context of his law school classes:

Our classes are a hundred people on average, so
you don't get called on that much. I always have
my hand up. I'm always getting into it. Because
I think you learn from your mistakes. I think mistakes stand out more in your mind than successes
do. I don't think I say, "Wow! What did I do right
to answer that question last time?" I never say that.
But I always say, "Wow! I loused that up. I'm not
going to do that again." I guess you've got to take
a lot of risk to get somewhere. I'm comfortable with
that. But I think a lot of people are not. I noticed—
believe it or not—the women in our law school
classes never speak. I have about six women friends

and stuff, all ages. I'm always like, "When are you
going to say . . . ?" [or] "I haven't heard you talk
all semester." They're like, "I don't want to talk."
It's pretty weird.

Valerie also described group discussions as promoting independent thinking:

Case studies, group discussions, learning to interact with other people—I think that really helped
you make your own decisions instead of spitting out
acts that somebody has told you to memorize. You
really make your own decisions, and you think sub-
jectively and objectively about things, and you decide what you want to do and what you think about
that.

Many individual-pattern students also focused on a way
to think about knowledge as an approach to learning. Kurt
searched for words to describe this notion as he discussed two
classes that he took his fifth year. He began by saying that the
courses were based on application. Asked to elaborate, he said:

I guess when I say application I mean the fact that
it makes sense. [I don't] necessarily see it actually
occurring—but it goes much farther than just an
example of it. When you can apply it, you can take
it into yourself, and I think I actually believe what
they say. Not that I don't believe what my professors are telling me, but I can—wow, this is tough.
I believe what they say, and I can see it as being
true instead of just listening to what they're saying
and thinking that it might be true.

After a brief pause, he continued:

When they can present it in such a way that it can
take on that personal relevance (and I'm kind of

using all of those words *personally relevant* and *application* as synonymous)—when that is done, I gain a lot more value out of the class and out of the information I'm learning. Simply because it's more important to me. Once I see it applying or once I can see it as actually happening in society or actually happening wherever it might actually happen, then I'm aware of it. I'm kind of stressing words like *being aware* of it, being able to *apply* it, having it have *more value* to me. All of those things are due to the process that I think that I internalize when I'm learning. I guess I'm seeing the big picture of things, and I can fit things into the big picture.

What Kurt seemed to be suggesting was that learning took on meaning for him when it went beyond providing information to permitting him to think about it in a way that made sense.

Individual-pattern learners preferred instructors who allowed them to make sense of things in their own way or to define their own learning goals. Lowell's favorite senior class was one in which students met twice at the beginning of the semester and then worked in groups to produce a paper. Describing the instructor's role, he said:

Largely secondary. It was just kind of a guidance. And if we needed, if we were trying to find something, he'd have his experiences to draw on and say, "Well, you can look here, and they might be able to help you." Guidance and kind of setting deadlines. Just kind of pushing us. We learned how to push ourselves from that.

Lindsey had similar experiences his senior year:

Basically, you were in a group, and you were given a certain company and certain situation with all types of background information. And you had to go through and extract and separate, "Where does

accounting come into this? Where does the finance
come into this particular case?" It was never specifically stated to us, but we knew we needed to look
at accounting, finance, marketing, and economics.
We naturally just kind of went to what our own
interests were. That's the way it should be.

Candace found an opportunity to learn her own way during
student teaching, as is evident in her comparison of her two
cooperating teachers:

In the junior high, she didn't let me go as much
as I wish she would have. When I went to the high
school, he pretty much let me have and do what
I wanted. He was out of the classroom a lot. I felt
like I got a better experience there because it was
a lot more like what I was getting into.

Another class that Lindsey particularly liked also gave the students considerable influence:

He let us run the class. He let us answer questions;
he let us ask questions. He told us from day one,
"This class is going to be as boring or as fun as you
make it." I learned more in that one class than any
other class. In fact, I know I did. There were not
tests, just writing papers. Everything in this class
was learned through discussion and arguments. It
was amazing; I liked it a lot.

Lindsey's elaboration on the discussion aspect of this class
illustrates the individual-pattern perspective that peers are expected to think independently. He described their exchanges
in this way:

The instructor would say something and say, "What
do you think about that?" And one person would
raise his hand and say, "Well, I feel that maybe this,
this, and this, and it's not right." And as soon as

that opinion came into it, it was no longer a discussion. You'd see someone's hand shoot up and
go, "But wait a minute." They weren't ugly arguments; it was just, "Well, I don't think so because
what about this, this, and this?" And then the other
guy would say, "Yeah, but don't forget that they
do that, that, and that." That's where I did the bulk
of my learning—through these people's arguments,
I guess you'd call them. Yeah, you could call them
discussions, I guess.

Lindsey made it clear that these were not "ugly" arguments but
that he learned a great deal from peers' challenging each other's
ideas. Andrew enjoyed his senior-year group projects for the
same reason. He said:

People would remember things differently. And
you'd hash them out, kind of debate with each other
what exactly you should be doing on the thing. So
you formulated your own opinions and learned the
facts, and then you had to defend them. Somebody
in the group invariably ends up playing devil's advocate, whether they mean to or not. And it helps
you really think and remember what you did and
learn that you need to base it on something.

These students' thoughts on evaluation of their work also
centered around independent thinking. Max described what he
perceived to be effective evaluation in his literature classes:

Most professors, if you can support what you say
with evidence and show it—and you're trying to say
it's this and they say it's that—if you can support
what you say, then they'll generally give you a good
grade because they can't really tell you it's wrong.
But if you just say something and don't support it,
and it's not what they believe, then it's wrong. Or
maybe not wrong, but it's not supported, so it's not
so credible.

Asked to elaborate on what he meant by support, Max continued:

> If they say, "What does this mean in this poem?,"
> you say, "Well, it means such and such." And then
> you take examples from the poem showing that. If
> you can support it with evidence, then you'll gener-
> ally get a good grade, whether it agrees or disagrees
> with them.

Emphasis on independent thinking also characterized Amy's favorite evaluation techniques:

> You had to keep a journal. And it was anything
> you wanted to write about. You were supposed to
> try to relate it to your experience as you went
> through the class and your past experiences with
> death or things related to that. Then we had three
> tests where they gave you people from different writ-
> ings. You could choose three and make a discussion
> between them and yourself, showing their views.

Whereas Amy's comments focus on choosing what to write about, Sidney's stress responding to questions independently. Discussing his senior-year law class, he noted that he thought essays would have been better "to express yourself, giving opinions and how the court might rule," but he thought the multiple-choice format worked for this reason:

> Basically, a case would be given, and then he'd ask
> [for an] answer—all four would be right, but you'd
> have to pick the one that was the most correct. So
> there was room for argument on some of the ques-
> tions. We were able to change some of his answers
> just based on giving a good oral argument as to why
> you thought something was right.

As was the case with their interindividual-pattern counterparts, independent thinking made career decisions difficult for individual-pattern learners. They tended to delay a decision by doing something that encompassed many interests, or they just postponed the decision. Steve had majored in history but was always interested in music. The year after graduation, I found him managing a record store, and he had this to say about his plans:

> I considered going back to school for the music thing. But at the same time, I'm not sure I'm ready to jump back into school. Right now, I'm sending out résumés to record companies for positions as label representatives, promotional positions. Music school could be further down the road, or that would be an option if I went into the audio or production side of it. I was interested and thinking about going into environmental issues. I almost signed up for classes for that in January, but I decided to wait a little longer. It's probably a good market. But I'm kind of doing this music thing first because that's what I've really wanted to do. But if I could incorporate both of them. There is a movement to get rid of CD boxes and things like that that produce so much waste. I don't know about that.

Hugh also explored numerous options as he tried to decide what to do after graduation:

> I wasn't really sure what I wanted. I was a finance major. I wasn't sure if I wanted to get more into the analytical side or the sales side—i.e., being a stockbroker or insurance. So I interviewed for both. I decided on the bank situation because it combined a little of both. I looked at sales as something I could always do. And I looked at the bank situation as still building my base. So I was really looking to gain experience. I came to the realization that when I came out of college, I was nothing spectacular.

You go from being top at college — you know, you're
a senior — to being zero on the experience level. I
thought that the bank was the best place to learn
about the business world and maybe decide from
that point where I wanted to go. So in a sense I
kind of put my decision off for now.

These students remained individual in their approach to
knowing; they placed their views at the center of the learning
process. In one way, they became more individual than in previous ways of knowing because their own perspectives emerged
as separate from that of authority figures for the first time. In
another way, however, they became less individual than previously because they tried harder to listen to peers' views. Before,
the ideas of classmates were important only to the degree that
they served to challenge the learner and to foster mastery and
achievement. In independent knowing, these students showed
heightened interest in others' views; Lowell described the desire
"to *really* listen, not to just hear it and let it go through." Yet
individual-pattern knowers insisted on the equality of their own
views and made efforts to persuade others to take them into account. It is possible that demanding that one's view be treated
as equal takes on increased importance because others' views
are genuinely considered for the first time and because authority is no longer the ultimate arbiter.

Individual-pattern learners moved away from authority
figures as sources of their knowledge and also as leaders in the
process of learning. They preferred to be given freedom to define
their own learning goals, run their own classes, and pursue the
exchange of ideas freely. It seemed that they had become masters
in their own right and thus wanted little more from authorities
than the feedom to exercise their own authority.

Interindividual and Individual Patterns Compared

The equality of numerous views in the face of prevailing uncertainty made possible individually formed perspectives and independent thinking. Equality of viewpoints also changed the rela-

tionship of the knower to peers and to authority. For interindividual-pattern students, this change prompted greater connection to peers and to authority. Relationships with classmates
were important for interpersonal transitional learners, but interindividual-pattern knowers became more open to peers' views.
Exchanges became interindividual by virtue of these learners'
using their own voice. When the potential hazards to connection posed by criticism were removed by equality of views,
interindividual-pattern knowers connected more intensely with
their peers. The connection freed them to express their voices,
which appear to have existed internally before that point. The
adjustment to independent knowing came in finding their ideas
equal to those of peers and of authority. Interindividual-pattern
knowers reconnected to authority once their own voice was
legitimized. Thus, the interindividual pattern represents a union
of the individual's and the group's perspectives.

        For individual-pattern knowers, the equality of perspec-
tives had a different effect on relationships with peers and authority. The role of classmates was to create a relationship that
bordered on becoming a connection. Individual-pattern knowers
struggled to hear peers clearly; the adjustment to independent
knowing came in the form of including other voices as equal
to their own. In other words, their voices, expressed routinely
in previous ways of knowing, were slightly threatened by the
genuine consideration of other ideas. Their wish for and attempt
to find a balance appeared to mark the beginning of genuine
connection to others. At the same time, a sense of the equality
of views seemed to free individual-pattern knowers from authority to pursue their own independent thinking. This pattern therefore emphasizes both individually formed knowledge and the
ideas of others, with the scale tipped toward the former.

        The variation between interindividual and individual
knowing can also be cast in the language of *communion* and *agency*
(Bakan, 1966). Communion involves connection and relationship with others, whereas agency involves separateness. Both
patterns moved toward communion: interindividual-pattern
knowers became very open to classmates' views; individual-
pattern students moved toward real consideration of the opinions

of others. Students in both patterns also came closer to agency in generating knowledge, and individual-pattern knowers approached agency in their separation from authority in the learning process.

Movement toward communion or agency is best understood in light of the degree to which either was perceptible in earlier ways of knowing. Receiving- and interpersonal-pattern students earlier demonstrated communion, but agency represented a shift for them. Mastery- and impersonal-pattern knowers previously manifested agency, so that communion represented a change for them. Thus, although interindividual-pattern knowers still lean toward communion and individual-pattern knowers are still inclined toward agency, they are moving closer together than in previous ways of knowing.

Chapter Six

Contextual Knowing: Integrating One's Own and Others' Ideas

The analytical thinking that you learn in the classroom settings and the ability to think critically that came up from
discussions really prepare you for the real world.

— Gwen

Thinking for oneself was the hallmark of independent knowing. It remains the defining characteristic of contextual knowing, but there is a change from thinking totally independently
to thinking for oneself within the context of knowledge generated by others. Reginald described moving from total independence to thinking in context as a responsibility within a community:

> In terms of explaining self-responsibility, that you
> begin to use your own mind entirely. I always
> thought that I had an original idea and that I was
> never basing myself on what someone else had done
> before me. And I guess I was a bit pompous or
> wanting to think that I could be creative and origi-
> nal. Yes, I can be creative and original in my
> thoughts, but to base it on something is okay. So
> that's sort of like returning to the community in
> terms of your self-responsibility. I mean, you're not

168

alone. To look at it as you're not alone instead of being, "I'm being infringed on by these other people's ideas. And it's their ideas that are really showing their power instead of my ideas being creative and innovative." But no, I got to look at that from a different viewpoint of, "Okay, I can base something on what someone else has done and then my ideas" — then you're getting into self-responsibility if you can entirely put your ideas on the line innovatively and use those other ones to support, acknowledge, and work with yours. And it makes it much stronger. It's much more difficult, much more of a struggle. You really have to ask yourself, "What do I believe?"

What Reginald seemed to describe was a transition from the complete freedom of independent knowing to a way of knowing that entailed judgment about what to believe. As an independent knower, he used his mind and could choose to believe whatever he wished. As he approached contextual knowing, he had to consider the ideas of others and the relationship of his point of view to others'. The latter process, which he considered "much more difficult," required judgment within a context. It is what Gwen called analytical, or critical, thinking.

Deirdre described this same transition as she discussed a class she took her senior year. She said:

I took literary criticism, where we were introduced to all these new ways of looking at literature that no one ever talked about in high school. You know, it was always formal and always had to do with the things that were in the text. Nothing was taken out, nothing cultural or historical, no other perspective, no Marxism or communism or anything like that. Those tools were never yours to use. And once I had taken that class, then I got my feet wet about that, and I could buy into some of that. And then the more and more I thought about it and the more and more I read after,

I began to see that the idea—there was just too
much there for you to ignore, too much to the argument kind of thing. I don't know. Am I being
really vague?

Deirdre found it difficult to explain her point, possibly because
she had not entirely resolved it herself. Initially, her comments
seemed to reflect independent knowing. However, she was not
only seeing literature from a wider lens but also trying to use
the new tools to learn and think about literature. She went on
to say that this experience "made me reevaluate just about everything I had learned, right down to my choice of major. Everything kind of just got reworked." This reworking implied that
she was bordering on making judgments in the learning process.

Contextual knowers still viewed knowledge as uncertain
but no longer endorsed the "everything goes" approach. Judgments were possible based on evidence in a particular context.
The exchange of perspectives with others took on a new dimension in that ideas were compared in order to come to conclusions about them. Peers and instructors were expected to make
valuable contributions to the dialogue. The dialogue focused
on thinking through problems rather than just talking about
them, and on integrating knowledge to apply it in a context.
Experts, who could be instructors or supervisors, were expected
to participate in this evaluative dialogue and to help critique
views. Experts and learners were seen as working together to
learn and measure progress. The core assumptions held by contextual knowers are summarized in Table 6.1.

Contextual Knowing

Contextual knowers' assumptions are evident in six areas: the
varying value of ideas, expertise, learning, teaching, evaluation, and decision making. Each area will now be discussed,
to describe the contextual perspective.

Some Ideas Are More Valid Than Others

Contextual knowers believed that some views were more valid
than others, depending on the available evidence. Sean, preparing

Table 6.1. Epistemological Reflection Model.

Domains	Absolute Knowing	Transitional Knowing	Independent Knowing	Contextual Knowing
Role of learner	• Obtains knowledge from instructor	• Understands knowledge	• Thinks for self • Shares views with others • Creates own perspective	• Exchanges and compares perspectives • Thinks through problems • Integrates and applies knowledge
Role of peers	• Share materials • Explain what they have learned to each other	• Provide active exchanges	• Share views • Serve as a source of knowledge	• Enhance learning via quality contributions
Role of instructor	• Communicates knowledge appropriately • Ensures that students understand knowledge	• Uses methods aimed at understanding • Employs methods that help apply knowledge	• Promotes independent thinking • Promotes exchange of opinions	• Promotes application of knowledge in context • Promotes evaluative discussion of perspectives • Student and teacher critique each other
Evaluation	• Provides vehicle to show instructor what was learned	• Measures students' understanding of the material	• Rewards independent thinking	• Accurately measures competence • Student and teacher work toward goal and measure progress
Nature of knowledge	• Is certain or absolute	• Is partially certain and partially uncertain	• Is uncertain—everyone has own beliefs	• Is contextual; judge on basis of evidence in context

for medical school during his senior year, reported that his professors had changed their approach. In previous years, they had given him material to master, but during his senior year he perceived that they were asking him to figure out whether the material was legitimate. Asked how he decided on the legitimacy of material, Sean explained:

> I need to work through it for a while. I usually ap-
> proach it by reading through the material that we're
> talking about, or at least going over the sources
> several times and being able to get off where noth-
> ing else is going on — no radios are playing or what-
> ever. Just sit and run it over in your mind, think
> about different perspectives, intentionally bring up
> things that you know are wrong and just go with
> it to see where it's going to end up. And just try
> to analyze it through enough different viewpoints,
> if you can get them, to see if you feel in your own
> judgment that it's solid all the way around or if it's
> got some flaws. But it's much more sit back and
> reflect on it. You can work through it back and forth
> until you come up with some kind of conclusions,
> hopefully, satisfactory conclusions.

Sean used different viewpoints to analyze the material, relied on his own judgment to determine the soundness of an idea, and focused on coming to some conclusion. Jim expressed a similar approach in talking about expertise in his senior business classes. I asked how he recognized expertise, and he replied:

> I don't know if you can make a cut-and-dried state-
> ment on that. I think the biggest is supporting ar-
> guments. If somebody makes a statement and then
> goes on, I don't believe them. It's kind of like, "I'm
> from Missouri, the 'show me' state. Show me how
> I can believe this." They have to present an idea
> and then support it with some either facts or sto-
> ries or some legitimate ideas. You can go up there

and say, "Well, the world's round." "Well, that's great, but can you show me a picture from Mars, show me a globe or whatever, some models?" So I think that's really how you can justify the opinion. There's not a certain way to say, "Well, that's right" or "that's wrong." It's based on what you've learned, what you believe in, and what kind of supporting arguments they have.

Jim clearly articulated that deciding is not automatic or easy. In order for opinions to be taken as valid, they must be based on legitimate ideas and strongly supported. Jim combined what he had learned previously and what he believed in with supporting arguments to make a judgment.

Gwen, whose experiences were detailed in Chapter Two, spoke of the soundness of others' views. She clarified the difference she perceived between a response and a reaction, the former being sudden and spontaneous and the latter taking more facts into account and allowing them to jell. Her thinking process paralleled that of Sean and Jim:

> As you hear other people's opinions, you piece together what you really think. Who has the valid point? Whose point is not valid in your opinion? And come to some other new understanding. Even if it's the same basic belief, maybe be able to look at it from a more dimensional perspective.

She stated that deciding which points had merit was "super subjective" — weighing opinions and facts against what she already knew and the degree to which others could support their stance.

Considering evidence was essential in Lowell's mind during his first year in a graduate international studies program. He enjoyed debating a variety of perspectives and often found himself trying to decide what to think. He explained:

> Especially when people bring up facts that I didn't know. You're going to have a theoretical opinion,

and that, hopefully, is based on facts that you have learned. In the Soviet Union class, there're a lot of things now that I'm learning that I didn't know and that make what my answers would be different, just because I know something that I didn't know before. So I don't think my beliefs or my values have changed. But if you know something to be a fact and it's different from what you believed — if you don't change, if you're not pragmatic, then you're going to just sink. And if you close your eyes to the truth or what other people see as truth, then you're going to fail.

Thus, Lowell takes facts and what others see as truth into account.

Heather approached making judgments by evaluating their consistency. She felt strongly that she had to decide what she believed to avoid being hypocritical. Her process worked in this way:

I spent time getting a general feel for the topic as a whole before I made any generalizations. And then after that, I started piecing together general ideas that I believed in or general principles that I then tried to defend or follow through the rest of the semester. And if it seemed like I was going against that principle too often or disagreeing with it too often, then I would sit down and reevaluate. Like maybe I'd learned something new that changed my way of thinking. So then I'd have to sit down and reevaluate that and then possibly change my mind accordingly.

Heather judged new evidence against her guiding principles and made adjustments as she encountered new information. For all five students quoted here, knowledge hinged on reviewing and judging various claims to determine what was valid.

Contextual Expertise

What counted as evidence for contextual knowers came from experts. Experts were not automatically defined as instructors or supervisors but were individuals who had gained expertise in a particular context. Recall Mark's comment from Chapter Two about instructors' "supposedly" being experts; he remarked that having a Ph.D. did not automatically make a person an expert. Contextual knowers conferred expert status on classmates when they had valid knowledge. For example, Lowell relied on the expertise of his peers in a senior-project class in international studies. He commented:

> We gave each other quite a bit of criticism and praise and constructive criticism. That was helpful. People were studying different areas. Mine was Western Europe, and people studied others. And this paper was about Africa. So I had missed some subtle innuendos that someone who had studied Africa more picked up or knew. He could say, "Well, your suggestion is good, but here's why it probably won't work in this context." So teaching each other, really, about different stuff. I was an economics major, and this was on the debt crisis. So I had criticism for others that was more of an economics nature in the same vein.

Lowell's classmates who had studied other countries could enlighten him in those areas, and he could share his knowledge of economics. It is clear from Lowell's description that students made contributions about subjects they knew, as opposed to sharing opinions without justification.

Contextual knowers expected these contributions on the part of their peers because they felt that it enhanced learning for everyone. Reginald shared this perspective in a discussion about the degree to which his peers contributed in class. He reported that open exchange took place in some classes but not

in others. In the latter case, he felt frustrated that he was not
given access to peers' knowledge and believed that students who
were more concerned with grades than with sharing were not
being responsible. He expressed his hopes for classroom dialogue:

> I want them to be as excited about the knowledge
> and the dialogue and that you're going to be learn-
> ing from everybody. I'm giving them credit in terms
> of, "Look, I really respect what you think. And you
> have some knowledge that not only expands but is
> in addition to the instructor. And I expect you —
> well, I would really appreciate it if you would speak
> out and put that into the dialogue."

Deirdre also expected to learn from her classmates, as she did
in her graduate English classes. Her peers' knowledge came from
their experiences:

> It's a very different atmosphere being in class with
> someone who's forty-five and who has gone out and
> lived and worked and things like that — which makes
> it really interesting because they bring a new per-
> spective, something that I haven't really gotten a
> grasp on at all. But then again, I bring something
> that they can't because things that he's having us
> read and the more theoretical ideas that he intro-
> duces I'm very familiar with. And these people
> who've been out of school for so long aren't. Peo-
> ple are there because they really want to be, and
> they bring a lot of their own selves to the discussion.

Deirdre felt that she and her peers supplemented each other's
expertise in these classes. Her comments also make the connection between personal and intellectual life that she mentioned
in Chapter Five.

Learning Contextually

Contextual knowers incorporated the exchange and comparison
of views in their learning process, which was aimed at thinking

through knowledge claims and integrating information in order to apply it within a context. Mark offered an example of this learning process during his senior year:

> One independent study was this group idea of a reading group. The instructor didn't force himself into the picture but was always available if we wanted to come talk to him. Instead, we just got together and talked amongst ourselves. In that way, it wasn't divorced from your everyday intellectual life. And so, at the end of the course, you didn't feel as if, "Oh, I have to have this answer." It was more or less how does this knowledge plug in to what I've learned here? And then, looking back on it now from law school, I can pick up some of those strings and bring them into what I'm thinking now. Because I didn't necessarily come to any concrete conclusions or closure. So that was good, I thought.

Mark was working through ideas with his peers, relating their conversations to knowledge he had previously learned, and carrying ideas forward into the new context of law school. He stressed that he did make judgments, but they were flexible. He said: "I have definite opinions about things, but they're always amenable to new knowledge."

Thinking through ideas was also part of Lowell's learning process, which he distinguished from his earlier approach:

> I guess before, it was getting a lot of the facts down. And now, it's you truly try to analyze, try to really think. You can look at an issue from both sides, and it's still history, and you're still getting those facts and different people's opinions about things. And then that's kind of the basis. And now taking that and working with it to come up with some sort of conclusion, or maybe not a conclusion, and that's the conclusion in itself. Instead of regurgitating and saying, "Okay, I know this fact," saying, "All right, well, here's how this fact fits into the world."

Lowell works through facts and opinions, determines how facts fit into the larger picture, and comes to some sort of conclusion, which may not be a final answer.

Both Mark and Lowell illustrate an emphasis on integrating knowledge and incorporating new ideas as they come along. Tracy also focused on integration:

> I try to really read it and kind of digest it. Then, after I've read that and some of the related articles — so kind of, how do these all relate? Generally, we'll read either the original study or a discussion about the original study. Then we'll read a modification or two that were done on the study or something counter to the study. Then, in addition to that, I'll look at it in relationship to other articles that we've read in the past or other things that I've experienced in different classes. I'll try to bring my knowledge from all my other classes to this. It helps in the discussion. So when I read things, I kind of read them, think about them, in a broader view, almost in a holistic sense, rather than just "This is Marketing 451; this is what I'm reading."

Tracy tried to connect what she was reading for one class to her previous knowledge and experience to develop a comprehensive picture of the issue at hand. Knowledge from one course alone was insufficient and needed to be related to other strands of knowledge in order to be useful.

Contextual knowers also held the view that knowledge out of context was less useful than knowledge applied to a particular context. As Chuck explained, having a base of information is necessary but not sufficient. Talking about his first-year law school classes, he commented:

> You have to know it, and then you have to know how it pertains to a specific problem or a specific situation. It's so vague, just to know it. I mean, they use words like *reasonable*. Those mean nothing un-

til you apply it to a specific situation. Then you can
evaluate what those terms mean. There are not that
many correct answers because it remains to be seen
whether your client would win or lose. But there
are strong arguments, and then there are weak
ones.

Thus, knowing the law is essential, but knowing how the law
applies to a particular case is also necessary. Barry described
a similar situation in learning the sales business:

You really can't see how it applies or how it really
works until you get out there. You really don't see
the feedback that you get when you make a sale.
We'd make pretend sales calls. Well, it's all pretend;
you really don't know what the actual feedback is
going to be. Yeah, I know how to get over some
of the obstacles, or I've learned some different
methods. But I don't know which method's going
to work for me, and I don't know which method
is best for the industry. Those are the kinds of things
that only in application am I going to be able to
learn.

Barry suggested that sales methods are only useful for a particular salesperson and a particular industry. Although he has a
variety of methods at his disposal, he cannot judge their worth
until he applies them in a particular context.

Teaching Contextually

The core assumptions discussed thus far—thinking through
knowledge claims, evaluating each other's expert perspectives,
and validating knowledge in a context—form the foundation
for contextual learners' expectations of instructors or supervisors. Gwen appreciated the instructor of her national issues forum class because that person facilitated the evaluative discussion of issues. She remarked:

At the time, it was just really quite something, with
all the changes in Eastern Europe, all about the issues here really coming to a head. For instance,
AIDS and recycling and drugs and education and
all these different day-to-day issues that were in the
newspapers. And to discuss those with people who
really seemed to have an interest and knowledge
of them, I found really exciting. Classmates who
watched the news, read papers. These were things
that interested me, and they kept up with them.

Gwen stressed that the discussion was stimulating because other
students were knowledgeable. She also appreciated that her supervisor in her job after graduation accepted her evaluative comments about the company training program. Although Gwen's
peers in that setting did not choose to engage in that discussion, the supervisor did. This was Gwen's response:

You set your own limitations and live within them.
And if you set your boundaries wide and vast, you
have so much room to grow. That is my new philosophy: that I will continue to think critically and
challenge that around me, because so far, it's working wonderfully.

Gwen perceived that she was learning and growing more as a
result of this approach.
Evaluative discussion involved a combination of considering and questioning other ideas, as Deirdre explained while
describing a teacher she felt was ineffective:

We were supposed to kind of assess the character
of Achilles, and he's a very stereotypical, very traditional, masculine figure — very, very violent and
very aggressive. [The instructor] made some comment about how Homer feels about Achilles. Is he
a hero, or is he someone that is just very violent
and kind of like a sociopath? I was writing that — I

used some kind of phrase, I think it was the "masculine ego" in the journal I did, talking about the men and women and their roles and everything. I was saying it's based on an exchange of women in a way and trying to really grapple with how Homer thought about Achilles. Because I think that he was sensitive to it, and I think that it was a very antiwar piece. Or it could be read the opposite way. And I was trying to work out how I felt about it. He had underlined everything, and he just made some comment almost teasing me, like, "Oh, are you some feminist?," or something like that. I didn't write anything anymore after that. I thought he was narrow-minded. I thought there was really no point. I don't risk anything in class because he challenges everything I say. I think there are certain ideas and ways of viewing the world that are very much valid and need to be talked about. And the fact that he just seemed so closed off to that, and his whole stance, his whole pedagogy—he's always very defensive about it.

Deirdre's complaint was twofold. First, the instructor did not listen to her perspective prior to challenging it. Second, his response to her journal and his position in class led her to conclude that he was unwilling to include her ideas in the dialogue. Her attempt to decide how she felt about Homer's thoughts on Achilles was impeded by the instructor's failure to genuinely consider her thoughts.

Contextual learners also appreciated opportunities to apply knowledge in a particular situation. Barry had an opportunity to apply what he knew in a senior course that entailed a major group project. The group was charged with developing a new marketing plan for a company. The instructor had arranged for the students to work with actual companies, matched to the students' career interests. Barry said that the instructor offered guidance about how to organize their work and how to collect data and put the research together. Then the students contacted actual clients of the company to solicit their needs and preferences, analyzed the data, and formulated recommendations to present to the company. Barry described the most valuable aspect of the project:

> Where you're actually out there, seeing the results coming back. And, again, it wasn't someone else doing the work, and then you just have a case study on it: "Okay, here's this, this, this. Now what do you recommend?" Well, we had to find out what this, this, and this is. And then we had to make a recommendation. And that was basically the true learning process.

Barry's distinction between the case study in which he was given the information and having to generate the information in this project involves applying knowledge in a particular context. His comment also clarifies the difference between the hands-on experience that transitional learners prefer and the contextual students' desire to apply knowledge in context. The case study would have been perceived by transitional knowers as practical application of the ideas they had learned. For contextual learners like Barry, specific results from a particular company were necessary to determine what recommendations were valid in that context.

Jim told a similar story about applying managerial skills. He talked with one of his instructors about gaining experience, and the instructor suggested that Jim assume a group-leader role in his business class. Jim was in charge of fifteen people working on a project for a company. According to Jim, it was one of the best experiences he had in college. He explained why:

> It was really interesting because you had to deal with a lot of different personalities, and you assigned people to groups based on their preferences. Then there were conflicts within those groups, and you had to deal with that. It forced me to reprimand people in certain situations, when they weren't pull-

ing their weight. It helped me get better prepared
for — you know, I already had to do an evaluation
for my secretary. I had done a little bit of it and
understood the whole idea.

Jim's experience in trying out these managerial skills in a real
situation helped him make judgments about how to apply them
in new contexts after graduation. Instructors or supervisors who
offered access to these opportunities were seen as contributing
substantially to the contextual knower's learning.

Evaluating Contextual Learning

Contextual learners also appreciated guidance in measuring the
progress of their classroom or job performance. They perceived
evaluation more broadly than in previous ways of knowing. For
contextual knowers, evaluation meant working together toward
a goal and determining progress together. Reginald came to this
perspective as a result of reflecting on his senior honors thesis.
He described the process in this way:

> You have an adviser. And the adviser would, you
> know, check up on how you're doing and give you
> some really good critical analysis, but, basically,
> "This is up to you. You do it." Even though it's a
> self-responsibility, you've got that adviser, or you've
> got that circle of people to critique and support you.
> I was impressed with my paper, but there was still
> room for critique. Discussions with the honors ad-
> viser and the thesis seminar group helped me un-
> derstand how self-responsibility really worked.

Reginald described taking responsibility for his project and his
thoughts, yet simultaneously soliciting criticism and direction.
He considered the reactions of fellow students, the honors adviser, and the thesis adviser in conjunction with his own assessment before being satisfied with his final result.

Adrian discussed working with others toward a goal as

one of the highlights of her job at an advertising agency. Talking about her work, she stated:

> I love it. There's always someone willing to help you out, willing to take the time that it would take to teach you something new. That's been a fantastic help. Informal feedback is almost constant. Problems can't go unresolved. But also, if you're doing things right, since it is a small agency, it's definitely rewarded on a very regular basis. And since everyone essentially knows what everyone else is doing, the vice president knows what you've done. People are promoted very quickly based on your skill, your area of interest, and how far you want to go.

Adrian got help from colleagues to do her work well, got feedback to resolve problems, and got rewarded when she did well. This environment enabled her to perform effectively and make progress.

Just as contextual knowers evaluated knowledge claims in a particular situation, they thought judgment of their performance should be related to context. Lindsey offered this perspective:

> An English class is designed not to test you on the basis of giving you a final exam. It's to test your writing abilities, whether that be through the course of the year or just all at once at the end. My management class, which was a group project, should have been graded on how well you worked within a group and how well you contributed and how you finally came up with a solution. The tests for that class weren't exactly very representative, I didn't think, of what the class itself was trying to teach you. The final didn't match with what the whole course was trying to emphasize.

Lindsey referred to a variety of methods for evaluating learning, including writing, tests, and judgments about participation. He assessed the effectiveness of these methods on the basis of what the course was trying to teach, so that some methods were better in some contexts than others. Jim experienced an evaluation system that was compatible with the group-management experience that he described earlier in this chapter:

> My fifteen people evaluated me; at the same time, the instructor evaluated me based on our final project, what we actually handed in, the quality of it and the content of it, the satisfaction of my members, did they learn anything. Then also just my interaction with the instructor—how many times I came in to see him and what I showed to him, my general process, did I have an agenda for my people to follow.

As the sources of Jim's evaluation were directly related to his role, he felt that they accurately measured his performance.

Decision Making in Context

Contextual knowers' emphasis on validating knowledge within a context carried over into decision making. Recognizing that numerous options were available in an uncertain world, these students weighed the information relevant to their decisions, calculated risks, balanced these against established priorities, and specified criteria upon which they based their decisions. Adrian illustrated this approach as she discussed her next career move. Having graduated a semester early, she had been in her first job for a year when we held her fifth-year interview. Despite her love for her job and the agency, she was planning to move to New York City the following summer. Her fiancé was studying to be a chef and wanted to go to New York to gain experience. She described her thoughts:

> He would like to work in New York City for a couple of years to get the experience under his belt. And we have an opportunity for a reasonably priced apartment through one of his classmates. My agency

is owned by a big agency in New York. And hopefully, I'll be able to transfer there. I don't ever want
to have children in New York City. So logically,
now is the time to go, if we're going to go. It's been
hard for me because my family's here and my mom
has multiple sclerosis. It will be hard not seeing her
every day to know exactly what's going on. We're
going with the idea that it's only for two years, maximum.

There were clearly drawbacks to moving to New York for Adrian.
However, her future husband's career was an important priority, and she judged the risks to be reasonable at that point
in her life. Other priorities for the future led her to conclude
that it was an appropriate time for such a change.

Deirdre spent more of her decision-making energies on
establishing her priorities. She described how she determined
what to pursue after graduation:

You think about it all through your senior year,
but you don't really think about it too hard because
it's so frightening. Because I really had no idea what
I was going to do when I graduated. I mean, counseling was an option, and I like talking with people individually about different things. But, like I
said, something didn't sit with me well about that.
I don't know. My understanding of things was kind
of coming from a different perspective now, and
it just didn't seem like a real option. The comparative literature class made me reevaluate my choice
of psychology. There was something about it, where
the emphasis was placed, that didn't strike me as
real anymore. I felt strongly about teaching now
the things I know. That's why I chose the graduate
program in English with certification in education.

Although Deirdre struggled with what direction to pursue, she
was able to establish the priority of teaching others what she
knew. This then enabled her to make a choice.

Jim had experiences during college that helped him establish priorities prior to graduation. He had already decided on a direction at the beginning of his senior year, based on work with a credit union and summer internships:

> My mom raised me always to be a giving person, caring, loving, that type of thing. And a lot of the philosophies and ideals that credit unions are formed on are based on people helping people. The idea of people who don't have the privilege of the big bank can pool their money together and then loan it out to provide a better service. And I want to be in business; I like the idea of managing people and objects. My major is finance, so I want to deal with money. And this is a way to handle all of the things I want to do and at the same time help people.

Jim's values and his interests provided criteria for his career direction. A year later, he shared how he had chosen his particular job:

> I knew I wanted to go into credit unions through my experiences with them. And then it was merely what area of credit unions do I want to get involved in? About half of it was based on what I had done the summer before. My exposure to the trade association was fun. It was a chance to get involved in a lot of different credit unions. Then, for my own self, I wanted—my goal right now is to be president of a trade association for credit unions. I sat down and did a little analysis of where did the current presidents come from. And a lot of them started out in a consulting role that I'm in right now or as examiners. I'm not an accounting geek; I don't want to be an examiner; I don't want to be the bad guy.

For Jim, Deirdre, and Adrian—and other contextual knowers— decisions were made on the basis of criteria within a particular context.

Summary

The key element of contextual knowing is an individually created perspective constructed through judging evidence in a context. Independent knowing is transformed from being completely independent of existing knowledge and context to being dependent on both. Reginald's term *self-responsibility* within community captures the essence of this idea. The increasing complexity of contextual knowing stems from the necessity of analyzing and assessing existing knowledge, weighing the particularities of the context, and developing one's point of view within these constraints. The awareness that some judgments are better than others increases the pressure to construct views carefully.

Because evaluating existing knowledge is essential to make valid judgments, the ideas of others are considered more carefully than they were in previous ways of knowing. The credible opinions of others must be integrated into one's own view, whereas previously they could coexist independently. Tracy's example of integrating readings from other classes illustrates this point. Contextual knowers focus on the opinions of experts or persons that they believe have gained appropriate experience in a particular area of knowledge. These persons can be authority figures, though these are not automatically experts. Experts can also be peers, because anyone who has developed expertise on a subject has an important perspective to share. Contextual knowers judge the soundness of ideas or knowledge claims on the basis of the expertise of their advocate and that person's supporting evidence.

Similarly, contextual knowers substantiate the views that they espouse by using the supporting arguments that led them to construct those opinions. They situate their perspectives in particular contexts and do not transfer ideas to new situations without reevaluating their validity. In some cases, such as Chuck's learning law and Barry's learning the sales business, a good approach cannot be determined until one is able to apply knowledge within the context. Contextual knowers defend their perspectives but are simultaneously open to new insights and new contextual constraints. As Mark put it, "I have definite opinions about things, but they're always amenable to new knowledge." Thus, knowledge evolves, continually reconstructed on the basis of new evidence and new contexts. Certainty returns to a degree but never in the absolute sense. The voice of authority, largely ignored in independent knowing, returns, but only in conjunction with the contextual knower's ability to judge its validity. The voice of self becomes stronger, based now on views that can be supported or justified.

Contextual knowing was not common during college for this group (as noted earlier, found in only 2 percent of the senior interviews and 12 percent of the fifth-year interviews). However, many of the examples from the fifth-year interviews were reflections upon the senior year. It is possible that contextual knowing developed for some students during that period but after their senior-year interview had taken place. Other examples of contextual knowing were in the context of graduate programs or work environments.

Given such small numbers, it was not feasible to identify gender-related patterns. Because contextual knowers integrated thinking for themselves with genuine consideration of others' views, it is possible that the gender-related patterns of earlier ways of knowing converged in contextual knowing. For example, receiving-, interpersonal-, and interindividual-pattern knowers' focus on connection to others is a central feature of contextual knowing when integrating other valid views. Mastery-, impersonal-, and individual-pattern students' individual approach is also a basic feature of contextual knowing, because students are ultimately responsible for their own judgments and constructed perspectives. The stories told here do not reveal whether variations in balancing this integration exist.

Chapter Seven

Relating the Patterns
to Diverse
Student Populations

> Do I sound pretty typical so far? I mean, do most people
> feel most of the same things that I've learned and ex-
> perienced?
>
> —*Hugh*

Hugh wondered if he was typical of the students in the study.
Readers are probably wondering if these students are similar
to those at other institutions. The ways of knowing and patterns I have named after hearing these stories are based on students of traditional age and mostly white, middle-class families;
they experienced college in a student culture characterized by
high involvement, academic focus, and tradition. I argued in
Chapter One that students' ways of knowing and the patterns
within them are socially constructed. Because their social construction stems from the interaction of unique characteristics
and the particulars of experience in a context, the ways of knowing and patterns within them described here cannot be automatically transferred to young adults everywhere. Many college students and settings differ considerably from these students
and the Miami setting. These facts undoubtedly prompt questions about the degree to which the perspectives generated by
this particular set of students can be applied more generally.

The transfer of insights from one set of students to another
requires caution. Constructivist researchers suggest that the

190

study of a set of particulars, such as the students' experiences recounted here, do not result in absolute truths. Rather, they create working hypotheses. The degree to which these can be applied to contexts beyond those in which they were developed depends on the similarity between the two contexts. Transferability is possible only when the researcher describes the context that produced the working hypotheses sufficiently for readers to judge its similarity to the contexts in which they wish to use the information (Lincoln and Guba, 1985). It is for this reason that Chapter One and the resources contain a detailed description of Miami as an institution, its student culture, and the characteristics of its students. The task for readers in similar contexts is to identify subtle differences in the mutually transforming interactions between students and their experiences that might alter the social constructions that result. Transferring the insights from the last five chapters to students with different characteristics in different contexts requires taking a step back from ways of knowing and patterns within them to underlying story lines.

By underlying story lines, I mean the threads that run through the collective student stories that are more general than the specific ways of knowing or patterns within them. The development and emergence of voice, the changing relationship with authority, and the evolving relationships with peers are three underlying story lines that form the foundation of parallels between the participants and other young adults. The development and emergence of voice story line show the transition from repeating what others say to developing one's own perspective. The story line about changing relationship with authority illustrates students' initial reliance on authority, their movement away from it, and their development of their own. The story line about relationships with classmates demonstrates peers' increasing value as knowers in their own right, as students rely less on authority figures for what to believe. The three story lines are summarized in the first portion of this chapter.

The remainder of the chapter explores two broad contexts in which these parallels might occur. The first context, which I call dominance-subordination, yields possibilities for how one party's dominance over another's affects voice and relationships. Parallels between the three story lines and this overall context are seen in three dominant-subordinate relationships: educator and student, objectivist and social constructivist perspectives, and majority and minority parties. Educators' dominance over students influences their view of authority figures, the nature of knowledge, and the value of students' own perspectives. The traditional dominance of objectivist perspectives in higher education encourages reliance on authority for knowledge, thereby hindering development of student voice. It also influences the type of relationships that educators have with students. Finally, majority dominance over minority parties affects the degree to which minority parties feel validated as knowers. Students who are subordinated are less likely to value their own abilities and express their voices freely. The second broad context, socialization, raises possibilities about how upbringing affects voice and relationships. Gender-related socialization can influence suppressing one's voice, as in the case of traditional female socialization, or expressing one's voice, as in the case of traditional male socialization. The socialization of African-American young people has the potential to affect relationships with authority, connections with peers, and, ultimately, the development of voice.

Though parallels between the story lines and the contexts just noted are intended to show the degree to which the understanding of particular students may apply to others, a caution is in order. True transferability can only be judged through dialogue with students. This dialogue offers the opportunity for students to explain their experience and to help the educator make sense of it in that particular context. I will return to a fuller discussion of dialogue at the end of the chapter to illustrate the role that it can play in transferring the ideas of this chapter to diverse students in varied settings. The four ways of knowing, reasoning patterns within them, and the three underlying story lines are summarized in Figure 7.1.

Voice and Relation with Others: The Underlying Story Lines

Despite considerable overlap among the story lines — student voice, relationships with authority, and relationships with peers — I have separated them here to clarify each one.

Figure 7.1. Overview of Ways of Knowing, Reasoning Patterns, and Underlying Story Lines.

Ways of knowing	Absolute	Transitional	Independent	Contextual
Reasoning patterns	*Receiving or mastery*	*Interpersonal or impersonal*	*Interindividual or individual*	*None identified*
	Echos authority	→ → Emergence of voice → →	→	Creates own perspective
Underlying story lines	Views authority as all-knowing	→ → Relationship with authority → →	→	Becomes expert in a given context
	Helps others understand authority's knowledge	→ → Relationships with peers → →	→	Becomes expert in a given context

Student Voice

Tracing student voice from absolute to contextual knowing shows
a dramatic change in this story line. There is no student voice
per se in absolute knowing because students assume that absolute knowledge exists and is the property of authority figures.
Because students can only obtain and repeat knowledge to
demonstrate their learning, the only voice that they express is
an echo of authority. The expression of the echo differs depending on reasoning patterns. Receiving-pattern knowers speak with
an echo voice at the request of authority figures and usually
refrain from employing it otherwise. Mastery-pattern learners
express the echo voice routinely, hoping thereby to improve the
quality of the echo and to show authority figures their interest
in perfecting it. Receiving-pattern students focus on repeating
authority's voice, whereas mastery-pattern learners stress both
imitating and repeating it. Toni and Tim, quoted at the beginning of Chapter Three, illustrate these approaches. There is a
hint of a separate voice in the comments of receiving-pattern
knowers — like the one Bev offered in Chapter Three. She suggested a distinction between "raw facts" and "how you feel about
at issue." Yet this separate voice was not expressed.

Transformation of the student voice begins to occur in
transitional knowing. The emergence of a student voice that is
separate from that of authority takes different forms depending
on reasoning patterns. The most dramatic shift occurs for interpersonal-pattern knowers. They seem to create two bodies of
knowledge: one that belongs to authority and one that is their
own. The body of knowledge belonging to authority is certain
and is mentioned only in passing. That belonging to students
is uncertain and is the focus of interpersonal knowers' attention. For example, Marla (whom we met in Chapter Four)
described the value of learning from her peers as inspiring different thoughts for her. She also commented in passing that these
ideas did not necessarily help her learn about the material in
the book. The voice of interpersonal-pattern knowers takes the
form of personal judgments about both bodies of knowledge.
However, that voice is usually expressed among peers rather

than to authority. By contrast, impersonal-pattern knowers continue to speak up to authority, perhaps because their voice is altered less than that of interpersonal-pattern knowers. Impersonal-pattern students still echo authority to some extent, while shifting from imitating the answers to imitating the process. Thus, their voice is still consistent with that of authority despite attempts to form their own opinion.

A genuinely distinctive individual perspective appears for the first time in independent knowing. Although interpersonal-pattern knowers formed a distinctive voice in some contexts in transitional knowing, they often did not speak with it. In independent knowing, both interindividual- and individual-pattern students created their own perspectives and expressed them freely. It is important to note that the voice of independent knowers is completely unrestrained and takes a "everyone's voice is valid" stance. Interindividual-pattern knowers work hard at this juncture to include their own voices as equal to those of peers and authority. They maintain an intense openness to others' opinions, as illustrated by Sheila's comments in Chapter Five. She said, "I'm so affected by everything everyone has to say to me: I'm so open to that that it's good." She also noted that she did not want to change anybody else. She fully acknowledged the ability to modify her own views as she chose but refrained from trying to get others to alter theirs. Individual-pattern knowers, on the other hand, struggle to include other voices as equal to theirs. Recall Lowell's comments from Chapter Five on his classmates' ideas: "To try to listen to theirs, to *really* listen, not to just hear it and let it go through." Lowell described himself and his classmates trying to hear each other out, not to change each other's minds, but to make sure that others took their ideas into account.

Contextual knowers maintain their own voices but place them in the larger context of existing knowledge and the particulars of a situation. Their voices are no longer completely independent. Those of others, which were of such great interest in independent knowing, are now carefully analyzed to judge their validity. Contextual knowers are more willing to change their minds and to try to influence others now that they view some knowledge claims as more valid than others, depending on the available evidence and the context in which it is applied. Contextual knowers demonstrate their ability to create and adjust their own ideas constantly, as they judge the validity of knowledge claims they encounter.

Thus, student voice moves from an echo of authority to the development of one's own voice in the context of existing knowledge. Although the process differs for students exhibiting different reasoning patterns, the transformation of voice is similar. As the story line and its variations unfold, transformations in relationships with authority and peers also take place.

Relationship with Authority

This story line seems to unfold in the opposite way to the preceding one. As the student voice gains strength in the shift from absolute to contextual knowing, the relationship with authority gradually loses strength only to return in a new form in contextual knowing. Absolute knowers view authority as holders of the truth; they depend on authority to provide information to them. Although both receiving- and mastery-pattern absolute learners exhibit this dependence, receiving-pattern students identify less with authority. They express interest in interacting with authorities only when clarification is needed or problems arise. Believing that it furthers their acquisition of knowledge, mastery-pattern knowers prefer regular interaction with authority. They believe that imitating the voice of authority will help develop their knowledge and that they will benefit from recognition by instructors. Rich, whom we met in Chapter Three, explained this perspective in his comments about sitting in the front of the class, participating to show the teacher that he was eager to learn, and volunteering to work at the board or read something in the class. Mastery-pattern students like Rich take on an apprentice role that is characterized by a strong attachment to authority.

The recognition of some uncertain knowledge that comes with transitional knowing makes relating to authorities as the holders of truth difficult. According to their reasoning pattern, students within transitional knowing make the adjustment differently. Interpersonal-pattern knowers detach themselves from authority to pursue their own ideas about the uncertain areas. They do appreciate a rapport with authority that allows students to share their experiences and takes these into account in evaluation. They do not rely on authority in the uncertain areas for guidance to the truth. For example, Kris commented in Chapter Four that she and her friends whispered opinions to each other in class about whether what the professor said was valid. She appreciated the instructor's willingness to listen when she and her friends challenged the material and explained their perceptions.

In contrast, impersonal-pattern transitional learners exhibited an attachment to authority driven by an interest in mastering the process of learning in a partially uncertain world. As Sean (Chapter Four) described learning, he expressed his belief that there was "some body of truth." Beyond that, he and other individual-pattern knowers focused on how to sort out conflicting information and often approached authorities for help in that process. Thus, on the one hand, authority figures play a facilitating role for interpersonal-pattern knowers; they help them to gain access to their own and others' experiences. On the other hand, authorities play a guiding role for individual-pattern knowers and help them to work toward mastery of the process. The place of authorities takes priority over that of peers for impersonal-pattern students, as it does with mastery-pattern learners in absolute knowing.

The expression of the individually developed voice in independent knowing results in these learners' becoming their own authorities. Yet for those who have been detached from authority — namely, absolute knowers using the receiving pattern and transitional knowers using the interpersonal pattern — the distinctive, individually formed voice facilitates reconnection with authority. Independent learners using the interindividual pattern now view their voice as equal to that of authority but desire to engage in dialogue. Thus, they include instructors in their quest to hear others' opinions, despite the perception that authorities are no more influential than peers. In Chapter Five,

Rosa and Stephanie make clear their own authority in an arena previously reserved for teachers. They both describe their role in evaluation of their work, student teaching for Rosa and a marketing experience for Stephanie, as equal to that of authority.

For students who were attached to authority earlier — absolute knowers using the mastery pattern and transitional knowers using the impersonal pattern — the voice the student has created leads to detachment. The achievement of equality frees independent learners using the individual pattern to pursue their own ideas. Individual-pattern students want to be left to do things their own way. For example, Lowell described his instructor's role as "largely secondary," and Lindsey's favorite class was one in which the instructor "let us run the class" (Chapter Five). The interindividual-pattern's focus on dialogue therefore leaves more room for the inclusion of authorities than does the individual-pattern's drive to establish an individual authoritative voice.

Contextual knowing requires listening more carefully than before to other opinions because one's own authority now depends on the support and justification of one's views. Other perspectives can no longer be accepted or ignored at will but must be analyzed to determine their validity in a given situation. Authority's voice is no exception. Authority is no longer automatically granted to authority figures; it is conferred only on those who have demonstrated expertise in a context. In the attempt to judge the validity of knowledge claims, the contextual knower relies on those with expertise, but not in the unquestioning manner of absolute knowing. The contextual knower consults the expert but simultaneously assesses the soundness of that opinion in light of other evidence. Thus, authorities, whether formal educators or peers, become partners in the process of sorting through knowledge claims to determine which ones are best within a specific context. Those who are granted expert status are more influential than authorities were in independent knowing, but they are not the final determinant. Contextual knowers remain their own authorities.

Relationships with Peers

This third story line is woven around and through the other two. Peers' role in knowing increases in importance during the progression from absolute to contextual knowledge. However, it maintains a higher priority throughout for receiving-, interpersonal-, and interindividual-pattern students than for mastery-, impersonal-, and individual-pattern ones. Relationships with peers, as they relate to knowing, take precedence over relationships with authority for absolute students using the receiving pattern and for transitional students using the interpersonal pattern. Balance is achieved as these knowers become independent and contextual. For mastery-pattern absolute knowers and impersonal-pattern transitional knowers, peers play a role secondary to authority. For individual-pattern independent students, classmates play a role secondary to the particular learner.

Absolute knowers view peers as collaborators in obtaining the truth. For receiving-pattern students, this perspective translates into supportive behaviors, such as sharing notes and creating a relaxed atmosphere for learning. This conceptualization of relationship emphasizes connections among peers to make learning possible. As Gale noted in Chapter Three, "It's good to have a small class because it's more intimate. You feel closer to the class and to the people in it. So you get to know the personalities — it's easier to ask questions." For mastery-pattern students, collaboration means debating and quizzing each other, in class or during studying, in an effort to test each other's knowledge. This conceptualization of relationship emphasizes autonomy among peers, as each person takes a turn at demonstrating his or her knowledge. Rob's comments in Chapter Three about peers illustrate the autonomy theme: "They help you in areas you are weak in and vice versa. Having a person drill me over things I am to know lets me know how well I have really learned it." Neither of these conceptualizations assigns legitimate knowledge to peers, but both view them as a means of obtaining the knowledge offered by authority.

In transitional knowing, relationships with peers are heightened for interpersonal-pattern knowers and maintained for impersonal-pattern knowers. For interpersonal-pattern students, peers become legitimate sources of knowledge by sharing their personal experiences. Thus, the interaction changes from exchanging notes obtained from authority to exchanging personal experiences. The intensity of these interactions increases as interpersonal-pattern knowers focus on gaining access to their own and others' experiences. They do not, however, try to reconcile differences in these experiences; the emphasis is on collecting, not challenging, each other's ideas. Adrian offered this perspective in Chapter Four when she said, "There are so many people here from all over; they've done all sorts of things. I think that's one of the most important things about going to college — meeting people from other places and hearing other things." For impersonal-pattern students, peers are not yet seen as legitimate sources of knowledge in their own right. Because the focus is on learning how to learn, impersonal-pattern students still rely on authority more heavily than on peers. However, the uncertainty of knowledge does increase the level of interaction with peers; discussion is viewed as important to understanding the process of learning. In describing discussion, Kurt said, "You get to learn more — the knowledge that you're talking about, certain theories or whatever — you get to learn more about them because you're defending them." Thus, the connection and autonomy themes in peer relationships remain in transitional knowing.

Regardless of their reasoning pattern, independent knowers believe that peers have legitimate knowledge, a belief that led to heightened peer relationships. The connection and autonomy themes take an interesting turn here. Interindividual-pattern students strengthen connections as they increase the intensity of dialogue with peers, yet increase autonomy as they struggle to include their own voices as equal to others'. Alexis's comments in Chapter Five show the tension between listening to others and deciding on one's own views. She vacillates between "listening to both sides," throwing some of her own views in, and going "with what you believe." Ironically, the autonomy that permits the expression of one's own views comes in part from a decrease in connection, described by some as no longer caring what peers would think of them. Thus, though the exchange of views creates greater connection, the lack of regard for others' reactions engenders less connection. The conceptualization of connection represents a shift from being defined by others to being able to join others. This shift is similar to what Kegan (1982) describes as an evolution from an interpersonal self-definition, in which one is defined by relationships with others, to an institutional self-definition, in which one has an identity beyond relationships with others.

Individual-pattern students strengthen their autonomy through expressing their own perspectives, but increase their connection by trying to hear others' views. Reginald described his attempt to listen to other points of view in his seminary classes but simultaneously held out hope that his classmates would see women's issues his way. The opinions of peers are important to individual knowers but remain secondary to their own.

Contextual knowers continued to value relationships with peers, although they analyzed peers' views more carefully than did independent knowers. When classmates were judged to be experts, their input was considered worthwhile. Lowell described learning from his classmates who had studied other countries and teaching them about economics, a topic in which he had expertise. Similarly, Deirdre learned from older students in her class about working and living outside of college, whereas she could offer them insights about theoretical ideas introduced in class. Interactions with peers in college classrooms and in work settings were prevalent in contextual students' descriptions of how they came to know. Because knowledge is constantly being constructed at this point, continued discussion and interchange of ideas with peers remain important to the ever-present task of deciding what to believe.

Contexts Characterized by Dominance and Subordination

As the summary of story lines demonstrates, it took a long time for students to claim to speak with their own voices. Most of those who told stories about expressing their own voice did so as they reflected on their senior year. (This situation is not unique to this study. For example, see Belenky, Clinchy, Goldberger, and Tarule, 1986; Kitchener and King, 1990; and King, Wood, and Mines, 1990). What types of environments produce this dependence on authority for so long? What types of contexts make it so difficult for students to claim their voices? One plausible answer could be environments characterized by dominant and subordinate relationships—between educator and student, objectivist and social constructivist perspectives, and majority and minority parties (the first in each pair playing the dominant role).

The Educator-Student Relationship

More often than not, educators play dominant roles because of the belief that they possess some body of knowledge and are responsible for bestowing it upon students. For faculty, this body of knowledge refers to their particular disciplines and the skills related to them. For student development educators, it refers to values, interpersonal skills, and leadership skills, to name a few. Often, educators in both realms begin their relationships with students with the assumption that students need to acquire some basic information before they can be included in the teaching process. Freire's concept of "banking education" captures this approach: "The banking concept distinguishes two stages in the action of the educator. During the first, he cognizes a cognizable object while he prepares his lessons in his study or his laboratory; during the second, he expounds to his students about that object. The students are not called upon to know, but to memorize the contents narrated by the teacher. Nor do the students practice any act of cognition, since the object towards which that act should be directed is the property of the teacher" (1988, pp. 67–68). Students are subordinated because what they think is not part of the process. They are automatically cast in the role of receivers, rather than constructors, of knowledge. Justin, a senior, described this context as he talked about his chemistry classes:

> Chemistry is just, "This mixes with this, and you
> get that." There're no questions about it. You know
> if the equation isn't balanced—well, it's wrong. You
> can't question it. It's just the laws of nature. The
> same goes for math and physics and stuff like that.

This conclusion appears to agree with the student quoted by Belenky, Clinchy, Goldberger, and Tarule who said "Science is not a creation of the human mind" (1986, p. 216).

The banking process occurs in student affairs settings as well. Although students are not often given information to memorize, they are expected to adhere to a set of rules. Despite student affairs professionals' awareness that behavior and development are a function of the interaction of persons and their environments (a version of the social constructivist view), environments are sometimes structured to apply identically to all inhabitants. For example, Rich complained that the visitation policy and other rules were the same for first-year and upperclass students. He remarked:

> It's just the principle of saying to twenty-year-olds and nineteen-year-olds, "You can't do this." I don't know where that comes from. Maybe it's my non-conservative approach being from the East, but I can't go down with that.

After suggesting a number of changes, he added, "All these, of course, I have no way of accomplishing, except for getting my voice heard." Rich implied with this last statement that he had to work to be listened to. His central complaint was being subordinated. Collective comments along these lines implied that it was not any specific outcome or rule that students resented so much as it was having little or no voice in the establishment of regulations.

Although the banking concept of education is endorsed by some, it is not intentionally adopted by many educators in the faculty and student development ranks. This latter group, however, often participates in banking education by default or unintentionally. Some educators participate in banking education because students have come to expect it and resist other approaches. Instructors, frustrated by unsuccessful attempts to solicit student participation in class, often revert to lecturing. Workshop facilitators who fail to provoke student interaction often end up stating their points directly as a last resort. These circumstances arise because students are trained in the art of receiving. The physical environment of a class or staff training seminar often emphasizes dominance or subordination. Rows of immovable chairs facing a podium make it difficult for an educator to overcome the banking approach. Institutional rules or expectations also dictate educator dominance. Instructors must evaluate student work; student affairs personnel must enforce disciplinary rules. Both may devise a way for students to play a role in these processes, but the educators are ultimately responsible for ensuring that the outcomes are fair.

There are more subtle, and thus more difficult to address, influences that lure educators into a dominant role. Most educators believe, for example, that they should appear knowledgeable and infallible as they interact with students. Faculty prepare for class carefully to have all the information necessary. They improve their scholarly writing by sharing it with a few close colleagues before publishing it for students to see. Student affairs professionals also prepare carefully for orientation or advising sessions so as to have all the information needed by the student. They perfect their presentations, programs, and policies before sharing them with students. This approach, though creating the impression that educators are well prepared and competent, reinforces the students' view of authority as all-knowing. Because they play no part in these processes, students do not perceive that they could come to know in any other way than to record the wisdom of their authorities. This situation is evident in the power of the deflation of authority as a learning experience. As Gwen described in Chapter Two, the instructor that said "I reject this role of professor" sparked Gwen's awareness of her role in learning. Belenky, Clinchy, Goldberger, and Tarule reported similar student reactions to the deflation of authority (1986).

Most educators also believe that they have a better sense of what should occur in a particular educational setting than do students. As a residence hall director, I spent many hours training my staff to handle the ever-present discipline problems that arose in our twelve-story hall. Yet their training was largely limited to playing roles in various scenarios and using prescribed techniques (complete with handouts) for addressing them. Looking back on these efforts, I regret that I never realized that learning set methods for dealing with rowdy students never came close to addressing the fears that made it impossible for undergraduate staff to confront their peers. I had set the stage in such a way that questions focused on techniques, rather than on the more crucial issues that prohibited the staff from using them. Despite this lesson, I still have to resist the temptation to use my elaborate overheads to teach student development theory instead of eliciting students' understanding of their experience. Thus, educators' decisions about what knowledge is introduced and recognized can place students in a subordinate role.

These decisions are influenced by forces beyond the particular educational setting in question. Giroux (1988) argues that they originate in the wider society. He challenges educators to consider "how wider forms of political, economic, social, and ideological domination and subordination might be invested in the language, texts, and social practices of the schools as well as in the experiences of the teachers and students themselves" (p. 130).

For example, the extent to which a higher education institution offers a liberal versus a vocational curriculum is tied to economic considerations involving the students and businesses the institution is intended to serve. Class size, certainly a dynamic that affects the nature of teaching, is based on economic concerns. Certainly, social and political considerations emerge in policy decisions such as whether to sell condoms on campus. In responding to a dean of students' letter asking for advice on this subject, the American College Personnel Association Ethics Committee attempted to balance two ethical codes: sensible regard for the social codes and moral expectations of the surrounding community and respect for the students' right of self-determination ("Dear Ethics Committee," 1988). Student affairs policies such as requiring entering students to live on campus (a common rule on many campuses) are in part economically driven and in part a result of the social belief that students are not yet able to live independently. Codes of student conduct and responses to violations are often aimed at avoiding behavior problems and negative publicity rather than providing an educational opportunity for students to learn to work and live together in a community. Campus attitudes sometimes lead to the devaluing of nondominant-population educators and students, as evident in instances of racism, sexism, and homophobia. Educational decisions are therefore often made on the basis of economic and political considerations rather than educational and student development theory.

The Objectivist-Social Constructivist Relationship

One aspect of the ideological domination to which Giroux refers has to do with ways of knowing. In his critique of conservative educational theories, he charges: "In this discourse, issues regarding what knowledge is of most worth, to what ends should students desire, and what it means to recognize that knowledge is a social construction so that students can learn to play an active part in its production both in and out of the classroom are ignored in the interest of 'reproducing' history rather than learning how to make it" (1988, p. 120). Not only is the notion of knowledge as a social construction ignored by the conservative educational theories that Giroux criticizes, but it has been placed in a subordinate position in academe for centuries. The way of knowing that has dominated for centuries, called positivism, is characterized by objectively pursuing knowledge that is then "summarized in the form of time- and context-free generalizations" (Guba, 1990, p. 20). The social constructivist perspective is characterized by the belief that generalization across time and context is not possible because multiple realities arise out of people's social construction (Guba, 1990).

One way to illustrate this distinction is to return to Coles's (1989) story, which I mentioned in Chapter One. There I drew upon Coles's experience as a psychiatric resident with two supervisors of different perspectives to understand my own way of knowing as it related to the students' stories. Coles's experience also puts the debate about ways of knowing into perspective. Coles initially valued the guidance of one of his supervisors

(Dr. Binger) more highly than the other (Dr. Ludwig). Dr. Binger was the supervisor who encouraged Coles to read more of the psychiatric literature and join him in "formulating" cases. Dr. Ludwig was the one who encouraged Coles to listen to his patients, to hear "*their* stories." Coles and his colleagues viewed Dr. Binger as a "brilliant theorist" as compared to Dr. Ludwig, who was regarded as an "affable old gent" (p. 5). Binger represented the positivist way of knowing; he believed that he, the writers of the psychiatric literature, and Coles could together solve Coles's client's problem without her input. Ludwig represented alternate ways of knowing; he insisted that the client's contribution was central to his and Coles's ability to understand her difficulties. Coles's realization that "no one else was preaching that line of psychological inquiry" (p. 22) and the slowness of his transition to Ludwig's way of thinking both demonstrate the difficulty of questioning the dominant view.

The dominance of the objectivist perspective over the social constructivist one is also evident in teaching and student affairs practices. The banking concept of education described earlier is one outgrowth of this dominance; the notions that educators should perfect their ideas prior to sharing them and that they know best what should be addressed in education also stem from this dominance. Although many educators have abandoned the banking concept and student affairs professionals gave up on in loco parentis long ago, like Coles, we have difficulty eluding the vestiges of the dominant perspective. We often leave students out of the process of organizing what knowledge is to be taught, both in and out of class. Whether the objectivist perspective still rules is a matter of opinion (see, for example, Lather, 1991, and Lincoln, 1990). The fact that other ways of knowing are labeled as alternative, new, and emergent and that those of us who endorse them still have difficulty making use of them shows the impact of positivism in most of our educations.

What does this dominance of positivism have to do with the story lines of voice and relations with others? The connection is clear in Eisner's comments: "When one operates on the belief that there is one way to validate knowledge, it is not a long step to the belief that students should learn that knowl-

edge. In other words, the primary mission of the school is to
see to it that the transmission of knowledge occurs and that students get it right" (1990, p. 99). The transmission of knowledge
in this context means that educators possess that knowledge.
Students' responsibility is to "get it right." This environment
makes educators dominant and students subordinate. Educators possess the authoritative voice; students should listen. In
this situation, the students' voice will be slow to emerge, and
their hesitancy to express it is understandable. Peers, according to the story lines summarized in this chapter, would sometimes seem to be collaborators in "getting it right" and at other
times conspirators in expressing the voice that is not legitimated
in the dominance-subordination context.

The Majority-Minority Relationship

Men's subordination of women and the racial majority's subordination of racial minorities are well-established ideas and need
no further examination here. The presence of both forms of
dominance in higher education is also documented in reports
on sexism in higher education (Hall and Sandler, 1982; Sadker
and Sadker, 1986) and the incidents of racism routinely reported
in the *Chronicle of Higher Education*. These situations also have
a potential connection to our story lines of voice and relations
with others. Students who are subordinated on two levels—
first, as students and, second, as women or minorities (or both)—
may be less likely to see their own voices as valid or to express
them than those students who experience less subordination.
    Deirdre's story in Chapter Six serves as an example of
this possibility. She described writing her interpretation of how
Homer felt about Achilles in her journal for a class. Her professor's reaction, "Oh, are you some feminist?," prompted her to
stop writing and to risk nothing. A return to Deirdre's story
shows that she had already perceived her view as valid but still
refrained from expressing it in this context. If students who already believe that their perspectives are worthwhile feel re-
strained by subordination, it surely has a similar, if not stronger,
effect on those who have yet to claim a voice. In another example,

Weiler (1988) recounts a story of a teacher who ignored an African-American student's reaction to a passage from Malcolm X's autobiography. She thought that the issue of socialization, which she had defined, was more important at the time than the student's concern about racism inherent in the passage. The student withdrew from the conversation after his point of view was not taken into consideration and withdrew from the class on the following day. A third example that illustrates this point in reverse is Mark's comment in Chapter Two that teachers "expect us to be more aggressive and to raise our hands all the time. [For] girls, I think, they don't encourage aggressive learning." If Mark's speculation is accurate (and corroborating evidence does exist that teachers work through interactions with men more than with women — see, for example, Sadker and Sadker, 1986), those who are encouraged to be aggressive may claim and express their voices with greater ease. Although instances of subordination or encouragement can occur for any student, history indicates that subordination is more often experienced by members of minority, or nondominant, groups.

In our story lines, the dominance of positivist over social constructivist ways of knowing appears in the majority-minority relationship as well. The abstract, rational, logical nature of the positivist approach has been generally associated with men, whereas the relational, experiential nature of the social constructivist perspective has usually been associated with women. Because the positivist perspective has dominated, the ideas of those subscribing to relational, experiential knowing have been assigned a lesser place. The receiving-, interpersonal-, and inter-individual-pattern knowers in our stories, regardless of their gender, are likely to experience more subordination than the mastery-, impersonal-, and individual-pattern knowers. Examples of this subordination are evident in faculty expectations for verbal participation that values mastery over receiving and in competitive student affairs settings that favor impersonal and individual approaches over interpersonal and interindividual ones. Expression of voice and relations with authority are likely to differ depending on the kind of environment that students experience.

I should note at this juncture that I have been citing examples of contexts that are consistent with the story lines as I heard them: delayed claiming of student voice, protracted dependence on authority, and uneven reliance on peers. This is not to suggest that education, both in the classroom and in student development, offers only these possibilities. Identifying these environments can, however, suggest new possibilities for freeing student voice. We will explore the contexts that encourage the use of voice, less reliance on authority, and positive relations with peers in Part Two of this book.

Socialization

Separating socialization contexts from dominance-subordination ones is difficult because considerable overlap exists between the two. One can argue that socialization practices produce, or at least maintain, dominant-subordinate relations; one can also argue that these relations create socialization practices. The utility of exploring various practices here is to consider the degree to which they contribute to the story lines of voice and relations with others. The following discussion of socialization as it relates to gender and to minority persons is intended to explore the degree of transferability of our story lines to persons socialized in these ways. These experiences, though not affecting everyone in these groups the same way, do have potential connections to the expression of voice and relations with others.

Gender-Related Socialization

Although socialization of female and male children varies in different societies, gender-related socialization does occur in Western cultures (Chodorow, 1989). Boys are said to be socialized toward separation and individuation, particularly because they must differentiate from their mothers in order to establish a masculine identity. Girls are said to be socialized toward connection, in part because they do not need to engage in this differentiation to establish a feminine identity. Chodorow (1989) and Gilligan (1982) both argue that these practices lead to boys struggling with relationships and girls struggling with separating from others. Concern for individuation, or autonomy, and concern for connection, or relationships, are evident in children's play. Lever's (1976) study of children's games revealed that boys often argued with each other about the rules of games in which they were engaged and seemed to value these disagreements as much as the game itself. Girls argued about rules less often and were more likely to discontinue the game rather than disagree. Thus, peers seem to reinforce boys' tendency to assert themselves and girls' tendency to refrain from jeopardizing relationships.

According to Brown and Gilligan (1990), girls on the edge of adolescence experience a crisis of connection. Whereas girls at age eight or nine express their thoughts readily, girls at age eleven or twelve hesitate out of concern for maintaining relationships. This shift is strikingly clear in Brown and Gilligan's conversations with a young girl named Jesse. At age eight, Jesse told a story about feeling left out while at a friend's house. Jesse explained her feelings to the friend, who also expressed her feelings by responding, "Just go home" (p. 11). At age eleven, Jesse told the interviewers that "if a girl doesn't like another girl, . . . she 'should pretend that [she] likes her'" (p. 16). Jesse's interviews show an increasing effort to become what the authors call "the perfect girl," one who is cooperative, kind, and good. Jesse avoids showing her true feelings for fear of jeopardizing her relationships and because she believes that others will want to be with her if she epitomizes the perfect girl. Thus, Jesse experiences a loss of voice. Although some girls try not to give up what they feel and know, it is not easy to resist. Brown and Gilligan quote Victoria's comments about what it is like to risk expressing herself: "I try to build, it's kind of bad really to do it, but I try to build a little shield" (p. 22). The stories of two other girls in the study, Anna and Tanya, reveal that some girls overcome the pressure to conform to the perfect-girl image and recover their voices. Others are unable to get past what Brown and Gilligan call the "wall of cultural prohibition."

Perhaps this is what Rich (1979) was referring to when she said women were taught to speak in "small, soft voices" (p. 243). Clinchy's (1989) interviews with college students demonstrate that hesitation to express opinions may continue into college. She noted that some college women were reluctant to engage in discourse characterized as argument. (Clinchy also discovered women who were accomplished in the art of argument, another reminder that gender-related differences are not generalizable or universal.) The men that Clinchy interviewed viewed argument as helping each other and were less comfortable trying to understand others' perspectives. Clinchy's findings agree with our story lines of delayed expression of voice, particularly on the part of receiving- and interpersonal-pattern knowers. They also confirm the story line about relationships with peers in that receiving-, interpersonal-, and interindividual-pattern students refrained from arguing, whereas mastery-, impersonal-, and individual-pattern students viewed it as a form of collaboration. Differing degrees of comfort with other perspectives were also evident in interindividual- and individual-pattern students' reasoning.

Brown and Gilligan (1990) also noted that the wall of cultural prohibition required girls to separate "the inner world of thoughts and feelings and the outer world of public knowledge— if they are to enter, without disrupting, the world they are to live in as young women" (p. 3). Some of the girls interviewed, like Jesse, reserved their feelings and what they knew from experience for their private sphere and expressed what was kind and good in the public sphere. Brown and Gilligan suggested that, as students progressed in school, teachers became less associated with them and more focused on the subjects they taught. This situation prompted further confusion for girls, who were then distanced from women who had important knowledge. These points of disconnection may be behind the interpersonal-pattern transitional students' creation of two bodies of knowledge: one for authority and one for themselves. Recall, once again, Marla's comments from Chapter Four about learning from sharing ideas with her peers, after which she said, "I don't know if I really necessarily learn anything more about the material in the book or anything like that." This division may occur earlier in absolute knowing, where one receiving-pattern student, Bev, drew a distinction between "raw facts" and "how you felt about a certain issue." Implying that it was separate from her personal beliefs, she also described what the instructor presented as "just hearing something you were taught."

Deirdre explained in Chapter Five what happened when these two spheres of knowledge reconnected in her experience of writing a journal for a class. Her comments bear repeating here:

> In school, you kind of leave your personal life and your personal experiences out of what you do academically. And everything's supposed to be kind of detached and formal. In the journal, you didn't pay any attention to what you were writing. I think any time you can learn about something and then somehow relate it to your personal life or some kind of experience you've had, it doubles—it makes the experience stronger. I think people need to get a chance to talk about the things they know, too.

She continued:

> I began thinking about things that I had read in high school and how everything I had learned has been from a very specific viewpoint that wasn't mine, that made me kind of look at myself as some kind of other, foreign thing. I look at my brother and my stepfather and the way they interact. And my brother and sister. And being able to look at the world personally and then publicly. And things just starting to click.

Thus, another context in which loss of voice occurs could be the objectification of knowledge (which as noted earlier has been the dominant process in education). This disconnection from teachers and public knowledge may also relate to receiving- and interpersonal-pattern students' detachment from authority. Reconnection of the private and public spheres, at least in Deirdre's case, has the potential to free the student voice and forge new connections with authority.

Additional stories of adolescents and college students suggest that females conceptualize autonomy in the context of connection, whereas the two concepts are separate for males. Stern's
(1989) interviews with adolescent girls yielded descriptions of
independence that did not reflect a separation from others. Independence for these girls meant being able to look beyond themselves, depend on others, and remain close to them. Straub's
(1987) interviews with college women also suggest a merging
of individuation and connection. Women described issues relating to intimacy in relationships as occuring together with their
development of autonomy and identity. College men, as reported
by Chickering (1969), developed autonomy as a precursor to
establishing identity, which in turn formed the basis for engaging in intimate relationships. Those students who focus on connection, regardless of their gender, may be less inclined to express their views if doing so would jeopardize relationships and
more inclined to use their voices in the context of peer relationships. Those students emphasizing separation, regardless of their
gender, may be more inclined to use their voices as part of being autonomous and as an attempt to give their individuality
a higher priority in relation to others.

   The intertwining of intimacy, autonomy, and identity,
along with the need to become the perfect girl that Brown and
Gilligan described, could predispose female-socialized students
to peer influence, already established as a powerful source of
socialization for both women and men. Studying peer culture
both at a black and at a white institution, Holland and Eisenhart (1990) identified a cultural model of romance and attractiveness that significantly influenced college women's behavior.
Holland and Eisenhart described the peer culture at those two
institutions as centered around "an ethos of romantic heterosex-
ual relationships" (p. 85). Prestige (a version of perfect-girl status?) for these women was based on their attractiveness to men,
a matter to which they devoted considerable time, often at the
expense of their own interests. Those who accepted this cultural
model gave up their academic aspirations as well as their relationships with other women. Some students, however, found
ways of avoiding this pressure, despite little collective support

for bucking the system. For those who bowed to peer pressure, a loss of voice seems inevitable. Ironically, this peer ranking system retained male dominance in that men were the judges of women's attractiveness and, thus, of their prestige.

The Socialization of African-American Students

Ward (1989) captures the essence of the socialization of African-American children in this quote: "As the black child sees herself as others see her, she knows that she is viewed in this society as a member of a devalued group. Transmitted daily to black children are messages that black people are undesirable, inadequate, and inferior" (p. 219). Ward further explained that awareness of belonging to a group that differed from others heightened the need for strong identification with a shared social identity, particularly during adolescence. Moreover, the adolescent girls that Ward interviewed reported strong support from their families in processing and coping with racial discrimination. Fordham and Ogbu (1986) also identified the notion of collective social identity, which they label "fictive kinship," as a way of opposing the social identity of white Americans. This takes the form of relationships resembling kinships (for example, brother, sister) among African Americans who are not related by blood or marriage. Similarly, an oppositional cultural frame of reference serves to protect the African Americans' identity and demarcate the boundaries between African and white Americans.

The collective social identity and cultural frame of reference combine to define certain behavior as "acting white" (Fordham and Ogbu, 1986). The African-American high school students that Fordham and Ogbu interviewed at Capital High School were torn between maintaining their collective social identity with black peers and engaging in behaviors perceived as acting white — namely, behaviors related to academic achievement. Although Fordham and Ogbu's students' stories are told in the context of academic achievement, which is not necessarily connected to the story lines of voice and relations with others, there are some similarities. Some of the African-American students

at Capital High performed less well than they could have to avoid
being viewed as "brainiacs" (acting white). Other African-
American students managed to perform well and simultaneously
avoid being viewed as brainiacs by establishing a clowning or
an athletic image that contradicted, and in a sense covered up,
their academic prowess. Students in both groups, however,
offered instances in which they withheld their voices. For example, Sidney, described as an underachieving male athlete,
revealed that he chose carefully whom he would interact with
in class for fear that those interactions would give away his academic potential and lead to his being called a brainiac. Shelvy,
an underachieving female, described a similar stance:

> Because once they find out you're a brainiac, then
> the first thing they'll say is, "Well, she thinks she's
> cute, and she thinks she's smart, she thinks she's
> better than anyone else." So what most brainiacs
> do, they sit back, and they know an answer, and
> they won't answer it. . . . 'Cause, see, first thing
> everybody say, "Well, they're trying to show off"
> [Fordham and Ogbu, 1986, p. 191].

The students who were high achievers at Capital High reported
similar approaches. Katrina, a high achiever, described holding back in class and letting other students answer to avoid being viewed as acting white. These experiences clearly prompted
these students to refrain from expressing their voices—in this
case, in class or with friends. Relationships with peers were also
strained by the effort made to avoid discovery of academic ability
and emphasize some other aspect of one's personality. What these
students described as "putting the brakes" on their academic
efforts (which took the form of missing class and not doing assignments) surely contributed to a detachment from authority.
Therefore, although the story lines of voice and relationships
with others do not dictate academic performance, the avoidance
of achievement can produce results like those we have seen in
these story lines.
      Studies of the development of racial identity create the

possibility that parental and peer socialization takes a variety of forms. Parham (1989) pointed out that the development of racial identity may be approached from a pro-black-oriented perspective by adolescents who have lived in predominantly black environments with parents holding Afrocentric racial attitudes. Adolescents who have lived in predominantly white environments with parents holding Eurocentric orientations may approach racial identity from a white-oriented perspective. Parham suggested that this latter group focused in late adolescence and early adulthood on integration and assimilation into the dominant culture, in some cases abandoning Afrocentric values of collective survival and mutual support. Experiences encountered at this point may call the white-oriented perspective into question. Positive experiences with black persons or negative experiences with white persons may result in questioning this nonblack identity. Those who begin to shift to a black frame of reference initially become preoccupied with interaction with black groups and activities and limit interaction with white peers. When the black identity becomes internalized, the inner security that results allows a freer interaction with a variety of persons, resulting in "bicultural success," in Parham's words. Thus, relations with peers and use of voice may vary throughout this process.

The type of socialization experienced in adolescence, combined with the versions of socialization that occur on predominantly white and predominantly black college campuses, results in a wide array of story lines about voice and relations with others. The prominence of the interpersonal environment is a central theme in numerous accounts of African-American students' experiences. Fleming (1984) asserted that the supportive interpersonal environment of black colleges explains why African-American students experience more positive development there than in predominantly white colleges. Friendships with peers, faculty, and staff help fulfill the need for connections and, therefore, assist intellectual growth. For African-American students in white colleges, isolation and loneliness lead to preoccupation with attempts to meet relational needs at the expense of other aspects of development. According to Fleming, African-American

males in black environments are able to establish relationships
with faculty and peers that result in their increased assertiveness (which, in our terms, relates to expression of voice). African-
American females become more outspoken and expressive in
white environments, where they are not dominated by African-
American men. In black environments, Fleming reported that
African-American women show a decrease in assertiveness,
which is replaced with a social passivity that does not conflict
with African-American males' dominant roles. These stories suggest that African-American college students' voices are modu-
lated in accordance with their relationships with peers and authority.

The interpersonal environment is also central to the stories that African-American women at Bradford College told Holland and Eisenhart (1990). Seven of the ten women studied approached college as something to be "gotten over" (p. 169). They
viewed college as a means to a better job and their role as fulfill-
ing the requirements to obtain a degree. Two quotes from a
student named Cynthia show clearly what this approach entailed:

> I felt like going to college would bring me a good
> job . . . and I wanted to become something. . . . I
> didn't want to just get out of high school and just
> set up and just wait for somebody to bring me some
> money. . . . If I can just pass, I'll feel all right. . . . I
> have to pass to get out of here. It's going to have
> to be done in order to get myself somewhere in life.
> It's just a step higher [p. 169].

Detached relationships with authority and minimal expression
of personal views are likely outcomes of such an approach. Expression of opinions and feelings was also infrequent, however,
with peers. As was true of their white counterparts at another
institution, they were susceptible to the cultural model of romance and attractiveness and preoccupied with romantic relationships with men. The African-American women at Bradford
also gained prestige by avoiding manipulation by peers. Despite
their use of kinship metaphors to describe relationships with

other women, they withheld information about their romantic affairs from other women to maintain control and independence. Some of their relationships with men were also not what they appeared on the surface, and men were expected to be able to assess women's intentions to avoid being hurt. Thus, the African-American women at Bradford appeared to have little or no outlet for their voices and minimal relationships with others, despite the importance of interpersonal relationships.

The interpersonal component was also prominent in Branch-Simpson's (1985) study of African-American seniors at a predominantly white college (summarized in Rodgers, 1990), particularly in the form of connection to peers and family. She found that African-American students described achieving identity through relationships with family and tended to stay connected to family in developing autonomy. The students also preferred the learning experience to be personal and connected and desired relationships with their teachers. These experiences were true for both women and men, although women were reported as achieving autonomy and intimacy ahead of men, whereas men appeared to be more oriented toward career achievement than were women. This focus on connection may have the implications for voice and relations already discussed.

The emphasis on connection figured in the experience of both African-American students in the Miami study. Kyle expressed an interest in connection with his teachers from the start of his first year; he expressed his preference for those who cared what he thought and were concerned about teaching him. Kyle built close connections with his peers and instructors, which contributed to his satisfaction with his major and the college experience. Carmen found less connection than she preferred. She described her college years as frustrating for a variety of reasons, all of which seemed to hinge on connection. She explored numerous majors and had difficulty finding one that seemed like a good fit. She often encountered instructors whom she perceived as more interested in covering the material or in their research than in whether she was learning. She often felt that what she was learning did not apply to real life. She described her peers early on as extremely competitive and ascribed some of her frustration with college to the peer culture's focus on appearance. She described it like this:

> A lot of it was just the looks complex they all have. "Well, you don't look like I do, and you don't wear the same name-brand clothes I do." Part of it was my desire not to. A lot of it was just I didn't fit in with them.

She went on to say that she liked classes that attracted students who did not accept these ideas and had "just a devil of a time with the atmosphere" in classes where the peer culture prevailed. She described finding one good friend who shared her feelings and who helped her cope with her frustrations. Carmen's collective experience led her to this reflection in our fifth-year interview:

> I'm learning to be more assertive because I just always took a back seat. That's one of the reasons I became an observer rather than a participant. So now, even though I do observe more, at times I can participate a little bit more and overcome that complex I had. I'm also more independent, because I've had to learn to be — I guess what you'd say is — a loner.

College for Carmen meant that she became an observer, whereas she had described herself as "on top" as a high school student. It also meant becoming a loner in order to establish her own identity and avoid "being mainstreamed." Her loss of voice and lack of relationship with others all seemed to stem from lack of connection.

Dialogue with Students

The discussion of dominance-subordination and socialization contexts creates possibilities for how our story lines may be relevant in other settings; environments have been identified where particular story lines can be expected to occur. Simultaneously, however, our discussion illustrates the variability of persons in each context. Some of the adolescent girls that Brown and Gilligan interviewed stopped expressing themselves upon encountering the wall of cultural prohibition, whereas others struggled ahead behind their "little shields." Some of Clinchy's college women avoided argument; others were expert at it. African-American students' relationships and their use of voice took numerous turns, depending on their racial identity, the connections that they were able to make in college, and the nature of the college cultures that they encountered. The relevance of our story lines to these contexts is evident, but Frye's caution that the prevailing winds do not affect everyone the same way suggests that these ideas should be explored with students. Thus, the judgment of transferability to any specific context still requires that dialogue.

The story lines form a foundation for the dialogue; educators can provide a context and opportunities for students to describe their experiences and, in doing so, make sense of them. Faculty have occasion in class and in small-group or individual interactions to discuss with students their expectations for a class, the roles that they expect to play, and the way that they see the instructor and themselves undertaking the task of learning. Student affairs professionals have extensive opportunities to engage students in rich dialogue about how they view themselves, the college culture, and their growth during college. These interactions not only illuminate student perceptions at that time but also open the door to experiences that build on those perspectives. The act of listening alone would enhance students' expression of voice and perhaps prompt a reformulation of the role of authority. Part Two of this book addresses how educators can listen to, validate, and respond to the student voice in a dialogue that creates new possibilities.

Implications
for Academic
and Student Affairs

The stories told throughout college by students in this study suggest that learning is a relational activity. Peer relationships played a central role for most students and a particularly important part for receiving-, interpersonal-, and interindividual-pattern students. Knowing in more complex forms was possible when students' genuine relationships with authority replaced detached or apprentice relationships. The connection of personal experience with subject matter enhanced students' recognition of and expression of their own voices.

Again, it is apparent that students are able to articulate what educators have come to know: that learning thrives in a communal atmosphere. Parker Palmer (1987) portrays knowing and learning as communal acts that "require a continual cycle of discussion, disagreement, and consensus over what has been seen and what it all means" (p. 25). This process requires connections among people and between people and ideas. Palmer asserts that "the act of knowing itself . . . is a bond of community between us and that which we know" (p. 24).

The students' stories also reveal something else that most educators know: that education is not often relational. The objectivism that has dominated education for centuries focuses on separation of the learner from knowledge. According to Palmer, this emphasis further spawns competitive individualism, rather than supportive collaboration. Supportive collaboration is necessary for discussing and disagreeing, for challenging each other to grow intellectually, and for developing student voice. The

223

task for educators, then, is one of reconnection — of students to their teachers, of lived experience to knowledge, of in-class life with out-of-class intellectual life.

Reconnection involves a balance between joining students "where they are," so to speak, and encouraging them to consider more complex ways of thinking. Student development educators refer to this as a balance of challenge and support (Sanford, 1962; Rodgers, 1980; Widick and Simpson, 1978). The challenge aspect asks students to call their assumptions about knowing into question, and support creates conditions that make this questioning less threatening. Too much challenge results in students avoiding evaluating their assumptions; too much support renders evaluating their assumptions unnecessary. Kegan (1982) offers an excellent framework through which educators can reconnect with students in a way that balances recognition of the students' current way of knowing with promoting the development of their own perspectives.

Kegan translates the notions of challenge and support into *confirmation, contradiction,* and *continuity.* He uses these terms to describe functions that the environment plays in people's growth. Following Piaget, Kegan views growth as a constant balancing of disequilibrium that results when one encounters new experiences that are incompatible with one's current view. The environment functions to confirm (hold, support) people as they face these changes. It also contradicts (lets go, challenges) them as they move to a new balance. Simultaneously, the environment offers continuity to aid in the transition and reintegration of the previous self into the developing one. The educational environment, then, should offer confirmation, contradiction, and continuity in order to promote intellectual growth.

The students' stories told in Part One of this book help determine what constitutes confirmation and contradiction for students with different ways of knowing. As a result, one might expect to find outlines of specific combinations of confirmation, contradiction, and continuity for each way of knowing in the next few chapters. Although it is tempting to pursue this approach, it is problematic for a number of reasons. First, educators rarely find a homogeneous group of students in any given classroom. Attempting to implement two, three, or four different approaches simultaneously would be confusing at best. Second, confirmation and contradiction are hard to separate in practice. For example, confirming the student voice at the same time contradicts authority as omnipotent. Third, and perhaps most importantly, developing specific strategies in the abstract violates the concept of connecting with students. For instance, applying strategies developed for absolute knowing as it is described in this book may overlook particular confirmations and contradictions for these students in a specific context. In order to connect learning to individual experience, educators have to determine what confirms and contradicts particular students in particular contexts. Katz and Henry (1988) advocate this approach: "As the essence of good teaching is the greatest possible individualization of the teacher's responses to students, any reliance on general formulas is in itself antidevelopmental and antieducational" (p. 4). Being flexible to entertain new possibilities, as well as maintaining continuity as students change, also requires a fluid approach. Defining specific strategies for each way of knowing tends to promote rigidity, rather than flexibility, in practice. Flexibility is essential given the dynamic nature of students' development, the diversity of ways of knowing and gender-related patterns in any given group of students, and the variety of sources for confirmation and contradiction in the college environment. Thus, I propose that we approach education as contextual knowers ourselves — that is to say, we should recognize the importance of context as we make decisions about educational practice.

Given the importance of context in defining educational practice, Part Two of this book revolves around the students in this study. Chapter Eight offers advice for classroom educators contained in the students' stories. I use students' accounts of what confirmed them in each way of knowing to help the reader judge whether that context is applicable to her or his classroom. Chapter Nine describes three principles that I identified from the stories that combine the use of confirmation, contradiction, and continuity across all four ways of knowing. Student stories are also used to illustrate these principles to establish the context from which they were constructed. Chapter Ten returns to advice to student affairs educators regarding confirmation for students in each way of knowing. Chapter Eleven uses the three principles defined in Chapter Nine to guide confirmation, contradiction, and continuity in student affairs practice. Although I cite others who have written about these issues when it clarifies the students' advice, most references to this research are found in the concluding chapter. That chapter places the insights generated in this study in the context of similar work on student development, effective teaching, and student affairs practice.

Chapter Eight

Teaching Responsively to Different Ways of Knowing

> After four years, there was a moment that it just hit me: there was a whole level of thinking that I didn't even know existed.
>
> —*Sheila*

The whole new level of thinking Sheila referred to was her ability to generate knowledge. Most educators would hope to promote this discovery in fewer than four years. Students' stories about their academic experiences offer rich insights into relationships with peers and authority that are conducive to learning and circumstances in which student voice can be claimed. Some of the stories describe experiences that confirm, or support, students' ways of knowing, whereas others recount situations that contradict, or challenge, student assumptions. As we saw earlier, development requires a balance of confirmation and contradiction that enables the student to constantly reevaluate ways of knowing in the face of new experiences (Kegan, 1982; Piaget, 1932). This chapter focuses on "matching" the classroom environment to students' ways of knowing, or providing appropriate confirmation.

In his extensive analysis of undergraduate education in America, Ernest Boyer (1987) concluded, "The central qualities that make for successful teaching can be simply stated: command of the material to be taught, a contagious enthusiasm for the play of ideas, optimism about human potential, the involvement with one's students, and—not least—sensitivity, integrity, and warmth as a human being. When this combination is present in the classroom, the impact of a teacher can be powerful and enduring" (p. 154). Our participants' stories about their academic experiences confirm Boyer's conclusion and elaborate on the meaning of his ideas for students using different ways of knowing. How students make sense of their experiences was influenced by these perspectives (and their advice was categorized accordingly). For example, absolute knowers expected the instructor to provide answers and judged those who used unguided group discussion as ineffective. However, transitional knowers expected student involvement and judged the same instructor more favorably.

The thoughts of students that could be useful for classroom educators fell into six categories: professors' attitudes, professor-student interaction, teaching strategies, class structure, evaluation techniques and systems, and knowledge contradictions. Within each category, prevalent themes show how educators can respond to students' learning needs. Table 8.1 shows the themes in each of the six categories for absolute, transitional, independent, and contextual knowing. These themes are, again, prevailing winds that did not affect all students identically. Despite that, the stories reveal experiences that can help educators understand what it is like to be on the other side of the educational enterprise.

Matching Absolute Knowers' Learning Needs

The majority of absolute knowers' insights came from sophomore-year interviews. Although there were many absolute learners in the freshman year, their experience was very limited because interviews were conducted as they began their first semester in college. The number of students who kept this perspective in their junior year was too small to make possible the identification of themes.

Table 8.1. Students' Advice for Curricular Education.

	Absolute Knowing	Transitional Knowing	Independent Knowing	Contextual Knowing
Professors' attitudes	Demonstrate helpfulness	Relate to and demonstrate care for students	Treat students as equals	Engage in collegial relationships with students
Professor-student interaction	Provide opportunity to know professor	Engage in positive interactions with students	Establish genuine relationships with students	Engage in collegial relationships with students
Teaching strategies	Make classroom active	Get students involved	Connect learning to real life	Create opportunities for mutual responsibility
				Look at the "big picture"
Classroom structure	Make classroom relational	Build in peer involvement	Create opportunities for independence, critical thinking, and peer collaboration	Create opportunities for interdependency
Evaluation	Help student understand grading	Promote thinking rather than memorization	Allow for freedom of expression	
Knowledge discrepancies		Introduce contradictory views	Value contradictory views	

Professors' Attitudes: Demonstrate Helpfulness

Professors' attitudes played an important part in learning for absolute knowers. They appreciated instructors who seemed to enjoy teaching, cared about students, and helped them. For example, Leah said:

> Teachers who want to be teaching are the best. I have one like that—he wants us to be interested, and he's excited about teaching. I have another teacher who just repeats what he's taught year after year—he doesn't even care.

Fran elaborated on the caring aspect:

> This year, my teachers are more personable. My calculus prof knows my name and makes me feel like he cares to go out of his way. He says, "Come to office hours and call for an appointment if you can't come [during regular] hours." The teachers this year don't seem against you. They care and will try to help you.

Spencer gave an example of receiving help from a professor:

> My physics prof gives letter grades for homework. He also hands it back and goes over it so you can see your mistakes. He offers a help session once a week. He goes the extra mile for you. Help sessions in math are only before tests. And if you have another class, you can't make the session. Having regularly scheduled sessions helps.

Some professors were not viewed as concerned and were characterized as having negative attitudes. Students reported the impact of negative attitudes in comments like "one professor is arrogant, acts like he is doing us a favor by being there— this intimidates me" and "ones who hated teaching and thought we were dumb made me hate to go to class." Encouraging these students' interest required showing an interest in teaching and in students' success and avoiding adversarial relationships.

Professor-Student Interaction:
Provide Opportunities for Students to Know the Professor

Even students who had no interaction with their professors or were afraid to approach them wanted to get to know them. For example, Valerie reported:

> I never talked to teachers until I had to in calculus because it was so hard. She was really nice and helped me a lot.

Others also discovered that interaction could be helpful, both in and out of class. Steve described class-related interactions:

> In my English classes, they would have conferences. You came to talk about your papers, and I just think that's really important—getting to know your professors.

Others talked of being invited to accompany professors to class-related events and being good friends with teachers. Despite some interactions, these students expressed an interest in knowing professors better. Providing opportunities to get to know their instructors would help students who are too intimidated to ask for help, as was the case with Valerie. It would also add a relational component to the learning process.

Teaching Strategies: Make the Classroom Active

Absolute knowers appreciated teaching strategies that involved interesting activities. Amy's comment captures the essence of this theme. She said, "I like doing things rather than just listening to the teacher and writing it down." The focus on "doing things" is evident in other students' comments. Eileen said, "In theater, she does ask people to come up and do demonstrations and asks questions — tries to include people." Valerie remarked, "The teachers give more analogies or talk about application rather than just giving definitions." Bernard's definition of doing things was that "the teacher didn't mind questions and did little experiments." Terry said, "I got used to lecture as long as they somehow got the class involved — let us ask questions or take a break half way through." Instances when the professor gave a demonstration or answered questions were interesting to students. Most of these students reported that this type of activity occurred only occasionally. Thus, increasing the activity level of classes would create interest for these students.

Activity, however, does not decrease the professor's responsibility to explain the material. Students appreciated explanations that they understood. For example, Hugh said, "He talks to us like it's a conversation — you talk about one thing, and, when it's done, you talk about another." Paul stated: "Professors who point out little things to back it up help me remember it." By contrast, Hugh reported having another teacher who "explains things assuming that we know everything — he doesn't know how to start from scratch, talks to us as though we are faculty members — I get confused." Maintaining an awareness of the knowledge level of the class helps keep explanations within reach of students' understanding.

Classroom Structure: Make the Classroom Relational

Most absolute learners reported that their classes were large lecture classes with minimal interaction. However, they preferred the few experiences that they had in small classes. They sought an intimate, relaxed atmosphere to foster learning. Getting to know others in the class was the main advantage of this type of atmosphere. Anita's response is a typical example:

> In small classes, we've had projects and exercises where we've been put in groups with other people. Having to work with other people, you get to know them pretty well. It's easier because you can have

them help you if you don't understand. You can
work it out together.

For Anita, the advantage of small classes lay in getting to know
others and becoming comfortable collaborating with other students. Bernard's statement shows the importance of working with
instructors as well:

> I've had only two small classes. Most are lecture.
> [If] it is big, there is a tendency to skip or fall asleep.
> I have a coaching class that is small, and you have
> to relate and get in with the instructors, verbalize
> through the whole class.

Opportunities to get to know peers, engage in interaction, and
participate in debate were valued by many absolute learners.
Although the students suggested these ideas in the context of
small classes, small-group work in larger classes could also answer these needs. Creating small groups that remain intact
throughout a course could provide a context for getting to know
classmates and increase students' case in interacting with others.

Evaluation: Help Students Understand Grading

Although absolute learners generally took evaluation for granted,
they often reported frustrations with it that seemed to stem from
not understanding the professor's feedback. Subjectivity in grading was one such issue. Hugh illustrated this concern as he explained his preference for essay exams:

> Essay exams are good because it's aggravating on
> a multiple-choice test when you don't know an an-
> swer but you know a million and a half facts that
> relate to the question. I like essays. This is the best
> way to evaluate the student, but I hate the subjec-
> tiveness.

It is hard to tell from Hugh's explanation what he dislikes about
subjectiveness. It is clearer in Spencer's situation:

In English, I would turn in a paper and get an A. Then two weeks later, I would turn in another paper and get a C. I didn't see that much of a change in my style or thoughts. I got kind of turned off by that. The comments would be vague, and I'd ask him about it but still not understand what I did wrong.

Absolute knowers were also concerned with figuring out what their professors wanted on tests. The stress of getting good grades heightened these concerns. Increased communication between professors and students would aid their understanding of the criteria and process used to judge their work and help them interpret the feedback more effectively.

Absolute knowers' experiences convey the importance of relational aspects of learning. Helpful, caring attitudes of professors and interactions with professors helped students learn and are indicative of connection between students and professors. Relational preferences were also clear in students' desire to be involved in class and peer interaction. Despite having only a few small classes, students clearly felt that opportunities to get to know peers, as well as professors, enhanced the learning setting. Knowing others helped increase students' comfort with learning.

Matching Transitional Knowers' Learning Needs

A rich array of information is available from which to describe transitional knowers' learning needs and preferences; some students exhibited transitional knowing as sophomores and many as juniors and seniors.

Professors' Attitudes:
Relate to and Demonstrate Care for Students

Transitional learners appreciated professors who could relate to students. A few typical comments included:

I like instructors who get to know you; it's more personal. I like them to know you, talk to you individually and in class. You can go to their offices, and they'll tell you more about themselves and ask more about you. It makes them more human.

— Megan, sophomore

The best professor is one who cares, who would help and encourage us. One gave us study guides. She was friendly and open. She reached out to us.

— Kelly, her junior year

I feel more comfortable with professors who can relate to students and enjoy what they are doing. They are not higher than the students. They can relate to students on their level, which makes it more interesting. They are accessible out of class to talk with you.

— Sidney, senior

I am very comfortable talking with my professors. They care. They make us know they are there for us. They treat us as future professionals, rather than just students. The level of respect helps me bring in more of my own ideas.

— Kelly, her senior year

One professor said it was her obligation to teach us. She was the most honest teacher I had. She felt strongly about what she was teaching, so I wanted to do well. She got you involved in wanting to learn.

— Clark, junior

Phrases like "know you," "reached out to us," "treat us as future professionals," and "not higher than students" emphasize the relational aspects of learning. According to these students, these attitudes encouraged them to bring in their own ideas, take learning seriously, want to do well, and be interested in learning. Yet, as we might think, attitudes such as arrogance, intentional attempts to intimidate students, prejudgment of students' abilities, lack of receptivity to student questions and needs, an impersonal approach, and lack of concern about student learning had the opposite effect. Relating to students and demonstrating care for them obviously influences their ability to invest and succeed in the learning process.

Professor-Student Interaction:
Engage in Positive Interactions with Students

Despite their experiences, transitional knowers clearly preferred helpful interactions with instructors. Typical interactions in class are described by Sidney and Eileen:

> I have five classes, and three of the five professors are friendly. I go to office hours — I need to now, due to the difficulty of the material. The lectures and book don't always provide an explanation. I look to one professor for career-planning knowledge. He gives me advice.
>
> — *Sidney*

> Professors treat juniors and seniors differently. They don't talk down to you but meet you in the middle — mutual respect. They are more laid back in class. People want to be there, so they don't fool around. The teacher is more of a person instead of Dr. So and So.
>
> — *Eileen*

Students also reported interactions that extended beyond the individual classroom. For example, Tracy said, "I have a professor for a summer school class who became my mentor; he helped me with my career direction and became a friend." Sean said, "I go uptown to get ice cream with one professor; not many go uptown with you, but one got out a book and showed me information that I was interested in." Students also appreciated being invited to professors' home as a class, playing sports together, getting assistance with internship applications and résumés, and getting help with job searches. Both in- and out-of-class interactions were viewed as increasing students' incentive and ability to learn.

The desire and ability to learn were inhibited by lack of interaction with professors (reported by some sophomores) and negative interactions (reported by some juniors). Negative interactions for juniors involved professors who had criticized their ability, questioned their integrity, and shuffled them out during office hours. These students also hesitated to acknowledge to professors that they did not understand the material. The combined result of these two factors was that contact with professors was avoided. Initiating positive interactions would help build rapport between professors and students so that, when criticism becomes necessary, collaborative assessment could replace adversarial interactions.

Teaching Strategies: Get Students Involved

The teaching strategy that transitional knowers valued most was student involvement. These learners defined *involvement* as promoting thinking, application, and understanding. This understanding is inherent in the quotes below.

> I lose interest in professors that just lecture, and there's no input. I like them to act as a facilitator, ask for class input, so we're all kind of running the class. People can ask questions and make comments to further understand.
>
> — *Will, sophomore*

> In one class, we do groups. The discussion aids understanding and application. There is a more open atmosphere. I don't feel inferior anymore if I don't understand. Discussion causes you to change opinions when you hear others' experiences.
>
> — *Candace, junior*

When you are involved in the conversation, you
can say what you think about the topic. You understand better because you talk about it. You have
to think about what you think, rather than just writing it down.

—*Alice, junior*

These comments suggest that involvement leads to increased
interest, understanding, application of knowledge, and thinking about what one is learning.

Some students emphasized involvement as a way to form
their own ideas. Justin stated, "Discussion classes let you form
your own opinions—allow you to think about it, allow insight
into myself and growing as a person." Similarly, Scott said:

In political science, we could ask questions, draw
logical conclusions through debates and discussion
with the teacher and class. I was able to sit back,
observe, absorb ideas, and draw my own conclusions.

Hands-on experience was another important component of involvement. Leah explained:

In public relations, we had to do a whole campaign.
We learned everything about public relations from
trying it. We learned how to work in a group. You
learn more by applying it.

Kris described a similar experience:

Student teaching. I learned more in six weeks than
in the previous three years about techniques, relationships, how teacher and student attitudes affect
each other. I'm a hands-on learner—I'm doing it,
making mistakes, learning from it—techniques are
becoming part of me instead of something I learned
from a book.

Some students advocated being forced to be involved. Hugh's comment represents this perspective:

> One professor has our names on cards and randomly calls on us. It is good because it makes you pay attention — you don't want to look like a fool. It is negative because he asks us things we don't know yet. And if you make the mistake of trying to guess, he attacks you. It is best to say you don't know. I'm more comfortable with this now; he makes you think when he focuses on one person. I'm not 100 percent fond of what he does, but at least he shows he cares about students and is trying to make us learn. This makes us learn.

Although many students agreed with Hugh that being prompted to think was important, they described other strategies that encouraged thinking. Kyle, a sophomore, described one in this way:

> In smaller classes, you think more because they want more from you. I had an English class that gave a lot of new insights that I'd never thought about before, and it made me think a lot. I like that better, where they challenge you to think, rather than spit it back at them.

Alice, a junior, noted that in family studies:

> The professor encourages conversation and discussion. She asked us about experiences we had — so you don't sound stupid. It caused us to think.

Tracy, a senior, said:

> The professor encouraged us to critique theory. He made it comfortable to do this because he was down to earth. He gave us real-life examples to relate to.

He played devil's advocate—I was initially intimidated because you're conditioned to accept the
teacher's view. But he rewarded us for challenging
him, and we learned more.

Collectively, these comments reveal that transitional learners
appreciated opportunities for involvement, even if these were
forced, that enabled them to think critically about what they
were learning. These opportunities validated the discovery that
students could analyze information, rather than merely collect it.

Some transitional knowers also valued practical application. The comments below illustrate this theme.

Our chemistry professor does things that help you
relate. Talks about chemicals that curl hair, for example, or nitrates in red meat. He puts it into real
life. Sometimes the information is just straight technical. It is hard to understand without ties to the
real world.

—*Art, junior*

Dietetics professors relate the material to experiences they have had. This is more helpful than those
who just teach and can't relate it to real-life experiences. That's boring—I can read the book. In
dietetics, you have to know facts, but to handle patients you need experience.

—*Jill, senior*

These comments all noted that relating classroom facts to concrete situations was necessary for understanding.

Transitional learners viewed teaching strategies that did
not entail involvement or practical application as ineffective.
The students described poor connections between lecture and
reading material, ineffective presentation, lack of student involvement, miscalculation of student needs and abilities, presentations that went through the motions without concern for genuine learning, and inability to connect with the students. These

strategies were inconsistent with transitional knowers' preference for involvement, thinking, application, and understanding.

Classroom Structure: Build In Peer Involvement

Consistent with transitional learners' emphasis on student involvement in teaching strategies was their focus on peer involvement in class structure. Peer involvement had two aspects: participation, or talking to understand, and discussion, or talking to hear others' views. Responses dwelling on participation concentrated on the value of discussion itself rather than of others' views. Janice offered an example:

> Class is set up so you're motivated to say something or participate or get in small groups and discuss something, instead of just listening to lecture. If classes are strictly factual, participation doesn't help. With participation, you can see if you know what you're talking about, stop and think about it, analyze a problem, think like you were on the job.

Similarly, Chuck said:

> Political science involves discussion. We question the teacher. You should question to get a better understanding. They want you to get a wide base of knowledge, to think for yourself. It helps to know how others think. Students who take the class know we are going to be debating.

Although both students implied that group discussion was helpful, their focus was on their own learning. Another view of the role of discussion was described by Michael and Dawn. Michael said:

> It's interesting and good to hear other people's views because it gives you a chance to think about something in a different mode than before. It is usually

not effective if everyone is defending their own
views because people close their minds and won't
listen. I tend to change my view as I learn more
about things.

Dawn commented, "Any person we come in contact with has
a lot to teach us and we them; interaction is a good way to learn."
For these two students, the opinions of others have an effect on
the learner.

Transitional knowers also valued peer involvement to get
to know their peers. Knowing classmates helped Lauren learn.
She remarked:

With group work, you know people better, make
new friends. They help you solve problems; you
aren't on your own.

For Reginald, it was just more fun:

In the first two years, I only met a couple of people in large classes. Now, in smaller classes, I meet
more. I get to know people in theater and honors
courses. You're friends because you were in a skit
or shared something. Friendship helps learning because it's personable; you learn in fun ways.

Rosa noted that knowing peers increased the exchange of views:

Now that I know students and am comfortable, I
want discussion. We understand each other's views.
I know them on a personal level, too.

Thus, knowing classmates on a personal level provided support,
friendship, and access to other ideas.

Evaluation: Promote Thinking Rather Than Memorization

Transitional learners valued evaluation techniques that promoted understanding, application, and thinking, as opposed to

memorization. The examples below represent the range of responses about assessment:

> I like essay tests where I can voice my opinion and see what the teacher thinks about what I'm thinking. On the multiple-choice tests, the professor doesn't care what I think about the question. With essays, it makes me think, not just memorize facts.
> — *Marge, sophomore*

> In cost accounting, I didn't get any of the five questions right, but I got an A because I rationalized and explained what I did, even if it wasn't the answer he was looking for. This was the highest form of learning — not just getting one specific answer but understanding everything that went into it and being able to use the pieces to get a result.
> — *Sidney, junior*

> Essays are best. They give you a chance to integrate all your thoughts from different areas — that's what teachers are looking for at this level. Apply thoughts to a situation. The real world will ask us to apply — not multiple-choice questions.
> — *Stephanie, senior*

In addition to specific types of tests, students also reported that peer and faculty feedback promoted thinking. For example, peer critique was described by Deirdre:

> In creative writing, we wrote stories, had small groups critique them, rewrote them, and handed them out to the whole class. Then we would go through them — it was eye-opening. The same thing happened in drawing. We would critique drawings — instant feedback.

Other students commented on constructive feedback from professors. Kris offered an example:

We turned in a journal. She would write comments
on just about every page. Some were critical and
offered things to think about, and some were praise.
She offered suggestions about lessons. Constructive
criticism was very beneficial.

Professor's approaches to evaluation (beyond types of tests)
were important to some transitional knowers. For example, Will
remarked:

Professors now acknowledge that it is tough to grade
students. I like professors who take effort into account and offer diverse options. In economics, he
gave us a choice of tests. I've had professors who
say an A on a cumulative final means an A in the
course. I like these options.

Other students talked about approaches in the context of fairness. Fair tests contained reasonable questions on material that
had been covered in class. Predetermined decisions about the
number of students that would get each grade and tests on which
the majority of students performed poorly were judged as unfair. These students also appreciated more frequent evaluation
opportunities that counted less toward the grade.

Students complained about evaluation techniques that
they felt did not promote understanding, application, and thinking. Some students commented that they felt they had to repeat
the opinions of authority on tests. Repeating these views was
sometimes a matter of "going with what the professor is looking for — sometimes they are looking for a specific point of view"
(a senior). In other cases, it was writing what the professor believed, as Anita (a junior) explained: "I had one professor who
was right about everything — he didn't want to hear your opinion; you had to write what he wanted — it was unfair." Some
seniors also judged much of their evaluation to be ineffective
in that it did not reflect what they had learned.

Knowledge Discrepancies: Introduce Contradictory Views

Transitional knowers, with the exception of sophomores, found encountering contradictory views to be a regular part of their learning experience. Being exposed to diverse opinions led to increased awareness of new ideas and the need to make choices. For example, Kris said:

> In class, we read and discuss articles. The professor points out biases in the articles and exposes me to this. This is a push for being more critical.

Similarly, Anita stated:

> In women's studies class, I'm encountering all these different notions. It's hard to change the way I've thought all my life because I was ignorant on the subject.

Both reveal an opening of their thinking as a result of hearing these ideas.

Many of the encounters with contradictory views occurred in group work, where students often focused on resolving the differences. Janice described this reaction:

> Some groups have disagreements, but eventually you come to the same general conclusion. This gives you an opportunity to work with other people, which you have to do on the job. You compromise, or agree with the other idea if you missed something.

Others concentrated on supporting their idea even if it contradicted others'. Andrew explained:

> In honors economics, we studied a new controversial theory. I like to hear both sides and make my

own decision. I like someone to challenge me and
make me defend where I'm coming from. You have
to weigh ideas for yourself. My management teacher
encourages you to disagree and debate as long as
you defend your position.

Their experience with contradictory views prompted some students to be more aware of diverse opinions, some to strive for
compromise, and others to work on defending their perspectives.
    Together, the transitional knowers' preferences identified
student involvement as the key to learning. The individual student was involved in learning by talking about the material,
which in turn led to thinking about it and understanding. Involvement consisting of the expression of classmates' views also
aided thinking and understanding. Transitional learners preferred professors who used teaching strategies that allowed for
involvement, thinking, and real-life application and evaluation
techniques that measured understanding, thinking, and application. Knowledge discrepancies were encountered regularly,
often through peers' views in group discussion. Caring attitudes
on the part of professors and positive interactions aided transitional knowers in thinking about what they were learning. The
themes that we see in transitional knowing begin to identify the
teaching strategies, professor attitudes, and class formats that
activate the student voice.

Matching Independent Knowers' Learning Needs

As you will recall from Chapter Two, independent knowing was
not common in college; only 5 percent of the juniors and 16
percent of the seniors fell into this category. However, by the
fifth-year interviews, 57 percent of participating students had become independent learners. These students reflected on their
experiences during their senior year, and these remarks are included here. Some comments from fifth-year participants about
their work environments are also included because they shed
light on effective learning situations for independent knowers.

Professors' Attitudes: Treat Students as Equals

Independent knowers appreciated professors and supervisors who treated them as equals, as adults. Marla manifested this attitude in one of her senior classes:

> One teacher is very open-minded. Someone will bring up something, and she'll say, "Oh, I never thought of that," or "that's a good point." Or someone will ask a question, and she'll say, "I don't know." Just honest, no pretenses. She also gives you a blank paper with your multiple-choice test so if you think a question is ambiguous you can explain yourself. She may give partial or full credit. It makes you feel like she cares what I have to say; she thinks that I have a brain. And that I may not put the thing that she wanted me to put, but at least I have my own reason for why I did it.

Sheila expressed her displeasure over not being treated as an equal:

> The one thing that can really upset me these days is being put in the position of a peon. When a professor addresses me as a peon, I lose all respect for the professor. They ask for what students feel about an exam, then tell the students they are wrong. He is just reaffirming his own presence as master of the class. Anybody who's worried about losing control of the classroom, I have a problem with. The best things happen when there is that loss of control, and everybody's just so excited about learning and discussing and getting into it that ideas are bouncing off the walls. It's not somebody saying, "You're ridiculous. You should know what I wanted you to put down. And just listen to me because I know all the answers." That's reprehensible.

Both students valued their independence and wanted the instructor to acknowledge their contributions. Some students felt that they were treated as equals only after graduation. For example, referring to his job setting, Ned said:

> Here I'm an equal; in school, I was definitely not an equal. They didn't really treat me as an equal or as somebody really capable, but as kind of a young, naive person — which may be the case, obviously, since a lot of people are young and naive. But I kind of resent the fact that they somehow were more superior. Now I'm much more motivated to put my best foot forward and really impress somebody in whatever I'm doing because I am on their equal level. Looking back, I was treated like a kid — and some college students are rational, intelligent, mature adults.

Lindsey also commented on being considered an adult on his job. He was surprised that older people asked him questions, something he had never experienced, other than his mom's asking him how to operate the family VCR. These comments imply that treating students as equals or as adults validates their voices and thus enhances their motivation for and confidence in learning and knowing. Students who are treated as adults apparently join the learning endeavor more readily and with greater investment.

Professor-Student Interaction: Establish Genuine Relationships with Students

Independent knowers valued friendships with their instructors or work supervisors. Lindsey described one of his most important experiences in college:

> Getting to know teachers a little bit — you know, becoming friends with teachers and actually keeping tabs on them and talking with them and deal-

ing with them after class one on one, person to person, not student to teacher. That's something that sticks in my head. And I wonder how those people are doing now; I think about them. And I wonder if they think about me.

Dawn liked being on a first-name basis with professors and other students:

> From my standpoint, it makes me feel like I'm an individual, I'm an adult, I'm a responsible person. That adds to your self-confidence and [sense] that I'm not just another student who's another face in the crowd. It's been wonderful for me because it's made me very outgoing. Sometimes it's hard to go to another class where you can't call someone by their first name and you can't talk to them. The intimacy of the way our department is set up, we all know each other. It's just a very comfortable setting.

Ned described his friendship with his boss as making it easier for him to ask for advice and to feel free about what he could say. Thus, open, genuine relationships with professors or supervisors allowed independent learners to join their professors or supervisors as equals in the learning setting.

Teaching Strategies: Connect Learning to Real Life

The teaching strategies preferred by independent knowers centered around connecting and applying learning to the real world. These strategies all entailed active involvement on the part of students. Connection to the real world took place for Sheila in her flight-attendant training experience:

> It's kind of a mental war game. You're in a classroom situation, and everything you do and say is counted for or against you. They weigh you in at

weird hours. It's like boot camp. Utter information
overload. They'd put you in a simulator. And the
simulator rocks, or there's smoke, and you have to
evacuate the plane. I messed up on one, and the
instructor just screamed at me and said, "I hope
you're happy. You just killed thirty people." You
have to be very sure of yourself. I'm much more
steel-willed. My thinking is less theoretical. I have
to think on my feet so much more quickly now. I
can't sit around and go, "Well, how would Dante
consider this?" It's not as philosophically important
what I'm doing, but a lot of times it does have something to do with another person's safety. You learn
to let other people be. I am more willing to see
another person's right to be.

Sheila implied that the stress of this type of training was justified
by the importance of people's safety. Others described less intense experiences, but they also involved interaction with people. Remember Sandra's comments in Chapter Five:

I've learned ten times more in one year of working
than I did in four years of college. Every day I learn
something new about alcoholism or about teenagers
or about people in general. I learn most from patients,
and they don't even know that they're teaching you.

Similarly, Rosa said:

Student teaching was my best experience. You sit
in a classroom and hear what to do with kids. But
when you're actually put in the situation with that
child sitting next to you, that's the best learning experience. You make a thousand decisions a day.
The kids will just have question after question.

Sandra's connection with the teenagers, Rosa's with the children, and Sheila's with her future passengers seemed to play

an important role in the significance of these learning experiences.

Teaching strategies that promoted skills to use in the work
setting were viewed as equally valuable. Evan said:

> The best learning experience was a seminar class,
> which was to come up with a thesis for your major
> and research the thesis and prove it — give an oral
> presentation in front of a panel of students and
> teachers. You submitted a paper after that. I still
> use things from that, research techniques, editing
> techniques, presentation techniques.

Andrew offered a similar perception:

> I think some of the best things were giving presen-
> tations and also writing essays in the sense that col-
> lecting your thoughts and then being able to present
> them to somebody else. Because when you go out
> in the world, they don't ask you multiple-choice type
> questions. They ask you to explain something and
> to justify it and back it up. And you need to be able
> to verbally communicate that information.

For Evan and Andrew and others who described such experiences, it was important not only to learn how to apply skills
later but also to think for yourself in the process. This dimension is also evident in Sheila, Sandra, and Rosa's comments
about making decisions that affect others.

Classroom Structure: Create Opportunities for Independence

Thinking for oneself or independence in the learning process
was the major theme of independent students' needs and preferences in classroom and work environments. Amy appreciated
classes in which she could contribute her own ideas:

> Little things that people had heard from another
> class or things that you personally had read. It

wasn't like the professor knew everything. And I
liked it when the professors were like, "Gosh, I really
don't know that. I'll look it up, or maybe you can
look it up. I can give you a book on that because
I'm not up to date on it." When teachers criticize
students and say, "That's not so," then I felt like,
"Gosh, I'd better not say anything because obviously I don't know anything." But I liked it when
people gave me confidence that I was contributing,
because the teachers were interested in what you
said.

Alice commented on a similar class, about which she said: "I
really got the most out of those classes where they let us take
our own direction a little more." Lindsey's response to this type
of freedom is clear in his comment (portions of which appeared
in Chapter Five):

I'll tell you one class that I had which I thought was
absolutely fantastic. It was an economics seminar.
We read one book every two weeks, all about current topics, things that matter today, that "adults"
talk about at parties. Then we'd write papers on
these books afterwards. This guy was amazing because the way he handled this class was almost like
an honors class. He led us perfectly in conversation. He let us run the class. He told us from day
one, "This class is going to be as boring or as fun
as you make it." I learned more in that class than
any other class. That's strange for me because I'm
the math person and I'm the analytical person that
needs concrete things to work with. Yet everything
in this particular class was learned through discussion and arguments.

The freedom to "run the class" led to a high student involvement that Lindsey valued despite his preference for "concrete
things."

This same theme appeared in remarks about work settings in the fifth-year interviews. Steve, a record store manager, said, "They kind of let you do whatever you want as long as the store's running well and the money's doing well." Regarding his job at a radio station, Phillip said:

> If you don't know how something's going, you've got to figure it out. Sometimes, you may have to use your own wits as opposed to asking somebody. When I was in college, I could ask my prof, "How else can I do this?" And he or she would take the time to let me know how to do things. But when you're out in the world, you're just on your own.

Anne described her best learning experience in her accounting job:

> When they give me projects to work on and I have to dig in and figure them out for myself. Sometimes at first, I'd watch over someone's shoulder, and I'd pick up a few things. But until I actually get in and do something, I don't really understand what's going on as much. My supervisor pretty much stays out of the way, as long as I'm doing what I'm supposed to.

Although Phillip hinted at the value of support when he was in college, these statements suggest that independent knowers like environments where they have the freedom to do things their own way.

Classroom Structure:
Create Opportunities for Critical Thinking

Independent knowers wanted to engage in critical thinking. Tracy described believing what she read until she had teachers who advocated another approach:

The profs say, "Stop and think a minute about this.
Don't just accept everything that we tell you is true.
Critically evaluate this." And I think, as far as that
goes, with other people critically evaluting, then
everybody bringing their thoughts together, it helps
me think of things. Then I have lots of different
viewpoints to look at and choose from.

Amy's history teacher also emphasized critical thinking. Amy
described her like this:

She was a big one on not just spitting out the notes
that she'd talked about in class, but reading other
things and seeing how you could back up what you'd
learned in class with the outside reading by different viewpoints and examples of why this thing happened. She wanted you to understand why everything was happening, what its influence is on the
future. If you got the ideas and the workings, plus
you backed it up with examples that were relevant
to what you were saying, that was the way you were
to get an A.

Chuck encountered classes that encouraged his critical facul-
ties both in college and in law school. He explained:

I'm just more of a critical thinker now. I think you
learn how to look at things critically, especially in
law school, they do that, too. You say, "Is this really
right?" or "Does this really sound good or not?" I
just look at things under a different light than my
friends who didn't go to college. They believe what
they read. I took some poli sci, and I just know that
what you read is not what goes on. I know how to
argue both sides of every issue now, instead of being one-sided. There's always another side to something.

These comments reveal that independent knowers view critical thinking as understanding why things happen, not taking things for granted, and seeing more than one side of an issue. These experiences prompted them to examine further what they were learning, an approach consistent with developing one's own perspective.

Classroom Structure:
Create Opportunities for Peer Collaboration

The focus on freedom to influence the direction of learning and careful scrutiny of ideas provided an important role for peers in the learning process. Independent knowers advocated peer collaboration in the form of mutual assistance and challenge. Sheila emphasized the assistance of other people in her airline training:

> There were fifty of us in the class, and we really pulled together to make it through. There was a sense of community. I think that we all managed to see the good in another person. We saw each other's strengths and weaknesses and helped each other out.

Dawn said of her acting classes:

> We all become an instructor for each other. We work closely together; we know one another; we're all learning at the same level. We take in so much from each other. I admire the opinion of everyone else in my class because I think we all know something, maybe from different aspects and in different areas. You really learn to take criticism. It's healthy because I think we aren't usually exposed to criticism from our peers.

Kurt also emphasized interacting with various classmates and responding to their criticism. He said:

Interactions with peers were important to my learning experience. It's also important to be able to disagree with your peers. And to not be defensive
about that, to be open-minded when somebody disagrees with what you said. It contributes to that
value that you can get—it provides you with a
different perspective that you can take to something.
It also makes me look more into the perspective that
I am taking. My peers are going to ask why, and
you have to come up with those kinds of examples.
When they make me defend my position, then I
have to analyze it more for myself.

Andrew offered a similar perspective:

Senior year, you got a chance to work in groups
more—which now, being out and working, is an
invaluable skill. You do mostly individual [assign-
ments] going through college until senior year. In
group work, what you thought about some of these
things, what you remembered, you'd try to say to
people. People would remember things differently.
And you'd hash out, kind of debate with each other,
what you should be doing. So you formulated your
own opinions and defended them.

For Andrew and Kurt, the challenges of classmates helped them
formulate their own ideas more effectively. Peer collaboration
for independent learners extended beyond the involvement that
transitional knowers advocated to include a genuine exchange
of views.

Evaluation: Allow for Freedom of Expression

Freedom to form and express ideas was paramount for independent knowers in the evaluation of their work. Their preference
for expressing their own opinions is clear in Laura's perspective:

In literature, you could misunderstand the essay but still do well if you developed support for what you said. In most classes, though, I write the professor's perspective. There is a lot of pressure for grades — if I wasn't under the stress of trying to get scholarships or financial aid, I would say whatever I want. You can have your own thoughts and opinions, but that may not be what the teacher wants.

Others described being restricted in expressing their thoughts as promoting memorization and negative feelings about learning. Some, like Monica, described opportunities for self-expression:

In one class, we had a question [for the exam], and you take what you have read and tell the professor what you think. You could disagree with what you had read. Just because it's been published doesn't mean it's right. It's what he thinks. And someone else thought that what he thought was worthy enough to be published. So disagree with it if you can back it up. As long as you have factual evidence and reliable beliefs, then every person is entitled to a personal opinion and viewpoint. It's just being open to a new opinion or perspective.

Alice described this freedom of expression in the evaluation system of her psychopathology course:

We read novels. And then we had to try to diagnose and fit these characters from the novel. We based our papers on that. You really just took your own approach to it. At first, we tried to nail down the prof to "What do you want here?" At the time, it was so frustrating because he wouldn't tell us. But I learned to focus more on quality. He just wanted to see that you were thinking about the material

in original ways and trying to come up with some
reasoning in the papers.

Despite the differences in these students' experiences, they all
valued opportunities to express themselves. In most cases, freedom to voice ideas helped in the struggle to develop personal
perspectives. Phrases like "support what you said," "back it up,"
and "come up with some reasoning" show the beginning of
justifying personal opinions.

Knowledge Discrepancies: Value Contradictory Views

The learning needs and preferences of independent knowers in
every category hinged on the existence of different perspectives.
Unlike transitional students' emphasis on encountering contradictory views, independent knowers stressed acceptance of
contradictory views. As we have seen in the preceding quotes,
these students emphasized the importance of instructors' listening
to students' views, of instructors' avoiding attempts to sway students, of peers' valuing each other's views, of thinking critically
about material and questioning whether to believe it, and of
expressing opinions freely in discussion and evaluation.
     At first glance, the thread that connects the independent
knowers' perspectives seems to be active involvement. However,
because its purpose is different from the involvement described
by transitional knowers, the central element is best described
as independent thinking. Involvement was the major means of
expressing this thinking. Independent knowers collectively conveyed that they had their own perspectives to contribute to their
learning and that of their peers. Other views, from instructors
or peers, were valuable in that they enriched the individual student's ability to create a personal perspective. Despite the emergence of a distinctive voice, independent knowers maintained
the focus on relational learning settings. Close relationships with
professors or supervisors promoted speaking in such a distinctive voice; learning strategies connected to real life and exchanges
with peers helped develop that voice.

Matching Contextual Knowers' Learning Needs

The learning needs of contextual knowers emerged during their senior year or in their graduate school or work environments after graduation. As a result, advice about professors' attitudes, teaching strategies, and class structure are expanded here to include supervisors' attitudes, supervision strategies, and job structure.

Attitudes and Interactions: Engage in Colleagial Relationships with Students

Contextual learners emphasized colleagial relationships with professors and supervisors. Deirdre described a class that she had as a senior in which this type of relationship occurred:

> There were only four of us in comparative literature. The lecture actually was kind of divided among the five of us. The teacher would listen, and we just kind of all interacted. There wasn't a real teacher-student relationship there. That was really, really weird. It was a good class.

Deirdre described the students' relationship with one of her graduate instructors similarly:

> There's a respect between the student and the teacher. We're not treated like kids; we don't act like kids. We're all adults in there. And there's a kind of respect and listening to each other, and it's less master-slave.

She described this experience as inspiring interest and making learning "worthwhile and interesting and relevant."

Jim also developed a colleagial relationship with one of his professors as a senior. He described how it occurred:

> He was always, "Why don't you come in and talk to me?" I started stopping in to see him first semester

senior year. We really developed a friendship. It
was no longer a teacher-student thing; it was a Dave
and Jim type thing. We still keep in touch. I think
that was real important for me as far as developing as a person. He was able to contribute a lot of
experiences that I hadn't experienced yet. He showed
me how he evaluated job opportunities, and we
went over evaluating my job options.

For some, colleagial relationships often meant the support to take risks. Jim appreciated his chief executive officer in
his job after graduation for this reason:

The previous CEO left no room for mistakes. You
had to be perfect. That's why things were so slow,
because everybody wanted to make sure they did
everything perfectly. Then this CEO said right out
the first day, "Look, if you don't make one mistake
a week, you're not working hard enough." He is
very open to what we think and the whole idea of
participative management. Basically, you've got the
freedom to do whatever you want.

Reginald found the support to take chances in one of his senior
classes. He described the effect on the papers he wrote:

If you had the knowledge that they're going to let
you do it again or at least clear up your ideas and
make it so it's readable, it was much more of a relief,
and you can really maybe take—I was going to
say—take some risks. It is a risk to do those papers.
And to struggle with what you believe rather than
regurgitate what had been said out of concern for
the grade.

Support to take chances and relationships in which students or
employees felt like partners in learning and working provided
the freedom that contextual knowers preferred. Although in-

dependent learners also described wanting to be treated like adults, colleagial relationships for contextual knowers extended beyond an attitude to concrete interactions in which the distinction between teacher and student was diminished.

Teaching/Supervision Strategies:
Create Opportunities for Mutual Responsibility

The liberty to express themselves and pursue their own interests were the major preferences that contextual knowers demonstrated in comments on teaching and supervisory strategies. Deirdre encountered these opportunities in undergraduate classes for teacher certification. She said:

> I've got papers and a lot of journal writing, but it's much more of academic and interpersonal interspersed in the writing. That's what makes it so relevant — sort of brings everything together and makes the learning experience that much more powerful. You're finally given an audience to listen to how you feel and kind of legitimize it, just finding a voice and kind of exploring how you got to where you are. That's a lot of what the writing is about.

In her job after graduation, Adrian was able to learn anything she wanted to pursue. But she wished that these opportunities had been available in college:

> In college, there's always some paper that needs to be written and some chapter that has to be read and some tests that have to be taken. I don't think you get a chance to stop and think, "What would I really like to learn about this subject that's either not being presented in class, or just more information that [I] would like to learn."

For both Deirdre and Adrian, having their voices legitimized enhanced their ability to develop their own thinking. The same was true for Mark, who described what he felt was effective:

> Independent study projects that let you go at your
> own pace and study what you want to study. Work-
> ing directly with a mentor or independent study
> groups, even of students who will get together and
> talk about issues they're interested in without a
> professor even being there. Once you've tasted
> academia at its best, as far as doing what you want
> to do, you can't go back to any kind of forced model.

Reginald agreed, quoting his seminar professors as saying, "This
is your education. Go for it." He noted that their perspective
resulted in meaningful dialogue in the class.

Freedom went beyond self-expression, however, for contextual knowers. They also had opportunities to take responsibility for their thoughts or their work. Lowell and his classmates
in a graduate class took responsibility for class discussion:

> The professor acts as referee, and we kind of throw
> arguments back and forth at each other. He'll sum-
> marize things and say, "Okay, here's this, this, and
> this," or he'll tell us a fact that he's seen because
> he's worked so closely with it. And then we discuss
> it and say, "Well, you know that's wrong," or "They
> shouldn't have done that."

One of Barry's undergraduate classes was organized in a similar fashion:

> I had one class that really did pick your brain. I
> had a media law class that was really good. He'd
> say, "Always read the chapter before. I expect you
> should know that material. You're all seniors; you
> should know how to read and comprehend the ma-
> terial. Then we'll just talk about it and give it ap-
> plication." So that's what we did in class.

More opportunities to take responsibility were evident
in work environments during the fifth year. Gwen (see also
Chapter Two) initially described her job this way:

> It's kind of a downer because you start off learning
> a lot of—it's the insurance business and it's high-
> risk insurance. They like for you to become very
> technically proficient. It's interesting at first, but
> it gets to be a grind. They told me I would do that
> for six months. I had been there six weeks, and I
> thought, "You are joking."

As we saw earlier, Gwen subsequently complained about the
training program and sought additional responsibility that eventually resulted in her being promoted early. Adrian had a similar experience:

> I did a project that had to do with billings. My su-
> pervisor told me, "That's what I need to know. Do
> it any way you can." That's what I think is won-
> derful about the job. You can go as far as you want
> and take on as much responsibility as you want.

Jim, who commented on the openness of his CEO, also found
that though he had the freedom to set goals for his department,
he had to make sure that they were reasonable. Thus, classroom and work settings that offered contextual knowers opportunities to direct and take responsibility enhanced their learning and their contextual thinking.

Teaching/Supervision Strategies: Look at the Big Picture

Some contextual knowers commented on one additional issue
in teaching strategies. They felt that college lacked a focus on
what they called the "big picture." Mark said that there were
not enough broad issues addressed in college, such as spiritual
or "huge philosophical" questions that he felt he would have to
confront in his life. He complained, "I have no tools whatsoever
to leap at all into any kind of religious philosophy; I think that's
a serious lapse in my education." Jim's version of the big picture related to interdependency in the work world. He said:

> There's not enough group interaction [in college].
> I mean, like my job right now, I am so dependent

on everybody in my organization. I think colleges
often force you into, "This is an individual, and
your grades are individual. Everything you do is
individual." And it's not. I mean, our world is such
an interactive place. You're so interdependent on
each other.

Classroom/Job Structure: Create Opportunities for Interdependency

The encouragement of interdependency was also preferred in
classes or jobs. The experiences that contextual learners valued
most centered around good interaction with their classmates and
co-workers. Gwen explained that her national issues forum class
provided this interactive component:

> The class was case-study groups. We had two or
> three lectures. But we had presentations of all these
> groups and then discussion of it and went on to the
> next issue and had a presentation and then a dis-
> cussion. So it was very interactive. Not only were
> you working with the people in your individual
> group on your given topic, but [you were] also try-
> ing to formulate some feedback on others. At the
> end, we had to put together a complete report on
> it all. This was a class where people took these
> things rather seriously, and that was just kind of
> the unspoken expectation.

As if she anticipated the question in my mind, Gwen added,
"How you establish things like that, though, I really don't know."
She did offer a suggestion, though, in relation to an advanced
creative-writing seminar that she enjoyed:

> It was critiques and feedback by your peers, your
> fellow writers, so to speak. For people who take it
> as seriously as we all did, it was really a commu-
> nity, I suppose you could say. We felt like it was

us, you know—*we* were the writers. I think the tone
is largely set by an instructor who really and truly
thinks the world of his subject matter and is on fire
to teach it to people who are interested.

Thus, though the instructor set the tone, the interactions of a
community of peers gave the class merit. Jim had a similar view
of his management class, which he described as one of his best
college experiences because it required that students work together. He said, "There were a lot of people that were C students or even low B students who really came alive in that class
because it was a chance for freedom." The class involved a group
project in which the instructor played a minimal role. Lowell
had a similar experience:

> We had one or two introductory lectures, and then
> we were set free and did a lot of reading. From all
> the reading, we only wrote a paper of about twenty-
> five pages each. Then we put together a final paper
> as a group. It was a group paper. We all had to
> do different parts of it. And then that was the in-
> teraction between the fifteen group members. And
> then we subdivided ourselves and so on. But we
> still had to kind of keep in contact with each other
> and have meetings so we were all in the same vein.
> I enjoyed it a lot more than individual papers, be-
> lieve it or not. It was kind of fun to do something
> different, and I think I learned a lot more about
> the subject in addition to skills that I can use now
> and in the future.

These interactive experiences were often labeled teamwork or
collaboration. Adrian credited projects that received group
grades in her senior year for preparing her for her work role.
In her company, teamwork entailed thinking about what was
best for the client and relying on co-workers for help. Lowell
enjoyed the collaborative atmosphere of his graduate classes and
suggested that it resulted in a focus on learning, rather than

grades. Remember that Mark felt that the absence of grades in law school also contributed to collaboration:

> There're no grades, basically. There's no class rank ever computed, and no GPA ever computed. No grades basically. You're dealing with hypercompetitive people. The grading system encourages people to work together and not be selfish about note sharing or helping with projects.

Thus, interdependency was valued as a means to learn from each other in a variety of settings.

These accounts of contextual knowers' experiences reveal two key elements: freedom and interdependency. Colleagial relationships with professors or supervisors yielded freedom to pursue their interests and express themselves and the support to do so even when risk was involved. Students or employees felt more like partners in the process than apprentices, a circumstance that allowed them to contribute in a meaningful way. The strategies used by teachers and supervisors also reflect these two key elements. Courses and assignments that promoted free expression were preferable and also contained opportunities to judge perspectives. Deirdre's comments on figuring out how she got to a particular perspective and Lowell's explanation of how his class judged the topics that they discussed reveal that self-expression is not free of judgment. Ideas about work environments also contained this notion in the form of responsibility. Although interdependency was the main preference in class or job structure, the comments there also reveal a desire for a combination of freedom and interdependency. Interdependent peer relationships encouraged free expression in the form of ideas or feedback. As individuals seriously engaged in this process, they became interdependent on each other's thoughts. The contextual knowers' preferences combined a focus on the individual (freedom to express one's voice, pursue one's interests, take responsibility) with relational (interdependency) approaches.

Summary

Students' academic and, in some cases, professional work experiences offer useful advice regarding how educators can confirm various students' learning needs and preferences. Most of this advice centers on relational learning settings, although *relational* takes on meanings that vary according to ways of knowing. As these increase in complexity, confirmation takes on qualitatively different characteristics.

Confirmation for absolute knowers depends on the professor's behavior. These students are confirmed by the helping attitudes of teachers and by opportunities to get to know them. Further benefit comes from professors who do demonstrations in class, entertain questions, and provide opportunities for students to get to know each other. Making clear what is expected in evaluation also assisted these learners. Thus, for this group, instructors were the key element in learning, because their attitudes, teaching strategies, interactions with students, classroom structures, and evaluation methods all determined the success of student learning.

Confirmation for transitional knowers relied on a combination of professorial behavior and student involvement. Professors who related to students, cared about them, and engaged in positive interactions with them assisted learning. However, more emphasis was placed on involvement. The individual student's own involvement, as well as that of peers, was aimed at understanding. The views of peers were therefore regarded as helpful new ways to think about material. Evaluation formats that promoted thinking and understanding, rather than memorization, were also successful.

Independent knowers found confirmation through independence. They preferred genuine relationships with professors who treated them like adults. They enjoyed opportunities to learn independently, think critically, and collaborate in interactions with peers. The exchange of views with all parties to the learning task was viewed as key to thinking for themselves and helping each other. In addition, freedom of expression was important in evaluation and the acceptance of contradictory views. Exploring how learning would connect to their actual life experience also provided confirmation for independent knowers.

Contextual knowers found confirmation through interdependence. They still preferred freedom to express themselves and support to take risks but added the element of judging perspectives. The notion of responsibility changed the sense of freedom to an interdependency among peers in class or on the job. Colleagial relationships with professors or work supervisors also represented interdependency.

The stories in this chapter clearly reveal the importance of confirmation in heightening students' interest in learning, strengthening their investment in that process, creating comfortable learning atmospheres, and developing relationships that foster understanding. However, this advice must still be considered in light of two dilemmas. The first is that most classroom settings are occupied by students with a variety of intellectual approaches. Thus, what works for one group may not help another. Second, achieving complete confirmation is not entirely desirable if we agree that growth requires a balance of confirmation and contradiction. Sheila's comment at the outset of this chapter shows the danger of too much confirmation. The next chapter explores a balance of confirmation and contradiction by defining principles that promote development of students' own voice in all four ways of knowing.

Chapter Nine

Developing Students
in the Classroom

I got a little more confident of myself as having a valid point
of view. And I saw professors and I guess what I'll call
professional grown-ups, people over age twenty-five, as not
being the invincible, always-right people. And started questioning, being a little bit more of a critical thinker.

— Ned

The advice in the previous chapter is aimed at matching ways
of knowing with teaching strategies that build connection with
students. This connection furthers educators' understanding of
students' frames of reference and confirms students' ways of
knowing. Confirmation sets the stage for students to participate
in learning and to become creators of knowledge, rather than
recipients of it. Boyer's (1987) comment on the undergraduate
experience is relevant here: "The undergraduate experience, at
its best, means active learning and disciplined inquiry that leads
to the intellectual empowerment of students" (p. 151). The ways
of knowing and gender-related patterns described in this book
suggest that ongoing confirmation is necessary for students to
participate in active learning and to become intellectually em-
powered. Intellectual empowerment, from the standpoint of ways
of knowing, translates into students' developing a voice, or in
Ned's words, not viewing authorities as "invincible, always-right"
people.

Yet confirmation alone is insufficient for promoting the development of voice. That requires contradicting some ways of knowing, first, to help the student voice emerge and, later, to assist learners in developing their voice and making reasoned judgments about what to believe. Too much confirmation would result in what Piaget (1932) called "assimilation," or forcing new experiences into current ways of knowing. Assimilation leaves the current process intact. Equilibrium between confirmation and contradiction is necessary to prompt what Piaget called "accommodation," or adjusting one's way of knowing to account for new experience. Continuity is necessary to help students through the transitions as they reevaluate and alter their intellectual approaches.

This balance can perhaps be achieved using three principles that underlie the specifics of practice in a given context. These can be used to generate specific strategies within particular contexts — what Cross (1990) calls "classroom research." On the basis of the students' stories, I have identified these principles as validating the student as a knower, situating learning in the students' own experience, and defining learning as jointly constructing meaning. Defining learning in such a way automatically joins educators and students. Situating learning in students' own experience also connects them to the process. Validating students as knowers stems from the other two principles and takes different forms depending on the situation. The interaction between student and educator that comes from using all three approaches allows the educator to assess what confirmation and contradiction the student already experiences to determine what else needs to be offered to balance the two.

These three principles stand in stark contrast to the more traditional underlying assumptions in education: individualistic learning, student subordination, and objectification of knowledge. Gray (1989) calls our attention to these assumptions in this comment: "Picture a typical classroom in our educational system. There are row upon row of separated desks, lined up in order and facing an open space filled with one desk or one speaker's podium. What are the unspoken assumptions that lie behind this arrangement of furniture for the learning process?"

(p. 335). Of course, the arrangement of the furniture is merely a symbol of the assumptions or values that guide educational practice. Gray defines the unspoken assumptions in her response to her question:

> Clearly, it is because we conceptualize an education as a solitary and autonomous experience. To sit down as a first-grader at a separated desk in one of our school systems is as solitary an experience as for a runner in a track event to put his or her feet in the blocks and take [his or her] mark. We are to start running our own course, start learning our letters and math by ourselves, start competing with others for grades, start racing all the others to gain prizes and scholarships and, ultimately, better jobs in the real world that come after the educational world, the real world of adulthood. . . . Academic courses, and the educational curriculum as a whole, are highly individualistic, each student is to be alone and autonomous, and all are to be competitive from the time we sit down at that first separated desk [1989, p. 336].

Gray's depiction of education does not support the relational version of learning espoused by the students in this study. Encouraging relational learning that does not emphasize individualism at the expense of connection with others requires more than rearranging the furniture. It requires rethinking our assumptions about the educational process.

Our ideas about education are so ingrained in our own experiences and ways of knowing that not only are they unspoken, as Gray suggests, but they are also often unconscious. A few years ago, I would have xeroxed Gray's statements and sent them to my department chair to bolster my protests about the rooms available for my graduate classes. I would have argued that the placement of the furniture was the final impediment to an interactive environment; I already used small-group techniques, was on a first-name basis with students, and solicited student input regarding class assignments. I viewed my approach as particularly progressive in light of the admonishment I had received from a few colleagues that I was not properly asserting my authority with students. Yet reflection on my own teaching throughout the years of interviews has made it clear that my assumptions were no different from those of the colleagues whose criticism I disdained. Although my interpersonal style increased comfort in my classroom, I still valued my voice over that of my students, my judgment about the best content over my students' experiences, and my ability to make meaning over my students' less experienced learning perspectives. I have come to understand my students' perception of classroom openness in relation to their socialization in Gray's "culture of separated desks."

Rearranging these long-held assumptions about education is crucial in light of the data provided by the students in this study. Their experiences, particularly those that promoted more complex thinking, confirm Palmer's (1987) claim that learning is a relational activity. Even the students who might be expected to benefit from the individualistic approach — the mastery-, impersonal-, and individual-pattern knowers — spoke of the value of relational components in learning. Those components were a central focus for receiving, interpersonal, and interindividual knowers. Both the individual and relational themes were important to contextual learners, those who exhibited the kind of intellectual processes that education attempts to foster. Thus, rearranging our assumptions begins with broadening our view of education to encompass the development of the individual voice within a relational learning community. Boyer (1987) underscored this combination by saying that though competition was necessary for stimulating achievement, cooperation was just as essential and should be incorporated into classroom settings. In this chapter, students' insights are combined with those of educators to offer suggestions for designing practice consistent with these principles. Despite the considerable overlap among these three principles, I have separated them here for the ease of discussion. I also refer to student stories in Chapter Eight rather than repeating them here.

Validating Students as Knowers

I, as a freshman, am still learning how to learn in
college course work, and therefore do not feel that
I could be handing out advice to anyone on this
subject matter.

                                                    — Kyle

Kyle's response to the question about advice on how to learn
in college clearly reveals that he does not regard himself as an
expert on this topic. Neither he, nor his peers who are absolute
knowers, believe that he is equipped to assess course content.
The student voice story line summarized in Chapter Seven finds
no individual perspectives in the beginning, because verbal and
written expressions are echoes of the voice of authority. When
knowledge is the property of authorities, students can only obtain and repeat it. Those students do not begin to view themselves as knowers until the learning environment implies or states
directly that they have something of value to say. As uncertainty
arises in transitional knowing, the beginnings of a student voice
appear, particularly for interpersonal learners. However, they
attach this voice to personal, rather than to academic, understanding. A genuine, individually authored voice did not appear until the independent-knowing phase. Failure to validate
the student reinforces absolute and transitional ways of knowing.
    Promoting complex thinking entails promoting the de-
velopment of voice. Complex forms of thinking, such as independent or contextual knowing, require that students develop their
own voices and ideas based on evidence within a context. Students' naming their experience generates possibilities for learning and knowing. The challenge to educators, then, is to convey to learners that their voices are valuable and that expressing
them will help them to mature. Creating this atmosphere requires a delicate balance of Kegan's (1982) functions of confirmation, contradiction, and continuity. The student voice, fragile
in the beginning, needs confirmation, both for its emergence
and development. However, it often needs contradiction in order
for the student to consider other ideas. If contradiction over-

whelms confirmation, the voice will be silenced. Continuity is also necessary for the transitions that result from the optimum balance of confirmation and contradiction. I want to argue here that validation of the student should begin during absolute knowing rather than waiting for the student voice to emerge somehow.

As the story lines in Chapter Seven indicate, student voice develops as the omnipotent power of authorities dissipates. Validating student voice can be achieved through confirming student voice and deflating the sense that authorities are all-knowing. The themes of caring attitudes and assistance from professors show how building student voice and decreasing that of authorities can be accomplished. Recall the student stories about their academic experiences in Chapter Eight. Absolute knowers described caring instructors as those who "don't seem against you" and who will "go the extra mile for you." Transitional learners described the effects of concerned professors: "it makes them more human" and "the level of respect helps me bring in more of my own ideas." Descriptions of interactions with professors centered around similar themes. The students appreciated professors who actually helped them and those who did not hold themselves "higher than the students," and they liked getting to know professors. The kind of help that these students described was routine: answering questions, having office hours, being receptive, and scheduling occasional help sessions. These responses suggest that professors do not need to spend more time with students; what is required is a concerned attitude. This caring attitude offers confirmation of students and their ideas and gives them a chance to know the professor better. Increasing recognition of the teachers' humanness contradicts the notion that they and their knowledge are beyond the reach of students.

The students' stories confirm Noddings's (1991) idea of the importance of concern in the teaching relationship. Noddings portrays the caring teacher as one who receives not only what students say but the students themselves. Starting with respect for the students' interests, caring teachers make themselves present to the student. Although they maintain their own ideals, the concerned teacher recognizes the student's choice of what

is significant. Noddings concurs that it is the quality of the encounter that is important: "The time interval may be brief but
the encounter is total" (p. 180).

The contradiction of professors as omnipotent authorities
is necessary in more direct forms as well. Students' stories about
teaching strategies and class atmosphere offer examples of how
this contradiction can occur. Gwen described in Chapter Two
how one of her professors said, "I reject this role as professor."
Gwen noted that beginning in her junior year, professors began teaching differently: "[before] they'd tell you what to think
as opposed to now, when they say, 'What do you think?' And
you [say to yourself], 'Oh, I'd better think of something.'" Gwen
also advocated instructors who "get to know you on your level
rather than trying to set up the hierarchical structure." Asked
how this approach affected her, she offered:

> The student is less intimidated. And although you
> know that your experience and your background
> and your knowledge of the subject are not what your
> instructor's are, you still feel that your opinions and
> your ideas are valid.

These teaching strategies enabled Gwen to feel that her ideas
were worthwhile despite her awareness that her instructor had
greater expertise. Mark reported a similar experience. One of
his teachers in a sophomore class stayed out of the discussion
unless the students got way out of line. Mark liked this technique because the students could learn from each other's perspectives.

Opportunities actually to challenge the professor's views
in class also contributed to recognizing student voice while mut-
ing that of authority. Tracy (Chapter Eight) described a professor
who encouraged students to critique theory. She said that it was
comfortable because he was down to earth and rewarded them
for challenging him. She described being intimidated initially
because "you're conditioned to accept the teacher's view." Apparently, his down-to-earth style and the rewards were sufficient
to balance confirmation and contradiction. Kris (Chapter Four)

described a similar situation in which she and a group of her friends would discuss what the professor said among themselves. As you may recall, she reported that the professor was receptive to their comments, listening and allowing them to express themselves. Kris stated, "Sometimes they would reconsider and say that might be an alternative. Sometimes they would just prove us wrong."

The value of these students' ideas was clearly acknowledged. The emphasis placed on student opinions made it clear that the professors did not feel that they held absolute knowledge; the expertise that they did possess was also placed in a perspective. The professors listened to students, praised them for their contributions, and continued to offer their point of view when the students' ideas needed contradiction. These professors used their authority to help their students further develop their own perspectives. Belenky, Clinchy, Goldberger, and Tarule (1986) called this "midwife teaching." As they describe it, it involves aiding the emergence of student voice, preserving the "fragile newborn thoughts" (p. 218), and supporting the evolution of thinking. It focuses on the students' knowledge rather than that of the teacher. Being careful to balance confirmation and contradiction, the teacher introduces her or his knowledge in the context of the students' evolving thinking. Romer and Whipple (1991) label this same process a "dialogue of authority" (p. 69). They suggest that this collaboration requires that teachers silence or temporarily suspend their authority to solicit and absorb that of students. This suspension is necessary to overcome the power automatically granted to the teacher and to set the stage for true collaboration in which both teacher and student are learners.

Validation of student voice is probably most difficult to achieve in evaluating students' work. Objective testing and right-wrong answers reinforce the omnipotence of authorities and the students' echo voice. However, some participants told stories that indicate how these evaluation methods can affirm student voice. Valerie gave an example:

> I had a class last semester, business law, and we
> had multiple-choice exams. But if we chose an an-

swer and we thought that another answer might be right also, we got to explain why we thought it was that answer, which I think really helped a lot. If two answers seem really alike to you, but you can explain the difference between them or explain why you think this one is more the right answer than the other one, I think that's a lot better. Rather than "Okay, I chose *a,* but the answer was *b.* So my answer was completely wrong." Whereas you might think your answer was not completely wrong.

In this case, the value of the students' perspective was recognized in the opportunity to explain a response and it was given consideration in evaluation. However, kinds of assessment that offer greater opportunities to express opinions and obtain feedback are probably preferable to the multiple-choice exams described by Valerie. As a sophomore, Marge reported that she liked essays "where I can voice my opinion and see what the teacher thinks about what I'm thinking." Sidney described essays as furthering his learning because he could explain what he did and understand everything even if he did not arrive at the answer that the teacher was looking for. Kris described turning in a journal on which the teacher would write extensive comments. She said, "Some were critical and offered things to think about, and some were praise." Again, the instructor was balancing confirmation and contradiction.

Some instructors also encouraged students to express their own opinion in tests and papers even if it disagreed with that of the instructor. Recall Monica's comment in Chapter Eight about telling her professor what she thought. She commented, "Just because it's been published doesn't mean it's right." As her instructor expected students to say what they thought, she concluded that "as long as you have factual evidence and reliable beliefs, then every person is entitled to a personal opinion and viewpoint." I doubt that Monica would have come to this conclusion (that what is published is just what one person believes) unless her professors had confirmed that she, too, could have a worthy opinion if it was properly supported.

Teachers' weighing of opinions must be done with care.

If the contradiction outweighs the confirmation, the student's voice is stifled instead of affirmed. Remember Deirdre, who said, "I don't risk anything in class, because he challenges everything I say." As you may recall from her more detailed comments in Chapter Six, she was describing a professor who did not respect her perspective. Deirdre was silenced by her professor's response to a journal entry in which she was "trying to really grapple with" how she perceived Homer's feelings about Achilles. She said: "He had underlined everything, and he just made some comment almost teasing me, like, 'Oh, are you some feminist?,' or something like that. I didn't write anything anymore after that." Deirdre refused to value her teacher's challenges until he first listened to what she had to say. She thus lost the opportunity to work out her own perspective from the class experience. This story illustrates the care that professors must show to support fragile student voices.

Finally, knowers grow more self-confident as they increasingly view knowledge as uncertain. This fact suggests that introducing knowledge discrepancies is another way to contradict the omnipotence of authority and create occasions for the use of student voice. Most absolute knowers did not encounter such knowledge discrepancies. Only one described two teachers who held different views about economics; he felt that the contradictory views helped him see both sides. He thought this was good experience, even though he did not know how to decide between the alternatives. Transitional knowers had more experience with contradictory views. Kris (Chapter Eight) noted that her professor pointed out biases in articles, and pushed the students to be more critical. These experiences were commonplace for independent and contextual knowers. Thus, discussing biases and contradictory views helps students see learning knowledge as more open to their participation. Clarifying that the information presented comes from a particular perspective and is generated by other human beings is essential for students to begin to see themselves as capable of forming their own perspectives.

Situating Learning in the Students' Own Experience

In school, you kind of leave your personal life and your personal experiences out of what you do aca-

demically. And everything's supposed to be kind
of detached and formal. In the journal, you didn't
pay any attention to what you were writing. I think
any time you can learn about something and then
somehow relate it to your personal life or some kind
of experience that you've had, it doubles — it makes
the experience stronger.

— Deirdre

Deirdre's comments (repeated from Chapter Five) illustrate the
most powerful learning situations reported by the students in
this study: those that related to their own experience. Mark
described it as engaging the material, which occurred for him
when "it resonates with your personal history." This approach
recognized students as people who bring their personal lives to
the classroom, appreciates their feelings about learning, and incorporates their actual experiences into the process. Bruner
(1986) describes this recognition of students as people with a
story about one of his teachers, who shared with her class her
sense of wonder that water freezes into ice. In inviting her students to wonder with her, she became, in Bruner's terms, "a
human event, not a transmission device" (p. 126). In the students' stories, the most common example of the instructor's importance as a "human event" was in an enormous communica-
tions class taken by numerous participants. Barry put it best:

It's 298 people. But he does make it — I've never seen
Frank Sinatra, but I've heard that Frank Sinatra
in a huge stadium with a huge audience can make
you feel very personal, like in a small bar. I think
it's the same thing with Dr. Glover. He makes it
seem like it's a much smaller class because he just
is so personal. It's just unbelievable how active he
is. He moves around a lot, walking up and down
the aisles. You know that he wants people to come
to class. He cares about students.

Others described the personal nature of this instructor as due
to his coming to class early to talk to students. He often asked

those who needed a ride home for the weekend to raise their hands, then asked others going to those locations to raise their hands if they could take a passenger. The students appreciated this instructor's recognition of their everyday lives. Barry offered another example of Dr. Glover's understanding:

> We just had a test, and he talked about cheating. He said, "You know, I really don't blame a lot of people because there's so much pressure, it's that three-point [average], and you have to get a job." He's just like, "I'll ask people to cover their papers." That was a much better attitude than "I'm going to nail you." He says you're going to hurt yourself. He looks at the students' side because a lot of times the temptation is there. He realizes that. He cares.

Despite its size, which necessitated a lecture format, students felt that the class was personal, that Dr. Glover was a human event, because he resonated with their lives. He made the class less detached, less formal, and more related to them, even though its academic content was not necessarily connected to their experience. Another professor was often mentioned as having a human approach because he brought his children to his psychology class to demonstrate physical growth. The students enjoyed the reality of the demonstration but placed even more importance on viewing him as a father rather than just a teacher.

Making learning more central to the experience of students avoids marginalizing them. Students feel marginalized when they cannot identify with the core experiences of a particular learning setting. For example, using "he" as generic aids men in visualizing the idea at hand but causes women to "blank out" because the imagery does not apply to them (Thorne, 1989). Using the experience of a particular race or class group as the norm in teaching, a practice that Weiler (1988) suggests stems from the teacher's own experience, helps those of that race or class group but alienates the others. Marginalized students become silent and invisible; as Thorne describes it, they feel not quite at home, anxious, and full of self-doubt. For example,

Chuck recounted in Chapter Five that he was comfortable learning from his mistakes in discussions at law classes. However, he noted that the women in the class never spoke. When he inquired why, they told him that they did not want to speak, and he concluded that they were uncomfortable with the participation format. He was probably correct; it is likely that though he could identify with this approach, they could not — another example of contradiction outweighing confirmation.

Even students who do not yet view themselves as knowers value connection. The absolute students' comments noted earlier in Chapter Eight demonstrate this fact. Amy wanted to do things, rather than just write down what the teacher said; Eileen liked her theater teacher because she tried to include people; Valerie preferred teachers who gave more analogies than just definitions; Terry wanted lecturers to get the class involved, even by asking questions. This "activity" focus and the personal and caring approach discussed earlier are important ways of connecting students with learning.

The development of student voice seems, however, to require a connection to students' actual experience. Recall Art's suggestion (Chapter Eight) that chemistry was hard to understand "without ties to the real world." Art identified better with the material when it was couched in experiences he related to: hair curling or red meat. When class subjects were relevant to students' own lives, they felt more able to become part of the learning process. Adrian told us in Chapter Four about the effect of having had an experience to which a class topic was relevant. A student from Webster Grove happened to be in her class when they watched a movie about it. She valued the Webster Grove student's perspective, which she felt increased the entire class's understanding. The freedom that student enjoyed to tell about his or her home town affirmed all the students. This "narrative mode of knowing," as Bruner would call it, leads to "good stories, gripping drama, believable (though not necessarily 'true') historical accounts" (1986, p. 13). Withrell and Noddings (1991) believe that personal narratives like the one of the Webster Grove student help students "penetrate cultural barriers, discover the power of the self and the integrity of the other, and deepen their understanding of their respective histories and possibilities" (p. 4). These outcomes are evident in Alice's comments (Chapter 4) about her class on rural America. A student from Japan added useful insights, and Alice found herself explaining away stereotypes about small towns. Alice gained insight into Japanese culture and big cities from other students who talked about their experiences in those settings. She valued their points of view (which offered her contradiction), yet acknowledged the contribution she could make (confirmation) as she enlightened them about her life in a small town. Sharing stories may therefore have another consequence: the development of student voice.

Tappan and Brown (1991) suggest that telling their own stories enhances students' moral development. They state: "By representing the cognitive, affective, and conative dimensions of their own moral experience through narrative, students will therefore be encouraged to reflect on their own experience from the standpoint of their own moral perspective. This will lead to not only an increased sense of authority and authorization on behalf of that perspective but also an increased sense of responsibility for action" (p. 184). The student stories in this study seem to corroborate Brown and Tappan's belief and also imply that it applies to intellectual development. Consider the story that Kris told in Chapter Four. She described "listening to other students contribute their ideas and putting in my own inputs" as making her think more. As she and her classmates considered the material, they reflected upon how it related to them and considered actions. Thus, she illustrates the cognitive (what they thought), affective (what they felt), and conative (what they would do) functions that Tappan and Brown identify. Kris later commented that this process prompted "internalizing and making this stuff my own," a comment that reflects the creation of her own perspective.

Telling one's story does not have to be a verbal exercise. In Chapter Eight, Deirdre offered a striking account of how telling her story via journal writing aided authorship. Some of those comments and some additional ones are quoted here:

> I liked writing a journal a lot. I could be a lot more personal and writing about things that really were

foremost in my mind. I kind of got them out of my head and dealt with. I could look at things a little more objectively and kind of know better where I stood or how I felt about something. I've got papers and a lot of journal writing, but it's much more of academic and interpersonal interspersed in the writing. That's what makes it so relevant — sort of brings everything together and makes the learning experience that much more powerful. You're finally given an audience to listen to how you feel and kind of legitimize it, just finding a voice and kind of exploring how you got to where you are.

Getting her most prominent thoughts on paper helped her to deal with them, to know better where she stood. Having an audience to listen and legitimize her feelings enabled her to find a voice. Expressing that voice then led to the ability to reflect upon it. Deirdre's experience supports Cooper's (1991) contention that we develop our own voice in the process of telling our stories to organize our experience. It also underscores the power of confirmation.

Deirdre's story, moreover, clarifies that the technique of journal writing alone does not automatically lead to the development of voice. Recounting a journal-writing experience in another class, she made these comments:

We keep a journal, but it's so structured. We've got to pay special attention to mechanics; he takes off for spelling errors. We've got to write our spelling words twenty times if we get them wrong. Things that I did in fourth grade, you know. We're supposed to take something that he says and respond to it, which is kind of limiting. It's like you don't really get to write about how you're feeling about what you read or what he's saying. It's just frustrating. I feel so — my sentences are like dut, dut, dut.

In this instance, she had no audience. The requirement to respond to what the instructor said was limiting — perhaps marginalizing—in that she could not incorporate her own experiences in her response. Her sentences became mechanical because she could not write about how she felt and because of the focus on correct spelling. This, by the way, was the same instructor whose comment "Oh, are you some feminist?" silenced Deirdre. This example of journal writing obviously did not situate learning in the student's experience or validate her perspective.

Yet effective use of storytelling does not require that students have a ready-made contribution (like the students from Webster Grove or Japan). In many instances, students benefited from opportunities to engage in an experience that also gave them the chance to develop their own stories or perspectives. Rosa's example about student teaching and Sandra's experience with teenage alcoholics (both in Chapter Eight) demonstrate that connection to others and to the experience make learning more powerful. The same was true for classes that created real-life environments. Perhaps the most prevalent example was participation in Laws Hall, a four-credit interdisciplinary course in which students develop promotional advertising campaigns for real corporate clients. Megan's perception of the experience was typical of the many students who participated in Laws Hall. She said:

Laws Hall and Associates was probably the best learning experience that I had in the four years I was at college. Just because we were given a practical case, and it seemed like a real-life experience. We were judged by peer evaluation. It seemed more like a work-type atmosphere. You really had a sense of loyalty to the project and wanted to put a lot of time and energy into it. We lived and breathed Laws Hall for a whole semester. It was great. We followed the philosophy that you have to have research to back everything up. Our client gave us a lot of research. But we tried to do our research and see if it supported what their research said because we didn't want to just go on what they had.

We did telephone surveys and tons of library research. And we let our research speak for itself when
it came right down to actually planning the strategy.

Megan's comments make it clear that the real-life nature of the
experience was important, as was peer evaluation (a topic we
will turn to later in the chapter). Active involvement in collecting research data gave Megan's team a basis upon which to plan
their advertising strategy. Her story implies that the team was
able to develop their own strategy because it grew from their
experience collecting data. She also talked about debate among
team members over what to do, which they resolved by returning to their data. Thus, they often experienced contradiction
of their views as well. Other students reported similar outcomes
from projects incorporated into classes. For example, Deirdre
said:

In multicultural education, we have group projects
where we actually go into a community, which has
us really working—I mean, directly related to something in your life. You go in, and you have these
talks with just whoever [is] on the street, asking
about the different groups that make up this community and how these groups work together. You
get a lot of license and a lot of chance to take an
issue and kind of get out of it what you put into it.

Deirdre repeats an emphasis on matters that directly relate to
students' lives. Her statement about license and control over
what she gained suggests that the experience gave her the opportunity to develop her own ideas and sense of responsibility.
Barry recounted a similar experience in devising a marketing
plan for a company in one of his classes. He and his peers were
responsible for analyzing what the company was doing, developing recommendations, and presenting them to the company executives. Barry emphasized the seriousness of presenting to the
executives what they needed to do to improve, as well as the
decision making required of the group.

Finally, connection to students' own experience is possible even when the topic is history or noncontemporary literature. Makler (1991) discusses helping students to connect to history by creating fictional characters whose behaviors, thoughts, and feelings were developed using information about a particular historical period. This "historical imagination," as she called it, was intended to enable her students to "understand that the historian writes an interpretation of the past that is, in essence, a carefully constructed argument for plausibility rather than an exposition of dead certainty" (p. 30). Thus, she contradicts the view of knowledge, particularly historical knowledge, as "dead certainty" and confirmed students as knowers. Schniedewind (1987) asked students to relate dilemmas in their own lives to those they read, a practice that again draws personal connections to the material. I ask those in my student development theory class to contribute stories of their own development to use in understanding students and critiquing theory.

As we see in these stories, connecting learning to the experience or understanding of students recognizes their contributions and thus leads to their greater investment in the process. When given opportunities to reflect upon experience and share those reflections, students can begin to sort through their perspectives and author their own. This strategy offers further validation, as the students' experience becomes part of learning. It also offers contradiction when students have different experiences or change their beliefs based on new experiences. Continuity comes in the form of processing these experiences with students in a way that helps them refine their voice. These connections between student and knowledge represent Palmer's (1987) view of the act of knowing.

Defining Learning as Jointly Constructing Meaning

When we met Mark in Chapter Two, he offered some advice that is relevant here. Advocating that his law school instructors should have both intelligence and a sense of humanity, he said:

For instance — and none of my professors did this the first day, but I thought they should have — if

they had said something like, *"We're engaged."* And
I think people could do this at the undergraduate
level, too, to make it clear to the student that the
teacher's also a student and that we're all in the classroom engaged in kind of a joint venture. "I can learn
from you, you can learn from me" approach.

Had his professors done as Mark suggested, they would have
been employing the educational approach that Schniedewind
(1987) supports. She suggests that "we enter into a dialogue with
our students, meeting them as human beings, and learning with
them in community" (p. 179). This approach incorporates the
previous two principles — validating students as knowers and situating learning in the students' own experience — but goes beyond them to bring together students and teachers in the process
of making meaning. It is the view that the educational interaction will be relational; it will shape both students and teachers.
Teachers give up their omnipotence and enter into a mutual
exchange of experience with students. This does not mean that
teachers abandon their expertise, only that they allow it to interact with students' feelings, experiences, and expertise.

Dialogue has been described as "the moment where hu-
mans meet to reflect on their reality as they make it and remake
it. It is the quintessential human act, the social moment wherein
we establish ties, and where we have authentic recognition of
the other" (Shor and Freire, 1987, pp. 98–99). This definition
emphasizes reality, or knowledge, as socially constructed and
the relational nature of truly recognizing someone else. Although
Mark was ready to participate in this dialogue as a student, many
others had not had experiences that led them to believe they
could construct meaning together with their instructors. This
may be because many educators do not participate in dialogue
as Shor and Freire describe it. Belenky, Clinchy, Goldberger,
and Tarule (1986) discuss how our underlying assumptions as
educators sometimes work against recognizing students as partners in constructing meaning. They note that instructors often
prepare their thoughts in private, before class, so as to be properly prepared. As a result, the students do not see the instructor's thinking process; the results simply appear full-blown in

class. Nor does the instructor participate in the dialogue, but rather facilitates the conversation from a previously considered perspective. Contrary to teachers' belief that "not knowing" is being unprepared, students' stories show that "not knowing" is often respected. As Marla noted in Chapter Eight, not having a definitive answer is often perceived as open-minded. Recall that Marla admired the teacher who recognized that students brought up points she had not thought about and acknowledged that she did not know the answers to some questions. Marla's teacher also gave students a blank sheet on which they could explain their answers on exams. Marla's reaction was, "She cares what I have to say; she thinks that I have a brain." Marla's teacher did participate in a dialogue. She appreciated the original thinking of her students. She entertained their thoughts on test questions, sometimes giving them credit based on their explanation. She allowed the students' ideas to shape her own even though she still made judgments about their explanations. The teacher's reaction to her students created a dialogue and affirmed their abilities.

When I first heard Marla's story in the interview, I remember feeling somewhat relieved, given that I often said, "I don't know," or "I had not looked at it that way" in my classes. I also tried to engage students in discussion and often changed my perception based on something one of them said. I discovered, however, that being willing to participate in a dialogue is not a sufficient condition for its occurrence. One afternoon, we had a lively discussion in my student development theory class. At the break, a student approached me with a diagram that she had constructed about the communication pattern of the group during the previous hour. (We had studied communication patterns in another class—somehow, these things always come back to haunt you.) The pattern, which traced the path of conversation from person to person, showed that conversation flowed largely to and from me, despite the involvement of all but two or three students. Thus, the sense that I was the authority still crept into the discussion. The student suggested that I might have a different effect by sitting elsewhere in the circle rather than in the front of the circle. I thought the suggestion was rather odd until Mark arrived for his senior interview. As you will recall from Chapter Two, his opening line was, "I would definitely like to address having had the best professor of my career." He continued, "She'd sit on the side of the classroom — out of the position of asymmetrical relations — the power source being in front of the room." He went on to describe the dialogue that took place in the class.

We often do not realize how much we exude power as instructors. Not only do we organize our thoughts in private to appear knowledgeable, but we develop the course goals, the expectations, the assignments, the grading process, and the daily agenda. It is not surprising, then, that students do not perceive themselves as partners in constructing meaning. Schniedewind (1987) offers an example of sharing leadership with her students. Negotiating as necessary, they describe their expectations for the course. As the course proceeds, the group discusses perceptions and changes that may be needed to improve the course, both on their part and on the instructor's. Schniedewind makes it clear that she does not give up her power totally but shares it with students to enhance the experience. The chapter on independent knowers gives numerous examples of shared leadership in classes where the instructor "let us run the class" or "let us influence the direction of the class." These behaviors communicate that instructors and students are "engaged in a kind of joint venture." Subsequently, engaging in dialogue requires more than a friendly relationship. It requires one in which the instructor openly participates in learning with students.

The instructor's participation in dialogue also encourages students to take part, as Bruner (1986) suggests: the student "becomes party to the negotiatory process by which facts are created and interpreted. He becomes at once an agent of knowledge making as well as a recipient of knowledge transmission" (p. 127). Bruner concurs with Palmer's (1987) idea of learning as a communal activity and notes that "it is not just that the child must make his knowledge his own, but that he must make it his own in a community of those who share his sense of belonging to a culture" (p. 127). This brings us to the relational context of students' dialogue with other students.

Jim commented on relational learning in Chapter Eight as he described being dependent on his colleagues in his work after graduation. He complained that college had often forced him into individual activity rather than preparing him for the interactive world that he found upon graduation. Jim, incidentally, had been in Laws Hall and had been a student manager in one of his classes that worked for a business client. Yet he still confirms the existence in college of Gray's culture of separated desks. Perhaps this culture was perpetuated by activities that occurred in groups but did not entail genuine dialogue — in other words, activities focusing on individual achievement, not mutual construction of meaning. Mark's comments on this subject (Chapter Two) are perceptive because he was able to reflect on a change in his own participation in peer discussions:

> I'd take extreme positions early on. I'd look at their position and extrapolate on that, take it to its farthest reaches, and make their argument ridiculous because of these implications. Then I'd show my position, trying to undercut all their positions. Now I'd maybe suggest there are some ramifications that we don't see for understandable reasons, and then try to find some common ground. Instead of shifting our arguments away, bring them together. I definitely think that people are more willing to build toward some common ground than stake out their own place against it.

Mark's initial approach to participation encouraged anything but dialogue. His focus, like most of the mastery-, impersonal-, and individual-pattern knowers, was on his own achievement. Now he "suggests" ramifications, adds that "we" don't see them for "understandable reasons," and searches for common ground. Note that he includes himself in the group that did not see the ramifications — even though he brought them up — and understands their being overlooked. This attitude is in sharp contrast to his earlier one.

You know from Chapter Two that Mark experienced this shift partially as a result of his interactions with women. He noted that "guys are more prone to stake out their ground and dominate," whereas women have "that building-towards-community attitude." The distinctions between the two patterns in each of the first three ways of knowing support Mark's contention. Thus, dialogue does not occur naturally for all students. It requires what Noddings (1991) calls "interpersonal reasoning." She describes interpersonal reasoning as "open, flexible, and responsive. It is guided by an attitude that values the relationship of the reasoners over any particular outcome, and it is marked by attachment and connection rather than separation and abstraction" (p. 158). This interpersonal reasoning is often not addressed in college, which emphasizes impersonal knowledge and skills (Eisner, 1985). Eisner concurs with Jim's assessment that interpersonal reasoning is essential in the work world, where successful interaction is a communal activity. If learning is a communal activity, how do educators help students to develop the interpersonal reasoning that Mark learned from his women friends?

One possibility is changing the "rules for talk" in classrooms. Thorne (1989) argues that "rules for talk in college classrooms are anchored in male, as well as white and upper-middle-class subcultures . . . . Talk among women tends to be more collaborative and participatory" (p. 319). She suggests engaging students in creating and negotiating the rules for discussion — in other words, allowing their particular voices to shape the nature of the classroom environment. This process confirms all students as equal partners in the dialogue. Michael suggested in Chapter Eight that hearing other opinions is good but "not effective if everyone is defending their own views because people close their minds and won't listen." If given the opportunity, Michael and the interpersonal and interindividual knowers we encountered in Part One of the book could offer many suggestions that would assist interpersonal reasoning.

Educators could also stress that learning is a risk and requires trust from the student, an element that Dawn emphasized in describing her acting class:

> In a lot of acting, you have to give yourself, you
> have to just totally open yourself up and let some

things come up that maybe you don't want to. You
have to be willing to trust people that you can open
yourself up and give them everything and they'll
take care of it. They won't hurt you in some way
outside of what you're doing.

The hazards that Dawn described are not, of course, limited
to acting. In developing a voice, in trying to create our own
perspectives, we risk sharing raw ideas that reveal our way of
thinking. Instructors and students alike have to feel confident
that these will not be abused. Dawn offered an example of how
this trust was developed in her acting class:

A perfect example is a project we had to do last
semester. We had to present our life from birth to
where we are now, and we had ten minutes to do
it in. You have to pick and choose the elements that
you want to present to people, but it became a
chance to let each other know who you really are
and the events that have formed your life and made
you what you are today. It's a scary thing because
there are a lot of things that people don't want to
talk about. It was a real risk. There has to be a lot
of trust in order to put all that out into the open.
It was a wonderful experience. It was just that sort
of experience where I can just say, "This is me. I
hope you like it." Nothing changed, and that really
reinforces the trust that you have in people if you
can show them a dark side of you, maybe, and they
take it along with everything that's good.

I suspect this technique may be even riskier than Dawn described
because some students may not accept the "dark side" of others
so willingly as Dawn's classmates did. Her story, nevertheless,
illustrates how revealing personal experience builds trust. Talking about the learning experience and fostering a caring atmosphere could similarly build the trust needed to take the risks
involved in genuine dialogue.

Finally, recasting collaboration in the context of trusting, caring relationships and dialogue would encourage those students who would like to approach learning as interpersonal reasoners and help others to do so. As we saw in Mark's comments in Chapter Two, this approach does not mean dismissing other kinds of reasoning:

> There was a lot of unity in one class; we discussed personal issues. I think that's important regardless of what classroom you're in. It's important to know something about other students in the classroom and get a sense for them. Even if you don't agree with that student, if you know where the person's coming from, you can divorce the critiques of their views from critiquing the person. It's a fine line between geting too far away from the material and getting it just personal and then engaging the material so much that your personal views don't come into it. It's a tough negotiation. It's rare, but it happens.

Mark's perspective implies that there should be a balance between interpersonal reasoning and engagement with the material. "Divorcing the critiques of their views from critiquing the person" reveals the ability to disagree while still respecting others as knowers. This kind of balance inspires both the development of individual voice and joint construction of meaning. "It's rare, but it happens" sums up the challenge for us as educators.

Summary

Kegan's functions of confirmation, contradiction, and continuity offer a framework for integrating the three principles discussed in this chapter. Confirming students' abilities is essential to the development of voice, authorship, and complex ways of knowing. Acknowledging, as Marla's teacher did, that students have a brain and that they have something valuable to say and convincing them that they are capable of constructing meaning are all ways of affirming them. Situating learning in students' own experience recognizes that experience, sets the stage for validating their reflection upon it, and thus further confirms their ability to know. Perceiving learning as a relational activity is also central to the development of complex ways of knowing. Contextual knowing requires constructing one's own view, taking other ideas and information into consideration. Thus, it requires access to this information and to others' thoughts, as well as the ability to interact with them. This dialogue is what we have been referring to as jointly constructing meaning, which is, in turn, a necessary condition if students are to recognize themselves as makers of meaning.

Contradicting the sense that authority is omnipotent is also essential. Teaching students that knowledge is not absolute and that authorities can disagree creates the possibility that students can learn in ways beyond collecting authorities' ideas. Sharing with students how we as educators form our own perspectives, and that our ideas are often in disarray before we arrive at a coherent view, makes the thinking process accessible. As long as instructors do not reveal the difficulties inherent in learning, students will not perceive that their struggles to understand are part of that same process. Contradiction of individual achievement as the sole focus of learning, at the expense of connection to others, is also imperative. Establishing connections requires more than instituting group activities and peer involvement. It necessitates facilitating genuine dialogue among students. It requires helping mastery-, impersonal-, and individual-pattern knowers learn how to appreciate interpersonal reasoning. This attitude would alleviate the problems that individual-pattern knowers experienced as they tried to "really listen" to their peers on the edge of contextual knowing. This is not to say that mastery-, impersonal-, and individual-pattern learning has no value; individual achievement is also necessary for students to create their own perspectives. My point is that both individual and relational modes of knowing are essential. They must exist in what Palmer (1987) calls "creative tension," each playing a part, but neither dominating consistently over the other. I think this balance is what Mark meant by "it's a tough negotiation" between being ruled by a personal approach or by engagement with the material. Dialogue helps learners using one pattern experience contradiction from those using another. This contradiction is effective as long as it exists in creative tension with the confirmation noted earlier.

The function of continuity is to "stay with" the students as they negotiate the difficult process of creating their own perspectives. Connecting to students' experiences in the teaching process offers an opportunity to stay with them. Working from their knowledge, rather than our own, we can understand knowledge construction from their perspectives and keep abreast of changes in them. Genuine participation in dialogue with students accomplishes this same goal. Dialogue also helps us recognize when a new meaning has replaced a previous one so that we can continue to balance confirmation and contradiction, the specific forms of which change as the learner moves from one way of knowing to another.

I approached this chapter with the hope that the three principles would help readers to relate to students' experience with the learning process, not to create distance from that experience by providing an abstract list of "do's and don'ts." More specific techniques for promoting development of voice in any context will stem from the meaning that readers construct with the learners there. The next two chapters explore possibilities for educators in student affairs roles, because the participants' stories also demonstrate that life beyond the classroom also affects the development of voice. The same three principles guide that discussion in hopes of generating ideas for the integration of the academic and cocurricular aspects of the college experience in assisting the development of the student voice.

Chapter Ten

Supporting
Patterns of Knowing
in the Cocurriculum

> I think some of my best experiences were outside of the
> classroom, where I could take what I learned in the class-
> room and apply it. Miami afforded me a lot of opportuni-
> ties to do that. Everybody at Miami is busy as can be. You
> could never sit back and watch the world go around. You
> had to be a part of it.
>
> — *Andrew*

Andrew's comments speaks to the central role that the cocurricular environment plays in the college experience. Students'
stories about their most significant experiences were often in
the cocurricular realm. As a result, the stories are full of examples of the confirmation, contradiction, and continuity that students experienced through interpersonal relationships, organizational involvement, everyday living, and employment. Life
beyond the classroom intensely involved students. They were
consumed, sometimes positively and sometimes negatively, with
roommates and other relationships. The success of these relationships often affected the students' perceptions of themselves
and the quality of their academic work. Involvement in organizations helped students build confidence, learn skills, make
career decisions, build friendships, develop leadership qualities,
and feel comfortable. The tasks of everyday living and work-

296

ing yielded insights about individual functioning, responsibility to others, and values. Relationships with others in all of these contexts broadened students' perspectives about human diversity and their own place in the larger community. The strong relational quality that can be seen throughout the stories about cocurricular life may explain the emphasis placed on this environment in the students' view of the college experience. In this chapter, their perceptions are translated into advice for student affairs educators. This chapter focuses primarily on "matching" cocurricular environments to students' ways of knowing. Advice regarding balancing confirmation, contradiction, and continuity across ways of knowing is found in the next chapter.

Students' ways of knowing affected the meaning they made of cocurricular experiences: relationships with roommates and friends, participation in student organizations and activities, and the overall student culture of the campus. For example, absolute knowers expected career counselors to provide answers to their career questions, whereas transitional knowers expected career counselors to help them with that process. Similarly, absolute knowers struggled to determine what was right in interactions with persons with different opinions, whereas independent knowers were likely to accept these differences as routine. Subsequently, advice for educators about the cocurricular environment is categorized here within students' ways of knowing.

The collective stories contained advice for student affairs educators in the categories of peer relationships, student organizations, living arrangements, internship or employment experiences, educational advising, general campus environment, and international experiences. Within each category, prevalent themes identify how student affairs educators can confirm students in their attempt to learn from these experiences. The themes in each category for absolute, transitional, independent, and contextual knowers are shown in Table 10.1. As was the case in Chapter Eight, the themes represent prevailing winds that did not affect all students identically. However, they do provide a framework from which cocurricular opportunities can be purposefully shaped to enhance students' ways of knowing.

Table 10.1. Students' Advice for Cocurricular Education.

	Absolute Knowing	Transitional Knowing	Independent Knowing	Contextual Knowing
Peer relationships	Create oportunities for positive peer interaction	Encourage development of support network of friends Help students respond to peer influence Help maximize learning about diversity	Support peer interaction that fosters appreciation of diversity Encourage efforts to balance personal needs with those of close friends Teach students how to create new support networks	Reinforce peers as legitimate source of knowledge
Student organizations	Create opportunities for positive peer interaction Create opportunities for student responsibility	Promote leadership development Offer opportunities for practical experience Use as a source of friendship and dealing with diversity	Validate voice through leadership opportunities	Provide freedom to exercise choice

Living arrangements	Create opportunities for positive peer interaction Create opportunities for student responsibility	Organize around themes of responsibility and community		Reinforce expanding horizons
Internships/employment		Build human relations skills Offer practical experience	Help students process insights gained Reinforce self-confidence gained	
Educational advising	Create opportunities for student responsibility, combined with support from authority	Provide direct experience and stress-management assistance		
General campus environment	Create opportunities for student responsibility	Provide opportunity for self-discipline		Create possibilities for freedom and development of voice
International and/or cultural exchange		Provide direct encounters with diversity	Create opportunity for students to reevaluatae their beliefs	

Matching Absolute Knowers' Learning Needs

This advice comes predominantly from the sophomore-year interviews because the first-year absolute knowers had been on campus only a few weeks by the first interview and very few remained in this category by the junior year.

Peer Relationships: Create Opportunities
for Positive Peer Interaction

Positive peer interactions helped students learn to get along with others, to become more comfortable at college, and to deal with cultural and social differences. Gale told this story:

> The most important thing about my freshman year — well, the thing that really makes me happy when I look back on my freshman year — is my corridor. Everyone in my corridor, I was crying to say goodbye to them. They were all my best friends. We are still all so close. I feel like I could tell them anything. And my roommates were the best experience because one was like me and one was really different. By the end of the year, we were all best friends. I really, really got a lot out of what went on in that room.

Anita also focused on learning from others' differences:

> I learned to get along with other people. I learned a lot from having two roommates last year. We're all very different people from different places, and I had to learn about what other people believe and differences in background. Just learning to share and do things on your own.

These two stories emphasize learning from differences and building relationships, including close friendships, with others. Apparently, sufficient confirmation existed for these experiences to be positive. Friendships also made the college experience more comfortable. For example, Art compared his sophomore year to his freshman year:

> This year is a lot different. Last year, I had a girl friend at home and no close friends here. This year, one of my friends transferred in here, and my girl friend goes here. That's a lot more relaxed. I don't think about too much outside the university this year — last year, I was always thinking about getting out of here to get home. This year, I've got people to talk to, and I feel more comfortable.

Bernard expressed a similar idea:

> Leaving home was kind of easy because I had a lot of guys in the corridor, so we became good friends. And then I got into a fraternity, so I always have people around me that I can talk to if there are any problems.

Friends served as a support, or a source of confirmation, for these students.

Learning to deal with others and being more comfortable at college also stemmed from interaction with peers in general, even if they were not close friends. One of the most important things that Lydia learned came from peer-group interaction. She said:

> To adjust to different people, most definitely, because — they're not so different here from where I lived before — but the group I was in in my high school was a lot different than the people here. Not as far as values and morals, but the way they go out and have fun, the way they just blow off classes, I guess, more. I had to adjust to the people more than anything.

Finding study partners also helped. Valerie described it in this way:

> This year, I study more with other people that I know from last year or that are in my sorority and my classes. More people are doing things together, like doing our projects together and our homework assignments together and studying together, sharing notes with each other. I get more of another side of an opinion or more clarification on something, or maybe they take better notes than I do. And I learn more about them and how they feel about things.

Other students commented on the positive influence of classmates. This is clear from Clark's comment:

> This is the best learning environment I've ever been in because of the fantastic students. You become a better student because of the other fine students — success breeds success.

These stories imply that developing friendships and interacting with peers happen in the natural course of college life. Living arrangements and organizations are natural settings in which these opportunities exist. Most student affairs educators know, however, that many students do not cope with these experiences as comfortably as those quoted here. Efforts to guide students in dealing with roommate differences would help create the outcomes quoted here for more students. Structured attempts to help students meet and interact with peers would assist those who are less likely to establish these connections on their own.

Student Organizations: Create Opportunities for Student Responsibility

Some absolute knowers joined organizations to acquire responsibility. For example, Rosa explained:

> Last year, I was going to join a sorority, but I didn't know anything about them. So I waited a year, and now all the girls in my hallway are in it. I just learned from them what sororities were like, what they had to do, what their responsibilities were. From that, I decided it was something I wanted to do, something I wanted to belong to. In high school, I was really active in a lot of things, organizing stuff. So this year, I decided to join to do something besides going to school.

Other opportunities for responsibility arose from being in college or from living arrangements. Most absolute knowers saw themselves as being more independent as a result of these opportunities for responsibility. Lauren described the outcome of her first year:

> I really gained a lot of independence. I matured a lot. My parents feel the same. You're on your own; everything is up to you; your responsibilities are your decision. If you wanted to do something you did it; if not, that was your problem. You didn't have someone there telling you, "Do this" or "Do that." You had a lot of temptations to do things you normally could not have done at home, so depending on what your values are, you acted accordingly, showing your maturity as a result of that.

Spencer described a similar experience:

> I had to learn to live on my own. I get a lot of help from the guys I live with and people I work with. For the most part, I have to tell myself what to do, whereas back home I had Mom to tell me to do my homework. It's really made me aware of the responsibility it takes to be an adult. It's made me respect my parents more. Even though we have some very different attitudes about certain things,

they've really helped me develop a sense of independence. I can make decisions easier now by drawing from my experiences and applying them to the
situation.

Students emphasized that college life prompted them to take
on some of the responsibilities that had been previously handled by their parents. Sufficient confirmation was available for
these students to begin to do things on their own, thus providing validation for their emerging independence.

Educational Advising: Balance Opportunity
for Responsibility with Support

Despite the overwhelming report of new-found independence,
the predominant theme in decision making was reliance on authorities. In other words, although students wanted responsibility, they also needed support, particularly when deciding their
college major. The dilemma is apparent in Toni's experience:

I switched my major four times last year. It was
just a big thing for me, because you're all alone and
you have to do this on your own. And Mom's not
here to help you any more. I had to learn how to
go find the resources myself and talk to the teachers
and advisers. I asked my friends for advice. Then
I asked my RA [resident assistant] who gave me
a number to call. I called the number and got hold
of some people, and they gave me advisers' names.
I talked to them then.

Although Toni felt she had to make this decision on her own,
she looked for substitute authorities because her mother was not
there to give her advice. Hugh described a similar combination of independence and reliance on authority (as we saw in
Chapter Three):

When I came here as a freshman, I just put down
economics because I had an economics class that

was interesting. You don't really know as a freshman. I think it's kind of unfair to ask freshmen to
state a major. I went to a finance club meeting the
other night, and we had a finance professor there —
the adviser of the group — and he said some things.
And I was just smiling because I was so happy because I agreed with him. I must be a finance major.

Hugh and Toni's struggle is probably an indication that as absolute knowers, they still felt that only one right major existed.
Although absolute knowers could make decisions about how to
behave and when to do homework, making a mistake on choice
of major was too large a risk. Responsibility in this area may
be a contradiction rather than a confirmation and thus must
be balanced with confirmation.

The overwhelming focus of these students' cocurricular
experiences was on adjustment to college. This emphasis is no
doubt partially due to their being (mostly) sophomores, but it
also reflects their view of the world. From their vantage point,
the nature of college is determined by authorities, and the student's role is to learn how to experience it correctly. Friends
and campus authority figures were the two mediums for adjustment for absolute knowers. The theme of friends as an important part of the college experience was salient for these students
in helping them learn about others and making college life more
comfortable. Perhaps the most important insight from the peer-
relationship experiences is that they were a source of differing
viewpoints — a characteristic that students did not perceive in
their academic environments.

Absolute knowers described the role of authority and the
emergence of independence simultaneously. Although most perceived that they were on their own, often noting parents' im-
mediate absence, they sought out authority figures for making
major decisions. They clearly recognized that they were supposed to be functioning on their own and did not consciously
recognize their reliance on authority. The opportunities to interact with friends and authority figures in the cocurricular environment offered absolute thinkers a bridge between reliance
on parents and reliance on themselves.

Matching Transitional Knowers' Learning Needs

Transitional thinkers abounded in the sophomore, junior, and senior years. As a result, their stories yield extensive advice for student affairs educators.

Peer Relationships: Encourage the Development of Support Networks of Friends

Friendship was a major source of confirmation for transitiona' knowers. Leah explained:

> I think friends are so important. I don't know what I would do without my friends. I live in a house with thirteen girls, and it's kind of good because it's like everyone is so different. You're an individual, but you get all their ideas on life, how they act. They give you support — when you're down or when you just need somebody to talk to. When you get upset, you can go to them. They lighten things up. They've got their own problems. So then if you get involved in their problems, you don't even think about your own.

Bev described a support system that she had coming into college:

> I had a boy friend when I came here. I never had to look for guys at college. And I know a lot of girls go through that. They need it so much. So I guess I've been lucky in that regard. I never felt much of a need to meet people because I already had people I knew here.

For some, the friendships were developed after arriving at college. For example, Reginald said:

> I made very close friendships. In one case, we both had problems that we needed to discuss, and we went to each other, supported each other, and talked and listened.

Comments like Leah's "I don't know what I would do without my friends" were common, and revealed that friends' support was a major source of affirmation.

Peer Relationships: Help Students Respond to Peer Influence

Transitional thinkers often described friends as an important influence on their attitudes. For example, Alexis said:

> I think that the attitude of your friends and your peers, people that you're with all the time, they really affect how hard you work. It just seems like the people that you're surrounded by, you tend to fall into the same rut they do. I find that if so-and-so's working harder, then I will. If they aren't going to study, I don't either.

Eileen described how roommates' feelings affected hers:

> I think the people you live with have a big aspect on how you view things and how well or badly things go. My roommate is not very self-confident. A lot of times, I want to go home, and she doesn't like to stay by herself. And I feel guilty, but then I think, "Well, I shouldn't feel guilty because she's twenty years old, and, I mean, grow up a little bit." Sometimes that just affects me, and I know it shouldn't. But I'm one of those people that worries about what she thinks.

Friends' attitudes influenced how students felt, as well as how they behaved. Students gave no indication of the ability to act in ways incongruent with peer pressure. Perhaps because friends were such an important support network, individualistic behavior was a risk not worth taking. Student affairs educators could help students learn how to respond to peer pressure in

ways that would maintain relationships and encourage independent thinking in many areas of their lives.

Peer Relationships: Help Students Learn
as Much as Possible About Diversity

As was the case with absolute knowers, transitional knowers
noted experiences with people as a source of awareness of diversity. Tracy illustrated this point:

> I think one of the most important things I've learned
> is that people are different and you have to accept
> them the way they come. I've come into contact with
> people that—you know, when you first look at
> them, just on appearances, you kind of raise your
> eyebrow and wonder about them. A lot of people
> have a lot of neat ideas that normally, if you just
> look at them and judge them as being something,
> you'd never get to know them. But I've come to put
> that aside and learn more about the inside of people.

Candace remarked:

> I come from a town of two hundred where most of
> my friends are married and have babies. I learned
> a lot about people's social values, a lot of things I
> never really thought existed.

In these two cases, sufficient confirmation was available for these
students to learn from these encounters. In instances when interactions occur in an organized setting, such as a student organization meeting or an educational program, educators can
heighten the chances of positive experiences with diversity.

Some students do not learn to accept diversity, as evidenced by some transitional knowers' concern over what they
called "closed" attitudes on the part of peers. Classmates were
accused of being materialistic, superficial in their interactions,
and unaccepting of differences. Lowell complained, "A lot of

people can't get their views out — I try to show mine; one person called me a name — she was unable to hear my view." Gale expressed her frustration like this: "People here are so materialistic — trying to impress everyone else; I feel like shaking some of them. I escape with my boy friend." Another woman, Megan, reported preparing with extra diligence for class to convince others that communication majors were intelligent. Guidance might have helped these students to approach their peers more openly and increase the effectiveness of peer influence on broadening students' perspectives. This guidance could be provided through programming efforts, peer education systems, or individual advising.

Student Organizations: Promote Leadership Development

One of the major advantages that students saw in organizational involvement was gaining leadership experience. The comments below illustrate the effects of leadership opportunities:

> I helped start a student organization and served as president. I learned things like letter writing, talking to people on the phone, soliciting money. It's neat to go into business classes now, because I can apply what I'm learning to the organization.
> — *Jim, a junior*

> Leadership experience is important to have on your résumé, and it gives you experience in dealing with people, working in groups, and managing your time. It helps you be successful on your own and formulate your own opinions.
> — *Al, a senior*

> I'm a social chair in my sorority, so that requires a lot more responsibility. I have nine chair people under me. So if they don't get things done, I'm the one who has to pick up the slack. It's taught me how to handle certain people under certain condi-

tions. How to approach them, to use the right word-
ing to get what you want across to them as being
a positive experience. How to get up and speak on
your feet and come across like you know what
you're talking about.
                                              — *Lydia, a senior*

These stories show that students gained a variety of skills through
these responsibilities, which they felt would benefit them in future contexts. The confirmation that they experienced in these
settings helped them apply academic knowledge in practice, formulate their own opinions, and work effectively with others.

Student Organizations: Offer Opportunities for Practical Experience

The second theme of gaining practical experience is closely
related to responsibility and leadership, as the examples below
indicate:

I got involved with various organizations. You need
interpersonal skills and a rounded personality in
the real world. You aren't going to be locked up
in a laboratory for the rest of your life.
                                              — *Ned, a sophomore*

Getting involved in activities is great. One, you can
take things you learn in class to use. I can take my
finance and accounting and apply it working as a
business manager. You can test out things in your
major, get experience for it.
                                              — *Andrew, a senior*

I'm in a marketing organization. A group of us in
the advertising division are doing an entire promotional campaign for a client with fifty-two stores in
New York. I have learned more, I think, in that
experience than I could ever learn in the classroom.

It's practical, hands-on — we're actually doing what
you could be learning, the steps in how to do it in
a practical sort of way.

— Adrian, a junior

Students viewed these practical experiences as augmenting classroom learning and preparing them for their future work.

Student Organizations: A Source of Friendships and Dealing with Diversity

Many students cited organizations as a source for building close
friendships. Rosa described making friends through her sorority:

My sorority is important. It was a good outlet,
something else to do than just going to class and
coming home. They have social events. One of my
best friends now was in my sorority. That's how
I met her. Even in your classes, there's always someone you know. And even when you go uptown,
there's always someone you run into you know because they're in your sorority.

Organizations also offered opportunities for learning to
deal with diversity, as we see in the following comments:

I have learned that people are motivated at different levels for different things. I have learned that
not everyone thinks the same way in the fraternity.
You have to learn to deal with the way different
people are.

— Lowell, a sophomore

I'm in a fraternity. I have these opportunities to interact with people — it's really neat. And it's important because I'm just becoming open to different
ideas and different ways of thinking. Just dealing
with problems between people.

— Ned, a junior

As was the case with peer interactions in general, the results of organizational involvement seemed to occur naturally. However, intervention by student affairs educators for students who need more than what naturally arises would help promote friendship and greater acceptance of diversity.

Living Arrangements: Organize Around
Themes of Responsibility and Community

What happens when students move off campus? This question has surely caused many sleepless nights for parents. The answers are not what some parents might expect. Juniors and seniors, many of whom had moved off campus, talked about living arrangements that promoted independence and responsibility. The students quoted below explained the essence of their experience:

> I have some different attitudes about things because I've found living off campus that you have more responsibility. It helps you to budget your time more; it makes everyday life more of a learning experience just in general and about commonsense things. A lot of times your work gets neglected because you have responsibilities, and you have responsibilities to the other people that you live with, too. You don't have any rules. So you have to do more or less what you think is best for yourself all the time. It makes you think about it more.
> —*Alexis, a junior*

> I think moving off campus was really important for me because it enabled me to find out that you've got to pay your rent and bills. And there is some degree of responsibility in living on your own. It's great because there's all this flexibility. I can eat what and when I want, go to bed when I want. It's how you tell what kind of people you want to live with in the future.
> —*Justin, a senior*

Having to make decisions on one's own and take care of everyday details were perceived by these students as preparing them
for the future. Student affairs educators could provide similar
experiences in campus housing by adopting policies that give
students responsibility for their living environment. Justin's comment about learning how to choose people to live with leads to
a related theme: students learn how to deal with people through
living with others. Will explained:

> People learn a lot from the community in residence
> halls. I found my ideas and morals were challenged;
> I enjoy good conversation which I think is meaning-
> ful. I got a lot out of people challenging me. I think
> people learn about themselves and people coming
> from different backgrounds. You have to accept
> people's right to think what they want.

Lindsey offered a similar perspective:

> When you live with a bunch of guys, you have to
> get along with everybody. Once you get in the real
> world, you're going to have to get along with every-
> body you work with. So that teaches you how to
> deal with certain individuals you may not wish to
> deal with at certain times. If you have a problem
> with something somebody else does, you have to
> deal with it.

"Having to deal with it" was not always easy, even with friends.
Lauren discussed this dilemma:

> One thing that living off campus showed me the
> most is that it's really hard sometimes to live with
> your friends and be good friends with them at the
> same time. I lived with my best friend last year,
> and that might have been a mistake because we
> fought over trivial matters. But it turned into big-
> ger things. This year, we are in the same house but
> on different floors. We haven't had a fight yet. It's

important to learn that they're your friends; however, you can't eat, breathe, and live twenty-four
hours a day with them.

Getting along was important due to the support gained
from living with friends. Hugh defined this support; and, in doing so, he offered his perception of gender differences in this
regard:

I'm living with seven other guys I'm pretty close
to. We're good friends. And that whole atmosphere
is pretty nice because of the support — being able
to go and talk to anyone about anything you may
want to talk about. Especially being a guy, I think
it's good to just talk to someone about something.
I'm not trying to make this a big difference between
guys and girls, but girls tend to maybe talk about
themselves and their situation more with their girl
friends. Guys, I think, have to be a little bit closer
with each other. And we have that in the house.

Despite Hugh's interpretation of gender differences, the importance of good relationships with housemates or roommates was
evident for most students. Community seemed to be the thread
that held them together and enabled them to struggle with their
responsibilities and relationships. Although this community atmosphere occurs naturally in some settings, intentional efforts
to create it in campus housing would encourage students to see
themselves as responsible persons and to think in more complex ways.

Internships and Employment:
Build Human Relations Skills

For students, the primary outcome of internships and employment opportunities was learning about other people or themselves. The students quoted below illustrate the variety of ways
that students learned:

I'm a supervisor in a dining hall. That's taught me a lot about how to get along with people and to tell people what to do without being bossy. In the beginning, I guess, I was a little bossy. But it's hard when you haven't had a leadership position because it doesn't come natural to many people. You have to learn how to get people to do what you want them to do without making them angry at you. So that's something I learned.

— Lowell

My summer job was valuable because it taught me a lot of things in regard to learning how to deal with people and learning how people usually come in with an attitude. If you're nice to them right when they come in, they'll usually be nice to you back. But I learned how to deal with people yelling at me because something wasn't right. I think that helped me a lot with my temperament as far as relating to people.

— Gavin

I have been a resident assistant and a tutor. These have helped me in dealing with people and learning about people and managing people. And all those kinds of skills you don't get from reading books. I feel that no matter how many numbers I can crunch, if I can't get along with people, then it's not going to help. The experience helps you because there're always new situations and there're always new people to deal with and different personalities you run up against all the time.

— Heather

These experiences helped students learn how to approach others, how to react in particular settings, and how to adjust to people and circumstances. Some students emphasized learning about themselves through these opportunities. Heather described the effect of her work on her self-understanding:

My resident-assistant job puts me in the position of getting to know people and forcing myself to be more outgoing. I have to meet and talk to people, when I'd rather put my head down. So that's helped me a lot because it's really hard to be a shy person and make it, especially in the classroom, when you need to interact. I also come into contact with different problems I've had to deal with. A lot of them are value judgments, and you really have to know yourself before you can help somebody else out.

"Helping somebody else out" was also an outcome of employment or internship opportunities, as Stephanie described:

I work at the crisis and referral center as a paraprofessional counselor. It is such a change from everything else that I do. Everything else I do is so business-oriented or practical-oriented. I think it's easy to lose touch with people or how people feel. It's relieving for me to help someone else with their problems. It puts me in a totally different frame of mind just to even walk into the place.

Internships and Employment: Offer Practical Experience

Students appreciated opportunities to gain practical experience beyond that related to managing people. Carl described what he gained:

I have co-oped for three semesters now in a paper mill. It is related to my field. It helped me decide a bit more what I want to go into because I got involved with a little bit of research. And it also helped me to see some of the stuff we've been talking about in class. That way, I could understand it a little bit more. It will also help me get a job.

Muriel offered a similar comment:

> I work in the campus development office. You find out a lot of different things about the university working there, all about alumni and who donates money and where it goes. I also learned how to run a telethon, in case that ever helps me in the future.

For Hugh, the experience involved major responsibility:

> I worked in the collections department of a bank this summer. I had a lot of responsibility for someone my age. I was doing the same things that people that were forty or older were doing. If I didn't do my job, I could really mess up a lot of people's lives. I knew there was no goofing around.

Collectively, the students's ideas about internships and employment suggest that transitional learners valued both the interpersonal and the work-related skills that they acquired through these experiences. They were apparently confirmed as knowers as they gained skills in working with others, insights about themselves, and practical experience.

*Educational Advising: Provide
Direct Experience and Stress-Management
Assistance to Help Students Make Decisions*

Choosing a major was the decision most often mentioned by sophomores and juniors. For seniors, it was the job search. Some transitional knowers described making decisions about their major through direct experience. Megan's experience was in class:

> All these guests came in to class to talk about advertising and public relations, all different technical aspects of communications and media. I listened to them and decided I couldn't do any of those things. So I switched majors.

Justin's direct experience was a job: "I changed my major to geology; I got a job at the Outdoor Pursuit Center, and I like the outdoors." Other students described additional influences, such as internships and interesting courses, as well as external restraints, including grades, required courses, and parents' demands. The stress created by these decisions was another theme, as articulated by Chuck, a sophomore:

> There are always decisions—majors and stuff. It is more stressful. Even on holidays, you have to think about the future. You start worrying about what to do with your life, getting jobs. A million decisions.

Students who still have the transitional perspective as seniors talked about the simultaneous pressure of the job search and the opportunities inherent in it. Heather described one side of the story:

> There is just such pressure, as far as careers. Especially here, especially in my school. There is a lot of competition for jobs out there right now. Everybody's talking about it, all excited. But individually, everybody's worried, "Am I really going to get a job?"

Sidney offered a view of the opportunities presented by the job search:

> With all the interviewing I've been doing, I think I've really learned a lot more about myself, and my confidence level has definitely increased. Just dealing with the professionals, people who have been working for twenty-five, thirty years, making lots of money, having jobs that I'd like to hold—you become more focused.

Perhaps the uncertainty faced by these students for the first time accounts for their focus on the stress related to important decisions. Direct experiences helped the students to make choices in the face of uncertainty, but the stories recounted here suggest that they could have benefited from assistance in processing those experiences. Student affairs educators could assist transitional students by providing more opportunities to see what various majors and careers are like, examine those encounters with students, and provide advising and programming to help them with the anxiety involved in such decisions.

Campus Environment: Provide
Opportunities for Self-Discipline

As students discussed the general campus atmosphere, they commented on their role within the campus community. Some found living on campus stifling. Max, a junior, complained:

> On campus they baby you — always checking up on you, taking care of you, making sure you do this and that; the rules are the same for upper-class and freshman students.

Others found opportunities for self-discipline, as Adrian described:

> Self-discipline — there's no one else but me. I learned that I can do it if I set my mind to it. You're forced to find out what you can do without your parents or any of your friends from home.

Another sophomore added, "I'm a lot more independent, less worried about what other people think and more worried about what I think." Students appreciated opportunities to move toward opportunities to become more independent in managing their daily lives. Max's comments clearly indicate that, in some cases, policies could offer a more significant role for students in monitoring their behavior.

International and Cultural Exchange:
Provide Direct Encounters with Diversity

Five of the transitional knowers had opportunities to travel
abroad. Their comments demonstrate the value of this kind of
experience. Two students who visited Japan and England emphasized their increasing awareness of diversity as a result.
Heather said, "I learned a lot about culture and people and how
different it is from Western ways of thinking; it gave me a whole
new perspective." Anita concurred: "It was a shock to see people living different kinds of life-styles. I have a different perspective now." The other three talked about the effect of meeting people from other countries. Julian commented, "You realize
other people don't think the way you do. It was an eye-opener;
I am much more open now." Evan, who visited the former Soviet
Union, said:

> I made lots of friends. It is important to see that
> people over there are like us; they do the same
> things we do. I learned that you could trust them.
> It changed the way I feel about people over there.

These direct encounters with other cultures prompted all five
students to view themselves as more open to others.

Collectively, transitional students' descriptions of the
cocurricular environment focused on expanding their ability to
function in the world. This emphasis is evident in the themes
regarding learning responsibility through living arrangements,
learning responsibility and leadership experience through organizational involvement, gaining skills through internships or
jobs, and achieving more independence. These students also
learned about others through living arrangements, friendships,
and organizational involvement. All of these circumstances were
characterized by connection to others or to experience. They
also created opportunities for students to claim and express their
voices. Decisions were based on experience, rather than on authority figures' advice. The emphasis on the stressfulness of decision making reflects an increasing awareness of uncertainty
and the necessity to choose without having an absolute answer.

Thus, the student voice was emerging but was not yet completely confident.

Matching Independent Knowers' Learning Needs

Educators and parents alike await the day when students think for themselves. As the students' stories show, however, we do not always nurture self-reliance. Perspectives on peer relationships, student organizations, employment, and international experience all focused on independence and diversity. These ideas come from the junior, senior, and fifth-year interviews.

Peer Relationships: Support Peer Interaction That Fosters Appreciation of Diversity

Independent knowers learned to appreciate diversity through their relationships with peers. Candace, a student from a very small town, described learning about differences and the impact it had on her when she returned to her home town to teach:

> Sometimes you just want to smack people and say, "Open your eyes. The world is not like this." The community I teach in is very racist and very chauvinistic. It's not that I'm not used to dealing with people like that; it's just that I don't like it. At Miami, people came from so many different places. The population of black students is still pretty low, but it was a lot for me when I went. It helps that I'm not afraid to talk to the black students at my school now. It sounds strange, but some of the high school students are afraid. I tell them they'll change when they go to college. You know — "Most of you will get a better opinion of life in general."

Kyle, a junior, reported a similar experience:

> This last year, I met so many different people that it was good for me because I learned to deal with other people. I'm more tolerant; I've learned to ap-

preciate and understand others. This just happens
through talking to people.

Tracy and Rob offered more specific instances of learning about
diversity through peers. Tracy explained:

> Through some friends, I was exposed to someone
> who had some Eastern views as far as things about
> basic, you know, holistic views. We talked about
> reincarnation and got into a big religious discus-
> sion. It was really neat, and it kind of put a new
> perspective on looking at things. I'd never been ex-
> posed to it before. It was something new and in-
> teresting to me, that I wanted to learn about. It's
> kind of opened my eyes on some things.

Rob learned appreciation of other opinions through his best
friends:

> I learned that best friends disagree — you're going
> to have problems you have to straighten out. You've
> got to make allowances for other people. I'm not
> as self-centered as I was in high school. I've met
> different people that think differently.

These comments go beyond the "dealing with people" attitude
expressed by transitional knowers to an appreciation of differences. Inherent in that appreciation is a recognition that other
views are valid; they are not just something that has to be taken
into account to deal with people effectively. Learning that other
opinions are equally valid confirms independent knowing and
thus sparks development of voice.

*Peer Relationships: Encourage Efforts to
Balance Personal Needs and Others' Needs*

Independent knowers valued close friendships and support from
peers, yet were concerned about their own needs as well. Stu-

dents described appreciating friends while not being consumed
by what they thought. Deirdre explained:

> As you get older, you don't try so hard to impress
> each other, [you] think about what you have to offer
> instead of looking for it in other people. I don't
> know. I guess — not in a selfish way — but I put my-
> self first more than how people think of me. I don't
> care if I stay home on Thursday night or don't feel
> like I need to find a boy friend. I'm just really con-
> cerned with what I feel like doing and just being
> with my friends. My good friends have always been
> really important to me, just keeping close relation-
> ships with them.

Alice also felt this tension between valuing a close friend and
pursuing her own interests when she went to graduate school
at the same university that her boy friend attended. She said:

> It's been different because my boy friend goes here.
> We've been dating five years. The whole time I went
> to Miami, he was here. I've never had to [juggle]
> academic time with my time with him before. I've
> never had to choose. I had to sort out my priori-
> ties and make a separation between the two.

For Phillip, dealing with peers in school helped him recognize
the need to look out for himself:

> I got a better idea about how to deal with people.
> I used to be friendly to everybody. You soon real-
> ize that people are going to take advantage of that
> and walk all over you if you're not careful. Being
> in that situation — where you're dealing with all
> types of people from all walks of life — helps you
> realize that, so that you can live your life more effec-
> tively. You've got to watch yourself and be a little
> bit careful when you're dealing with somebody,

whether they're taking you for a ride or whether
they're actually saying what they mean. That's what
I got out of senior year, [letting go] the naiveté.

Deirdre's "putting myself first," Alice's "sort out my priorities,"
and Phillip's "be a little bit careful" all suggest that these students figured out ways to meet their own needs in the context
of interacting with others. They were able to think independently
in deciding how to handle these situations. Student affairs educators could provide confirmation for independent thinkers by
helping them balance needs the way Deirdre, Alice, and Phillip did.

Peer Relationships: Teach Students How to Create New Support Networks

Independent knowers in their postgraduation work settings often
commented on the lack of support due to the absence of people
their age. Anne, an accountant for a paper mill, shared her feelings about this issue:

> I love my job, but it's been really hard because I'm
> so used to having roommates around, and there's
> always someone your own age to do something with
> in college. Here I work with a lot of older people.
> I'm the only female in our department and work
> in a male-dominated mill too. I get picked on a lot;
> people don't take me seriously at first. I really miss
> having my roommates and women around. So I'm
> really trying to meet people.

Ned, working in a sales position out of his home, concurred:

> I was continually surrounded by people my age and
> my interest level in school, fifteen thousand of them.
> Now it's kind of a lonely feeling, when you come
> home to your apartment and you've only got one
> or two friends. You're not always in contact with

good friends that you can backslap and laugh with. It's more of a serious nature, when you're with clients. It's just kind of a little bit of wishful feeling that, "Hey, I wish it were always these high human-contact situations all the time."

Some of the students viewed peer support as a component of their achievement or success. Andrew described the work world like this:

There are very few people that you just sit down and start talking politics with or just sit down and start debating things. I miss that. I don't feel I'm challenged when it comes to bases as I was. I just feel sometimes I'm just getting mentally lazy, and that really frustrates me. You get in a routine that stifles your creativity and learning. And society is a lot different [from college], as far as you're not supposed to challenge. Miami challenged me to do this, that, get involved. You step out in the real world, and it's easy to get depressed and disappointed. Some people are just happy doing what they're doing and don't want to advance or go any farther. In college, everybody seems to have drive. And you step out in the real world, and boy, that is not the case.

Andrew missed the stimulation and motivation provided by his peers in the college environment. These three students' comments underscore the benefit of interventions by student affairs educators in the arena of peer interactions. Even for students who experienced these interactions during college, it was difficult to establish networks after college. Because these networks offered so many advantages, not the least of which is that they function independently of authorities, students could benefit from learning how to create them. Educational programming addressing how to establish and maintain interpersonal relationships both in college and in the work world would thus be useful.

Student Organizations: Validating Voice
Through Leadership Opportunities

These students appreciated the chance to function independently in organizational settings. Students described positions and participation in organizations as furthering their ability as leaders. Sean articulated this theme well:

> I've taken on leadership positions. It changes how I think about things, how organized I am, the way I see myself in relation to other people. I think it makes a difference to have the responsibility to try to run an organization and coordinate people into a pretty effective system and create something on my own. It allows me to work on other skills, how well I communicate with people, organize things.

Sean's focus is on learning to increase his individual effectiveness through these opportunities. Ned agreed:

> I'm a lot more self-confident. That probably just came from being involved in a lot of leadership activities. I went through being in a lot of new situations, and I came out of all of them pretty well. So I think that gave me confidence that I could walk into many different situations with different types of people and be successful at it.

Ned also reported gaining basic communication and leadership skills from his organizational involvement. Lindsey also reported gaining such skills:

> I learned to be an arbitrator through my fraternity. I was vice president. That was my job, to be the enforcer of rules and the arbitrator at times. That definitely helped me learn how to better manage people. And I learned probably to better manage myself than I did before.

Independence and self-assurance are inherent in all three students' comments.

Internships and Employment: Help Students Process Insights Gained

Student employment opportunities enabled independent knowers to gain important insights about careers. Lowell described what he had learned:

> I've been working since day one. I'm a student supervisor in the dining halls. Dealing with students as an authority figure and controlling your temper — that's probably the hardest thing to do. I've made great strides toward that. Just dealing with a bunch of different types of people, some who aren't motivated, some who are highly motivated, and everybody in between. This is all very helpful, especially down the road, to what I want to do.

Phillip also gained understanding that he felt was important to his career success through an internship. He explained:

> It opened my eyes. It wasn't a completely positive experience. However, it did let me know where my interest lies and what it's going to take for me to get where I want to go. I finally realized that just because you've graduated from college, people aren't going to lay down the red carpet and welcome you into their business. You're pretty much going to have to fend for yourself. So that helped, I guess.

Phillip valued these insights, but his "I guess" showed his hesitation over the value of learning how things were. Andrew had mixed feelings, too:

> I had my job [postgraduation] at Thanksgiving. Then I got to work as a manager at the campus

radio station. The pressure of job hunting was over
with, so I really poured my heart and soul into the
radio station. And I fell in love with that type of work.
And that's not exactly what I went into. So I miss
music and those aspects. They're always in the back of
my mind. I love my job now, but it's an odd feeling. I
love my job, but I still think about the other.

Knowing that he loved the radio station work, Andrew wondered about his career in accounting and financial development,
even though he liked it as well. He added, "Now I'm questioning whether I'm actually in the exact career that I want to be in."
    For some, employment opportunities helped resolve such
questions. Alice described her job in social work as helping her
with "a sense of priorities, what's really important and what's
really not." Her volunteer work at a crisis referral center also
netted her a successful job lead. Dawn reported this outcome
of her summer job:

It forced me to take some big steps toward being
a responsible adult. I'm much more on top of things.
I'm more responsible; I'm much more organized
as to what I do.

The stories about employment opportunities suggest that students arrived at these insights independently. Perhaps assistance
from student affairs educators would have helped those who were
not quite sure what to do with their ideas process these experiences more effectively.

Internships and Employment: Reinforce Self-Confidence

Self-confidence was another outcome of student employment opportunities. Sheila gained confidence through her job at the computer center:

I worked in the computer lab for professors and
graduate students. I was hanging around with people who were very science- and math-oriented, and

that was completely not my orientation at all. So that was good for me, because I learned different things, and I picked up the fact that I wasn't as stupid as I thought I was. I guess I'd always been tracked as an English, kind of art person. Being thrown in that environment and being forced to cope was very good for me because I learned I could pick up things. I could work with computers, and I could do math and science. I was capable; it was just a matter of processing them in a different kind of background and processing them in my own vocabulary.

Tracy's increase in self-confidence came from getting a summer job in a business where she had no connections:

I didn't know anybody there. I went in and managed the interview, and I got through that okay, and I got the job. Then I was kind of like, "Most of these people are older; I hope I can meet their standards." And everything went well. I made some really good friends there. I feel a lot more confident about myself; I've had some positive feedback. My friends [there] say, "Oh, you did a good job." I still don't know what I'm going to do, but that's beside the point. I know I'll get where I'm supposed to go.

Tracy's newly discovered self-confidence reduced her anxiety about her future because she now believed that she would succeed. Self-esteem is essential if independent knowers are to maintain their new-found voices. Student affairs educators can help by creating opportunities for students to develop their self-confidence.

International and Cultural Exchange: Create
Opportunities for Students to Reevaluate Their Beliefs

Many of the independent thinkers had opportunities to experience different cultures. Students who had participated in exchange programs in Korea, Germany, Italy, and Spain reported being more independent and responsible, thinking differently, having a different point of view, and engaging in self-examination. For example, Laura said this of being able to go to the country where she was born:

> College gave me this opportunity that otherwise I wouldn't have been able to pursue: to go to [my country]. I had a lot of problems with my identity. I always ignored that. The fact of who I was and about my heritage. And college gave me this experience to go out and search for this person I didn't really understand.

Marla described the effect of encountering a new culture:

> You get even a greater sense of being totally on your own—a new culture, language, being absolutely responsible for everything. Finding yourself in circumstances you would never find yourself in here and that you had to think of how to get out [of] yourself and that you had to deal with. And just the whole culture thing and meeting people from another culture was so fascinating.

Gary focused on diversity:

> It was a great cultural experience. I became more aware of racial attitudes and differences in race. I feel more aware and a better overall individual because of the experience.

The effect on her thinking was articulated by Sheila:

> I kind of wish everybody had to leave campus for a year and go to some strange place and come back and totally rebuild their life. Because that's the best thing—the whole rebuilding and self-examination.

Learning to spend time with yourself and learning
to educate yourself.

Referring to this experience again in her fifth-year interview,
Sheila said it "taught me to trust my own judgment, be less naive,
and cope in a different culture." Similarly, Barry emphasized
the independence that the exchange program had fostered:

The biggest thing I learned was how to make decisions. Each day is different. You had a lot of decisions
to make — where to go, when to go, should you miss
class. A lot of times over there, you failed, you missed
the train, you stayed in the wrong place, you didn't eat
the right thing. All the time in the back of my head,
it was "All right, if I do this, will I die?" And if the
answer was no, I'd go ahead and do it. If you made a
wrong decision, it wasn't the end of the world. I
learned to take risks and handle problems.

The common theme in these stories is independent thinking and functioning. The students emphasized experiences that
prompted them to think about something differently. They were
no longer overly influenced by peers, but developed their own
perspectives. Interacting with others often offered opportunities to gain insight into diversity, which could be valued because
of these learners' sense that all perspectives are valid in an uncertain world. Independent knowers were no longer reliant on
authority figures in the cocurricular environment; they appreciated experiences that would help them function independently
and successfully in the future and gain insights about themselves.
Some of the stories suggest that student affairs educators could
join students as equals in assessing these experiences to help in
developing students' voice.

Matching Contextual Knowers' Learning Needs

The advice of contextual participants is gleaned from their fifth-
year interviews. Some of the experiences occurred during their

332 Knowing and Reasoning in College

senior year and some in graduate school and work settings after
college.

Peer Relationships: Reinforce Peers
as a Legitimate Source of Knowledge

Contextual knowers emphasized learning from peer relationships. Learning took the form of shaping one's future, changing attitudes, being more open-minded, and exploring ideas with
peers. Deirdre listed friends as one aspect of her college experience that prepared her for the future:

> The friends I made, getting some people from dif-
> ferent geographic locations, and just the very in-
> terrelationships we formed. Some of my friends,
> the one in California, for example — she had a very
> big influence on me. She's kind of the mature per-
> son I want to be some day. My friends had a big
> influence on me, introduced me to new things,
> things I didn't know existed.

Jim also listed interaction with classmates as an important component of college life:

> I think the general theme of what I got out of my
> college career was just a chance to work with a lot
> of different people and a chance to see so many
> different perspectives on life through my male-
> female relationships, through my fraternity, brother-
> hood relationships, through my acquaintance rela-
> tionships. A lot of it was just the interaction with
> people and a chance to see things in different ways
> and really grow as a person. You'd take up issues
> like abortion and how your opinions evolved through
> your college years. And dealing with women. When
> I first came into college, it was like the woman
> should be the subordinate-type person and that type
> of thing. And now, from my involvement with

> people in school, I've kind of gotten away from that,
> where it's more of an equal-type position.

Jim credited a relationship with a woman and work with a women's association through student government as major influences in these changes. Barry also experienced changes in his perceptions of others through interacting with fellow crew members at a construction job that he took temporarily after graduation:

> Now I've got some friends out there I met through
> work, in my crew. We're from all different walks
> of life. People who were college-educated and peo-
> ple who were just serving time. But basically, I'll
> look at some people I maybe would have made a
> stereotype about before and now will take a sec-
> ond guess.

Gwen also learned a valuable lesson about impressions of other people:

> I tend to always believe that people are good and
> they're always going to tell you the truth. And that
> if people are honest and do the right thing, they
> will be compensated for that. Not necessarily com-
> pensated, but that will never harm them. I've found
> little by little that that was not true; people were
> not always nice, and people did not always tell you
> the truth. People whose interests you may have
> looked out for don't look out for yours. Those are
> unfortunate things, but I think that a little caution
> never hurts anyone. It's more of an open-eyed view
> than a pessimistic view.

Although Gwen labeled what she learned as "unfortunate," she still felt it was important to know.

Learning from peers cut across curricular and cocurricular arenas. Lowell described a valuable lesson learned in his fraternity that carried over into the classroom:

I learned not to be so confrontational. I think that's one of the biggest learning experiences that I've had. Stand by your point, but don't go about it in a bad way. And that's a "feely" thing; you have to just kind of feel it. It happened outside of the classroom — in my fraternity. I had to be a house manager. Learning how to motivate people.

Mark described classroom topics as spilling over into cocurricular life:

Engaging with other students. Here [at law school] you're able to do it outside of even structured, extracurricular programs because everyone there has a story and everyone is very intelligent and articulate. And I feel honored to be there because you can knock on your neighbor's door and discuss anything. In that way, it builds a community, and at the same time you're constantly learning outside a classroom.

Barry also felt that learning could occur outside the classroom. He said:

It was difficult at times to get into a really good discussion. Some of my real close friends, I could sit down with. But even striking up a conversation in a bar or something — you'd be talking about politics and different facets of it. And some people would be like, "Why are you talking about that?" I go, "Well, you know, I think it's interesting." And I think a lot of people are scared of it or just bored with it. You can learn just as much when you're having a beer as you can when you're holding a pencil.

Collectively, these contextual knowers advocated learning both academic and everyday-life lessons from peers. Classmates and work colleagues were viewed as legitimate sources of knowledge, and interaction with them in various environments enabled contextual learners to establish beliefs based on the information gained in the interaction.

Student Organizations: Provide Freedom to Exercise Choice

Contextual knowers appreciated organizational involvement that provided them freedom of choice. Gwen said:

> I think organizational and creative aspects that I learned from my extracurricular [life]. My extracurriculars were really important in my development. You are so the master of your own destiny at college. It's such a time of stretching and growing all the way around. You test the ground and see how it feels in a lot of different areas. And you are trying to fly off cliffs, and you crash a few times, and you soar a few times.

For Mark, there were specific opportunities that he appreciated:

> The scholar-leader program was excellent. A group of very dynamic people. It's not only leadership training, but within a fairly large school you can be grouped together in a community of people that is special. The opportunity to work with a small leadership honor society I was in. I really learned a lot about how to work together with people in an organization, how to plan events. There's a lot of self-determination at Miami, and I liked that a lot.

Jim, too, had a list of organizational involvements that affected him:

> Everything from hall government my freshman year, RA my sophomore year, campaign manager both freshman and sophomore years, student credit union, my fraternity — dealing with people, taking on leadership roles, a lot of good friends.

Gwen's term "master of your own destiny," Mark's phrase "self-determination," and Jim's long list of activities emphasize the freedom that these students experienced through organizational involvement. Freedom to explore and make choices is central to fostering contextual knowing. Students need experience to judge which choices to make and the opportunity to make them.

Internships and Employment: Reinforce Expanding Horizons

Contextual knowers also appreciated employment that offered freedom of choice and expanded their perspectives. Gwen cited her RA job as one such experience:

> You're pushed to your limits by situations, for instance, my RA job. Things like that push you to how far you really can—they force you to look at situations that you never thought that you'd know how to deal with. And, suddenly, you're dealing with them, and you're doing okay.

Deirdre described her work in a nearby city, which necessitated her driving home late at night, as giving her a sense of accomplishment. For Reginald, the RA job also had a significant impact:

> The RA experience really took the academics and incorporated it with, I guess, the social. Social in terms of the people. It put me in a position of sight where I could see that this wasn't just academics and it wasn't just social. That was praxis. It gave me the broader learning aspect.

Although it sounds as though these students responded to challenge out of necessity, their views must have been open to expansion for these employment opportunities to have had this effect.

Campus Environment: Create Possibilities
for Freedom and Development of Voice

The notion of freedom was also part of contextual knowers' vision of the overall college environment. Mark felt restricted by what he called the "Mother Miami" attitude. He said, "I felt that a lot, and I didn't need it; it was beyond the bounds of reasonableness." Adrian reacted quite differently:

> I think I'm interested in more things, just because I'm open to more than I was before I went to college. And I think that had to do with Miami having so much going on, very diverse possibilities.

Whereas Mark felt his freedom was restricted, Adrian perceived the environment as offering possibilities. Identifying aspects of the environment where students can exercise choice would help contextual knowers continue to develop this way of knowing.

Two common themes emerge from the contextual knowers' experiences: freedom of choice and learning acquired as a result of peer relationships. The combination of these two implies that contextual knowers had established their ability to function independently sufficiently to engage in the learning community without losing their own voices. They appreciated opportunities for self-determination and control over their own destinies; they chose to explore their limits and gain as much as possible from diverse opportunities. Their stories clearly demonstrate that contextual knowers were instrumental in shaping their experiences in organizations and work settings. Simultaneously, they valued peers as a source of learning for both academic and everyday life and genuinely engaged with them as partners. This equality of self and others may account for the relational tone of the contextual knowers' cocurricular stories.

Summary

These students' ideas illustrate the types of environments that confirm students in each way of knowing. Although some of the advice seems to overlap, it does take on different dimensions in absolute, transitional, independent, and contextual knowing. The absolute knowers' focus on adjustment to college translated into confirmation in three main forms. Positive interactions with peers helped them feel comfortable in the college environment; initial opportunities for responsibility launched their journey toward independence; and support from authority figures in making educational decisions helped define the right choices. Transitional learners shifted their attention to preparing to function effectively. As a result, confirmation for them included developing leadership in organizations, acquiring practical experience in organizations and employment, gaining human relations skills through employment, and learning responsibility through living arrangements and the general campus environment. Transitional knowers also became increasingly interested in how to deal with diversity and found confirmation for doing so in a variety of settings. Peers' influence strengthened, as transitional knowers relied less on authority figures.

Independent knowers' discovery of their own voices yielded new forms of confirmation. Validation of their own voices occurred in student organization leadership positions and international experiences. New insights and confidence gained from employment confirmed their independent functioning, as did the ability to balance their own needs with others'. Appreciation of diversity became possible because a variety of perspectives were recognized as equally valid. Contextual knowers began to use their voices to influence their experience and demonstrated an interdependence with peers. Confirmation for them came from freedom of choice, possibilities for creating their own perspectives, and opportunities to expand their horizons. Peers became a legitimate source of knowledge from which to make decisions about everyday and classroom concerns.

Stories about the cocurricular experience underscore the role that peers play in students' ways of knowing. The story line of relations with peers takes center stage in the cocurricular stories. Peers provided steady support during all four ways of knowing despite changes in what that support entailed along the way. Peers had a substantial influence on students' behavior until students discovered their own voices, at which point they began to make decisions about peer influence. Peers also made the students confront diversity, increased awareness of diversity, and eventually fostered its appreciation. The extensive support that students gained from peers probably balanced the contradictions that they introduced. Other students, particularly close friends, provided continuity by staying with students during the transitions from being dependent to independent to interdependent with peers.

Relations with authority were not a major factor in the cocurricular stories beyond absolute students' reliance on authorities for career decisions. Many of the opportunities for confirmation through student organizations, living arrangements, and employment may have been engineered by student affairs educators. In some cases, students noted how a student affairs educator had identified an opportunity or helped them make the most of it. However, many stories contained no mention of these educators. More intentional intervention in some cocurricular experiences might balance peer influence and help students process them in ways that lead to more complex ways of knowing. Despite extensive involvement in cocurricular experiences, most students in this group did not form their own perspectives until late in college or after college.

In addition to confirmation, the cocurricular environment offered some contradiction that was not available in students' curricular lives. In some cases, such as for absolute knowers, contradictions that were not a part of their academic environment were part of their cocurricular environment through peer interaction. Hands-on learning, advocated by transitional knowers but occurring less often than they would have liked in the academic environment, existed in the organizational and employment opportunities that students found in the cocurricular environment. Contradiction in the form of direct experience, confirmation from peers and accomplishments in other areas, and continuity provided by peers and support groups created an atmosphere where the student voice could develop. The enhancement of contradiction, confirmation, and continuity in the cocurricular environment, as well as the integration of the cocurricular and the academic environment, would offer additional possibilities for development. Chapter Eleven addresses this task.

Chapter Eleven

Promoting
Cocurricular Learning

Independence is instilled because in certain situations,
there's nobody there to tell you, "That's right; that's wrong.
You shouldn't do this; you shouldn't do that." You make
your own decisions.

— *Gavin*

At the outset of Chapter Nine, I described promoting student
voice in curricular life through the use of three principles: validating the student as a knower, situating learning in their own experience, and viewing learning as constructing meaning with
others. These same principles apply to cocurricular life. In fact,
the relational nature inherent in these ideas, so often obscured
in academic settings due to the dominance of objectivism, is
usually more visible in the cocurricular environment. However,
relational learning opportunities are often restricted by the subordinate position that student affairs has historically occupied in
the academy. A brief exploration of this situation is necessary
to bring to light the assumptions that must be reconsidered if
we are to use these three principles to develop student voice in
cocurricular life.

When the expansion of the number of students in the
early 1900s made it unlikely that faculty could address their total
development, responsibilities were divided. "The faculty was
charged with intellectual development of students, and such

340

specialists as deans of men and women were assigned responsibility for extracurricular student affairs" (Knock, 1985, p. 15). It was at this juncture that kinds of development other than intellectual, such as aesthetic, affective, or interpersonal, were relegated to the "extracurricular" domain, with the assumption that they could be separated from the intellectual sphere. With such strands of development designated as *extra* (or supplemental), student affairs was assigned a subordinate status from the beginning.

"To be on the margin is to be part of the whole but outside the main body" (Hooks, 1984, p. ix). Hooks's statement describes the dilemma faced by student affairs in light of its historical marginalization. Fenske (1989) describes student services as "a ubiquitous but almost invisible empire in virtually every institution of higher education" (p. 6). *The Student Personnel Point of View* (American Council on Education Studies, 1949) did take a philosophical stance advocating that students be considered as whole beings, whose development in all areas was related. The authors suggested "attention to the student's well-rounded development—physically, socially, emotionally and spiritually, as well as intellectually" (p. 1). Despite this comprehensive perspective, their conceptualization of the role of student affairs was confined to the "other" developmental domains and touched intellectual concerns in only two areas: admitting capable students and providing remedial services to increase academic success. They took a service-oriented approach to the student affairs aspects of development and noted that these could hinder intellectual progress if not effectively addressed. This acceptance of the bifurcation of intellectual and affective development has survived despite considerable challenge by noted writers in the profession. Fenske (1989) recounts repeated attempts dating from the start of the twentieth century to integrate intellectual and affective growth. Many other writers have argued for this integration, and some (for example, Brown, 1972; Miller and Prince, 1976) have articulated specific plans for how it could be achieved. Others (for example, Knefelkamp, 1974; Widick, 1975) provided research data demonstrating that intellectual development could be fostered through the application of student development theory. The conceptualization of new student service roles, particularly the student development educator and the campus ecology manager, held promise for integrating intellectual and affective development. However, Fenske's (1989) contention that most student services professionals continued to accept a complementary role to academic affairs seems true. As recently as 1987, a document to commemorate the fiftieth anniversary of the original 1937 edition of *The Student Personnel Point of View* identified as its first priority: "The academic mission of the institution is preeminent. Colleges and universities organize their primary activities around the academic experience: the curriculum, the library, the classroom, and the laboratory. The work of student affairs should not compete with and cannot substitute for that academic experience. As a partner in the educational enterprise, student affairs enhances and supports the academic mission" (American Council on Education and the National Association of Student Personnel Administrators, 1987, p. 10). This position appropriately confirms the importance of intellectual development but is narrow in that it limits that development to the curriculum, library, classroom, and laboratory. The partnership is construed as one in which academic affairs stands at the center and student affairs provides service from the margin. As a result, objectivism continues to be endorsed at the center, and relational approaches are relegated to the margin.

   This perspective fails to recognize that relational modes of knowing (termed narrative, aesthetic, affective, or interpersonal by various writers) are central to intellectual development. The student stories in this book confirm that this kind of knowing is central to the development of voice for many students. It is also essential to complex ways of knowing. These ideas come as no surprise to many student development educators who have studied the theories evolving in the last twenty years. They know autonomy and interdependency (or the capacity to join others in a relationship that appropriately balances autonomy and dependency) are necessary if the student voice and complex perspectives are to emerge. They know that participation in genuine relationships is a major source of the dissonance that calls upon students to reshape their ways of knowing. Perhaps most importantly, these professionals realize that development of all kinds stems from relational opportunities to interact and experience feedback from others, to differentiate previous perspectives and reintegrate them into new ones and that it is nurtured in contexts offering confirmation, contradiction, and continuity. What these professionals may not realize is that their relational perspective is valid and should be incorporated into the center of the academic enterprise.

Many of the philosophical underpinnings of student affairs support my contention that it should join (not replace) academia at the center. Caring for students is a fundamental concern of student affairs, which has held sacred that students are unique individuals whose differences must be celebrated; student affairs has also emphasized "that the major responsibility for a student's growth in personal and social wisdom rests with the student himself" (American Council on Education Studies, 1949, p. 3). Many student affairs divisions have endorsed the recent focus on developing communities in which students care for each other, celebrate diversity, and function interdependently. Kuh and others (1991) concluded that institutions that stress to students their responsibility for their own affairs encourage involvement. These ideas clearly support our three principles: validating students as knowers, situating learning in the students' own experience, and defining learning as jointly constructing meaning. Yet student affairs practice does not always reflect these notions.

I noted earlier Thorne's contention that marginalized groups become silent and invisible. Perhaps this thesis explains the contradiction between student affairs practice and the beliefs of professionals in the field. We gave up in loco parentis as a philosophy in *The Student Personnel Point of View* (American Council on Education Studies, 1949). We believe students must take risks, make their own decisions, and manage the outcomes in order to develop, even if this behavior creates a disruption of routine campus life. Yet we know that we are accountable to those at the center for "managing" student life in a way that does not interfere with the central mission. Thus, our underlying assumption of student affairs at the margin prohibits us from negotiating a community with our faculty colleagues in which opportunities for development that may be risky can occur. Perhaps being silenced and made invisible explains why student affairs professionals who are so committed to relational approaches choose not to share them with faculty colleagues who could benefit. Changing the basic assumption that student affairs is marginal to the academic mission and that affective development has little to do with intellectual growth is crucial to helping students develop voice and complex ways of knowing. Such a change is crucial to freeing student affairs professionals to implement policies and practices based on the principles I have described. As we explore the role of student affairs in these principles, other underlying assumptions that warrant our attention will emerge as well. The students' stories in Chapter Ten illustrate how these principles relate to the student affairs function. Rather than repeat them here, I often refer to those cited earlier.

Validating the Student as a Knower

As the story lines summarized in Chapter Seven indicated, students with absolute or transitional ways of knowing do not perceive that what they have to say is of great value. Initially, this situation would seem to apply mostly to the academic sphere, but the stories of absolute learners suggest otherwise. Despite their perception of increased independence in everyday life and decision making, they often revealed their reliance on authority. Recall Toni's experience of changing her major four times. Toni felt all alone and totally responsible for her decision. As a result, Toni went to friends, her RA, and then advisers for help. Her mom's absence led to Toni's feeling of independence, but she described what she did on her own as finding authorities to take her mom's place. Toni gave no hint of self-reliance in this important decision. Students like Toni approach career counselors with the assumption that the counselors know more than they do about what they should major in. Peers sometimes took the authority role in other situations, as many students explained how roommates had helped them learn how to live on their own. I want to argue here, as I did in Chapter Nine, that validating students should begin during absolute knowing, rather than waiting for their voices to emerge.

The students' stories about their cocurricular lives show that they found validation in student organization leadership opportunities, work environments, and cross-cultural experiences. Lydia recounted in Chapter Ten how her role as social chair in her sorority helped her "handle certain people under certain conditions." She described learning how to approach people and to "come across like you know what you're talking about." In order to influence her peers, she had to become more adept in both her individual and collective dealings with them. As she told her story, it was clear that, by "coming across as if she knew what she was talking about," she had actually come to see herself as competent. Ned gained similar validation and self-confidence from leadership activities that were new situations for him. He noted that he "came out of all of them pretty well." The connection between self-confidence and autonomous learning is clear in Sean's comments about the effect of his leadership positions. He reported, "It changes how I think about things, how organized I am, the way I see myself in relation to other people." The opportunity to take responsibility for an organization and other people led to Sean's ability to "create something on my own." In that light, his comment about the way he saw himself in relation to other people might refer to seeing himself as a knower.

Students found this same kind of confirmation in their roles as student employees. Stories about work experiences from Chapter Ten demonstrate this point. Gwen described her RA job as pushing her to her limits. Being forced to deal with situations resulted, in Gwen's case, in "doing okay." This outcome confirmed her sense that she could do more than she had imagined. Sheila had a similar experience in her job in the computer lab. She described being around "people who were very science- and math-oriented," through which she learned new things. As a result, Sheila went from believing she was stupid in math and science to stating unequivocally, "I was capable."

Functioning as an authority figure also helped students confirm themselves as knowers. Heather explained how her RA job forced her to "be more outgoing." She said that coming into contact with different problems necessitated that she understand herself in order to help her residents. Carrying out her RA responsibilities forced Heather to view herself as mature and independent, even though she did not feel like that. (Her comments about the problems of shy persons in the classroom, where interaction is required, also support my contention that affective learning is central to intellectual development.) Lowell also learned about himself as a student supervisor in the dining halls. He said, "Dealing with students as an authority figure and controlling your temper—that's probably the hardest thing to do. I've made great strides toward that." His role as an authority figure helped him learn how to function like one.

As we saw in Chapter Ten, the development of voice that comes from viewing oneself as responsible and competent is clear in the student stories about cross-cultural experiences. Marla reported a "sense of being totally on your own—a new culture, language, being absolutely responsible for everything." She found herself in many situations that she had never encountered. She returned from this experience pleased with her ability to figure out how to get out of situations herself. Sheila also valued thinking for herself as a result of what she referred to as going to "some strange place" and coming back and "totally rebuilding" her life. She found this to be a process of self-education. Barry described the same process in his comments about his cross-cultural experience. Recall that Barry's decisions hinged on the question, "All right, if I do this, will I die?" If he thought the answer was no, he would proceed. He described the result of learning "to take risks and handle problems." What is arresting in Barry's story is that he was not always "forced into" new experiences but chose them on the basis of his predictions of survival—in other words, Barry had confidence in his ability to think before these experiences. All three of these stories demonstrate that successful functioning in a new setting helped confirm students as knowers.

Barry's view of himself as an independent thinker before

his cross-cultural experience is in contrast to the stories discussed thus far that focus on "forced" contradiction; students described being "pushed," "forced into," and "thrown into" situations. Use of these terms implies that the situation contained significant contradiction. Yet the students reported successful outcomes, which suggest that they were confirmed as knowers. Our understanding of the necessary balance between confirmation and contradiction requires a closer look at their stories. The careful reader has already discovered that the ones I have summarized here came largely from students in independent and contextual knowing; they had probably developed at least some voice previously. Yet a review of the comments of absolute and transitional knowers about organizational and work experiences reveals that the outcomes were friendship and support rather than development of voice. Thus, providing these opportunities is not in itself a sufficient plan for validating all students. Balancing confirmation and contradiction is essential if experiences like those discussed here are to help student voice develop.

Many organizational leadership positions, student affairs opportunities such as resident-adviser positions, and most international exchange experiences are reserved for upper-division students. In the case of leadership and work opportunities, the students with the most individual achievement have a better chance of acquiring these positions. As I think back on my years as a residence hall director, I remember that I always sought the best undergraduate staff members and hall government officers I could find. The ones that I sought were self-confident, could analyze a situation and make a good decision, and could work interdependently with their peers. Placing such students in these positions not only reduced the number of unwise decisions that I then had to deal with but also supposedly served the student population more effectively. Yet my approach meant that I offered opportunities only to those who had already begun to develop a voice. How can we make developmental opportunities available to those who do not yet view themselves as knowers and still balance the need for effective service to students? It seems to me that there are at least three workable solutions to this dilemma.

The first approach entails being more flexible in our expectations of students in organizational leadership roles. By more flexible, I mean less concerned about avoiding uncomfortable situations and more concerned about making them into educational opportunities. Take, for instance, the story about the controversial T-shirt, a version of which has probably occurred on numerous campuses. A student group designed a T-shirt for its members in the spirit of group cohesion and community. Additionally, in the spirit of being clever and creative, they arrived at a design that was interesting and unique. Being caught up in this process, the designers failed to reflect carefully on how the design could be interpreted by others. The T-shirt, which arrived in mass quantities (as T-shirts always do), was offensive to various campus populations.

This scenario is every organization adviser's nightmare. The questions come from administrators. Where was the adviser when this T-shirt was being designed? Did the adviser approve this design? Why did he or she let the group order a T-shirt that had not been approved? And then the students have questions. If we cannot sell or distribute the T-shirts, is the division going to reimburse our organization for the purchase? Why should we be told what we can and cannot do with our money? The outcome of the story usually includes one consistent change: future T-shirt designs must be approved in advance.

The aim of preventing such incidents, particularly when they devalue other student populations, is understandable and justifiable, yet such situations arise every day in many contexts where intervention is not possible. The T-shirt controversy, however, can be turned into an opportunity for education and development. Exploring students' thinking about the design's implications (both with designers and others), assisting students in processing their thinking and feelings, and helping students to hear varying perspectives are opportunities to confirm that students have something valuable to say, to contradict perspectives that are narrowly construed and are insensitive to others, and to support students' struggle to find an acceptable solution. The outcome that would be profitable for future situations would involve staff in an ongoing dialogue with students (in the process of the T-shirt design, for example); dialogue continues the learning experience, whereas approval shuts it down. Dialogue affirms the value of student perspectives without necessarily validating any particular one. Knowing that students often hold ideas that we would like to challenge, we might be wise to watch for these opportunities, rather than to create rules to make sure they do not arise in organized settings. Palmer (1987) suggests that conflict, or "the ability to confront each other critically and honestly over alleged facts, imputed meanings, or personal biases and prejudices" (p. 25), is essential for knowing and makes for a healthy community. Knowing that students are not automatically skilled at this type of confrontation, we ought to look for as many chances to teach and practice it as possible.

A second approach involves broadening student participation beyond leadership and student staff positions. Student leaders and staff routinely complain that they do all the work. Group members who were so enthusiastic at the beginning of the year have disappeared when it is time to implement plans. Although apathy is certainly one explanation, the failure of students to perceive their worth and of leaders to reveal it to them is an equally plausible one. Student leaders are often focused on achieving individually and acquiring confirmation for their own developing voice. This emphasis is particularly true of mastery-, impersonal-, and individual-pattern knowers. Lowell described learning how to "tell people what to do without being bossy. You have to learn how to get people to do what you want them to do without making them angry at you." Lowell emphasized learning to manage people effectively. Effective leadership, according to many experts, involves empowering rather than managing people: "To empower followers means that the leader must share his or her power—converting followers into leaders and being shaped by, as well as shaping, one's followers" (Rogers, 1988, p. 6). If student affairs staff helped student leaders learn how to share their power with others and to engage in mutually beneficial interactions with them, those not yet in leadership positions could be drawn in and experience the validation needed to increase their involvement. This action, of course, requires that student affairs staff treat students in the same way—a central component of the third approach to our dilemma.

The third approach concentrates on confirmation in arenas where all students are "involved" from the outset of their college experience. Living arrangements and student-conduct policy are two such areas that touch all their lives. The stories about living arrangements reveal that validation of individual authority occurred largely in off-campus living arrangements. Many students valued the friendship and support that they received living on campus, but the development of voice was described as a result of having to take responsibility for their everyday life. Alexis's comments from Chapter Ten bear repeating here:

> I have some different attitudes about things because I've found living off campus that you have more responsibility. It helps you to budget your time more; it makes everyday life more of a learning experience just in general and about commonsense things. A lot of times your work gets neglected because you have responsibilities, and you have responsibilities to the other people that you live with, too. You don't have any rules. So you have to do more or less what you think is best for yourself all the time. It makes you think about it more.

There are a wealth of insights in Alexis's comments. She had more responsibilities and had to make decisions about how to balance them. She recognized that she had obligations to her housemates that had to be juggled with the rest. She had to decide what was best in the absence of rules, a situation that caused her to reflect more upon her choices. It is important to note that the absence of rules did not translate into doing whatever she wanted. Rather, it translated into wise decisions and a recognition that she had obligations to herself and others. Her autonomy came without the cost of irresponsible behavior. Of course, three hundred students living in a residence hall is quite a different situation from ten students living in a house or two students in an apartment. A complete absence of rules is not feasible in any campus-housing unit. Yet if students are aware, as Alexis was, of their obligations to others with whom they live, their inclusion in discussing group norms within living units could be positive. Most students do not advocate being insensitive to others, harming others, damaging others' property, or creating unsafe living conditions. Group discussions about these matters might result in standards that are closer to staff expectations than they might predict. Students and staff agreeing on living-unit norms would validate students and give them opportunities to take responsibility. There might also be creative ways in which students could assume some of the residence hall duties that are currently undertaken by overburdened resident advisers.

Student participation in student-conduct discussions is another way of fostering self-reliance and independence. Recall Max's complaint about the campus environment: "They baby you—always checking up on you, taking care of you, making sure you do this and that. The rules are the same for upperclass and freshman students." Max does not appear to be arguing for an absence of rules but for expectations appropriate to his maturity. Max would probably feel more affirmed in the campus community if someone listened to his ideas and treated him as an adult who has a reasonable perspective on student behavior. This strategy would be consistent with the philosophy outlined in *The Student Personnel Point of View* (American Council on Education Studies, 1949) that students are responsible for their own growth. It would also constitute a caring approach, in Noddings's (1984) terms. She describes caring as "starting from a position of respect or regard for the projects of the other" and stresses that the one caring "does not abandon her own ethical ideal in doing this" (p. 176). Translated to student affairs, I take this statement to mean that staff would start from a position of respect for students' ideas, yet not abandon their standards about nonnegotiable conduct rules, such as those determined by law or the safety of others. Taking this approach would, of course, increase the risk that things would not always go smoothly. However, the investment of other students in rules of conduct is likely to carry far more weight with those prone to rule violations than the abstract warnings of staff. Engaging students in this kind of dialogue requires changing our assumptions that they will not participate wisely and becoming more comfortable justifying this approach as an educational activity to those at the academic center.

Situating Learning in the Students' Own Experience

What student affairs is responsible for teaching students is less clear cut than it is in academia. *The Student Personnel Point of View* (American Council on Education Studies, 1949) committed student affairs to the physical, social, emotional, and spiritual domains. I have argued that we should also include intellectual development. An entire field of literature is available on how to promote each of these aspects of development. One framework that allows us to discuss how this learning might be situated in students' experience is the Carnegie Foundation for the Advancement of Teaching's (1990) six principles for defining community. Using the student stories to illustrate these principles helps clarify how student affairs can enhance learning in a setting that naturally involves the student's experience. It also offers guidance for how student affairs can move from the margin to the center of educational practice because the conceptualization of community contains the creative tension between objective and relational modes of knowing. *Community* is defined as purposeful, open, just, disciplined, caring, and celebrative.

In advocating a purposeful community, the report calls for members of the community to work together toward educational goals. One avenue for this is an "'out-of-class curriculum' where the intellectual, aesthetic, and social dimensions of campus life thrive" (p. 14). Part of the out-of-class curriculum for Adrian was her student marketing organization. In Chapter Ten, she told us about a promotional campaign that her organization was doing for an actual client. She said, "I have learned more, I think, in that experience than I could ever learn in the classroom." The central point of Adrian's comment seems to be that the experience was real. "We're actually doing what you could be learning" implies that doing and learning are conceived as separate entities. "Doing" connects to Adrian's experience and creates one for her to reflect upon. Andrew's business manager position in a student organization helped him apply what he had learned in class to his organization and to test out ideas to see how they worked. Both Adrian's and Andrew's stories reveal that they were invested in these activities. Organizations that function to integrate learning with students' experience contribute to the educational mission of the community. Drawing on academic experience in these organizations might help more students make the connection.

The principle of an open community dictates that students speak and listen to each other in a way that allows free expression, yet affirms civility. Candace expressed her surprise in her first-year interview that most of her peers had not given any consideration to marriage. In her home town of two hundred, most of her friends were already married and had children. She said that she "learned a lot about people's social values, a lot of things I never really thought existed." She learned these things initially through roommates who were from cities. They shared their experiences and took turns going home with one another. Returning to her home town four years later, she reported wanting to say to people there, "Open your eyes. The world is not like this." Candace's insights came from the fact that she and her roommates, and later other friends, were able to express themselves freely and learn from each other about differences. Tracy reported a similar experience about coming into contact with people who were different. Initially, her reaction was, "When you first look at them, just on appearances, you kind of raise your eyebrow and wonder about them." She later realized that they had many good ideas that she would miss if she did not get to know them. Although Tracy did not say directly how this came about, we know it was through some sort of contact. Somehow, those she wondered about expressed themselves in a way that allowed her to see the value of their ideas. In both Candace's and Tracy's cases, civility (confirmation) was apparently present to balance the free expression (contradiction) of differences. This balance was not apparent in all the stories, however. Lowell reported that "one person called me a name — she was unable to hear my view." Gale used her boy friend to escape her peers because of her frustration at their attempts to impress everyone. Thus, civility and free expression are not automatic but take place in contexts where openness is encouraged by others. The more controversial the topic is—as is the case with racial- or sexual-orientation differences—the less likely that civility and free expression will be balanced.

The possibilities for encountering those from differing backgrounds and cultures abound in cocurricular life. Students live with others, have extensive interactions in organized social groups, work together on tasks in student organizations, interact with peers as student leaders, and play on recreational and organized sports teams. The contradiction stemming from these encounters is inevitable. The confirmation that allows free expression, promotes civility, and facilitates dialogue, so that students can reflect upon their differences, must be created by student affairs staff. So must continuity, as students' exchanges and reflections lead to changes in their perceptions. Creating opportunities for exchange prior to the breakdown of civility is also wise. However, if programming aimed at diversity issues is to be effective, it must be situated in the students' experience. Had a panel of presenters told Candace or Tracy that others have different values or that people cannot be judged by their appearance, their perspectives would not have been changed by the abstract nature of this encounter. Organizing programs in which students can either share experiences that they have already had or create new ones by exploring their differences balances speaking and listening. It also gives students a chance to encounter each other's varying approaches to learning and helps them devise their own.

The principle of a just community extends beyond merely allowing the free expression of diverse opinions in a civil environment to valuing those differences. The Carnegie report (1990) states this idea as honoring the sacredness of each person and pursuing diversity. By her fifth-year interview, Tracy had moved from "accepting people the way they are" to being appreciative of another person with different views. This change occurred as a result of an impromptu discussion with a person who had "some Eastern views" that she met while visiting some friends; Tracy came into contact with a new perspective that she wanted to learn more about. Rob also noted appreciating other perspectives: "I'm not as self-centered as I was in high school." Again, it took the student's own experience to move from self-centeredness, to acceptance, to appreciation.

Most of the instances of coming to value and pursue diversity came about because of interactions with friends. The fact that it was by accident that Tracy met someone who caused her to reassess her opinions attests to the tenuous nature of this experience. Many students who live at the center of campus life will never meet students who live on the margins and vice versa. Establishing activities and programs that involve the perspectives of both groups are needed to bring them together. Encouraging the balance of individual and relational modes of knowing in cocurricular life helps learners within each pattern to encounter the other. Ensuring that groups on the margin are included in student leadership positions is another way to bridge these worlds. Bringing the students together, however, is not enough. Student affairs staff must provide the confirmation needed for these groups to engage in civil and genuine exchanges and must help students learn how to value each other.

A disciplined community is one in which individuals accept their obligations to the group. The Carnegie report (1990), taking alcohol use and abuse as an example, advocated education about alcohol rather than its prohibition. This is advice relevant to other areas as well. Banning particular behaviors attempts to force students to abide by their obligations; it does not help them accept those responsibilities. Assisting students to arrive at their own decisions about their obligations promotes their development and increases the likelihood that they will act on those obligations. Rich's complaint about the visitation policy shows the impact of prohibiting certain activities:

It's just the principle of saying to twenty-year-olds and nineteen-year-olds, "You can't do this." I don't know where that comes from. Maybe it's my non-conservative approach being from the East, but I can't go down with that. That could be changed.

Rich's issue is not so much about the actual policy as it is that it states, "You can't do this." Anita shares this point of view as she described people taking responsibilities away from her generation:

> Like visitation. I think that if you give people the responsibilities or the privileges to make decisions on their own, they're going to do what's best for them in the end. Maybe they'll go a little crazy for a while, but I think—I don't know. It makes you angry, the visitation thing. I can't see any justifiable reason for it. Supposedly, we live in a democracy. And I think if you took it to a vote, there'd be an overwhelming majority of people who wanted to abolish that. My roommate is completely independent. She pays everything on her own. And for somebody to tell her that she can't do something like that, I think is just really oppressive. It's kind of like, "I'm doing all this proving I'm an adult; I can take responsibility, but I can't have somebody in my room after twelve o'clock." It doesn't coincide with it. It's hard because people are always telling you, "Act like an adult." It's kind of, in a way, you need to be able to learn how to do those things for yourself. College is a time when we should be able to make choices like, "I don't want people making a lot of music around me." I think if you gave people the choices to make for themselves that other people would have respect for each other. And you would learn what's right for you.

Although Anita personally disagrees with the content of the visitation policy, her real point is that students need to learn to make choices, to create their own perspectives as adults. She predicts that students would then accept their obligations. Tonya speaks to this issue from experience:

> The term *in loco parentis*—they seem to go a little overboard in that respect. And it makes me more

rebellious, a litte more liberal, more determined to break the rules, more determined to do what I'm not supposed to, just because I think they're over-stepping their bounds when they try to get you to do it. And it has a lot to do with how I was brought up; my mom didn't really tell me what to do all the time. I had guidelines, and I followed them. When I screwed up, I screwed up pretty badly, but I learned from them. So the conservatism has made me a lot more liberal; I used to be a lot more con-servative.

This is clearly a story of policies that have backfired. Tonya is out to break rules because they were imposed on her. She had had the previous experience of making her own decisions and learning from her mistakes. All three students' comments emphasize the need for teaching responsibility to others in a way that includes and relates to them, not by abstract pronounce-ments of the rules. Helping students negotiate guidelines, make choices, live with the consequences, and reflect on their needs and those of others is the best encouragement of responsibility.

A caring community is necessary to achieve all of the tasks discussed thus far. The Carnegie report notes that "the unique characteristic that makes these [the previous four] objectives work, the glue that holds it all together, is the way people relate to one another" (1990, p. 47). The report defines *caring* as the sensitive support of community members for one another and the encour-agement of service to others. The relational cocurricular world plays a major part in achieving this goal. Many students talked about the support they received from friends. Hugh's comments in Chapter Ten focused on the importance of being good friends with his seven housemates. The special relationship between Hugh and his housemates provided him with the help he needed. When Leah had a problem, she could also talk to one of her house-mates, who listened to her and sometimes diverted her attention by talking about her own concerns. The caring that Leah re-ceived from her housemates at times helped her work through her problems or even avoid them. At least, when she pushed them aside, she did so by showing concern for someone else.

Caring for others was sometimes also a way to receive care. Stephanie's story about working at the Oxford Crisis and Referral Center is a good example. She found that she often got overwhelmed by her own problems; she felt "like the whole world's coming down on your shoulders." However, helping someone else provided relief and put her own situation in perspective. Stephanie's service to others had the same effect and kept her in touch with how other people felt, a priority that stemmed from a previous experience:

> Part of the problem with last year, [when] I felt that there was so much tension, was that I had certain friends and acquaintances that really tended to be like that, very into themselves or into their own problems — kind of not caring about the people that were around them as much as what *they* wanted right then. I think it was a reaction to that and to my feeling that I didn't really want to do that; I didn't want to step over other people.

Eileen also volunteered her time to serve others and found it rewarding:

> I'm pretty active at Oxford View Nursing Home up the road. I'm vice president of GAP, which is the grandparent adoption program. It's nice to go there and do bingo and things because they just love — you can just walk in after going through a tornado, and they say, "Oh, you look beautiful." They just love people. And it's nice to go over there; it kind of puts things in perspective every once in a while. Makes you kind of realize how lucky you are and how young you are.

Confirmation like that received by Eileen and Stephanie also came to Hugh, by being a big brother through his finance association, and to Spencer, through being a secretary for a service fraternity. These opportunities to care for others not only helped students find support, but it also undoubtedly helped them to be more sensitive to others. Developing a caring attitude, giving full attention to other people, responding to them in a flexible way that explores possibilities, and cultivating relationships are the characteristics that Noddings (1991) uses to define interpersonal reasoning. These are likely outcomes of experiences like the ones described here.

Stephanie's story makes it clear, however, that not all students are concerned about others. It is an attitude that no doubt evolves from receiving care or experiencing the reward of providing it — a fact that again underscores the importance of situating learning in the students' experience. Hugh commented that although he enjoyed having a little brother, he had not been socialized for it. Mastery-, impersonal-, and individual-pattern learners may need confirmation of their ability to care and opportunities through which they can develop this capacity. Perhaps interpersonal reasoning and caring should be a focus of living-unit programs and educational programming about building relationships. Workshops that teach student organizations how to function might include components on interpersonal reasoning. Experiences like those of Stephanie, Eileen, Hugh, and Spencer, as well as opportunities to volunteer in soup kitchens, build housing for the homeless, and help at-risk youth, should be made more available to students. Contradiction of noncaring attitudes in cocurricular life are also essential to emphasize the importance of care. For example, Lowell found out by being a fraternity house manager that confrontation did not work; he learned through this contradiction to be less confrontational: "Stand by your point, but don't go about it in a bad way. And that's a 'feely' thing; you just have to kind of feel it." Lowell is describing the flexibility of interpersonal reasoning. Certainly, student affairs staff must themselves exhibit concern and interpersonal reasoning in interactions with students to encourage this behavior. Thus, careful attention to students and flexibility in responding to their needs are important. The development of the capacity to care would improve students' ability to work together, speak and listen to each other, appreciate differences, and accept their obligations to others. A caring community makes possible the sixth principle: that communities celebrate their traditions and changes in them. Only in a community that encompasses the first five principles can celebration include both those at the center and those on the periphery.

Defining Learning as Jointly Constructing Meaning

Situating learning in students' own experiences and developing community are still not sufficient for developing student voice. Within these experiences, genuine dialogue among students and staff is necessary to help students create their own identity and their fashion of relating to others in the communities they join. As was the case in teaching, interactions between student affairs staff and students should be seen as shaping both. This perspective agrees with the majority of functions of the student affairs profession. For example, the counselor role is based on appreciating the student's individual perspective and on nonjudgmental interactions; counselors listen to the student rather than using their personal perspective to guide the interaction (Forrest, 1989). The counselor's interpersonal skills are aimed at aiding the development of clients and avoiding establishing power over them. In addition, the belief in genuine interaction with clients underscores that the counseling encounter is the type of mutually transforming dialogue noted by Schniedewind (1987) and Shor and Freire (1987) in Chapter Nine. Similarly, the student development educator views the student as an integral part of the process (Brown, 1989). The student development educator provides experiences to facilitate student development based on an assessment of the student and of the goals that the student and educator mutually determine. Student development educators alter the opportunities they provide as students change, a process that requires an ongoing dialogue. The campus ecology manager focuses on designing environments that also promote student development. Such design is developed on the basis of jointly chosen educational values and goals, student perceptions, and reactions. In all of these roles, the student affairs professional does not minimize her or his expertise but allows it to exist in creative tension with the students' voices. The expertise is not applied to students but offered as part of a dialogue that values their voices.

Constructing meaning jointly with students replaces hierarchical staff-student interactions with heterarchical ones. Rogers (1992) says that educators should "make meaning rather than make rules" (p.249). She argues, "Making meaning requires a transformative leader to identify and articulate a shared vision, to empower followers, to shape a collaborative culture, to focus on the common good, to model cooperation and to take a multiperspective view" (p.249). Each of these requirements is relational and involves the acknowledgment of others and of the mutual nature of interaction. Each entails sharing with students how we think, judge, and decide, while offering them an opportunity to engage in the same process. Adopting such an approach means giving up control, or at least the illusion of control, in exchange for joint participation. Not making standard rules means giving up the efficiency and consistency that arise from applying the same rules to everyone and to all situations, the kind of efficiency that is essential for services offered from the margin. Making meaning requires that student affairs practice be designed to promote student voice — the kind of practice based on the educational purpose of the center.

The participation of student affairs professionals in the dialogue would aid student involvement in it. Empowering students would promote their speaking and listening to each other, discovering and accepting their differences to create an open community. A "multiperspective" view would help students appreciate differences, as is necessary in a just community. A focus on the common good, in conjunction with openness and justice, would assist students in accepting their obligations to others to form a disciplined community. A collaborative culture that demonstrates real cooperation promotes caring, celebrates inclusiveness, and includes everyone in striving toward educational goals. To teach students the lessons of community and simultaneously to promote their autonomy, every aspect of cocurricular life should embrace these attitudes. The competition for entrance to student organizations stresses individual achievement; open participation would emphasize inclusion and collaboration. The hierarchical operation of some student organizations gives leaders more power than members; "heterarchical" operation would increase everyone's involvement. Living units should focus on developing collaborative groups that by mutual agreement accept their obligations to others. Making meaning instead of rules would enhance collaboration among student staffs as well. Heterarchical interactions between the student affairs division and student government promotes collaborative rather than adversarial efforts related to conduct expectations and campus activities. These suggestions do not deny the importance of individual achievement or staff authority. They do, however, require that individual achievement and staff authority should not be the priority; instead, they should be placed within a relational context in which they do not supersede the focus on student development. The importance of students' ability to influence their environment and their experience is evident in Gwen's and Mark's comments, two students who (as you recall from Chapter Two) experienced growth to the most complex forms of knowing. Remember this comment of Gwen's in relation to cocurricular involvement. She added:

> You are so the master of your own destiny at college. It's such a time of stretching and growing all the way around. You test the ground and see how it feels in a lot of different areas. And you are trying to fly off cliffs, and you crash a few times, and you soar a few times.

Mark said of his participation in a leadership honor society, "There's a lot of self-determination at Miami, and I liked that a lot." Offering students the opportunity for self-determination, for soaring and crashing, is essential if they are to function in complex ways when they leave college.

Summary

Developing one's voice requires exploration. Thinking in complex ways requires that the individually formed perspective ex-

ist and function interdependently, along with individually constructed voices of others. The dual tasks of establishing self and
relationships with others is what Kegan (1982) describes as the
evolution of the self. Balancing what is part of self versus what
is other is an ongoing task that results in truces. Balancing and
rebalancing occur as a result of the combination of confirmation, contradiction, and continuity in the environment. Thus,
developing voice is more complex than developing an opinion
on a specific topic. To develop their own knowledge, students
must be able to perceive themselves as autonomous. To engage
in complex knowing, they must be able to move beyond autonomy to interdependence.

As students explore who they are and what they believe,
experiment with new behaviors, and try new beliefs on for size,
support for their ability to choose and reflect upon those choices
confirms them as autonomous. Some student choices warrant
confirmation, whereas others warrant contradiction. Yet even
in the latter case, the student can still be confirmed as a person
who is cared for and respected. Giving student opportunities
to participate in dialogue in various aspects of their cocurricular life emphasizes both their autonomy and the importance of
considering others in a relational context. It also creates opportunities for student affairs staff to process ideas, beliefs, and community values with students that might otherwise occur only
by chance. Sharing how staff make choices about their values
and behavior can help students struggle with the multitude of
decisions that they face in college. Recognizing staff as people
who also struggle might help students build trusting relationships with them in which discussion of their ideas could take
place.

Contradiction is inherent in participation in a relational
community and in genuine dialogue. Students encounter others
with different experiences, values, ways of knowing, and patterns within ways of knowing. An environment in which exploration and reflection about the meaning of stereotypes or
closed attitudes toward others are confirmed keeps contradiction within the productive range. Too much contradiction threat-
ens students, particularly those whose voices and identities are

not yet strong enough to withstand the challenge. Contradiction of an overemphasis on individual achievement automatically occurs when students are in environments where they have to work together, such as living units or organizations. Contradiction of dependence also occurs as students challenge each other to define themselves. Staff can help students work through these contradictions that occur naturally in cocurricular life.

Continuity offers students a support system as they struggle to understand themselves and the nature of their relationships with others. Staff who maintain their connection with students through their various definitions of themselves offer the stability that may not be available from peers or faculty. Constructing meaning together with students helps staff stay attuned to their development in order to adjust the holding environment accordingly.

As is clear in the students' stories, many find the confirmation, contradiction, and continuity that they need through their interactions with peers. This finding might lead some to wonder why student affairs staff should interfere. I would argue, however, that it is surely not wise to expect students to accomplish the daunting task of defining themselves simply by relying on each other. The students in this study struggled for most — or, in some cases, all — of their college life to view themselves as knowers both in academic and cocurricular realms. Although many opportunities for exploration existed, they were often left to their own devices to learn from these experiences. Leaving crucial aspects of development to chance interactions risks that they will not take place or that students will be unable to help each other create new possibilities for making meaning. Staff efforts must reflect an intentional approach to creating opportunities to describe experience, make meaning of it, and create new possibilities for viewing the world and relationships to others. Students are not left to learn the knowledge of their disciplines on their own; they receive guidance from faculty. This comes both in a proactive form, as the instructor prepares a syllabus and course of study, and in a reactive form, as the instructor responds to particular students' needs. In student affairs, our marginal role in education has led to greater focus on reactions—helping students when they struggle and resolving crises as they arise. The roles of student development educator and campus ecology manager call for the proactive stance needed to aid student development in a purposeful way. As is apparent from these students' stories, the mere existence of opportunities is not sufficient to result in complex knowing. They must involve genuine reflection on experience, a component that can be enhanced through staff participation. This approach reflects the type of educational practice that takes place at the core (not the margin) of the educational enterprise. Joining academia at the center of the educational enterprise also requires reconfiguring the partnership between student affairs and academic educators. This issue is addressed in the concluding chapter.

Chapter Twelve

Becoming Responsive
to Ways of Knowing
in Higher Education

I can usually listen to a story better than I can listen to
a lecture.
                                                    — Kris

The major purpose of this book has been to listen to students
like Kris describe their experience to create new possibilities for
understanding ways of knowing and improving educational practice. I resisted the temptation to cite often the extensive literature on student development and learning in order to keep the
focus on the students' stories. Now that they have been told,
setting them in the context of relevant literature and the realities of higher education clarifies what the stories can contribute.
     The new possibilities created by these stories are discussed
first in the form of major findings regarding students' epistemological development, or ways of knowing. Discussion of these
findings in relation to relevant literature illustrates the transferability of the underlying story lines, the insights that emerged
from studying both genders, and the role of relational knowing
in promoting the development of student voice. A discussion
of discoveries about educational practice — highlighting connections between these and the literature on collaboration, experiential learning, and student affairs practice — follows. Consideration of new approaches is not complete without a discussion of

barriers to their use. The realities of higher education as they impinge on these possibilities are noted, as are ideas for working within them. Finally, relational knowing on the part of educators and students is advanced as the key to transforming education.

Major Findings: Epistemological Development

The details of the epistemological reflection model, as described by the stories, are summarized in Chapter Two (Table 2.1) and Chapter Seven (Figure 7.1). I plan to focus here on four major findings from the collective stories that extend the current literature base regarding epistemological development. Although considerable overlap exists between them, I have separated these findings here to emphasize the essence of each.

Two parallel reasoning patterns cut across most ways of knowing. The key to this finding lies in the word *parallel*. The identification of two reasoning patterns within absolute, transitional, and independent knowing provide a more detailed picture of the possible approaches to each one. The emergence of these patterns also demonstrates two important points: (1) both cut across most of the developmental picture, and (2) both are equally complex ways of making meaning of experience.

The mastery-, impersonal-, and individual-reasoning patterns match Perry's (1970) descriptions of positions two, three, and four relatively closely. Mastery-pattern learners' attempts to "master" the material sound very much like Perry's position two thinkers' efforts "to learn to find the answers for ourselves" (p. 78). Like Perry's position three thinkers, impersonal-pattern students maintained their loyalty to authority even as they tried to discover the process for learning the right answers. Individual-pattern students reflected Perry's position four stance of everyone's having his or her own opinion. All three patterns reflect an objective approach to knowledge similar to that described by Perry. This "main line of development," in Perry's terms, was adopted to interpret the thinking of college students in general (despite Perry's own objections). One likely reason for accepting Perry's descriptions as relevant to most college students is that they made sense within the objective, or paradigmatic (Bruner, 1986), view of learning.

The receiving-, interpersonal-, and interindividual-reasoning patterns coincide with Belenky, Clinchy, Goldberger, and Tarule's (1986) description of women's development relatively closely. Toni's quote (receiving pattern) at the beginning of Chapter Three, "You see it, you hear it, and then you write it down," mirrors their definition of received knowing as "receiving, retaining, and returning the words of authority" (p. 39). Interpersonal-pattern learners' intense interest in their own and others' experiences is similar to the subjective-knowers focus of Belenky and others. Interindividual-pattern knowers share a common characteristic with Belenky and others' connected version of procedural knowing: an attempt to understand and find ties to others' perspectives. All three patterns reflect the focus on understanding inherent in the connected, or narrative (Bruner, 1986), approach.

The existence of parallel reasoning patterns in three of the four ways of knowing also extends Belenky, Clinchy, Goldberger, and Tarule's notion of separate and connected knowing. These two versions of knowing appeared in their interviews with procedural knowers. Separate knowers doubted what they heard, and argued the opposite of what others said, similar to the way that individual-pattern students operated. Connected knowers believed what they heard and tried to understand why a person held a particular point of view, much like the interindividual-pattern students. Belenky and others described the separate approach as focused on knowledge, which they said "implies separation from the object and mastery over it" (1986, p. 101). The connected approach focused on understanding, and, as such, required intimacy with the subject matter. This same distinction appears in slightly altered form in the mastery and receiving patterns and in the impersonal and interpersonal patterns. The paradigmatic and narrative approaches, then, are evident in absolute, transitional, and independent knowing. They also seem to converge in contextual knowing, a matter discussed in more detail under the fourth finding.

Belenky, Clinchy, Goldberger, and Tarule's picture of women's development represented a major contribution to the epistemological development literature because it suggested another possibility for approaching the main line of development. Often, other possibilities are considered to be deficient when compared to the existing description of development. This is certainly possible with the alternative version of epistemological development because the narrative approach it represents has traditionally been valued less than the objective or paradigmatic approach. However, as stated earlier, students' stories in this book reveal that the two approaches are equally complex, that one is not superior to the other. Both receiving- and mastery-pattern students share the core assumptions of absolute knowing; interpersonal- and impersonal-pattern learners are guided by the same assumptions in transitional knowing; and interindividual- and individual-pattern students have the same fundamental understandings during independent knowing. The patterns simply represent different learning preferences and behaviors that stem from the basic assumptions used to make sense of experience. This evidence refutes the argument that learning arising from connections to others and intuition is inferior to the objective version traditionally characterized as the male approach.

The two parallel patterns relate to, but are not dictated by, gender. As we saw earlier, receiving-, interpersonal-, and interindividual-reasoning patterns were used more by women than men, and the mastery-, impersonal-, and individual-reasoning patterns were used more by men than women in this study. However, no pattern was used exclusively by women or men. Additionally, some students combined the two approaches in different domains of their thinking or used one pattern within one way of knowing and another during the next. This finding clarifies the assumption that emerges logically out of comparing Perry's and Belenky, Clinchy, Goldberger, and Tarule's developmental schemes — that is, one pattern represents men and one represents women. Because those studies focused on men and women separately, it is not surprising that the primary themes to emerge from each study would reveal one of the two patterns but not both.

The fact that these patterns are related to, but not dictated by, gender is important for a number of reasons. Mixed use of the patterns shows that women are capable of an objective approach and men of a narrative approach. The employment of both sets of patterns by women and by men also helps maintain an awareness that the two perspectives are equally complex. Historically, developmental schemes have been derived from the study of men. When women were then studied, the resulting picture was compared to the existing one and judged as different, or, in many cases, deficient. Patterns revolving around connection were traditionally associated with women and viewed as inferior to those centering on autonomy. Finally, their mixed use offers hope that more women and men can use both patterns, a condition that appears necessary for the most complex forms of knowing.

The gender-related nature of the patterns is similar to distinctions in moral development, an area closely related to epistemological development. Kohlberg's (1969, 1984) theory of moral development, drawn originally from studying men, centered around the concepts of rights and justice. Gilligan's (1982) version of women's moral development revolved around the concepts of care and responsibility. In Lyons's (1983) exploration of these ideas, she found that persons with a separate-objective self-definition (based on impartiality and distancing self from others) used considerations of justice in moral decisions, whereas persons with a connected self-definition (based on interdependence and concern for others) used care considerations. Lyons also reported that care was the predominant focus of women and that it was used less frequently by men. Similarly, concern for justice was the predominant response of men and less frequently one of women. Lyons's work suggests that self-definition may be the key to gender-related distinctions.

Position vis-à-vis authority affects the transition from certainty to uncertainty. Studying both genders simultaneously and sketching the story lines by gender revealed nuances in the relationship with authority and the development of voice. Although the direction of the story lines is similar to the underlying themes in Perry, Belenky and others, and Kitchener and King (1990), students' connection to or detachment from authority emerges in the transition from certainty to uncertainty. These story lines are detailed in Chapter Seven, but an overview here helps illustrate this finding.

For mastery-, impersonal-, and individual-pattern knowers, the story line starts with attachment to authority and leads
to detachment from it. Mastery-pattern absolute knowers depend on authority for the truth and take the apprentice role to
learn to become authorities. This attachment remains in the impersonal transitional learner, who relies on the teacher's guidance
to approach the process of learning in an uncertain world. Upon
arriving at independent knowing, the individual-pattern student
claims his or her voice and becomes free of authority. This new
voice takes its place as equal to authority, and the student then
concentrates on pursuing an individual course without direction or interference from authority.

For students in the receiving, interpersonal, and interindividual patterns, the story line starts with detachment and
moves to attachment. Although receiving-pattern absolute knowers view authority figures as holders of the truth, they do not
believe that regular interaction with authority is necessary to
learning. They listen and record information and interact only
when clarification is needed. The comments of receiving-pattern
learners that students could feel differently about an issue than
what they had been taught hinted at the existence of a voice
other than the echo of authority. This was also the first indication that feelings about what students learned were not expressed
because they were not considered part of the academic learning process. This hidden voice comes to the forefront when
interpersonal-pattern transitional knowers discover uncertainty.
Although it was not always expressed, many interpersonal transitional students shifted quickly to knowing through their own
experience and that of others. They appreciated authority figures
with whom they had a rapport to help them gain access to others'
experiences but did not rely heavily on instructors for learning. The distinctive, personally formed voice that emerges with
independent knowing helped interindividual-pattern knowers
connect or attach to authority. Interest in engaging in dialogue
about equally valid opinions included authorities, even though
their opinions were not superior to those of peers. This dialogue
represented the first genuine connection to authority for
interindividual-pattern independent knowers.

These differences indicate that mastery- and impersonal-

pattern knowers, although subordinate to teachers by virtue of
being students, occupied a privileged position vis-à-vis authority because the dominant objectivist mode of knowing validated
their approach. Receiving- and interpersonal-pattern students
occupied a less privileged position with respect to authority because their narrative perspective was not valued in the objectivist tradition. Thus, those in the more privileged position identified with authority more readily than those who were less
privileged. Perry's description of men's linking "authority-right-
we" (1970, p. 59) and Belenky, Clinchy, Goldberger, and Tarule's
description of women's linking "authority-right-they" (1986, p.
44) suggest this same distinction.

        Contrasting these two versions of the story lines suggests
the possibility that mastery- and impersonal-pattern knowers'
attachment to authority made their acceptance of uncertainty
gradual, whereas receiving- and interpersonal-pattern students'
detachment from authority led to their embracing uncertainty
more readily. For those attached to authority, uncertainty posed
a challenge to the relationship with authority and the dominance
of their approach. For those detached from authority, uncertainty created an opportunity to incorporate the hidden voice
into the learning process, to validate the narrative approach.
Belenky and others note that when women in their study found
support for reliance on themselves, they "move full speed into
the subjectivist position" (p. 68). The differences in the authority and voice story lines offer new directions for research to explore how a dominant versus subordinate position vis-à-vis authority affects the development of a distinctive voice.

        These nuances in the transition from certainty to uncer-
tainty reveal some consistency with Kitchener and King's (1990)
reflective judgment model. That model, constructed on the basis
of both women and men, addresses the transition from certainty
to uncertainty of knowledge in stages two through five. Stage
two parallels absolute knowing because all knowledge is certain
and, if not observable, can be obtained from authorities. In stage
three, temporary uncertainty emerges, and learners use their
own biases until absolute knowledge is possible. I read this as
a combination of the impersonal transitional knower's holding

out for absolute knowledge and the interpersonal transitional knower's switch to reliance on experience (one's own biases). Interpersonal-pattern transitional knowers, however, do not seem to view their new-found uncertainty as temporary. They appear closer to Kitchener and King's description of stage four, when some knowledge is perceived as permanently uncertain. Kitchener and King describe judgment of knowledge claims in this stage as based on one's own biases, others' biases, logic, and available data, a combination yielding idiosyncratic evaluations of knowledge claims. Stage four most closely matches independent knowing, with interindividual-pattern students focusing on collecting others' biases and individual-pattern learners emphasizing logic and available data. The only discrepancy here is that, in independent knowing, most knowledge is perceived as uncertain, a characteristic of stage five in the reflective judgment model.

Despite the difficulty in trying to match exactly the stages in these two models, they describe the transition from certainty to uncertainty similarly. It is possible that the reflective judgment model stages represent a picture that includes rather than separates the patterns. Although the model was constructed using both women and men, gender was not in the forefront of developmental issues when it was developed. Accounting for data from both women and men may have resulted in descriptions that merge gender-related patterns.

Connection, or relational aspects of knowing, may be the key to complex forms of knowing. Contextual knowing as described in this book incorporates the threads of objective and narrative modes. Whereas the individual learner is the primary focus in the mastery, impersonal, and individual patterns, the student strives to "really listen" to others in contextual knowing (recall Lowell's story in Chapter Five). The receiving, interpersonal, and interindividual students' primary focus on others is replaced in contextual knowing with an equalizing of self and others. This suggests that autonomy and connection are both required for complex forms of knowing.

The story line of peer relationships contributes to this finding. Classmates play an important role in receiving, interpersonal, and interindividual students' learning. For receiving-pattern absolute knowers, connection, in the form of getting to know peers, provides a supportive learning atmosphere. For interpersonal transitional students, connection with peers increases as they share and collect each other's personal experiences. The interest in sharing views remains in independent knowing; however, interindividual-pattern knowers begin to try to balance their own voices (autonomy) with those of others (connection). Their ability to express a distinctive perspective comes about in part from a decrease in connection with peers because their opinions matter less. This change in connection is similar to Kegan's (1982) description of the transition from an interpersonal to an institutional definition of the self. He described the interpersonal definition of self (which he calls a truce) as defining the self through mutual relationships with others. These relationships are a key part of the definition: the person does not have a separately functioning self. When the self-definition changes, resulting in the institutional truce, the person can "have" relationships rather than "be" them. A separate self emerges that joins in, but is no longer defined by, these relationships. Interindividual-pattern independent knowers separate from classmates enough to express their own voices but maintain the connection to them in order to exchange perspectives. This shift may represent a change in their self-definition.

Peers are important to mastery- and impersonal-pattern students, but they are secondary to the individual learner. Classmates help the mastery-pattern absolute knowers practice their knowledge acquisition. Peers help the impersonal-pattern transitional knowers learn more by challenging them to defend their ideas. In both cases, autonomy is primary, and connection exists only in its service. Individual independent learners strengthen autonomy by expressing their voices but also increase connection by struggling to hear others' views. When the notion of links to authority is added to the picture, connection runs throughout the ways of knowing for mastery-, impersonal-, and individual-pattern students. They are connected to authority in absolute and transitional knowing and to peers in independent and contextual knowing. Thus, autonomy alone is not sufficient for complex forms of knowing.

The importance of connection to complex forms of thinking is an important finding for two reasons. First, the dominant objectivist view of knowledge does not emphasize connection. Perhaps this fact explains why so few students in this study used contextual knowing during college. Other studies also indicate that college seniors do not usually employ contextual approaches. Kitchener and King (1990), summarizing ten years of research on the reflective judgment model, reported that seniors were generally in stage four of that model. King, Wood, and Mines (1990) similarly found that seniors tended to use stage-four thinking and that some graduate students moved to stage five (comparable to contextual knowing).

Second, the concept of autonomy has enjoyed a favored status in the student development literature. Autonomy was described by psychosocial theorists as a precursor to successful identity development (Chickering, 1969; Josselson, 1987). In Chickering's model, connection to others came later, in the form of intimacy made possible when a separate identity had been achieved. Separation from others, particularly family, was necessary to arrive at Josselson's identity-achievement status, despite her belief that "communion is central to female development, and women are likely to opt for preserving attachment before pursuing their agentic needs. For many women, success in communion, in relationship, is itself an expression of agentic needs for assertion and mastery" (1987, p. 171). Straub (1987), however, provided evidence that some women achieved intimacy prior to autonomy. In the context of ways of knowing, the stories in this book demonstrate that connection played an important role for both women and men in achieving autonomous voice. The value of connection broadens our understanding of student development and places the importance of connection within the development of both women and men.

Major Findings: Educational Practice

I have used the term *educational practice* throughout the book to refer to curricular and cocurricular educational settings. Chapters Eight through Eleven detail teaching and student affairs practices that provide Kegan's (1982) confirmation, contradiction, and continuity for students in various ways of knowing. Four major findings from this data integrate insights from students' stories for educational practice. These findings overlap one another but are separated here to highlight each one.

Validating students as knowers is essential to promoting students' voices. Until students feel that what they think has some validity, it is impossible for them to view themselves as capable of constructing knowledge. As most participants made meaning of their experiences from absolute or transitional perspectives when the study began, they needed recognition of the value of their ideas to move toward the development of voice. Their curricular life, characterized by lack of encounter with knowledge discrepancies and by large classes with minimal interaction, initially offered no such recognition. Their cocurricular life—with its opportunities for student responsibility and for exposure to diversity via peer interactions—did foster confirmation. As they increased their responsibilities in their cocurricular lives, involvement in curricular settings, and interactions with authorities, students began to entertain the notion that teachers were human like themselves. When authority figures expressed respect for students, asked their opinions, and directly encouraged self-reliance, this confirmation helped build the student voice. Speaking in their own voice through class involvement, evaluation techniques, leadership opportunities, and peer interactions helped students come to see themselves as sources of knowledge.

Much of the current literature on teaching and promoting student development speaks to this validation of the student. Katz and Henry (1988) derived seven basic learning principles from their extensive projects with faculty and students. Although all seven in some way relate to affirming the student as a knower, four in particular convey that idea. One such principle is "the transformation of student passivity into active learning" (p. 6), which, in Katz and Henry's terms, "means helping students become investigators and coinquirers, approximating for themselves some of the ways in which the knowledge was originally developed" (p. 6). Inherent in their definition is that students generate knowledge by practicing the process of developing knowledge. A second principle, individualization, emphasizes the importance of understanding the students' frame of reference and recognizing that their unique approach to the world must be central to the learning interchange. A third principle, the process of inquiry, stresses the importance that students encounter the process by which knowledge is constructed, rather than only the outcomes of these processes. All three of these principles indicate that the student is an active agent in the learning process. A fourth principle that Katz and Henry advance is support. Support is considered necessary to engagement in learning, as Katz and Henry describe it, and is given by both students and teachers.

Katz and Henry's principles are consistent with Belenky, Clinchy, Goldberger, and Tarule's (1986) "midwife teaching," which suggests that knowledge belongs to the student. The teacher supports students in the thinking process, helping them bring forth their ideas and constructions of knowledge. Support is crucial to assist with the birth of new knowledge and the use of new processes of knowing. Much of the feminist literature on teaching concentrates on support for students in the process of knowledge construction. For example, Weiler (1988) summarizes the vision of feminist teachers and administrators as emphasizing "that students are knowers and the creators of knowledge" (p. 122). Similarly, liberatory approaches advocate these same ideas. The principle of affirming the student as a knower is an important component of most literature endorsing the narrative mode of knowing and education.

Supporting students as individuals capable of self-determination has also been a traditional foundation for student affairs educators. *The Student Personnel Point of View* (American Council on Education Studies, 1949) described students as unique individuals who were responsible for their own development. The authors of *Involving Colleges* (Kuh, Schuh, Whitt, and Associates, 1991) encourage creating environments in which students can be responsible as one way of increasing student involvement. They argue that students should be full members of the institution and in charge of their own affairs. The student development educator role puts these beliefs into action by working with students in assessing development, establishing goals,

mapping out programs related to these goals, and evaluating progress made toward them (Brown, 1989). Although the educator's
knowledge of development is a major factor in the process, it is not
applied to the student; rather, it is used to support students in
understanding themselves. Similarly, as we have seen, Kegan
(1982) advocates supporting persons in their current definition
of self, offering appropriate contradictions to that definition, and
providing continuity during the evolution of self-understanding.
This process hinges on validating the person's current definition
and placing the responsibility of change on that person.

    *Situating learning in the students' own experience legitimizes their
knowledge as a foundation for constructing new knowledge.* Recognizing students as constructors of knowledge simultaneously recognizes that their experiences went into forming their ideas. Students often view knowledge as abstract, as unconnected to the
real life about which they know. Recall Deirdre's story in Chapter Five about the formality of academic learning. Knowledge,
from this vantage point, is unattainable and remains the property
of authorities. Attaching knowledge to students' experience
bridges the gap between what they know and academic knowledge; it suggests the possibility that their everyday lives are
related in some way to what and how they come to know. This
possibility opens the door for students to be legitimate sources
of knowledge and gives them a role other than memorizing and
repeating the knowledge of authorities. It is the introduction
of the opportunity for them to interpret their experience and to
construct knowledge. Approaching learning within the context
of students' lives has other advantages as well. The variety of
these experiences automatically introduces diversity. This diversity and students' reactions to it were apparent in the cocurricular stories. The experiences of others prompted students to become aware of other viewpoints, adjust to dealing with different
people, and eventually appreciate diverse perspectives. Incorporating students' experiences into learning also personalizes
learning, or in Deirdre's words "doubles — it makes the experience stronger."

    Students' observations in this regard are consistent with
what many educators have been arguing for years. Proponents

of experiential learning, liberatory learning, feminist approaches to education, and student involvement all emphasize the importance of situating learning in students' own experience. This principle is perhaps at the heart of the narrative approach in its integration of experience with knowledge construction. Kolb (1984) defined experiential learning as "the process whereby knowledge is created through the transformation of experience" (p. 38). This definition confirms the literature previously cited regarding the construction of knowledge and suggests that a central component of the process is experience. Kolb suggests that students bring their prior knowledge to each learning situation, and their experience thus influences learning in each new setting. He believes that the learning process is facilitated by "bringing out the learner's beliefs and theories, examining and testing them, and then integrating the new, more refined ideas into the person's belief system" (p. 28). Kolb further states: "Knowledge is the result of the transaction between social knowledge and personal knowledge. The former, as Dewey noted, is the civilized objective accumulation of previous human cultural experience, whereas the latter is the accumulation of the individual person's subjective life experiences. Knowledge results from the transaction between these objective and subjective experiences in a process called learning" (p. 36). Clearly, in Kolb's view, experience is an important aspect of the transaction. Schön's (1987) reflection in action hinges on experience as well, as the learner continually reflects on what is taking place and readjusts her or his knowledge accordingly.

Shor and Freire (1987) portray a similar perspective in their discussion of a pedagogy for liberation. They propose a dialogue between teachers and students that is placed in the context of the "culture, language, politics, and themes of the students" (p. 104). They suggest that this kind of dialogue simultaneously motivates students because the themes are theirs and offers an opportunity to reflect upon these ideas critically. The dialogue is placed within the students' subjective realm but is also outside it — a situation that yields more advanced reflection. Shor and Freire view these tensions as transformative; they transform the students' thinking about their own experience.

Feminist approaches to education make similar proposals. Weiler (1988) described the goals of feminist teachers as interrogating consciousness, questioning meaning, and analyzing and criticizing the social world. Teaching, in these terms, respects the human value and cultural worlds of students. Feminist teachers seek to empower students to become aware of and critique their experience with social realities. Thus, the tension that Shor and Freire described can exist if students' experience is used as a basis for moving beyond it. Respect for students' experience is central to Noddings's (1984) perspective on teaching. Noddings affirms that the teacher leads the student, all the while recognizing that "he will learn what he pleases. We may force him to respond in specified ways, but what he will make his own and eventually apply effectively is that which he finds significant for his own life" (p. 176).

Perhaps Noddings's observation explains in part why students report learning so much through their cocurricular lives. The strong influence that peers have on students' learning is well documented (Pascarella and Terenzini, 1991), as is the role that involvement plays in heightening investment in learning (Astin, 1984; Boyer, 1987). Peers' influence, according to Pascarella and Terenzini's extensive review of the research in this area, affects a wide variety of areas, including intellectual development, values, personal development, and educational attainment. Changes appear to come from reflecting on experience with diverse peers and reexamining beliefs in light of those of peers. Peer interaction is significant to students' lives by virtue of its placement in everyday experience. Pascarella and Terenzini speculate that much of this interaction takes place in cocurricular environments, partially because the research they reviewed rarely separated peer and cocurricular involvement. Many of the cocurricular activities discussed in the student stories in this book involve interactions with peers, while others center around practical experience gained. In either case, cocurricular involvement brings students' experience to the forefront of the learning endeavor and thereby legitimizes it as a foundation for constructing new knowledge.

Defining learning as jointly constructing meaning empowers students to see themselves as constructing knowledge. The goal of validating students and situating learning in their experience cannot be completed without defining learning as jointly constructing meaning. To promote development of a distinctive personal voice, teachers must be willing to accept the result of the process — that is, the students' own constructions. Entertaining students' ideas does not necessarily mean acceptance of them, as both Shor and Freire (1987) and Noddings (1984) make clear. It does, however, require teachers to respect these perspectives, engage in dialogue about them, and be willing to alter their own as needed. The stage is therefore set for students to experience validity as knowers because the omnipotence of authorities is contradicted. The mutual nature of dialogue helps the teacher maintain continuity with students as transformations occur. The relational aspect of the dialogue connects the student to the learning process and links the players in the learning environment. The support of students' constructions of knowledge and the exchange of ideas between teacher and student model a contextual perspective.

Bruner (1986) noted the implications for education of what he called a "negotiation process," through which people agree on the meaning of social concepts. His version of negotiation is similar to the principle of defining learning as joint construction of meaning. The teacher's role in this negotiation process is to open ideas to speculation, to invite "the use of thought, reflection, elaboration, and fantasy" (p. 127). Students are thus afforded the opportunity to enter the negotiation process and to become active creators of knowledge. This process is consistent with what Palmer (1987) calls the "continual cycle of discussion, disagreement, and consensus over what has been seen and what it all means" (p. 25).

This negotiation is also central to Bruffee's (1984) version of collaborative learning. Bruffee argues: "We establish knowledge or justify belief collaboratively by challenging each other's biases and presuppositions; by negotiating collectively toward new paradigms of perception, thought, feeling, and expression, and by joining larger, more experienced communities of knowledgeable peers through assenting to those communities' interests, values, language, and paradigms of perception and thought" (p. 646). Bruffee believes that taking part in this conversation facilitates student learning, to some extent because the conversation itself demonstrates how knowledge is generated. Participation in the negotiation can help students learn how to construct knowledge. This definition of collaborative learning meshes well with two of Katz and Henry's (1988) basic learning principles: the ability to inquire with others and participation.

Bruffee emphasizes that collaborative learning is more than just putting peers together without guidance from a teacher. Shor and Freire (1987) discuss how the teacher and student connect during the process. They suggest that teacher and student come together to inquire about a given topic because it is not the sole domain of either party. Although the teacher knows about the subject, his or her knowledge is remade through examining it with the students. Shor and Freire describe this connection as follows: "The object to be known in one place links the two cognitive subjects, leading them to reflect together on the object. Dialogue is the sealing together of the teacher and the students in the joint act of knowing and re-knowing the object of study" (p. 100).

Student affairs professionals in recent years have advocated a campus ecology approach that represents a negotiation between students and the college environment. Huebner (1989) describes this as "focused more on designing (or redesigning) campus environments to meet the needs of members than 'adjusting' or 'treating' students so that they will fit into existing environments" (p. 167). The approach involves joint selection of educational goals arising from consensus about educational values, design of the environment based on these goals as well as on student needs, and redesign of the environment as a result of student reactions (Banning, 1989). This joint construction of meaning empowers students to join in knowledge construction.

The relational component evident in all of these three findings is essential to empowering students to construct knowledge. Validation via relational approaches confirms students as people and as knowers. Situating learning in students' own experience connects personal life and academic life. As Kolb (1984) claimed, knowledge results from the "transaction between social knowledge and personal knowledge" (p. 36). Starting with students' experience makes this transaction possible. Situating learning within students' experience also generates more interaction with authority figures. Thus, students relate both to knowledge and to authority figures. Defining learning as jointly constructing meaning connects educator and student. Shor and Freire's (1987) eloquent description of dialogue sealing together the teacher and student captures the intensity of this connection. The negotiation inherent in jointly constructing knowledge connects teacher and student, as well as connecting both to the process of knowledge construction.

Though connection has been largely regarded as a matter of greater importance to women (Chodorow, 1978; Gilligan, 1982), the students' stories in this book indicate that men also use patterns in which relationships to others are primary — namely, the interpersonal and interindividual patterns. The collective stories imply that the experiences that promoted complex thinking and a distinctive voice for both women and men relied on the relational aspects inherent in validating students as knowers, situating learning in their experience, and defining learning as jointly constructing meaning. The relational aspect of knowing thus seems essential to aiding all students to develop knowledge themselves.

Realities of Higher Education

Beyond the issue of overgeneralization, a topic that I addressed at length in Chapter One, there are a number of other issues that hamper the implementation of the findings of this study. Although the list that follows is not exhaustive, it highlights some of the realities that we face as educators and how they affect the approach I have advocated throughout the book.

Educators need a better understanding of the diverse student populations that will inhabit campuses of the future. The composition of the college student population is projected to change rapidly in the near future. Students of color, of nontraditional age, and from a variety of socioeconomic backgrounds will make up a greater portion of the population than they currently do; in some cases, they may even outnumber white, traditional-age students (Kuh, 1990). Yet much of the literature on student development and on teaching and learning is situated in the context of white, traditional-age students. Although my study adds to our understanding of gender-related issues and the longitudinal development of students' ways of knowing, it too has relied on mostly white, traditional-age students. Research is just now advancing in the study of women and just beginning on the study of nondominant populations. Not only is more of this research necessary, but educators should be wary in attempting to transfer the findings of this study and others like it to new populations without investigating their applicability.

Educators need a better understanding of the effect of context on learning. Research on student development and learning has historically been conducted using quantitative methods that arose from the objectivist school. After Pascarella and Terenzini's (1991) comprehensive review of the literature on the impact of college, Pascarella (1991) concluded that "the vast preponderance (perhaps 90–95 percent) of what we know about the impact of college on students (and we know considerable) comes from inquiry that is firmly rooted in the hypothetico-deductive, logical positivist, quantitative paradigm" (p. 463). The knowledge base constructed from those studies reveals extensive insight about the processes of development and learning and, in Pascarella's view, has served us well and will continue to do so. Yet Pascarella, more familiar than most with the extensive body of literature on this subject, expressed discontent with the limits of quantitative research in "capturing many of the subtle and fine-grained complexities of college impact" (1991, p. 463).

Many of these complexities stem from the context in which development and learning take place and the ways that context influences the process. Campus ecology proponents have always argued that student behavior "results from the interaction of the individual and the campus environment" (Rodgers, 1990, p. 32). Qualitative studies are more likely than quantitative studies to reveal the nuances of the individual student, as is evident in the student stories in this book. Interview studies like this one move toward consideration of context in their focus on student stories, particularly when students are asked to describe their environment and their reactions to it; yet they stop short of a full consideration of context inherent in observing cocurricular and curricular environments. Much of the recent qualitative research, however, takes this approach, studying particular classes or cocurricular environments intensely by prolonged involvement in these settings themselves. This research pays attention to the campus environment as well as to interaction. The underlying assumptions of the social constructivist perspective suggest that knowledge cannot be created outside of context. Thus, part of the task of judging the transferability of this book's findings is to study the specific contexts where they would be applied.

Understanding student development and learning requires studying particular students in specific contexts. I do not suggest that the extensive body of educational research has no relevance to educational practice. Nevertheless, given the unique nature of students and of the interaction of individual with context, educators must study their own students in their own settings. Pat Cross's (1990) notion of classroom research is relevant here. She advocates classroom research as a way for teachers to become actively involved in what students are learning, which includes both content and thinking processes. Although Cross presents the primary purpose of classroom research as "to get feedback from students on what they are learning while the learning is in process" (p. 12), it also studies the particulars of student and learning context. She urges that classroom research be adopted as a component of outcomes assessment to improve educational practice. The interaction inherent in such an approach also contributes to the relational dimension of education.

Development of a distinctive voice requires an environmental structure that encourages it. I suspect that a faculty member who teaches organic chemistry to two hundred students or a student affairs professional who coordinates 150 student organizations has been wondering how these ideas could possibly be carried out. The structure of educational environments is often indicative of the objectivist view of knowledge from which it was created. The lecture hall with immovable chairs facing forward symbolizes an educational approach in which a teacher disseminates knowledge at an assigned hour. Large classes usually stem from the assumption that education can take place as long as everyone can hear the instructor. The residence hall designed to house eight hundred students with one full-time staff member certainly does not convey that interaction is a component of education. Most of the advice from students in this book advocates interaction with students, an endeavor constantly complicated when the educator-to-student ratio is one to several hundred. On a hopeful note, there is evidence that educators can overcome this obstacle in the classroom (Katz and Henry, 1988) and the cocurricular environment (Rodgers, 1990). However, it will remain a struggle unless the broader issue of the nature of education is addressed.

Some educators believe that promoting development of the students' voice sacrifices content learning. Many of the ideas I have proposed, on the basis of student stories and other literature, make the educational process much more ambiguous. Validating students requires giving them opportunities to express their thoughts, which may often be incomplete. Coaching students along is more complicated and frustrating than giving them the information. Situating learning in the students' own experience puts the educator in the position of not knowing where the discussion is going to go. Classroom educators wonder how they will get through the course content if too much time is spent discussing students' experiences and perceptions. Student affairs educators wonder how a wandering discussion will develop the leadership of student organizations. Jointly constructing meaning complicates matters even further. By definition, it requires negotiation, disagreement, and eventually consensus, a process that every educator knows takes an enormous amount of time.

This issue is perhaps most salient in the classroom, where certain content is required in order to maintain success in future study. As I have had opportunities to talk with faculty about the student stories in this book, I am often asked, "What about getting through the material?" Nelson (1989) describes his initial feelings about this issue as facing a "tragic tradeoff: concentrating on biology left students uncritical but teaching thinking would require that I cover less biology" (p. 17). This concern, along with educational structures and the dominance of objectivism, probably explains why Boyer (1987) found that "today, the lecture method is preferred by most professors" (p. 149). Boyer further described the lectures that he witnessed as ones in which students passively received information. Noddings's (1984) warning that students will learn what they please is important here. Educators often assume that students learn if the material is thoroughly covered. Student stories, and much of the literature, would refute this assumption, however. Students often reported forgetting most of what they had learned, particularly when it was learned passively. Even those with high grade-point averages often noted that they absorbed material for a test, only to forget it a short time later. Their stories support Noddings's contention that they made their own only what was significant to them. Passive learning, according to the literature, often fails to make a topic relevant to students' lives.

When educators dispute the claim that covering the material yields learning, different approaches become a little more palatable. Nelson (1989) described trying new ways to teach biology due to his frustration with what he called content failures. He translated Perry's (1970) insights about students' epistemological development into teaching "moves" (p. 19) that encourage more complex thinking (Nelson calls it critical thinking). These involve teaching precise thinking, fostering the recognition of fundamental uncertainty, engendering an understanding of theory selection (which means articulating the criteria for deciding which ideas tentatively to accept), and fostering an understanding of the role of values. Making these areas explicit promotes critical thinking and helps to apply it to the study of science. Nelson also carefully specified the type of support needed to help students gain from his teaching moves, many of which match ideas in this book. Nelson's fears about the tragic trade-off were alleviated by the outcomes of his new approach. He reported that improving critical thinking also increased content acquisition; higher percentages of his students mastered difficult content. He believes that retention is enhanced if the content reflects examples of critical thinking and concluded that "the tradeoffs between the teaching of process and the teaching of content that once seemed so evident are, in practice, as imaginary as unicorn horns" (p. 25).

Tompkins (1990) also described taking a new approach to her teaching of English, calling it an "awkward lunge in the direction of creating a different world in the classes I teach" (p. 656). She described a class in which students choose topics of interest to them and work together to bring the information to the class. She reported that students are more active, talk more to each other than to her, and engage in the material more deeply than before. Although she describes the feelings of guilt that many educators feel when students do such work, she recognizes that it is important for the students to develop their skills and voice. After twenty-five years of teaching, Tompkins concluded, "A kinder, more sensitive attitude toward one's own needs as a human being . . . can bring greater sensitivity to the needs of students and a more sympathetic understanding of their situations, both as workers in the academy and as people in the wider world" (p. 660). Thus, though she described her foray into interactive learning as kinder to herself, she recognized its benefits for students as well.

Glidden and Kurfiss (1990) also provided research that supports collaborative learning in the form of small-group methods. Alternating lecture presentations and small-group techniques in two introductory philosophy courses, they tested various content areas and compared the results for the two teaching methods. Of six topic areas, students demonstrated higher achievement in three areas when the group method was used, similar achievement in two areas when group and lecture methods were used, and less achievement in one area when the group method was employed. Glidden and Kurfiss point out that even the lecture format used was highly interactive. They conclude that the group method is at least as effective as lecture and did not impair content mastery. This type of evidence is needed to convince educators that the risks involved in promoting development of voice do not endanger content.

Broader issues that affect educational practice need to be addressed if efforts to promote development of a distinctive voice are to be successful. Constraints such as class size, educator-to-student ratios, and physical arrangements have already been noted. In addition, definitions of what the educator's work consists of require rethinking. The stories in this book and my interpretations of them advocate defining the educator's task as facilitating knowledge construction rather than imparting knowledge. Educators therefore need knowledge about students' ways of knowing and training in group facilitation skills. Classroom educators need to understand that it is acceptable not to know everything and to let students discover, rather than be told. The idea that involving students in learning is irresponsible must also be abandoned. Of course, this type of teaching means more preparation for class. It requires innovation in planning, constant assessment of students' needs, adjustment and reorganization based on assessment data, and flexibility to respond to the directions sparked by students' experience. All this takes more time and effort than organizing and implementing a course on a predetermined plan. Student affairs educators for their part must appreciate that it is acceptable not to control all student behavior and that allowing students to learn for themselves in cocurricular life is worth the risks. The educational practice described in this book means more negotiation between student affairs educators and students about rules, practices, and student-group decisions. The assessment and adjustment functions noted above apply here as well. Rewards for teaching and student affairs work of this type must be forthcoming to implement these changes.

Finally, the separation of academic and student affairs is problematic. Academic affairs concentrates on curricular education and ignores cocurricular life. Student affairs focuses on cocurricular education to the exclusion of curricular life. The groups neither capitalize on each other's expertise nor collaborate in meeting educational goals. Students are subtly given the message that curricular and cocurricular life are unconnected. Allowing cocurricular life to stand outside the formal educational mission is misguided in light of students' stronger identification with this area.

Transforming Education, Educators, and Students

In Chapter One, I described my journey from the objectivist to social constructivist perspective of making meaning. Specifically, I described changing my approach from interpreting students' stories using categories I had learned from the litera-

ture to interpreting them drawing on a combination of students'
and my own perspectives. Although I studied Perry's (1970) work
for years, I never understood the real essence of his argument
that the meaning people make of their experience arises largely
from what they "have to say on the matter" (pp. 41–42). It took
the dissonance between my objectivist analysis of the students'
stories and my experiencing of their stories to recognize the
difference between interpretation based on my perspective and
interpretation based on both what they had to say and my own
understanding. Interpreting based on my point of view required
only recording and filing their ideas. Interpreting based on both
perspectives required connection: listening carefully, suspending my own ideas in order to hear the students' and negotiating
a reasonable meaning from the combination of the two. From
the objectivist approach, I interacted with students and their
ideas abstractly. From the social constructivist approach, I interacted with students relationally.

This notion of relation, or connectedness, is the central
message of this book. Education's historical use of the objectivist perspective has limited educators' ability to connect genuinely with students. By genuine connection, I mean taking students' experience into account and making meaning with, rather
than for, students. The dominance of objectivism hinders students' development of a distinctive voice—for example, by fail-
ing to link experience and knowledge. It poses additional barriers for students whose way of making meaning is inconsistent
with the objectivist perspective—namely, those who use the
receiving, interpersonal, and interindividual patterns. Students'
stories in this book illustrate that connection is essential to
promoting development of a distinctive voice for receiving-,
interpersonal-, and interindividual-pattern knowers and helpful for those using the other patterns. Thus, lack of connection
hampers *some* students, and a relational approach reaches *most*
students. Promoting development of voice and meeting the learning needs of a diverse population of students require a transformation from objectivist to social constructivist education.
This transformation mirrors what Riane Eisler (1987) calls the
transformation from a dominator to a partnership society. She
describes a dominator society as one in which one half of hu-

manity (men, in the context she discusses) dominates the other half. A partnership society is one in which both halves are equally valued. According to Eisler's account of history, making the transition will not be easy. However, all the principles I have advocated would transform education into a partnership society. The social constructivist view also advocates a partnership society.

The social constructivist view involves knowledge construction within a community, meaning that all members of the community negotiate a consensus on the meaning of their experience. The scarcity of this type of community interaction in curricular life impedes students' ability to think in the complex ways necessary for today's complicated world. When social conditions on campus are described in terms of drug and alcohol abuse, crime, lack of civility, prejudice, sex discrimination, and separation of in-class and out-of-class activities (Carnegie Foundation for the Advancement of Teaching, 1990), it becomes clear that a sense of community is no more prevalent in cocurricular life. Unless these conditions are changed, community will also be lacking in the larger society that these students will inhabit.

The key to community building is connection. Connection in curricular life can be achieved through validating students' contributions to learning, situating learning in students' own experience, and defining learning as joint construction of meaning. These principles, by their nature, entail connecting with students from various ways of knowing, within different gender-related patterns, and with a variety of learning needs and preferences. These principles point the way to contextual knowing, as well as to civility and sensitivity to others. They underlie knowledge construction, and in the process teach students how to develop their own distinctive voice. In a contextual perspective, that voice reflects the ability to evaluate knowledge critically, analyze complex situations, assess biased perspectives, and make wise choices. These principles create a community in which knowledge construction can take place.

The same principles create connection in cocurricular life. Implementing them in student affairs practice helps students learn to construct knowledge in cocurricular areas of their lives. These are where issues like racial prejudice, sex discrimination, sexual violence, civility, and obligations to others come to the forefront. Helping students process, or work through, these issues is essential for overcoming the unhealthy social conditions of campus life. Helping students create their own informed perspectives is crucial to promoting responsible community membership on campus and beyond.

Connection within curricular and cocurricular life is not sufficient for overcoming the dilemmas currently faced by higher education. The separation of the academic and student affairs spheres must be reconsidered. Both have an educational mission that could be better achieved by collaboration rather than by separation. Student affairs educators, who are experts in student development (including epistemological development), community building, and group facilitation, can share their knowledge of these fields with faculty. (These topics are required courses in most student affairs preparation programs.) Faculty educators are experts in knowledge creation and research methodology. They can aid student affairs educators, who have typically focused more on student interaction than on research, to acquire and apply these skills for the benefit of both educators and students. Strange and King (1990) place research as a crucial link in translating student development theory into action to improve student affairs educational practice. The resulting knowledge would be equally relevant to faculty. Collaboration between classroom and student affairs educators can heighten the sensitivity of each to the other sides of students' lives. Perhaps more importantly, it would convey to students a sense of connection between academic and social or personal life. It would form a foundation for campus community.

The stories in this book have convinced me that incorporating the relational component is the key to transforming education. Acknowledging that knowing is relational and acting on that assumption entail uniting experience and knowing, teaching and learning, students and their peers, and curricular and cocurricular education. I chose to convey the students' stories in a manner that created a connection between them and the readers of this book. Through that connection, I hope that these experiences can be used to inspire new possibilities for educational practice.

Context of
the Study:
Miami University

A social constructivist perspective requires that the reader be given as much information about context as possible to use in judging whether a book's findings can be transferred to other situations. Chapter One thus contains a description of the study participants and the larger student body of which they were a part. Here I provide additional information about the student culture and institutional dynamics that further describe the environment in which this study was conducted.

The Culture

The student body's preference for extensive on-campus involvement, as noted in Chapter One, can be realized in the student organizations that abound at Miami. Over three hundred exist, including honorary societies; career-related and military organizations; music, programming, and religious groups; and service and special-interest organizations. Students also participate in publications, a student credit union, and student government. One-third take part in Greek organizations. Membership and leadership opportunities in many of these organizations are competitive. The smallness of the surrounding community (which numbers about eight thousand outside of the student population), the thirty-minute to one-hour distance to the nearest metropolitan areas, and the almost-total ban on student cars combine to make the campus the primary source of recreational, sports, musical, and cultural entertainment.

Expectations of student conduct are aimed at maintaining community. All community members "are expected to observe standards of propriety, honesty, and integrity at all time. This implies thoughtful consideration of the welfare and reputation of the University and all members of the University community" (*Miami Bulletin,* 1990, p. 17). The focus of student life staff on the responsibility of students to behave as adult members of the community is sometimes overshadowed by rules that hint of in loco parentis. Students feel that having the same rules for first-year and upper-division students is restrictive and often view the visitation policy with suspicion. For example, one woman in the study commented:

> I'm sure the rules are necessary, but it just seems like they're so trivial—that they're trying to treat us like little kids. Even at home, I pretty much make my decisions and do what I want. It seems like I have more disciplinary rules here than I do there. I mean, really.

Another woman, Tonya, said, "The term *in loco parentis* is a school motto; they seem to go a little overboard in that respect." Some students call the institution "Mother Miami." Seeing it as isolated from what they call the real world, other students refer to the campus as the "Miami Bubble." Lindsey offered an example of this perception:

> Miami has this reputation of just basically mothering you. They try so hard to make it really nice for all the students here. It's not like Washington, where I'm from. It's kind of fake; it's not really the real world. It's a lot nicer. I'd like to be here for awhile.

Anita viewed the experience a little less positively:

> It's difficult because you lose track. Like my mother says, "Oh, wasn't that plane crash awful?" I'm like,

"What plane crash?" And she says, "What do you mean, 'what plane crash?'" And it's kind of like everyone jokes that we live in this little bubble. But it kind of sometimes feels like that.

These feelings are strengthened by the nature of the student population, which is relatively homogeneous: of traditional age, white, and middle class. Students from nondominant populations represented only 3 percent of the undergraduate population during the time of this study. In a walk around campus, one observes fairly conservative dress, ranging from corporate attire to organization- or event-related T-shirts. The diverse haircuts and dress that are a regular feature at metropolitan-area airports and shopping malls are rarely seen on campus. Students can be observed playing sports, studying on the lawns, jogging, and biking. The campus is relatively quiet except near the periphery, where loud music blasts from fraternity houses and student apartments in the warm months.

Traditions also reflect a degree of consistency and stability in the student culture. Homecoming and Little Sibs weekend are annual major events, as are the annual bike race and Founder's Day Ball. Unique terms, some of which have already been mentioned, describe other traditions and values. To identify the characteristics of colleges that actively involve their students in campus life, a research team interviewed Miami students during 1988 and reported:

Miami has an extensive cultural vocabulary. The phrases "Mother Miami," "cradle of coaches," and "mother of fraternities" connote nurturance and sense of family; the university is a source of life (of the mind) and nourishment (for the spirit), and a sheltering home for all her "children." Similarly, the "Miami Bubble" implies that the university is a safe place, a protected seat from which to observe, and occasionally experience, the "real" world. "Miami mergers" are marriages between Miami students; these couples annually receive Valentines from the

University, commemorating their symbolic affirmation of the Miami family. "Miami memos" are
the calendars that students keep in order to organize
their time "by the hours." The message of "Miami
memos" is "we are so busy"—students are so involved in so many activities that they must live by
precise schedules in order to get everything done
[Kuh and others, 1991, p. 99].

Although it is possible to escape the outside world by staying inside the "bubble," many students choose not to do so. The
concern for students and their education on the part of faculty
and student life staff supports service activities, such as adopt-
a-grandparent programs with residents at a local retirement community, a food sharing program between the dining halls and
local community food banks, and the construction of houses for
the homeless. Support for the celebration of differences has
helped create campus awareness of the rights of gay, lesbian,
and bisexual members of the community and has spawned a
campuswide unity through diversity program, which stresses
awareness and appreciation of cultural diversity. Thus, the expressed value of the cocurricular experience that appears in admissions brochures and student life publications is put into
practice.

The Institution

The student body and its culture exist within the framework
of the larger institution. The institution's values are evident in
everything from its physical appearance to curricular and cocurricular missions. Approaching Oxford, Ohio, from any direction, one encounters pleasant, artistic wooden signs that read
"Welcome to Oxford, Home of Miami University." Flanked by
neatly trimmed miniature evergreens, the signs mirror the pic-
turesque campus that appears within a few hundred feet of the
signs on the roads entering from the east and south. The
Georgian-style architecture gives the campus a uniform appearance. Nearly all of the approximately one hundred buildings

are of red brick, making it difficult to distinguish new buildings from those on the National Register of Historic Places. The manicured grounds, with their variety of trees, plants, and open spaces, add to the beauty and feeling of timelessness of this place. The aesthetic value of the campus is further enhanced by features like natural areas, a formal garden, and limestone bridges. Structures like the historic McGuffey Museum add to the campus's sense of history.

Indeed, history and tradition are mainstays of the institutional culture. The detailed story of the university, beginning with its founding in 1809, fills nearly four hundred pages of Walter Havighurst's *The Miami Years* (1984). This volume is given to new staff and faculty upon their arrival. Threads of the campus's history are routinely woven into campus speeches, stories, and publications. Dr. Phillip Shriver, a previous president of the university and a historian, is one of the university's most popular speakers, according to students on campus. He often gives a talk based on the mural of significant events in Miami's history that covers one entire wall of a large multipurpose room in the campus center. The room is aptly named the Heritage Room. Maintaining the history of the institution and its basic values is blended with a progressive approach to the future. This attitude is evident in the improvements to library collections and computer capability, the advanced technology found in the administration and in classrooms, the expansive recreational facilities, a major capital funding campaign, a substantive revision of the liberal education requirement, and the strong commitment to recruit minority students, staff, and faculty.

The mission of the university figures centrally in both the academic and out-of-class life of the campus. The major components of that mission are captured in this statement from the *Miami Bulletin:* "The mission of Miami University is to preserve, add to, evaluate, and transmit the accumulated knowledge of the centuries; to develop critical thinking, extend the frontiers of knowledge, and serve society; and to provide an environment conducive to effective and inspired teaching and learning, promote professional development of faculty, and encourage scholarly research and creativity of faculty and students" (1990, p. 6).

The *Bulletin* also includes other important statements, such as "Miami's primary concern is its students," "the University endeavors to individualize the educational experience," and "it educates men and women for responsible, informed citizenship, as well as for meaningful employment" (p. 6). These identify the values of the institution, values that are incorporated in the academic and student services divisions.

The commitment to educate students for responsible, informed citizenship is evident in the university's core requirements. This core consists of twenty-four credits from English composition and literature, humanities, social sciences, and natural sciences, and eighteen credits from outside the division of a student's major. Students are encouraged to meet these requirements during the first two years of enrollment. (Though in place during the time of this study, this core curriculum will be replaced in 1992 with the new liberal education requirement.) Approximately 130 majors are offered in six divisions, including arts and science, education and allied professions, business administration, fine arts, applied sciences, and interdisciplinary studies. Nearly nine hundred students participate in the honors program.

Individualized education is available in a number of forms. For example, senior thesis options are available in programs such as honors and interdisciplinary studies. These theses are publicly presented for the benefit of the community. Internship and cooperative opportunities are offered in many programs. The Miami campus in Luxembourg provides an opportunity for international study. Special programs, such as Laws Hall and Associates, offer experiential learning. In Laws Hall and Associates (simultaneously a four-credit course and a student-operated advertising organization), students work in teams to develop promotional advertising campaigns for real corporate clients. The program is interdisciplinary, cosponsored by the marketing, mass communication, and art departments.

The twenty-to-one ratio of students to instructional faculty is another indication of the concern for students. Women constitute 27 percent of the full-time faculty. Students in this study consistently reported that faculty were available, friendly, and

helpful. Many faculty members serve as advisers to student organizations and as faculty associates in the residence halls. The
faculty associates program aims to build informal relationships
among faculty and students by integrating faculty members into
the residence hall community activities. The interest in the welfare of students is also obvious in the cocurricular environment.

Approximately half of the 16,000 students enrolled on the
Oxford campus reside there; the remainder live within a two-
mile radius. Students are required to live on campus during their
first year unless they commute from home. Commuters make
up only 3 percent of the Oxford campus population. The thirty-
nine residence halls house from 75 to 350 students; none of the
halls is more than three stories high. The ratio of professional
residence-life staff to students is 135 to 1. In the first-year program, halls are staffed by full-time professionals with master's
degrees and graduate students in student personnel and related
graduate programs. These staff members are responsible both
for routine student services functions and for the academic advising of all first-year students in their buildings. Housing first-
year students together and having student services professionals
perform academic advising are intended to help these students
adjust to college life and address a combination of the academic
and cocurricular concerns. Upper-division halls are staffed by
graduate students, many of whom have had previous full-time
experience in student services. The residence hall system also
offers opportunities for students in paraprofessional positions
for each floor. These students receive extensive training in human relations, crisis intervention, and leadership skills.

Design and Methods Used in the Study

Chapter One traces my journey from quantitative to qualitative interpretation of the study's data. The original design of the study facilitated that journey.

Design

The design was grounded in previous cognitive development research methodology. Most notably, Loevinger and Wessler's (1970) work in ego development advocated using unstructured interviews to allow the students' frame of reference to surface. They also provided a process for analyzing data that began with establishing categories from responses, comparing new responses to those categories, and constantly revising them to account for the data. Using their work as a foundation, data collection and interpretation were informed by, yet not limited to, previous conceptualizations of students' epistemological development.

The longitudinal design allowed tracing the development of students' ways of knowing throughout the college experience. Starting at the outset of their first semester and continuing past graduation ensured that the entire experience would be reflected. The inclusion of both females and males was essential to explore gender similarities and differences in students' ways of knowing. The interview was selected as the primary mode of data collection because it is viewed by both cognitive development researchers (King, 1990) and naturalistic inquirers as providing the most accurate source of information. The labor-intensive use of interviews did limit my research to one campus, and thus the context of the study must be kept in mind. I used a written questionnaire to provide a second source of data on epistemological development.

Data Collection

A discussion of the implementation of data collection (including information on participants, the conduct of interviews, and the Measure of Epistemological Reflection) follows.

Participants

The 101 participants were randomly selected from the population of students entering in 1986. Although I no longer intend to generalize my findings (the original purpose of random sampling), the process did broaden the picture of students' epistemological development. The students had diverse academic majors but were homogeneous in socioeconomic status and race. (See Chapter One for a description of the student culture and study participants.) The first-year participants included 51 women and 50 men. The 95 students who continued to participate in the study during the second year included 48 women and 47 men. In the third year, there were 47 women and 39 men; in the fourth year, 43 women and 37 men; and in the fifth year, 37 women and 33 men. Thus, gender representation remained reasonably balanced throughout the study. The high retention rate (70 of 101 over the five years) is consistent with the 68 percent four-year and the 80 percent five-year graduation rate for the 1986 entering class. Fifty-nine of the 70 students participating in the fifth year of the study graduated within four years. The remaining 11 were to graduate during the fifth year. Of the 59 who graduated, 7 were pursuing additional education: 3 in graduate school, 2 in law school, 1 in seminary, and 2 in medical school.

Interviews

The first-year interview (see Resource C) was designed to address six areas of epistemological development defined by previous research (Kurfiss, 1977; Perry, 1970). Those included the roles of the learner, instructor, peers, and evaluation in learning; the nature of knowledge; and decision making. The roles of the learner, instructor, peers, and evaluation and decision making were introduced directly, but the questions were open-ended to allow the students to pursue any direction of interest to them. I intentionally avoided leading the students within the domain under consideration. The follow-up questions on the interview schedule are examples of how I responded if the students asked for clarification or how I went about prompting additional responses to clarify the students' perspectives. When students were unable to think of responses, I asked them to describe experiences they had encountered in the domain in order to stimulate their thinking without making specific suggestions. I asked for reasons for the perspectives that the students offered if they were not clear from the comments. Finally, I routinely summarized each students' comments to ensure that I understood them accurately.

The nature of knowledge domain was not directly addressed in the first-year interview. This area was pursued only if the student introduced the subject. This decision stemmed directly from concern about leading the response. The remaining four questions in the first-year interview were designed to elicit what students felt was most important (most significant aspect and value of things learned) and ideas that might not otherwise surface in response to the six domains (would the students like to change anything, and did they have anything else to add?) First-year interviews ranged from thirty to forty-five minutes.

After analyzing the first-year data, I modified the interview in two ways. Because the students interviewed in the previous year had seldom brought up the subject themselves, the first was to address the nature of knowledge directly. Question number six was thus added to ask students whether they had encountered discrepancies in the information they were studying. This question was posed only if the student had not introduced this idea earlier. The second change was to explain at the outset that learning took place both in and out of class and that students were invited to use whichever context came to mind. This approach opened the door to responses about significant experiences and valuable learning outside the classroom that were not specifically encouraged in the first year. Second-year interviews ranged from forty-five minutes to an hour.

I made additional modifications in the interview for the third year. The first involved asking more follow-up questions in each area (see Resource C) to get a more comprehensive understanding of the responses. Second, the out-of-class learning experience was addressed more directly (item three). These changes reorganized the interview to flow from the most significant experience, to classroom learning, then to out-of-class learning, and then to decision making. The interviews became more conversational as a result of reorganizing and my moving from one topic to another under item two based on how the student responded. The question about the value of what the student had learned was eliminated because it rarely produced much response from students in previous years. Instead, a question about whether the students had changed in any way as a result of their learning experiences was added. The follow-up ("How did this happen?") produced valuable information about the factors that affect learning and epistemological change. The same interview schedule was used for the fourth year and for students still in undergraduate school the fifth year. Third- and fourth-year interviews ranged from sixty to ninety minutes.

The fifth-year interview for participants who had graduated included three phases (see Resource C). Phase one, reflections on learning during the senior year, was intended to cover the same content as previous interviews for the time remaining in the senior year after the fourth interview. The most and least effective learning experiences were used to focus responses, yet still assess the areas of instructor, learner, peers, and evaluation. Question three was used to gain additional information on the learner's role. The decision-making domain was altered so that students could be asked how they made decisions about what to believe (this question encompassed knowledge discrepancies). Phase two focused on perceptions of learning in the participants' current settings, which included work environments, further education, and (in a few cases) job searching. The format of phase one was repeated, substituting the current setting for the senior year. Phase three asked the respondents to reflect on the overall college experience. Questions about the most and least important experiences were used to draw out insights, as well as environmental influences, on learning. The remaining questions referred to the impact of college as the graduates perceived it. Fifth-year interviews ranged from sixty to ninety minutes.

Interviews were conducted in the fall of each year, with interviews extending into February in the last two years. I conducted interviews in my campus office for as long as students were in school and interviewed graduates in the fifth year by telephone. Four trained interviewers assisted me by doing thirty of the first-year interviews; two of these interviewers conducted a few of the second-year interviews. I conducted all interviews personally in the remaining years. All interviews were tape-recorded. Participants were paid five dollars for their participation each year.

The Measure of Epistemological Reflection (MER)

This short-essay questionnaire, designed to assess epistemological development, was used to give students an opportunity to write about their ways of knowing and triangulate (test against another source) the interviews. The MER (Baxter Magolda and Porterfield, 1985) addresses the same six domains as the interview: the role of the learner, instructor, peers, and evaluation in learning; the nature of knowledge; and decision making. Short essay questions within each domain ask the respondent to state a preference about the introductory statement (see Resource C). Follow-up questions ask for reasons for the preference and for elaboration on the respondents' thinking. All of the questions are open-ended to allow participants to produce a response. This practice is believed to promote the respondents' using their own frames of reference (Loevinger and Wessler, 1970). The reasons given become the basis for interpreting the response because *how* people think or *why* they hold a particular view is more relevant to epistemological development than *what* they believe about a particular topic. The questions are spaced throughout the page to increase the likelihood of a response to each one.

The MER responses are coded with a rating manual that was constructed using Loevinger and Wessler's (1970) empirical validation process (Taylor, 1983). That process involved assigning the MER responses of eighty-four students to theoretical descriptions of Perry's (1970) positions one through five. Within those five categories, the reasons that students gave for their perspectives were sorted into themes called reasoning structures. Another seventy-one students' MER responses were then coded according to the five positions as well as to the reasoning structures. Those structures that were confirmed by the additional data were retained; those that did not reappear were omitted. The overall epistemological levels were then arrived at on the basis of the empirical data rather than the initial theoretical descriptions (Taylor, 1983). Because both genders were included in the original construction of the manual and in subsequent studies to refine it, the current manual reflects epistemological levels that encompass characteristics of both Perry's first five positions and Belenky, Clinchy, Goldberger, and Tarule's (1986) five perspectives. In the MER scoring process, the respondent is assigned an epistemological level and reasoning structures within that level for each of the six domains. The final rating for epistemological level is derived from the average of the domain ratings.

The MER's accuracy in assessing epistemological level was supported by consistent significant differences across levels of education (Baxter Magolda and Porterfield, 1988) and a .93 correlation with interviews (Baxter Magolda, 1987). Despite the fact that a written instrument generally results in less in-depth information, it was judged to be a viable means of gathering additional data about students' ways of knowing. There is also evidence suggesting that two independent raters can arrive at similar scores using the rating manual. Interrater reliability is supported by a .80 correlation ($N = 752$) and by interrater agreement (when both raters arrive at the same score) ranging from 70 to 80 percent (Baxter Magolda and Porterfield, 1985).

The MER was given to each participant to complete after the interview. Participants were asked to wait at least two weeks to complete the questionnaires, which were returned from two weeks to three months after the interview. All respondents returned the MER the first year. It was returned by seventy-seven of the ninety-five second-year participants, sixty-four of the eighty-six third-year participants, forty-five of the eighty fourth-year participants, and thirty-four of the seventy fifth-year participants.

Interpretation of the Data

A discussion of my interpretation of the interview data and MER responses and of the trustworthiness of my procedures follows.

Interviews

All of the interviews were transcribed verbatim by a professional audiotape transcriber. The MER rating manual was used to interpret the epistemological levels within the interview responses. This practice clearly placed the interpretation within a theoretical context established a priori (a concern in qualitative research that theory should emerge from the data). However, in my view, this particular theoretical context did not limit the possibilities of interpretation. The theoretical context embodied in the MER manual came from empirical data—that is, approximately one thousand previous college students' responses to the MER. Because this group included both women and men, whose education ranged from first-year to doctoral levels, the picture of development provided by the manual was sufficiently broad to serve as a starting point for interpreting the interview data. The theoretical context contained in the MER manual represents grounded theory as Lincoln and Guba (1985) describe it. They argue that grounded theory is "open-ended and can be extended indefinitely; and it is discovered empirically rather than expounded a priori" (p. 206). They also indicate that grounded theory can then be used in subsequent study. Perhaps more importantly, the a priori categories were explicitly stated. As such, it was easier to maintain an awareness of their influence than had they been less clear (as is the case with the unstated assumptions that most researchers naturally hold). In addition, an explicit process for noting new categories and reasoning structures was built into the MER rating process. New reasoning structures are noted if they do not match ones already in existence in the manual; the result is that the manual evolves with the data as opposed to limiting interpretation to already-established categories. When new reasoning structures appear repeatedly, they are added to the manual. Although the provision for adding categories also exists, no new categories have been added as a result of interpreting the interviews. However, the ways of knowing described in this book are refined and relabeled from those in the manual as a result of the interview data.

I rated all of the interview transcripts each year. I began by reading each response to identify reasoning structures in each of the six domains. The general interview questions were interpreted within the six domains, depending on the direction the student chose for the response. Domains were rated separately by identifying the primary reasoning structure in the response and comparing it to those in the MER manual for that domain. When a match was found, the corresponding epistemological level and reasoning structure were recorded. If a match was not found, I made a judgment regarding whether the response reflected one of the epistemological levels and, if so, noted the new reasoning structure. Once an epistemological level was assigned for each domain (or it was noted that one could not be determined because no clear reasoning structure was evident in the response), the domain ratings were averaged to arrive at a final epistemological rating. Overall epistemological-level ratings made it possible to compare women and men, a process that identified no substantial differences.

Because reasoning structures within the epistemological levels were recorded as a part of the process, gender comparisons were also possible on that level. Two steps were used for these comparisons. In step one, the number of women using each reasoning structure (within each domain and in each epistemological level) was used to identify the reasoning structures most used by women in each epistemological level. This process was then repeated for men. Although most reasoning structures were employed by both women and men, some were used more often by one gender than the other. These differences were recorded. To triangulate (confirm) the results of this process in step two, the data were then separated by gender, epistemological level, and domain. These sets were read to identify themes in the responses without knowledge of the gender and epistemological level of each set. Next, these themes were compared to those identified in step one. Step-two themes matched step-one reasoning structures in which differences in the percentage of women and men using them was 20 percent or more. In most cases, gender-related patterns reported in this book stemmed from reasoning structures in which the percentage of women and men using those structures differed by approximately 33 percent. Rereading the data for this last step also provided an opportunity to check the consistency of responses assigned to the same epistemological levels.

The curricular and cocurricular experience themes reported in Chapters Eight and Ten emerged from a separate reading of the interview data. For this process, a trained graduate student and I read the interview transcripts on an annual basis. The interviews were separated by epistemological level prior to this reading. Using Lincoln and Guba's (1985) version of the constant comparative method for processing naturalistic data, we independently recorded on index cards any comments describing a curricular or cocurricular environmental component that students had actually encountered and their reactions to it. Academic components were often located throughout the interview because much of it focused on classroom learning. Cocurricular components were most often found in the general questions and the cocurricular section of the interview. We read the entire interview, however, to search for ideas throughout. When we both had completed our recording, we compared our cards to identify variations. When one had recorded a comment and the other had not, we returned to the original interview transcripts to reread that section. If the comment was a component that the student had actually encountered and reported about, the comment was included. Otherwise, it was excluded.

Once our two sets of cards matched, we independently sorted these units into categories. This process involved placing cards with similar content into groups, labeling these groups to capture the essence of cards included, reviewing the groups to eliminate any overlap in categories, and identifying subsets or themes within each category. After completing this process independently, we compared our category sets for consistency. Differences were discussed and units resorted as necessary to reach consensus. When our final category set was established, we reread all data within the categories and themes to ensure that the assigned label captured the essence of all data in the set.

MER Responses

I and a second certified rater interpreted the responses each year using the MER rating manual. The primary reasoning structure for each domain (page in the case of the MER) was identified and then matched to those in the manual for that domain. The same provision for adding new reasoning structures described earlier was also used here. Rating resulted in an overall epistemological-level rating derived from the average of the domain ratings as well as reasoning structure ratings in each domain. We worked independently and compared our interpretations upon completion each year. The two-step process previously described for comparing reasoning structures by gender was also implemented with the MER data. The MER data yielded interpretations very similar to the interviews, both in epistemological levels and reasoning patterns. Due to this similarity and because fewer students submitted the MER each year than participated in the interview, the ways of knowing and gender-related patterns described in the book are drawn largely from the interview data.

Trustworthiness

These data processing procedures were chosen to enhance the value, or trustworthiness, of the data and interpretations. Because the value of qualitative findings cannot be discussed in the quantitative terms of *validity* and *reliability,* Lincoln and Guba's (1985) qualitative counterparts are used here to evaluate the data. Two of these, *credibility* and *transferability,* are applicable. The credibility of the data are supported by three of Lincoln and Guba's techniques. The prolonged engagement with study participants over a five-year period helped me understand the participants' experiences, become aware of any personal assumptions that interfered with accurate interpretation, and build trust between me and the students. Member checks (checking with the participants about my interpretations during the interview) increased my comprehension of their comments. Triangulation was implemented in the curricular and cocurricular themes by using two independent readers to process the data. The same was true of the MER rating. Working separately and then comparing our findings helped limit biases that may have altered the interpretation. Although I alone rated the interviews for epistemological level, the reexamination of the data for reasoning structure and the similarity between the interview and the MER ratings contribute to triangulation of that process. The degree to which these findings may be applicable to students other than those participating depends on the similarity of this study's context to that envisioned by the reader. The discussion of the context in Chapter One and the story lines in Chapter Seven are intended to assist the reader in judging transferability.

 Resource C

Study Interview and Questionnaire

The following interview protocols describe how the interviews were introduced and the questions asked each year. All questions were used, but the order was not rigidly followed. If the student introduced an area of interest in the course of another response, the interviewer was free to make a transition to that subject, particularly when it concerned knowledge discrepancies (included in the interview protocol starting in year two). If the student introduced the topic of knowledge discrepancies, the interviewer pursued that line of thinking to avoid suggesting the subject. The follow-up questions noted throughout were used only when the student did not initiate discussion of those areas.

Interview Protocol: Year One

Introduction

This interview is intended to solicit your ideas about your learning as a student. It will be an open-ended interview in order to allow you every opportunity to offer your ideas on each aspect of the learning experience that we discuss. Feel free to talk about any experiences or ideas that come to mind as we discuss each area.

Note to interviewer

The student will be encouraged to talk freely and elaborate or explain as necessary after each question to allow maximum freedom of response. The interviewer asks general questions and

411

encourages the student to describe experiences and ideas to avoid structuring the student's thinking.

Questions

1. Tell me about the most significant aspect of your learning experience in the past year.
2. As you think about yourself as a learner in the classroom, what role do you prefer to play to make learning more effective for you?
3. Let's talk about instructors. What do you expect from them to help you learn effectively? (Follow up if necessary: What relationship do you think instructors and students should have to make learning effective?)
4. What about other students in your classes? What kinds of experiences have you had with them that help you learn? (Follow up if necessary: What kinds of interactions would you like to have that would help you learn?)
5. As you think back over the work you've done in your classes the past year, talk about how you think learning should be evaluated in order for you to learn effectively.
6. Discuss your perspective on the value of the things you have learned in the past year. (Follow up if necessary: What things have you learned that you think are important? What concerns have you had about some of the things you have learned?)
7. I am interested in your perspective on how best to make decisions. Can you describe an important educational decision you made in the last year and talk about how you went about it?
8. Would you change anything about the learning environment you have experienced over the past year? If so, what?
9. Is there anything else you would like to share to help me understand your perspective on the learning you have experienced over the past year?

Closure

Thanks very much for your time and willingness to share your ideas. As you recall, your identity will be kept confidential.

Interview Protocol: Year Two

Introduction

Thanks for continuing with the study! Your willingness to continue makes it possible to study how students' learning preferences change in college. This interview is intended to solicit your ideas about your learning experience as a student. It will be an open-ended interview in order to allow you every opportunity to offer your ideas and thoughts on each aspect of the learning experience we discuss. Learning experiences probably have occurred both in class and in cocurricular experiences. Feel free to talk about any experiences or ideas that come to mind as we discuss each area.

Questions

1. Now that you have experienced your first year of college, tell me about the most significant aspect of your learning in the past year.
2. As you think about yourself as a learner in the classroom, what role do you prefer to play to make learning most effective for you?
3. Let's talk about instructors. What do you expect from them to help you learn effectively? (Follow up if necessary: What relationship do you think instructors and students should have to make learning effective?)
4. What about other students in your classes? What kinds of experiences have you had with them that help you learn? (Follow up if necessary: What kinds of interactions would you like to have that would help you learn?)
5. As you think back over the work you've done in your classes the past year, talk about how you think learning should be evaluated so that you can learn effectively.
6. This past year you have probably heard and/or read a great deal of information. Usually with that amount of information, you run across some discrepancies. Has this happened to you?
   If yes, how do you decide what to accept or believe?
   If no, what do you think you would do if it did?

7. Let's talk about decisions of a different nature. Can you describe an important educational decision you made in the last year and talk about how you went about it?

8. Discuss your perspective on the value of the things you have learned in the past year. (Follow up if necessary: What things have you learned that you think are important? What concerns have you had about some of the things you have learned?)

9. Would you change anything about the learning environment you have experienced over the past year? If so, what?

10. Is there anything else you would like to share to help me understand your perspective on the learning you have experienced over the past year?

Closure

Thanks very much for your time and willingness to share your ideas. As you recall, your identity will be kept confidential.

Interview Protocol: Year Three, Four, and Five (prior to graduation)

Introduction

Thanks for continuing with the study! Your willingness to continue makes it possible to study how students' learning preferences change in college. This interview is intended to solicit your ideas about your learning experience as a student. It will be an open-ended interview in order to allow you every opportunity to offer your ideas and thoughts on each aspect of the learning experience we discuss. Learning experiences probably have occurred both in class and in cocurricular experiences. Feel free to talk about any experiences or ideas that come to mind as we discuss each area. Note: Start each area A through E by asking for general observations. Follow-up questions are used if necessary to prompt elaboration.

Questions

1. As you think about the last year, what is the most significant learning experience that comes to mind?

    A.   What made it significant?

    B.   Why is it more important than other experiences?

2.   You spend a lot of time in classes. Let's talk about the classes you've had this past year.

    A.   Instructors

        What things have they done to help you learn?

        What things did they not do that would have helped?

        What interactions have you had with instructors? Did these help you learn?

        What relationships have you had with instructors? Did these affect your learning?

        What suggestions do you have for change?

    B.   Other students

        What interactions have you had in class with other students? Were these interactions helpful?

        What interactions have you had out of class with other students? Were these interactions helpful?

        What interactions with other students do you prefer? Why?

    C.   Yourself

        What methods of learning have you found that work for you?

        Why are these effective?

    D.   Evaluation

        What have you experienced that is helpful?

        What have you experienced that is not helpful?

        What should have been done? Why?

    E.   Varying points of view

        Have you experienced these?

        If so, how do you decide?

        What is the source of discrepant information?

3.   You learn outside the classroom as well, so let's talk about that.

   What aspects of your environment have helped you learn? Why?

   What aspects of your environment have not helped/hindered your learning? Why?

4.   Is there anything you would change about any aspect of the environment here to make learning more effective?

5. Decision making:
    A. What is the most important decision you made last year?
    B. Why is that one most important?
    C. How did you go about it?
    D. Are you finding decision making easier or harder as you are in college longer?
6. Are you different in any way as a result of your learning experience last year? If so, in what way? How did it happen?
7. Anything else of importance that I missed?

Closure

Thanks very much for your time and willingness to share your ideas. As you recall, your identity will be kept confidential.

Interview Protocol: Year Five
(for participants who graduated in May 1990)

Introduction

Thanks for your willingness to continue with the study! Although the study focuses on your ideas about learning as has always been the case, this year there are three phases in the interview. The first one relates to your experiences during senior year after our last interview, the second concerns learning in your current setting, and the third involves your perceptions of the impact of college. As usual, the interview is open-ended. Feel free to talk about anything that comes to mind. Remember that learning experiences occur in both curricular and cocurricular settings.

Phase One

Reflections on learning during the senior year (let person being interviewed choose curricular or cocurricular but cover both in questions one and two).

1. Describe the most effective learning experiences you had as a senior. Inquire as necessary about
   A. The nature of these experiences
   B. Instructor's role
   C. Your role as learner
   D. Peers' role
   E. How this work was evaluated by instructor and your perception of its effectiveness.
2. Describe the least effective learning experiences you had as a senior. Inquire as necessary about
   A. The nature of these experiences
   B. Instructor's role
   C. Your role as learner
   D. Peers' role
   E. How your work was evaluated by instructor and your perception of the evaluation's effectiveness.
3. Describe the role you assumed as a learner during your senior year.
   A. How did you approach learning? Why?
   B. Was this similar to or different than in previous years? Why?
4. Decision making:
   A. Did you encounter the need to make any decisions about what to believe in the subjects you studied your senior year? If so, describe the situation, how you decided, and why.
   B. What educational or career decision did you make senior year? Describe the decision, how you approached it, and why.

Phase Two

Perceptions of learning in current setting (i.e., job, graduate school, current activities).

1. Describe the most effective learning experiences you have had (in your current setting).
   Inquire as necessary about

    A.   The nature of these experiences

    B.   Instructor's/supervisor's role

    C.   Your role as learner

    D.   Peers'/co-workers' role

    E.   How your work was evaluated and your perception of the degree to which your work was evaluated effectively.

2. Describe the least effective learning experiences you have had (in your current setting).

    Inquire as necessary about

    A.   The nature of these experiences

    B.   Instructor's/supervisor's role

    C.   Your role as learner

    D.   Peers'/co-workers' role

    E.   How your work was evaluated and your perception of the degree to which your work was evaluated effectively.

3. Describe your role as a learner (in current setting).

    A.   How do you approach learning? Why?

    B.   Is your approach similar to or different from the way you approached learning as a senior? Why?

4. Decision making:

    A.   Do you encounter the need to decide about things you are learning (in current setting)? If so, describe the situation, how you decided, and why.

    B.   Have you made any major decisions (in current setting or since graduation)? If so, describe the decision, how you approached it, and why.

Phase Three

Perceptions of the impact of the college experience (looking at the undergraduate experience as a whole).

1. Describe the college experiences that you feel had the most important effect on you. Start with the most important and add others in order of their importance.

A. Describe the experiences. What impact did they have on you, how did they have this impact, and why is this important?

B. If person chose all curricular or all cocurricular, ask if there are experiences in other category.

2. Describe the college experiences that you feel had the least effect on you.

A. Describe the experiences, your perception of why they did not affect you, and how you feel about them now.

B. If person chose all curricular or all cocurricular, ask if there are experiences in other category.

3. What characteristics would you use to describe yourself now that you would not have chosen before you went to college?

4. Describe aspects of your college experience that you feel prepared you for your current role. How and why?

5. Are there aspects of your current role for which you feel your college experience did not prepare you? If so, describe.

6. Do you have other observations or thoughts about your college experience that you feel are important? If so, please describe them.

Closure

Thanks again for continuing with the study! I will keep in touch with you and call you again next year for the next interview.

Measure of Epistemological Reflection

INSTRUCTIONS: The questionnaire that follows has to do with your perspective on learning in college. Each of the questions on the following pages asks for your opinion or choice on a given subject and the REASONS why you have that particular perspective or opinion. We are interested in understanding your perspective as fully as possible. Please give as much detail as you can to describe how you feel about each question. Feel free to use the backs of pages if you need more space. Thank you!

Please Write Your Responses in Ink

Name: _____

Age: _____

Sex: (circle one)   male   female

College major: _____

Father's job: _____

Mother's job: _____

Today's date: _____

Class rank: (circle one)   Freshman
                                  Sophomore
                                  Junior
                                  Senior
                                  First-year master's
                                  Second-year master's
                                  Doctoral student
                                  Ph.D.
                                  Other _____

Measure of Epistemological Reflection   Protocol # _____

Page 2

Think about the last time you had to make a major decision about your education in which you had a number of alternatives (e.g., which college to attend, college major, career choice, etc.). What was the nature of the decision?

_____

_____

What alternatives were available to you?

_____

_____

_____

_____

How did you feel about these alternatives?

_____

_____

_____

_____

How did you go about choosing from the alternatives?

_____

_____

_____

_____

What things were the most important considerations in your choice? Please give details.

_____

_____

_____

_____

Do you learn best in classes that focus on factual information or classes that focus on ideas and concepts?

_____

_____

Why do you learn best in the type of class you chose above?

_____

_____

_____

_____

What do you see as the advantages of the choice you made above?

_____

_____

_____

_____

What do you see as the disadvantages of the choice you made above?

_____

_____

_____

_____

If you could give advice to anyone on how best to succeed in college course work, what kind of advice would you give them? Talk about what *you* believe is the key to doing well in college courses.

_____

_____

_____

_____

Measure of Epistemological Reflection   Protocol # _____

Page 4

During the course of your studies, you have probably had instructors with different teaching methods. As you think back to instructors you have had, describe the method of instruction that had the most beneficial effect on you.

_____

_____

_____

_____

What made that teaching method beneficial? Please be specific and use examples.

_____

_____

_____

_____

Were there aspects of that teaching method that were not beneficial? If so, please talk about some of the aspects and why they were not beneficial.

_____

_____

_____

_____

What are the most important things you learned from the instructor's method of teaching?

_____

_____

_____

Please describe the type of relationship with an instructor that would help you to learn best and explain why.

_____

_____

_____

Do you prefer classes in which the students do a lot of talking or where students don't talk very much?

_____

_____

Why do you prefer the degree of student involvement/partici-pation that you chose above?

_____

_____

_____

_____

What do you see as the advantages of your preference above?

_____

_____

_____

_____

What do you see as the disadvantages of your preference?

_____

_____

_____

_____

What type of interactions would you like to see among members of a class in order to enhance your own learning?

_____

_____

_____

_____

_____

Measure of Epistemological Reflection   Protocol # _____

Page 6

Some people think that hard work and effort will result in high grades in school. Others think that hard work and effort are not a basis for high grades. Which of these statements is most like your own opinion?

_____
_____
_____
_____

Ideally, what do you think should be used as a basis for evaluating your work in college courses?

_____
_____
_____
_____

Who should be involved in the evaluation you described above?

_____
_____
_____
_____

Please explain why you think the response you suggested above is the best way to evaluate students' work in college courses.

_____
_____
_____
_____
_____
_____
_____

Measure of Epistemological Reflection   Protocol # _____
Page 7

Sometimes different instructors give different explanations for historical events or scientific phenomena. When two instructors explain the same thing differently, can one be more correct than the other?

_____

_____

When two explanations are given for the same situation, how would you go about deciding which explanation to believe? Please give details and examples.

_____

_____

_____

_____

_____

Can one ever be sure of which explanation to believe? If so, how?

_____

_____

_____

_____

If one can't be sure of which explanation to believe, why not?

_____

_____

_____

_____

References

Admissions Office. *Freshman Class Profile.* Oxford, Ohio: Miami University, 1986.

American Council on Education and the National Association of Student Personnel Administrators. *A Perspective on Student Affairs.* American Council on Education and the National Association of Student Personnel Administrators, 1987.

American Council on Education and the University of California, Los Angeles. *Cooperative Institutional Research Program.* Los Angeles: American Council on Education and the University of California, 1986.

American Council on Education Studies. *The Student Personnel Point of View.* Washington, D.C.: American Council on Education Studies, 1949.

Astin, A. W. "Student Involvement: A Developmental Theory for Higher Education." *Journal of College Student Personnel,* 1984, *25,* 297–308.

Bakan, D. *The Duality of Human Existence.* Boston: Beacon Press, 1966.

Banning, J. H. "Creating a Climate for Successful Student Development: The Campus Ecology Manager Role." In U. Delworth and G. Hanson (eds.), *Student Services: A Handbook for the Profession.* San Francisco: Jossey-Bass, 1989.

Baxter Magolda, M. B. "A Comparison of Open-Ended Interview and Standardized Instrument Measures of Intellectual Development on the Perry Scheme." *Journal of College Student Personnel,* 1987, *28,* 443–448.

Baxter Magolda, M. B., and Porterfield, W. D. "A New Approach to Assess Intellectual Development on the Perry Scheme." *Journal of College Student Personnel,* 1985, *26,* 343–351.

Baxter Magolda, M. B., and Porterfield, W. D. *Assessing Intellectual Development: The Link Between Theory and Practice.* Alexandria, Va.: American College Personnel Association, 1988.

Belenky, M. F., Clinchy, B. M., Goldberger, N. R., and Tarule, J. M. *Women's Ways of Knowing.* New York: Basic Books, 1986.

Benack, S. "The Coding Dimensions of Epistemological Thought in Young Men and Women." *Moral Education Forum,* 1982, *7* (2), 297–309.

Bogdan, R., and Biklen, S. *Qualitative Research for Education.* Boston: Allyn & Bacon, 1982.

Boyer, E. L. *College: The Undergraduate Experience in America.* New York: HarperCollins, 1987.

Branch-Simpson, G. E. "A Study of the Patterns in the Development of Black Students at the Ohio State University." Unpublished doctoral dissertation, Department of Educational Policy and Leadership, Ohio State University, 1985.

Broughton, J. M. "Women's Rationality and Men's Virtues: A Critique of Gender Dualism in Gilligan's Theory of Moral Development." *Social Research,* 1983, *50,* 597–642.

Brown, L. M., and Gilligan, C. "The Psychology of Women and the Development of Girls." Paper presented at the annual meeting of the American Educational Research Association, Boston, Mass., April 1990.

Brown, R. D. *Student Development in Tomorrow's Higher Education: A Return to the Academy.* Washington, D.C.: American Personnel and Guidance Association, 1972.

Brown, R. D. "Fostering Intellectual and Personal Growth: The Student Development Role." In U. Delworth and G. Hanson (eds.), *Student Services: A Handbook for the Profession.* San Francisco: Jossey-Bass, 1989.

Bruffee, K. A. "Collaborative Learning and the 'Conversation of Mankind.'" *College English,* 1984, *46* (7), 635–652.

Bruner, J. *Actual Minds, Possible Worlds.* Cambridge, Mass.: Harvard University Press, 1986.

Carnegie Foundation for the Advancement of Teaching. *Campus Life: In Search of Community.* Carnegie Foundation for the Advancement of Teaching. Princeton, N.J.: Princeton University Press, 1990.

Chickering, A. W. *Education and Identity.* San Francisco: Jossey-Bass, 1969.

Chodorow, N. J. *The Reproduction of Mothering.* Berkeley: University of California Press, 1978.

Chodorow, N. J. *Feminism and Psychoanalytic Theory.* New Haven, Conn.: Yale University Press, 1989.

Clinchy, B. M. "The Development of Thoughtfulness in College Women: Integrating Reason and Care." *American Behavioral Scientist,* 1989, *32* (6), 647–657.

Clinchy, B. M., and Zimmerman, C. "Epistemology and Agency in the Development of Undergraduate Women." In P. Perun (ed.), *The Undergraduate Woman: Issues in Educational Equity.* Lexington, Mass.: Heath, 1982.

Colby, A., and Kohlberg, L. *The Measurement of Moral Judgment.* Volume 1. Cambridge, England: Cambridge University Press, 1987.

Coles, R. *The Call of Stories: Teaching and the Moral Imagination.* Boston: Houghton Mifflin, 1989.

Cooper, J. E. "Telling Our Own Stories: The Reading and Writing of Journals and Diaries." In C. Withrell and N. Noddings (eds.), *Stories Lives Tell: Narrative and Dialogue in Education.* New York: Teachers College Press, 1991.

Cross, K. P. "Teaching to Improve Learning." *Journal on Excellence in College Teaching,* 1990, *1,* 9–22.

"Dear Ethics Committee." *ACPA Developments,* April 1988, p. 22.

Deaux, K., and Major, B. "A Social-Psychological Model of Gender." In D. L. Rhode (ed.), *Theoretical Perspectives on Sexual Difference.* New Haven, Conn.: Yale University Press, 1990.

Eisler, R. *The Chalice and the Blade: Our History, Our Future.* San Francisco: HarperCollins, 1987.

Eisner, E. (ed.). *Learning and Teaching the Ways of Knowing.* Chicago: National Society for the Study of Education, 1985.

Eisner, E. "The Meaning of Alternative Paradigms for Practice."

In E. Guba (ed.), *The Paradigm Dialogue.* Newbury Park, Calif.: Sage, 1990.

Eisner, E., and Peshkin, A. (eds.). *Qualitative Inquiry in Education: The Continuing Debate.* New York: Teachers College Press, 1990.

Fenske, R. H. "Historical Foundations of Student Services." In U. Delworth and G. Hanson (eds.), *Student Services: A Handbook for the Profession.* San Francisco: Jossey-Bass, 1989.

Fleming, J. *Blacks in College: A Comparative Study of Students' Success in Black and White Institutions.* San Francisco: Jossey-Bass, 1984.

Fordam, S., and Ogbu, J. U. "Black Students' School Success: Coping with the 'Burden of Acting White'." *The Urban Review,* 1986, *18* (3), 176–206.

Forrest, L. "Guiding, Supporting, and Advising Students: The Counselor Role." In U. Delworth and G. Hanson (eds.), *Student Services: A Handbook for the Profession.* San Francisco: Jossey-Bass, 1989.

Freedman, E. "Theoretical Perspectives on Sexual Difference: An Overview." In D. L. Rhode (ed.), *Theoretical Perspectives on Sexual Difference.* New Haven, Conn.: Yale University Press, 1990.

Freire, P. *Pedagogy of the Oppressed.* New York: Continuum, 1988.

Frye, M. "The Possibility of Feminist Theory." In D. L. Rhode (ed.), *Theoretical Perspectives on Sexual Difference.* New Haven, Conn.: Yale University Press, 1990.

Gibbs, J. C., Arnold, K. D., and Burkhart, J. E. "Sex Differences in the Expression of Moral Judgment." *Child Development,* 1984, *55,* 1040–1043.

Gilligan, C. *In a Different Voice.* Cambridge, Mass.: Harvard University Press, 1982.

Giroux, H. A. *Schooling and the Struggle for Public Life: Critical Pedagogy in the Modern Age.* Minneapolis: University of Minnesota Press, 1988.

Glidden, J., and Kurfiss, J. G. "Small-Group Discussion in Philosophy 101." *College Teaching,* 1990, *38* (1), 3–8.

Gray, E. D. "The Culture of Separated Desks." In C. Pearson, D. Shavlik, and J. Touchton (eds.), *Educating the Majority.* New York: Macmillan/American Council on Education, 1989.

Guba, E. *The Paradigm Dialogue.* Newbury Park, Calif.: Sage, 1990.

Hall, R. M., and Sandler, B. R. *The Classroom Climate: A Chilly One for Women.?* Project on the Status and Education of Women. Washington, D.C.: Association of American Colleges, 1982.

Hare-Mustin, R., and Maracek, J. *Making a Difference: Psychology and the Construction of Gender.* New Haven, Conn.: Yale University Press, 1990.

Havighurst, W. *The Miami Years.* New York: Putnam, 1984.

Holland, D. C., and Eisenhart, M. A. *Educated in Romance: Women, Achievement and College Culture.* Chicago: University of Chicago Press, 1990.

Hooks, B. *Feminist Theory: From Margin to Center.* Boston: South End Press, 1984.

Huebner, L. A. "Interaction of Student and Campus." In U. Delworth and G. Hanson (eds.), *Student Services: A Handbook for the Profession.* San Francisco: Jossey-Bass, 1989.

Josselson, R. *Finding Herself: Pathways to Identity Development in Women.* San Francisco: Jossey-Bass, 1987.

Katz, J., and Henry, M. *Turning Professors into Teachers: A New Approach to Faculty Development and Student Learning.* New York: Macmillan/American Council on Education, 1988.

Kegan. R. *The Evolving Self: Problem and Process in Human Development.* Cambridge, Mass.: Harvard University Press, 1982.

King, P. M. "Assessing Development from a Cognitive-Developmental Perspective." In D. Creamer (ed.), *College Student Development: Theory and Practice for the 1990s.* Alexandria, Va.: American College Personnel Association, 1990.

King, P. M., Wood, P. K., and Mines, R. A. "Critical Thinking Among College and Graduate Students." *Review of Higher Education,* 1990, *13* (2), 167–186.

Kitchener, K. S. "Cognition, Metacognition, and Epistemic Cognition." *Human Development,* 1983, *26,* 222–232.

Kitchener, K. S., and King, P. M. "Reflective Judgment: Concepts of Justification and Their Relationship to Age and Education." *Journal of Applied Developmental Psychology,* 1981, *2,* 89–116.

Kitchener, K. S., and King, P. M. "The Reflective Judgment Model: Ten Years of Research." In M. L. Commons and others (eds.), *Adult Development.* Volume 2: *Models and Methods in the Study of Adolescent and Adult Thought.* New York: Praeger, 1990.

Knefelkamp, L. L. "Developmental Instruction: Fostering Intellectual and Personal Growth of College Students." Unpublished doctoral dissertation, University of Minnesota, 1974.

Knock, G. K. "Development of Student Services in Higher Education." In M. J. Barr, L. A. Keating, and Associates (eds.), *Developing Effective Student Services Programs: Systematic Approaches for Practitioners.* San Francisco: Jossey-Bass, 1985.

Kohlberg, L. "Stage and Sequence: The Cognitive Developmental Approach to Socialization." In D. A. Goslin (ed.), *Handbook of Socialization Theory and Research.* Skokie, Ill.: Rand McNally, 1969.

Kohlberg, L. *Essays on Moral Development.* Volume 2: *The Psychology of Moral Development.* New York: HarperCollins, 1984.

Kolb, D. A. *Experiential Learning: Experience as the Source of Learning and Development.* Englewood Cliffs, N.J.: Prentice-Hall, 1984.

Kuh, G. D. "The Implications of Demographic Shifts for Student Affairs." In M. Barr and M. Upcraft (eds.), *New Futures for Student Affairs: Building a Vision for Professional Leadership and Practice.* San Francisco: Jossey-Bass, 1990.

Kuh, G. D., Schuh, J. H., Whitt, E. J., and Associates. *Involving Colleges: Successful Approaches to Fostering Student Learning and Development Outside the Classroom.* San Francisco: Jossey-Bass, 1991.

Kurfiss, J. "Sequentiality and Structure in a Cognitive Model of College Student Development." *Developmental Psychology,* 1977, *13,* 565–571.

Lather, P. *Getting Smart.* New York: Routledge, 1991.

Lever, J. "Sex Differences in the Games Children Play." *Social Problems,* 1976, *23,* 478–487.

Lincoln, Y. S. "The Making of a Constructivist: A Remembrance of Transformations Past." In E. Guba (ed.), *The Paradigm Dialogue.* Newbury Park, Calif.: Sage, 1990.

Lincoln, Y. S., and Guba, E. *Naturalistic Inquiry.* Newbury Park, Calif.: Sage, 1985.

Loevinger, J., and Wessler, R. *Ego Development.* Volume 1. San Francisco: Jossey-Bass, 1970.

Lyons, N. P. "Two Perspectives: On Self, Relationships, and Morality." *Harvard Educational Review,* 1983, *53,* 125–145.

Makler, A. "Imagining History: A Good Story and a Well-Formed Argument." In C. Withrell and N. Noddings (eds.), *Stories Lives Tell: Narrative and Dialogue in Education.* New York: Teachers College Press, 1991.

Miami University. *Miami Bulletin.* Oxford, Ohio: Miami University, 1990.

Miller, T. K., and Prince, J. S. *The Future of Student Affairs: A Guide to Student Development for Tomorrow's Higher Education.* San Francisco: Jossey-Bass, 1976.

Nelson, C. E. "Skewered on the Unicorn's Horn: The Illusion of Tragic Tradeoff Between Content and Critical Thinking in the Teaching of Science." In L. W. Crow (ed.), *Enhancing Critical Thinking in the Sciences.* Washington, D.C.: Society for College Science Teachers, 1989.

Noddings, N. *Caring: A Feminine Approach to Ethics and Moral Education.* Berkeley: University of California Press, 1984.

Noddings, N. "Stories in Dialogue: Caring and Interpersonal Reasoning." In C. Withrell and N. Noddings (eds.), *Stories Lives Tell: Narrative and Dialogue in Education.* New York: Teachers College Press, 1991.

Palmer, P. J. "Community, Conflict, and Ways of Knowing." *Change,* 1987, Sept.-Oct., 20–25.

Parham, T. A. "Cycles of Psychological Nigrescence." *The Counseling Psychologist,* 1989, *17* (2), 187–226.

Pascarella, E. T. "The Impact of College on Students: The Nature of the Evidence." *The Review of Higher Education,* 1991, *14* (4), 453–466.

Pascarella, E. T., and Terenzini, P. T. *How College Affects Students: Findings and Insights from Twenty Years of Research.* San Francisco: Jossey-Bass, 1991.

Perry, W. G. *Forms of Intellectual and Ethical Development in the College Years: A Scheme.* Troy, Mo.: Holt, Rinehart & Winston, 1970.

Piaget, J. *The Moral Judgment of the Child.* (M. Gabian, trans.) New York: Routledge & Kegan Paul, 1932.

Rich, A. *On Lies, Secrets, and Silence: Selected Prose 1966–1978.* New York: Norton, 1979.

Rodgers, R. F. "Theories Underlying Student Development." In D. Creamer (ed.), *Student Development in Higher Education.* Alexandria, Va.: American College Personnel Association, 1980.

Rodgers, R. F. "Recent Theories and Research Underlying Student Development." In D. Creamer (ed.), *College Student Development: Theory and Practice for the 1990s.* Alexandria, Va.: American College Personnel Association, 1990.

Rogers, J. L. "New Paradigm Leadership: Integrating the Female Ethos." *Iniatives,* 1988, *51,* 1–8.

Rogers, J. L. "Leadership Development for the 90s: Incorporating Emergent Paradigm Perspectives." *NASPA Journal,* 1992 *29*(4), 243–252.

Romer, K. T., and Whipple, W. R. "Collaboration Across the Power Line." *Journal of College Teaching,* 1991, *38* (2), 66–70.

Sadker, M., and Sadker, D. "Sexism in the Classroom: From Grade School to Graduate School." *Phi Delta Kappan,* 1986, *67* (7), 512–515.

Sanford, N. "Developmental Status of the Entering Freshman." In N. Sanford (ed.), *The American College.* New York: Wiley, 1962.

Schniedewind, N. "Feminist Values: Guidelines for Teaching Methodology in Women's Studies." In I. Shor (ed.), *Freire for the Classroom: A Sourcebook for Liberatory Teaching.* Portsmouth, N.H.: Boynton/Cook, 1987.

Schön, D. A. *Educating the Reflective Practitioner: Toward a New Design for Teaching and Learning in the Professions.* San Francisco: Jossey-Bass, 1987.

Shor, I., and Freire, P. *A Pedagogy for Liberation: Dialogues on Transforming Education.* South Hadley, Mass.: Bergin and Garvey, 1987.

Stern, L. "Conceptions of Separation and Connection in Female Adolescents." In C. Gilligan, N. P. Lyons, and T. J. Hanmer (eds.), *Making Connections: The Relational Worlds of Adolescent Girls at Emma Willard School.* Troy, N.Y.: Emma Willard School, 1989.

Strange, C. C., and King, P. M. "The Professional Practice of Student Development." In D. Creamer (ed.), *College Stu-*

dent Development: Theory and Practice for the 1990s. Alexandria, Va.: American College Association, 1990.

Straub, C. "Women's Development of Autonomy and Chickering's Theory." *Journal of College Student Personnel,* 1987, *28,* 198–204.

Tappan, M. B., and Brown, L. M. "Stories Told and Lessons Learned: Toward a Narrative Approach to Moral Development and Moral Education. In C. Withrell and N. Noddings (eds.), *Stories Lives Tell: Narrative and Dialogue in Education.* New York: Teachers College Press, 1991.

Taylor, M. B. "The Development of the Measure of Epistemological Reflection." Unpublished doctoral dissertation, Department of Special Services, Ohio State University, 1983.

Thorne, B. "Rethinking the Ways We Teach." In C. Pearson, D. Shavlik, and J. Touchton (eds.), *Educating the Majority.* New York: Macmillan/American Council on Education, 1989.

Thorne, B. "Children and Gender: Constructions of Difference." In D. L. Rhode (ed.), *Theoretical Perspectives on Sexual Difference.* New Haven, Conn.: Yale University Press, 1990.

Tompkins, J. "Pedagogy of the Distressed." *College English,* 1990, *52* (6), 653–660.

Walker, L. J. "Sex Differences in the Development of Moral Reasoning: A Critical Review." *Child Development,* 1984, *55,* 677–691.

Ward, J. V. "Racial Identity Formation and Transformation." In C. Gilligan, N. P. Lyons, and T. J. Hanmer (eds.), *Making Connections: The Relational Worlds of Adolescent Girls at Emma Willard School.* Troy, N.Y.: Emma Willard School, 1989.

Weiler, K. *Women Teaching for Change: Gender, Class, and Power.* New York: Bergin and Garvey, 1988.

Widick, C. "An Evaluation of Developmental Instruction in a University Setting." Unpublished doctoral dissertation, University of Minnesota, 1975.

Widick, C., and Simpson, D. "Developmental Concepts in College Instruction." In C. Parker (ed.), *Encouraging Development in College Students.* Minneapolis: University of Minnesota, 1978.

Withrell, C., and Noddings, N. *Stories Lives Tell: Narrative and Dialogue in Education.* New York: Teachers College Press, 1991.

Index

A

Absolute knowers: and authority, 37, 85-86, 88-90, 96-97, 344-346; and classroom structure, 232-233; and cocurriculum, 300-305; and educational advising, 304-306; educational needs of, 267; and evaluation, 233-234; and instructor attitude and interaction, 230-231; and peers, 37, 77-79, 199, 300-302; and student organizations, 302-304; and teaching strategies, 231-232. *See also* Absolute knowing; Mastery-pattern knowers; Receiving-pattern knowers

Absolute knowing: case examples of, 29-36, 74-81; core assumptions of, 74; evolution of, 70-72; and gender, 37, 92; and mastery/receiving patterns, 37-38, 81-102; nature of, 36-37. *See also* Absolute knowers

Advising: and absolute knowers, 304-306; and transitional knowers, 317-319

African-American students, 217-220; male, 217-218; peer culture of, 214; racial identity of, 215-217; socialization of, 215-220; subordination of, 209; female, 218-219

American Council on Education and the National Association of Student Personnel Administrators, 342

American Council on Education and the University of California, Los Angeles, 25

American Council on Education Studies, 341, 343, 351, 352, 377

Arnold, K. D., 14

Astin, A. W., 380

Authority: and absolute knowers, 37, 85-86, 88-90, 96-97, 344-346; and college choice, 89-90; and contextual knowers, 188, 189, 198; and epistemological development, 370-373; and impersonal-pattern knowers, 125-126, 133, 197; and individual-pattern knowers, 165, 198; and interindividual-pattern knowers, 156, 197; and interpersonal-pattern knowers, 116, 123, 197; and mastery-pattern knowers, 96-97, 196; and receiving-pattern knowers, 85-86, 88-90, 196; and student voice, 274; and transitional knowers, 55, 344-345. *See also* Instructors

Autonomy: male, 214; and student development, 375

437